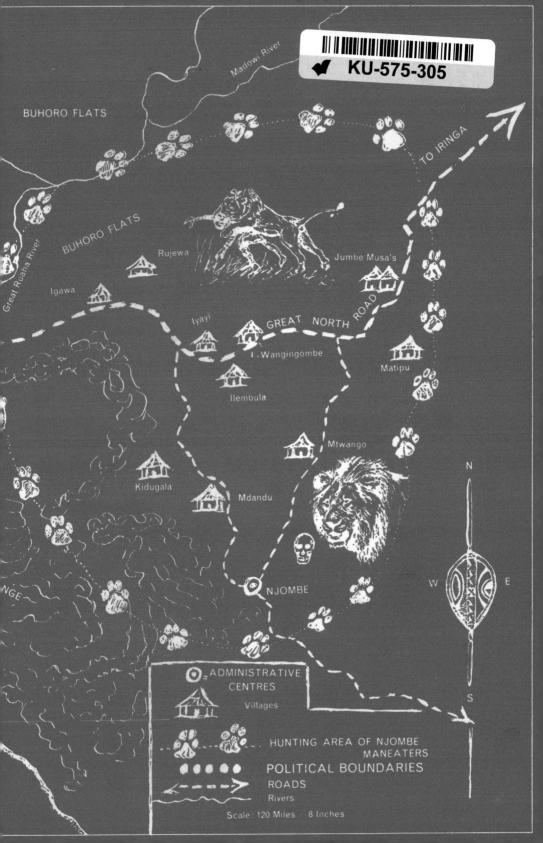

BUHORO FLATS

Madowi River

BUHORO FLATS

TO IRINGA

Great Ruaha River

Rujewa

Igawa

Jumbe Musa's

Iyayi

GREAT NORTH ROAD

I. Wangingombe

Matipu

Ilembula

Mtwango

Kidugala

Mdandu

NJOMBE

NGE

N

W   E

S

ADMINISTRATIVE
CENTRES

Villages

HUNTING AREA OF NJOMBE
MANEATERS
POLITICAL BOUNDARIES
ROADS
Rivers

Scale: 120 Miles : 8 Inches

THE HUNTER IS DEATH

Other Books by T. V. Bulpin

T. V. BULPIN

THE HUNTER
IS DEATH

GEORGE RUSHBY

Illustrated by C. T. Astley Maberly

NELSON
1962

THOMAS NELSON AND SONS (AFRICA) (PTY) LTD
301-305 Barclays Bank Buildings
Commissioner and Kruis Streets
Johannesburg

THOMAS NELSON AND SONS LTD
Parkside Works Edinburgh 9
36 Park Street London W1
312 Flinders Street Melbourne C1

THOMAS NELSON AND SONS (CANADA) LTD
91-93 Wellington Street West Toronto 1

THOMAS NELSON AND SONS
18 East 41st Street New York 17 New York U.S.A.

SOCIÉTÉ FRANÇAISE D'ÉDITIONS NELSON
97 rue Monge Paris 5

PRINTED IN SOUTH AFRICA
BY CAPE AND TRANSVAAL PRINTERS LIMITED
CAPE TOWN

TO

all those members, living and dead

of what was one of

the most select company of adventurers

ever known to man

THE PROFESSIONAL IVORY HUNTERS

AUTHOR'S NOTE

IN JUNE 1956, George Rushby retired from his position as Deputy Game Warden of Tanganyika. After three years of farming at Lupembe he eventually took his wife back to her original home in the Cape and they settled in the pleasant little naval port of Simonstown. George Rushby's retirement marked the end of what was without doubt one of the most remarkable careers of adventure ever known in Africa. His record as a hunter, poacher, wanderer, prospector and game ranger made him a legend during his day and a veritable prince of what is nowadays a vanishing breed of men.

On his retirement, George Rushby and the author commenced preparations for the writing of this book. The purpose of the work was not only to record a remarkable life, but also an uncommonly interesting and little-known segment of the often lurid history of Africa. In presenting what is a story of considerable complexity, the author was able to depend not only on George Rushby's vivid memory, but also on an exceptionally detailed series of letters written by his wife and fortunately preserved by her mother.

To research the background of the book, the author, in company with George Rushby, made a detailed tour to the sites of all the principal events featured in this narrative. In the course of this tour, the author had the pleasure of meeting many people, both African and European, who had been concerned with George in the events of his life. The author would like to thank all these good friends for information, advice and hospitality in remote places which, to a substantial extent, aided in the production of this book. Numerous government officials and missionaries also contributed their knowledge and information.

In connection with the remarkable cases of animalism and reputed lycanthropy which occur in this book, the hyena cult of the Mbugwe and Irangi people, the lion-men of the Singida district, and the bizarre man-eaters of the Njombe district with their almost unbelievable total of killings, the police files and district records of Mbulu, Kondoa, Singida and Njombe, together with the annual reports of the Tanganyika Game Department, will bear ample witness to the truth of details revealed in this book which might otherwise appear incredible.

CONTENTS

PRELUDE

IT WAS at the Salvation Army "Come and Join Us" meeting in the garden outside the General Post Office in Durban that George first met Green. Chance made them fall in together when the Salvationists marched them off to the soup kitchen and after eyeing each other warily for a moment or two, Green said in an Australian accent—

"Let's keep in step. Fanny with the tambourine gets really riled if we fall out. My name is Green, who are you?"

"George Rushby."

"New to this aren't you?"

"Yes, I've just gone broke."

Green grinned.

"Miserable luck, but if it's any consolation, we're all broke here. Where are you sleeping?"

"Down on the north beach, on the big sand dune they call Hill 60."

Green seemed to recoil.

"The deuce with that place. I was at the original Hill 60 in Flanders. A real bloody butcher's shop run by Sweeny Todd Haig, the demon general of the War Office. If half the good blokes he killed off had been able to emigrate to this country, South Africa would be another America."

He looked at George appraisingly—

1

" You couldn't have been in that mess. You're too young. You don't know what you missed."

" I've heard of it."

" What's the present place like?"

"A bit draughty, of course, but not bad. One advantage in going broke in a place like Durban is that the climate is warm. It must be pretty miserable being broke in the cold."

" True," said Green, " I must overcome my repugnance and try your hill. I've been sleeping on the embankment but it's noisy from the traffic and you cannot lie-in there, the police get officious before dawn. The good citizens of Durban have tidy minds. They know they have stony-brokes like us roaming around the place but they like us swept out of sight underneath the civic carpet in daytime."

" We have it quiet on the hill," said George. " I've never seen the police there, we are well out of view. Providing you can get to sleep in spite of drunks and dead-beats bickering over women and booze, nobody ever tries to wake you up. In fact, they only knew that one chap was dead when somebody noticed blow-flies boring holes through the newspapers he was using for blankets and the publication dates were all a month old."

Green laughed. He looked at his companion again. He saw a resolute young man, good-looking in a sturdy and ruggedly built way, and about 5 ft. 10 in. in height.

" How old are you? " he asked.

"As it happens," answered George, " this is my big day, the 28th February 1921. It's my birthday, I'm twenty-one."

" Well," said Green, " congratulations! You'll have to get an extra dollop of grub from the good old army."

They filed into the soup kitchen as he spoke, and queued up for the meal. It was quite an extraordinary assembly of human crocks, stiffs, dead-beats, freaks, and genuine out-of-works like themselves. Some were in rags, a few of the freaks in peculiar costumes, but most others just shabby. The man dishing out the soup regarded them all with such an impassive face that George giggled.

" That chap looks as though he wouldn't even blink an eye if someone in evening dress held out a bowl for soup, and the next customer was naked."

Green nodded. They received their portion, a big helping with thick slices of brown bread. They sat down with the others at a long trestle table and tucked in to the meal, trying to keep from laughing at the eating noises of some of their companions. The soup was hot, the men hungry, and the liquid could only be swallowed with a deal of blowing and gurgling. For the rest, there was a curious silence at the table. When the meal was over few men lingered to chat. George and Green went outside.

" Where now? " asked Green.

" I always go to the library and look at the evening paper for any situations vacant."

Green nodded. They went to the newspaper room of the library and awaited their turn to reach the current evening's paper on the reading stand. There was always a crowd at the library. Even if he was completely broke, a man could pass a pleasant couple of hours there, reading the periodicals and newspapers, or just watching the human oddities who were attracted like moths from the darkness into the place by its lights and shelter.

There was nothing in the situations vacant column. They walked down to the beach. George had a penny in his pocket.

" Let's buy a pineapple," he said, as they passed a fruit vendor. " It'll do for breakfast."

They went on, with George carrying the fruit and sniffing its pleasant odour. The ocean front was full of bright lights and decorations. Durban has a twelve-month holiday season. The only difference in weather is that it sometimes gets warmer. There is always some activity on the beach and with swimming free, George spent much of his spare time there in the daylight hours. At night the place was a large-scale amusement park with mechanical rides, fantastically dressed rickshaw-boys, gambling stalls, and displays of freaks.

They wandered through the throng for a little while. Barkers tried to lure them in to view such educational shows as two-headed goats, mermaids, the inevitable Pepper's Ghost, and a Zulu who danced with apparent impunity on broken glass.

" They never seem to have boxing booths here," said George disappointedly, " I used to make a little money in them in England. If you could last three rounds with a bruiser you won £1."

" Could you last?"

" Not always. Those chaps knew all the dirty tricks; but, mind you, so do I. They gave one a pretty torrid time, but I often held out. For £1 I'd stand against Dynamite Bill tonight. Let's go. This place attracts me, but I have difficulty in watching people throwing shillings away when I haven't sixpence to my name."

They walked on up the beach to Hill 60. It was a pleasant evening. The moonlight glinted on the sea and the music of the funfair rose and fell as it was carried along by the breeze. They reached the hill, and George showed Green around. It was occupied by about 150 assorted people who lived there in the shelter of a variety of structures as odd as themselves. Gunny bags, scraps of tin, soap boxes, or just holes excavated in the sand, acted as homes for these unfortunates. Some of them seemed quite indifferent to shelter. They just slept on the sand, rainy or clear.

It was still early. The two men made themselves comfortable, and listened to the distant music and the sound of the sea.

"How did you come to get here," asked Green, "or are you sensitive about that?"

George shook his head.

"No, it's just one of those things. I came out from England last year at the end of May in search of adventure, and I found Hill 60."

He paused a moment, and listened to the music.

"It's funny how things work out. It's just as well fortune tellers are frauds. So long as we have hope and health, things aren't too bad. If we could look ahead and see things getting any worse we might be inclined to run for it, or take a jump in the sea."

"Haven't you got any parents?"

"My father died when I was one and a half years old. I grew up with a stepfather, a drunken and bullying bastard. The best thing I ever saw of him was the last of him. He went off the rails eventually. He used to sing in bars for booze and what he earned was the end of him."

"Sounds as though you had a dismal childhood."

"It could have been worse, really. I was born in Nottingham, but my parents moved to Eastwood while I was still a baby. It was there that my mother remarried when my father died. I grew up largely with a crowd of gypsies who used to camp on our land. They half adopted me, especially one old couple, the Woodheads. The women used to carry me about slung in a cloth on their backs when they went around the villages selling clothes pegs and telling fortunes. I suppose I was valuable to them. I made the customers more sympathetic."

Green looked at him curiously.

"What were the men like?"

"First class. They taught me to box. About the earliest thing I can remember is being taught to box with their own young sons. Joe Beckett was one of the boys, and he's doing pretty well now as a professional fighter, so we had first class instruction. Then there was a farm-hand named Jack Gunn, living in a cottage nearby. He had a friend named Joe Flint. They were the village holy terrors on pay nights when they got drunk. They were famous experts on rough-house fighting. They also gave me instruction."

"Why were you so keen on learning the rough stuff?"

"So that I could handle my stepfather when I grew up. He was a man with troubles coming his way if he only lasted long enough. I used to go along nearly every mid-week evening to visit Jack Gunn. I had an old, battered set of boxing-gloves which had belonged to my father. I was very proud of them. Jack Gunn and Flint would kneel in turn on the hearthrug and give me lessons. If they had any money left from their last binge, they would send Gunny's old widowed mother out with a jug to fetch a quart of mild draught ale. They always gave me an egg-cup full of the stuff when the lesson was over. I used to feel terribly important, sitting on the hearthrug between them, drinking the ale and listening to them talk of fighting and poaching.

" They were great poachers. Nearly every Sunday morning if the weather was fair, I went out with them, with a dog, shot guns, ferrets, purse nets and snares. It wasn't always poaching, of course, but out of the goodness of their hearts they allowed a little boy to think it was, with a heavy air of secrecy to everything. Those chaps gave me the great pleasures of my life. They were my first real heroes. Even torture would not have extracted any information from me on their doings. And now here I am on Hill 60."

He lay on his back and looked at the stars.

" It's funny, I came out here thinking to see the Southern Cross a blazing formation in the skies. And it's nothing really, you can hardly see it. It's just something you cannot see in the northern hemisphere. I suppose people from here go north thinking to see the North Star almost as bright as the moon."

" Everybody has illusions. They make life interesting. What made you come out here?"

"A few books my father left me. There was a three-volume work, *Worlds of Adventure,* with many of its stories about Africa, and there were Selous' great hunting books. I almost read the print off their pages. I never wanted to be an engine driver or anything like that. I just wanted to come to Africa and hunt."

" Well, you can fight and poach; can you shoot?"

George laughed.

" Don't worry, I learned all the basic qualifications. I took my preparations seriously. By the time I was going to school we had moved to a village called Riddings. It was in beautiful country. I made a curse of myself against the birds and rabbits with an air-gun and became a dead shot with the thing. As for poaching, when I was thirteen we moved to Jacksdale. My mother married again to a well-to-do bookmaker named Simpson, and I went to Worksop College which was near Clumber Woods and the game preserves of the Duke of Portland. I had two pals, and we poached his game and trout from one end of his estate to the other. His gamekeepers didn't stand a chance. What a time we had, poached trout and game makes a meal that even a king couldn't equal. It has the subtle flavour of illegality added to the pot, and what a taste that gives. If we'd been caught, I suppose we would have been expelled. A hundred years ago we would have been shipped to Australia."

Green sneered. " What a fate! People pay to go there nowadays."

He sucked at his teeth.

" You make me hungry. Oh man, imagine one of the Duke of Portland's trout now."

George sighed.

" They were as fat and lazy as pigs. We caught them with worms while the Duke couldn't catch them on his most cunningly made flies. I grew hefty on those trout. When I left school I went to work with Oakes & Co., at **Pye Bridge**, to learn electrical engineering. It was then that I used to go around to the boxing booths. I was saving money to come to Africa. I'd do anything for a pound. I became a part-time motor-cycle mechanic as well as a boxer in order to save up money for my fare. So that eventually I could come to this."

" Did you come straight to Durban?"

" No, I'd seen some publicity poster showing passengers from a ship being unloaded at East London in a kind of giant basket hanging on the end of a donkey-winch. I thought that the place must be pretty primitive. So I booked to go there, steerage class, £25 a ticket from Tilbury Docks on the S.S. *Gaika*."

" When were you disillusioned?"

" I'm still not disillusioned, although I admit I went to the wrong place. I reached it in the beginning of June, last year. The basket affair was there all right. The ship lay at anchor, and they swung us over the side in the basket on to the decks of a tug which ferried us into the mouth of the river. That was where the romance of East London ended. It was just a pleasant little seaside place, with some first class beaches, a very sociable set of people, and some exceedingly pretty girls. I got a job there, and worked for a while. I played rugby and travelled around the countryside with the team. It was really a happy little place, but it wasn't what I came for. So I packed up, moved to Durban, and ended up here on the beach."

" What now?"

" Well, this is certainly not what I came to Africa for. I'll get a job sooner or later. Then as soon as I've saved up enough cash I'll clear out for the north."

" Do you think you'll find what you want there?"

" What do I want, a place where the Southern Cross looks brighter? Somewhere where elephants still wander? I don't know. On the boat coming out I met one big game hunter, a chap named Bill Buckley. He told me that the days of the hunters were through. He was going back to Mombasa to start a coconut plantation and settle down. But there must be something left in this continent. It can't all be as civilised as East London or Durban. There must be lonely places somewhere, where the bush is thick and the mountains are high, and a man can do very much as he pleases."

" There are such places," said Green. He lay back on the sand and tilted his hat over his face. " I've dreamed of them myself, but I've never had the courage to reach out to find them, for fear that my hands would touch only the empty sky and those places would vanish like a mirage. There comes a time when a man has had too many disappointments, and wishes to save himself from one more, so that he can at least keep something to dream about."

He sighed, and there was silence for a while.

" Tell me your story," asked George, but Green had fallen asleep. George leaned on his elbow for a few moments and looked at him. Then he lay back, as he had done on many a night, and listened to the sea and the distant music, until he drifted off to sleep himself.

It was a quiet night on the hill. They slept until the sun rose like Neptune in a blazing chariot from the cool blue bath of the Indian Ocean. Then they ran down to swim and enjoy their pineapple breakfast sitting on the beach while the warm rays of the sun acted as a substitute for a towel. Behind them the city slowly woke up with its first isolated sleepy stirrings of sound gradually merging into a rumbling roar. By the time they walked into the streets, there was a bustle and rush of business- and trades-people going to work, shopkeepers were removing their shutters, and the streets were flowing with traffic like rivers in spate.

They made the rounds of labour exchanges, the library to examine the situations vacant columns of the morning newspaper, and the central garden in front of the post office where out-of-works gathered to exchange news and rumours. The post-war depression in South Africa had set in with a freezing grip on the country's economy. Listening to the talk of the men in the garden was frustrating and miserable, like being caught without an umbrella in a never-ending drizzle. When George and Green tired of it, they went back to the beach. They could always fish for their supper. The fish may not have had the subtleties of flavour of the Duke of Portland's poached trout, but they were tasty grilled on an open fire, and if enough were caught, they could always be sold to provide pocket money.

There was one luxury which George had discovered by accident. He went to the Model Dairy restaurant once for some coffee. The waitresses were a pleasant crowd, and one of them asked him if he would like some cakes. The establishment was noted for a particularly delectable cream puff, a real confectionery bomb which exploded in your mouth as you ate it.

" Just love some," said George, his mouth watering, " but no money."

The girl fetched a plateful of cakes from another table.

" Here, finish these, somebody else left them."

They got talking while he disposed of the cakes. He saw her often afterwards. She kept any left-over cakes as a reserve for him, and occasionally slipped in a dinner on the house. It was a good change from Salvation Army fare, and the girl was a cheerful soul who rallied him if he was out-of-sorts and by allowing him to take her home occasionally, made him feel that at least somebody in the world had a liking for him.

Political meetings were another way of passing an evening, although these were pretty sterile affairs. There was a general election on in the country at the time and South Africans are prone to making a great noise about very adolescent politics. Green used to work up a temperature about some of the speeches but they left George cold. He was interested to hear the famous

General Smuts talk, but the man seemed to be just an expert thumper on the usual hollow political tub. To the unemployed he had no solution to any of their difficulties. The only thing which could be said about him was that his opposition seemed even dimmer.

" Governments in this country," said Green sententiously as they walked back to the beach, " are just a crowd of bloody tax-gatherers. The whole history of this country has been made in spite of them by little blokes like ourselves; hunters, traders, farmers, prospectors or craftsmen. Most of them came here to get away from wretched conditions and dud politicians at home. They battled through bush, heat, wild animals and cannibals; found the gold, and the tax-gatherers immediately came panting up to find them. Now everybody is battling to pull the country out of a hole. And what's the government doing? It's like a horse-fly pestering horses struggling to heave a cart up a hill. It gives no lead, it doesn't push, it doesn't pull, it's just a confounded nuisance. But the moment the horses reach the top of the hill, oh man, you'll hear that fly shout to the whole wide world, ' Look! alone and unaided I did it. They would never have got here without me.' And the trouble is, the horses are so shackled up with harness, they cannot reach out and kick the pest."

It was a few days after this that George found work. He happened to walk past the garage of Irvin, Maule & Mansergh and noticed a man in the act of putting up a sign, " Wanted, Electrical Mechanic. £17 a month." He walked in and within minutes was busy at work. It was an incredible relief. He could hardly believe his luck. For the first few hours he felt so much in the air that he was frightened to drop a tool in case the noise either brought him to reality on the streets again, or made some irritable foreman with a hangover sack him.

When the day ended, he could go and find a room in College Lane for £3 a month, and walk around to the pawnbrokers to ensure that they hadn't sold any of his pledges, as he hoped soon to be able to retrieve them.

It was really quite amazing how work changed his approach to life. It was only while he was completely broke that he had appreciated the real pleasure that lies in being able to select his own food and pay for it, instead of just being grateful for whatever he was given. It was a pleasure to wear clean clothes, to feel part of society again and not just be an outcast, to be able to take the girl from the restaurant to a cinema show, and stand Green some slap-up dinners of fish and chips or sausage and eggs at the Model Dairy, with real butter on the bread, and then stroll about under the trees around the post office where the colonies of mynah birds made such a fearsome clatter, and talk of the future and look at the girls and wonder whether to stay in the town or keep to his original intention and wander off again as soon as he had saved enough money to pay his fare.

It was two months later that George noticed an advertisement in the morning newspaper. The Delagoa Bay Development Corporation in the Portuguese port of Lourenço Marques had a vacancy for an attendant in their power house. George took an instant decision. Lourenço Marques was the next step up the east coast. The advertisement neglected to mention a salary, but on the assumption that it could not be much less than his present rate he rushed off an immediate application. With the effrontery of youth he added that he would be on the next ship in order to take up the appointment.

He had saved just enough to cover his fare on a British India Line ship, and at dawn three days later he sailed into the great bay where lay Lourenço Marques, the capital of the Portuguese colony of Mozambique. The seaward approach to the place was not particularly exciting: a line of sand dunes marking the encircling arms of an enormous bay, a lightship anchored over a sandbank, and a sallow looking pilot clambering up a rope ladder to guide the ship through the shallows to the as yet distant and invisible harbour.

As soon as the ship docked, George walked to the address of the advertiser. It was a British-owned firm and the manager and engineer who interviewed him seemed amused at his arrival. They were a kindly and elderly pair who made him think of the Jolly boys from Dickens.

" You've certainly got gumption," the manager said. " What will you do if we don't give you the job?"

George grinned.

" I hadn't thought of that. I left my bags on the ship, and I can stay on it until tomorrow, but after that they would throw me off."

The manager reached for his hat.

"Anyway, you can have the job. I'll take you down now and clear you through immigration. The Portuguese are a trifle sticky about such things. Then you had better get yourself a room at a place like the Miramar, and settle down."

The work was pleasant and reasonably paid. The company ran the local tramway service and supplied electric power to the town. George's position was as a shift engineer in the power plant. It was an old-fashioned plant with four generators all in use at peak loads, but it gave very little trouble and life was easy. The town was an attractive and vivacious little place, very hot and humid, with its population somewhat riddled with fever, but friendly and hospitable.

There was a fair-sized British community, and boating, fishing and swimming made the time pass in very congenial fashion. The only trouble was that there was no more adventure to life in the place than there had been in Durban or East London. George soon became bored. He was always afraid that he might get too entangled in the routine of such an easy-going place. Social obligations, conventions, romances and friendships could accumulate insidiously. Before you knew what was happening you could be settled down, married and talking of pension in such an amiable atmosphere. The prospect alarmed him. At the end of July 1921, he gave notice with some regret to

the two " Jolly boys ", and notwithstanding offers of a raise and other attempts at persuading him to remain, he sailed for Beira, the next major port
up the coast of East Africa.

He sailed with greater regret than he had felt when he left Durban. His
memories of that port were too flavoured by the taint of life on Hill 60 to
ever give him much pleasure. An experience such as that might steel a man's
character, but it can also leave bruises and scars. Lourenço Marques had
been a pleasant relaxation in comparison. He watched its lights vanish on
the evening he sailed. He felt almost a proprietary interest in their twinkle and
glow. For some intangible reason he felt certain that Beira, lying far away
in the darkness ahead of him, would see the start of his real life of adventure.
His past was just like the wake of the ship, a trail stirred up by his own
passage through the ocean of time, stretching back to the lights of a civilised
city, and lasting for just a little while before it was lost and forgotten with
only the cry of a seabird coming from the distance like the final goodbye of
a friend.

BEIRA.

CHAPTER ONE

THE HUNTING LIFE

BEIRA, in August 1921. At least it could be said that the place had nothing of the dissembler in its make-up. From the sea it looked exactly what it was on land, a listless and enervated hole, lying on a sandbank at the mouth of a typical river of Africa, muddy, fetid, and sulky looking. The life-blood of the town had long since been squandered on the feeding of mosquitoes. When George was ferried ashore in a rowing boat, the voracious insects came out in a cloud to welcome him, humming with glee at the prospect of some good red blood instead of the poisonous mixture of bad gin, third rate whisky, and impure drinking water which was about all the permanent residents of Beira could still offer in their veins by way of a meal for mosquitoes.

George turned and looked back at the ship. It was curious how you became attached to the things. He supposed it was because while you were on them with your fare paid you were the charge of the owners. With some paternal care they sheltered and fed you and then, at the end of their obligations, like a father telling his son that it was time he earned his own living, they saw you off at your destination and left you to your own means and devices. For a moment, George felt something of the regret of leaving home. Then his boat bumped against the landing jetty. Sentiment was forgotten in the urgency of looking sharp after his baggage while some two dozen porters brawled alarmingly with one another for the business of carrying a solitary suitcase which he would much rather have carried himself.

An immigration-cum-customs officer received him without visible emotion at the base of the jetty. The man was sitting at a table toying with an empty quinine bottle. He had a tic which kept one eyelid and one of his feet on the blink and the tap. George wondered whether the man had had the misfortune to be bitten in the two different places by the same noxious insect. The man was polite enough, however. He had a few words of English, and as George had picked up a basic knowledge of Portuguese in Lourenço Marques, they could make each other understand.

" Plenty, the English here," said the man as he stamped George's passport. " You come to work on the railway construction?"

" Maybe, if I can get a job. Are there vacancies?"

The man sneered.

"Always vacancies. Men always dying. Fever and booze bad."

" Could you recommend a hotel to me?"

The man leaned over the table and viewed George's suitcase appraisingly. He weighed up the worth of the thing by moving his head from side to side.

" You try the Queen's Hotel," he said judiciously. " Food bad but insects good."

George assumed that the man meant that the place was at least clean. He could always eat out. He picked up his suitcase.

" How much should I pay the porter who carried this thing for me up the jetty?"

The porter was a big man. He was standing waiting for his money with a determined expression on his face. He screamed as though on a rack when he heard the customs man suggest a coin of low denomination. George flicked the suggested coin at the man and gratefully slipped away, leaving the porter abusing the customs officer, who simply looked bored.

The principal civic amenity of Beira was discovered outside the customs shed. This was a line of narrow gauge trolley rails which ran up the main street from the boat jetty. The streets themselves were soft sand and the trolley rails at least permitted some wheeled traffic. Pairs of Africans pushed small trolleys along the rails. Each trolley had a slotted seat for three passengers and a certain amount of luggage space. The rails were only laid single track, with periodic loops as crossing points. There was some traffic right of precedence which George never properly comprehended. If two trolleys encountered each other in between crossing points the result was some of the most flaming language he ever heard anywhere in Africa, with a fine international range in vocabulary before anybody would agree to lift his trolley off the rails.

The Queen's Hotel was a corrugated iron structure supported in places by brickwork. The best establishments, like the Union-Castle Hotel, afforded brick, the lesser concerns were built of a mixture of tin and brick, while the joints were plain corrugated iron. There was a plethora of the latter type of enterprise. Practically every second building along the main street appeared to be a gin palace with an annex in the rear housing a collection of young ladies of assorted colour and price. The main shopping stretch of the street had a section of cement and wooden side walks. A few short side streets completed the town. Beyond that, it was hemmed in by the river, the sea, mud-befouled by the discharge of the river, and a flat, bush-covered hinterland.

Social life started at sundown. The bars seemed to be doing excellent trade, with most of the customers being a pretty rough and tough-looking crowd of construction workers employed by Messrs Pauling & Co. on the building of the new railway line to Nyasaland. They were a type of man George had never met before, a didn't-care-a-damn crowd, hard-drinking and incontinent but basically good-hearted and certainly open-handed.

In the first bar he visited, George met a party of construction workers who were in the port on a two-day binge. They were a pretty boisterous crowd, but before their entertainments became too phrenetic, George managed to put in a question about chances of work.

" No trouble about that," one of them, Barlow by name, told him. " There are always jobs going. If you want to try, travel back with us in the caboose on the construction train leaving tomorrow morning. Just be at the station by 8 a.m. and climb aboard. Nobody will ask any questions. Now join in our party and let's all tell one another why we ended up drunkards in this cursed hole."

George remained with them exchanging sympathies until the evening became somewhat hectic. There was a pretty hot three-piece band made up of a very blond Frenchman who chain-smoked as he played a piano whose tone was affected by the humidity, a very black American negro deserter from some ship who handled a saxophone as though it was a loud hailer, and an odd-looking nondescript character who managed the drums with the ruthless staccato rhythm of a machine gun. The soloist was a sultry-looking female of very cosmopolitan origin. She received a raucous welcome from the customers, but whatever talent she possessed had nothing to do with her voice. Long after George had slipped away to his room to sleep, he heard the music and the party end with a blowing of police whistles and a considerable confabulation in the street. The soloist worked herself up to a fine climax of sound. He heard some windows being opened by his neighbours in the hotel, but he was too tired to be interested. He fell asleep grateful that at least the band had been silenced.

He was up early the next morning, paid his dues, and was taken by trolley to the railway station. The Beira side of the line was fairly long established, originally having been built as a link with Rhodesia. The new rail section was being built as a branch leading northwards to Nyasaland from a place called Dondo which lay a few miles up the original Rhodesian line.

At the station George found the construction train being marshalled on a shunting line. He made his way to the caboose and climbed aboard without anybody paying much attention to him. There were about fifteen men already in the caboose, trying to make themselves comfortable. His friends of the night before were there looking slightly the worse for wear.

The caboose was under the control of a Welsh guard who, by the spleen and colour of his language, had a mortal feud with the Irish engine driver. The engine driver had decidedly the better of the argument. He could jerk the train to a fiendish extent every time it started or stopped, or even while it was still in motion. The effect on the caboose, at the end of a long line of goods trucks, was almost like a whiplash. The passengers and guard could hear a succession of crashes travelling down towards them as the couplings of each successive coach banged against the next. This warning at least allowed the men in the caboose time to secure themselves against the final jolt. The Welshman would then half-fall out of the caboose door, holding on to the rail with one hand as he sent a stream of vituperation and blasphemous demands for divine damnation at the head of the distant driver.

The one ambition of the Welshman was to win a sweepstake. He stated in his sing-song voice that he would then indulge in one final journey up the line, and conscientiously dislocate its entire working by locking every switch and signal in the wrong direction at unattended crossing points. He would then set fire to his train, shoot the Irishman, and vanish into the bush at a selected point where he had been careful to cache some means of making a quick getaway.

George found the man's frustrations amusing, but the other passengers had obviously heard the repertoire before. They whiled away the time by playing cards, drinking and talking rubbish about women and personalities. The scenery outside was equally dull. It was flat, sandy, bush country with hardly a sign of human habitation and never a glimpse of a wild animal.

From Dondo the train branched northwards up the new line of construction. The passengers started to disperse as they reached their respective working points. The railhead was then about fifty miles north of the junction. George was advised to continue to the end of the line where the normal mortality rate from blackwater fever was quite certain to provide him with the chance of finding employment.

The men at the railhead camp confirmed the advice given on the train. The contractors working ahead were bound to have some vacancy. After a night spent in the camp, George shouldered his case and walked ten miles up the trace of the future line to the advance working parties. He was directed immediately to the camp of an Italian contractor; a big, beefy, overbearing individual who rather offhandedly offered him the position as an overseer of a gang of African labourers building earth enbankments and cutting drains.

It was certainly a way of earning a living, but with even less of a future to it than the time it would take to complete the construction. The Italian had quite a reputation. In the camp that night, George met a pair of men who were working as hunters, shooting game and supplying the meat to the various contractors for use as rations for the labourers. Both of the hunters had tales about the Italian.

"He's not only the biggest rogue on the construction," one of them said, "but he's an impossible chap to get on with. He's always shouting, swearing and vapourising, if you get what I mean. He also talks to everybody as though they were dirt. He likes taking contracts on stretches of the line that go through swamps. He's pretty certain then that a good few of his men will die of fever and that saves him from paying them. You be pretty careful about taking your quinine, and if he doesn't pay you regularly, then get tough with him."

"How do you fellows live?"

"Fair. There's plenty of plains game around here; zebra, waterbuck, impala, buffalo; and there's always enough demand for meat to force the contractors to bid fair prices for it. Why don't you try your luck?"

"I haven't got a gun."

"That's no trouble. If you nose around the camp you'll find somebody prepared to sell you something. Even if it's an old ·303."

The prospect interested George. He had come to Africa to hunt, and this looked like a more profitable start to the life he wanted than giving service to somebody who presumably hoped he would die before he claimed a month's wages.

Over the next few days he inquired around the camp, and eventually found a man prepared to trade a rather battered-looking ·303 and some ammunition for a combination of old clothing and cash. George occupied his spare time in overhauling the gun, and indulging in some target practice, restricted of necessity by the shortage of ammunition. He looked for game around the camp, but the noise of construction and the hunting efforts of the labourers had driven the animals too deep into the bush. It amused him to think that if he embarked on a hunting career he would surely be one of the very few to have started such a life by never having seen an African game animal in any place other than a zoo or a picture book.

After ten days' work for the Italian, George found him insufferable. Squabbling with the man each day about trifles would be a waste of time. George extracted what money was owing to him from the Italian by dint of a few judicious threats, collected half a dozen of the man's best labourers who chose to leave at the same time, and set out with them for the bush at the start of his life as a professional hunter. As things turned out, it was quite a momentous day for him.

The Africans were local men, and pretty knowledgeable about the country. They had worked for hunters before and this certainly made it easier for George. They automatically took for granted all the basic routines which experienced hunters had taught them. Like a cyclist coasting down hill, George could sit back and leave them to guide him to a good game area in open country, and in a reasonably dry and healthy spot, build a camp of grass shelters for themselves, and racks for smoking the meat. For his own comfort George had acquired a sheet of canvas which was slung up underneath a tree to provide him with a sheltered sleeping place.

It was there that George spent his first night as a solitary white man in the African bush. The Africans built two fires, one for themselves and one for George. As the employer, he was not expected to join them in the evenings. He soon learned that if he did, his presence tended to cramp their conversation. They expected the boss to recognise the social distinctions of position, and in any case he spoke very little of their language.

He sat on his own at his fire, listening to their voices and their bursts of laughter and to the whispers and murmurs of the bush at night. He felt curiously relaxed and content. He had been dreaming of such a life since he had been old enough to read his father's hunting books. He had often imagined the camps of the great adventurers and explorers, and now at last here he was in a camp of his own. He lay back and made himself comfortable on the ground. One thing Hill 60 had done was break him of the habit of sleeping on anything soft. Being a light sleeper he had never been subject to any of the nervousness which most heavy sleepers have of being taken by surprise. With his rifle loaded and ready by his side he simply dozed off into a pleasant dream of successful hunts and a restless pursuit after a giant elephant which wandered for ever ahead of him through silent reaches of the bush.

Just before dawn he was awakened by the stirring of the Africans. A jackal was singing-out nearby with its high-pitched quaver. The birds were just starting to call reassurances to one another that they had survived the perils of the night. This would be the day of George's first hunt. He lay in bed for a few moments wondering what it had in store for him, hoping that at least he would end the adventure by evening with some credit to himself in the eyes of the Africans. He was self-conscious of his inexperience, and very desirous of being accepted as an expert by those who would witness his baptism of fire.

At dawn they set out. Two of the Africans accompanied George as trackers. He did his best to look knowledgeable. He was still wondering what the Africans would have thought if they knew that the only thing he had ever shot before was a rabbit, when the leading tracker suddenly stopped, pointed, and whispered excitedly " *inyama* " (game).

George looked in the direction the man was pointing. He strained his eyes but he could see nothing. Both Africans were excited and they obviously expected him to do something. He was quite tongue-tied, ashamed to ask them what they had seen. Then the animal moved. All he could see was an odd-shaped body low in the grass. He assumed that it was some animal lying down.

George raised his rifle, aimed, and fired. It was a clean miss. The startled animal shot straight out of the bush, directly at them. George thought that he was confronting his first charge. For a moment he was petrified. Then he saw what the animal was, an old wart-hog. At the same time the wart-hog noticed the hunters. He swerved sharply, and raced off into the bush. The last George saw of him was the odd little tuft at the top of his tail travelling just above the level of the grass like the observation lens of a submarine's periscope.

George became aware that the Africans had burst out laughing. They were looking at him, and he guessed correctly that they had noticed his confusion. There was only one thing for him to do, and that was join in the laughter. At least it covered up his embarrassment.

After a while they went on. They reached the verge of a swampy area. One of the trackers nudged George. Standing under the trees, some distance away, he saw his first large game, a family group of waterbuck, George was thrilled. The animals seemed enormous, with their shaggy coats and the magnificent spreads of horns of the males. He looked at them for a few moments and then tried to decide what to do. He had long since rehearsed in his mind a course of behaviour when he came across game. The expert hunters always started off by finding out the direction of the wind. The trouble was that the wind, when he tried to test it, seemed to be blowing erratically from several directions. He cursed his ill-fortune. A good, strong breeze would at least have dictated a positive line of approach. Now all he could do was trust to luck.

The waterbucks were regarding him with an unwavering stare. George decided on trying to work around them, for it would be useless making any direct approach. He began a careful movement towards the side. The waterbucks watched, tossing their heads and occasionally glancing behind them to ensure that they were not being surprised. They appeared to be at least as knowledgeable as he was in the ways of hunters, and obviously had no particular intention of being shot. George had progressed less than fifty paces in his manoeuvre when the waterbuck bull snorted a warning to his family, and the animals darted away.

George eyed the Africans to see whether any humour betrayed their opinion that he had fumbled another opportunity. They seemed impassive, however, and he was relieved to think that they admitted that the chance had been difficult.

The waterbucks had vanished into the bush. The trackers moved on. Half an hour later they came across a reedbuck. The animal, a medium sized antelope, was standing in the open, among some clumps of grass. The trackers pointed it out to George, and one of them went so far as to indicate a line of approach. The two men then sat down and left him to do the job. He was the only one with a rifle and it would be senseless to alarm the creature by staging a mass approach.

George felt like an actor nudged into his first solo role. He tried to remember everything he had ever read about method and technique. It all seemed terribly confused in his mind. Then his own hunting instincts took over. He forgot the books and set out to stalk the reedbuck in as simple and straightforward a manner as possible, exploiting what natural cover there was, and happy in the knowledge that at least the animal had had the misfortune not to have observed him.

At sixty yards George aimed at the reedbuck. He hit it first shot. He was tremendously pleased. He ran up to the animal and turned it over. In his enthusiasm and inexperience he was certain that he must have shot a record reedbuck, for the animal was possessed of a handsome spread of horns. The Africans came laughing up to join him. Their mouths seemed to be actually watering at the prospect of meat. They set about skinning and gutting the animal. Then they carried the meat back to camp. There it was cut into strips and placed for curing on wooden grids supported on forked sticks about three feet above slow, smoky fires. That night they all dined to capacity on venison. A reedbuck makes excellent eating. It is juicy and tender, with delicious steaks, and although they had no vegetables, one of the Africans made bread from George's solitary luxury of a sack of flour. They all went to bed very well filled and content. To George it was the most triumphant day of his life. He had rehabilitated himself in his employees' eyes, he was in business as a hunter, he had food for his men, together with a surplus for sale, and future prospects seemed marvellously exciting.

For the next few days he hunted with increasing success. Eland, buffalo, impala, zebra and hartebeest, were all numerous and his experience as a hunter expanded as he added to his first bag an assortment of fifteen of the animals. With the cured meat, he walked back to the construction camp and had the satisfaction of receiving the first cash from his efforts in his chosen profession.

For several months George hunted for the railway workers, moving further north with them as the construction extended. When they were across the Zambezi he could anticipate a dwindling of demand as labourers were paid off at the approaching end of the work. At this stage, fortunately, he heard that the British-controlled Senna Sugar Estate also bought meat as rations for its labourers. He visited the estate and saw the manager, an agreeable individual who would be happy to take as much meat by weight from any animal that George could supply. The estate already supported the efforts of several other professional hunters, but the demand was sufficient to provide opportunity for any other venturesome character to shoot a living out of the bush.

The new market seemed to offer George the basis of a permanent career. He was thoroughly enjoying the life. To be healthy and vigorous, and the master of his own life when he had only just turned twenty-two, seemed to him to be a dream come true. He was experienced, his shooting was accurate, he had invested his profits in a 9·3 mm. Mauser and a double-barrelled ·470-inch Rigby hammer gun acquired from a retiring hunter and, above all, he was supremely confident in himself.

There was a seemingly inexhaustible supply of game. Enormous herds of buffalo wandered along the banks of the lower Zambezi. They were great, heavy animals carrying substantial quantities of meat. There were also the prospects of elephants. He was already approaching the opinion of most hunters, that the elephant is the most rewarding of all trophies in Africa. The thought of securing with one bullet at least a quarter of a ton of saleable dried meat, with the added bonanza of ivory, left George very anxious to make the acquaintance of elephants. So far he had seen no signs of them, for he had not been hunting in elephant country. He could anticipate, however, an early meeting with them on the lower Zambezi, and the prospect excited him.

It was close to the banks of the Zambezi that he actually encountered his first elephants. The country was flat grassland, inclined to be swampy in the wet season. He had set out with his trackers at dawn in search of buffalo and it was shortly after the first light that they found the trail of elephants. From the tracks, there were about a dozen animals and their droppings were fresh and lying on top of the evening dew. It was a bright, crisp morning, with the elephants travelling into a steady breeze. Pursuing them gave George the most fascinating experience which a hunter can have, with a clear trail to follow, the innumerable interesting signs to interpret of the animals' behaviour, sex and size, and the knowledge that the end of the pursuit led unerringly to the richest of all hunting prizes.

The elephants remained on the move until afternoon. Then they rested in a well-trampled thicket, in order to pass the hot hours under some shady cover. The coolness of the morning had long since vanished and it was a pretty hot but determined George who eventually disturbed the peace of the elephants. When he first saw them dozing in the shade, their giant ears fanning the air with an easy movement, and their trunks swaying restlessly as they drove the flies away, he had no doubt that he was in the presence of the real kings of the African bush. The roar of the lion may be the voice of Africa, but the elephant is undisputedly monarch.

George crouched down behind a bush and watched the elephants closely. They were completely unaware of his presence. Their character and mannerisms fascinated him. They were always doing something interesting. He decided then and there that elephants should be his real life study and quarry. He felt that there could be nothing more interesting in the whole world of

animals, and elephant country would henceforth become his adopted homeland.

There was only one young bull in the herd, and his tusks were not very
considerable. He represented a substantial weight in meat, however, and the
financial aspects of George's interest in game made him visualise the creature
already being smoked on the racks. George tested the wind with a handful
of dust. Now that the kill was near, he felt tense. He had three Africans with
him, armed with spears.

" You stay here," he said to them.

They nodded and watched him closely as he went off, crouching close to
the ground and moving foot by foot towards the elephants. One of the cows
seemed inclined to be suspicious. Every now and then he had to freeze when
she looked towards him. The perspiration dripping down his forehead almost
maddened him with a desire to sneeze or wipe it away in the long minutes
when he had to keep still with the cow's eyes fixed steadily on him. A bush
tick also made the stalk a misery by crawling up his trouser leg with a
movement as inexorable as his own hunt, and eventually sinking its jaws
into a tender part of his anatomy.

At thirty-five yards, George lay down and waited for the young bull to
present the best target. The animal was dusting himself leisurely, doing the
job with something of the fastidiousness of a dandy. Suddenly he turned and
offered a heart shot. The ·470 bullet sent up a puff of dust as it connected
with the elephant's hide. It seemed to be dead on target. In the still air, the
sound of the gun was like a cannon explosion. The herd stampeded. George
gave the young bull a second shot in the flank as he twisted away. The
animals crashed off into the bush. George scrambled to his feet cursing his
aim. As he did so he heard a tremendous thud and a breaking of branches
from the bush. Then there was silence. It astounded him to think that twelve
great animals could vanish so quickly.

The three Africans ran up to join him. They seemed very excited. He
went off with them into the bush. About fifty yards away they found the
young bull. The first bullet had gone straight through his heart but as usual
his own muscular reaction had sustained him in a last desperate effort to
escape. The hunters walked up to him. George could hardly believe his success. The Africans cut the tail off the elephant. It was their traditional way
of establishing ownership of an animal and positively proving that it was
dead. An elephant has to be very dead to submit to the indignity of losing
his tail, while the man who possesses that appendage as a trophy can always
prove his ownership in any dispute by fitting the thing back again.

The Africans cheerfully came and presented the tail to George. When he
didn't seem to know what to do with it, they tied it to his belt. Then, while
he waited beside the carcass, they went to the distant camp. They moved
everything up to the elephant, for it is easier for man to move to such a

mountain of flesh, than have to carry wet and heavy meat for long miles through the bush. They built the new camp next to the elephant, erected the racks, started the fires, and commenced what seemed to be something like an industry in cutting up and curing the meat. George felt more content with himself than he had ever been in his life. The tusks were small twenty-five pounders, but the total proceeds from meat and ivory would represent a substantial addition to his finances. In the light of future events, he was very glad to have this money.

CHAPTER TWO

THE HUNTER IS HUNTED

FOR four months George hunted on behalf of the Senna Sugar Estates. He was making an excellent living. The restless, wandering sort of life pleased him. Notwithstanding the attentions of a mass of insects he was tremendously fit. He was also becoming astonishingly accurate with a rifle. He practised incessantly, selecting some difficult target, walking away from it to varying distances and at changing angles, whirling around as though taken by surprise, and firing rapidly from hip or shoulder. He was determined not only to become a hunter of deadly efficiency, but if fate ever made him the hunted, then whoever pursued him would find him formidable quarry.

Living in the bush sharpened his instincts and senses. In a town a man has little need for real acuteness of hearing, smell, or sight. In an environment of noise, stinks, and restricted views, sharpness of senses can be something of an embarrassment. But the clear air, the long views, and the overall silence of the bush makes a man strain to alert himself to the most furtive whisper, the slightest unnatural movement in a distant glade, or the most intangible odour floating in on an erratic wind. In some way, as well, intuition is also sharpened. That odd, indefinable instinct which sometimes allows a man a glimpse around a corner of his life, or a warning hint of his future, is the real birthright on which the creatures of the wild base their own hope of a reasonable

22

stretch of life in an environment of such constant hazard and uncertainty.

One night George was asleep. He still used his sheet of canvas as a shelter. It was suspended from a ridge pole slung between two thorn trees and the absence of walls allowed him the luxury of the faintest cooling breeze. It was about midnight when he awoke. It was a brilliant starlit night but he sensed rather than saw or heard, that something was moving around outside. Whatever that something was, it was furtively approaching the entrance to his shelter. George reached out his hand and silently picked up his rifle lying loaded by his side. Against the stars he saw the silhouette of a man with a spear in his hand quietly coming through the entrance. The man was almost upon him. George fired from his side without asking questions. In the silence of the tent, the explosion was deafening. The intruder simply collapsed on the ground. George scrambled up and lit his hurricane lamp. His African hunters came running in. They had heard the explosion.

They examined the intruder. The rifle had been loaded with a soft-nosed bullet and it had blown a hole right through the man's chest. He was stone dead. He was in tribal costume and his spear was a business-looking weapon with barbed edges. George looked down on him. He had never seen the man before.

" Who is he? " he asked the Africans.

None of them knew.

" He must be a robber from one of the villages," was all they could suggest.

There is certainly no pleasure in killing a human being, but neither was there any sense in shedding tears. The intruder had asked for what he had received. The Africans dragged the corpse outside, George reloaded his rifle in case the man had any friends, and everybody went back to bed. By the rapid snoring of the Africans, the affair did not seem to have worried them very much.

In the morning they buried the corpse. George broke up the camp and walked into one of the farms of the Senna Sugar Estate on the lower Zambezi. He would have to report the occurrence to the Portuguese, but he thought that it would be wise to ask the advice of the local estate manager beforehand. The manager had always been very friendly in the past, but he was certainly not very cheerful about the present matter.

" Look here," he said, " if you want advice, I'll give it to you. These Portuguese are charming people while things go well. But the moment things go wrong they become pure bastards. I don't doubt that they will believe your story. But you'll certainly sit in their local gaol for six months while their bureaucracy considers the case. And believe me, that would be punishment enough for even a cold-blooded murderer."

" So? "

" If I were you, I'd forget it. There's a river-boat passing through this afternoon. I'll pay your men off for you, or give them a job on the estate. You catch the boat. Tell people that your grandmother has died up country and you're off to the wake. By the time the corpse's relatives get around to reporting the matter, you'll be safe in Nyasaland."

The advice meant the abandonment of George's hunting business. The manager noticed the dismay on his face.

"Look here," he added hastily, "don't think that I want to get rid of you. I like you here. I'm just giving you my own private opinion."

George nodded. He had already learned that arguing the point with the Portuguese was not profitable. "I suppose you're right," he said unhappily. He drew what cash was owing to him from the estate, and took his belongings down to the bank of the Zambezi. He waited for the boat, sitting in the shade of a wild fig tree, watching the languid movement of the muddy river and thinking bitterly that fate had played him a scurvy trick. Just when things were working out well this idiot of an interloper had barged into his life and all he could save from the wreck was his experience, more capital than he had possessed on his arrival, and two good rifles, one of which had certainly been well blooded on a human being. Even the excitement of the crowd of Africans sitting around him failed to arouse him from his mood when the stern-wheeler came splashing up to the little jetty, with a great hooting, a churning up of mud by its paddles and no little bad language in a strong Scots accent. George went aboard with a sigh, feeling that he was ending the happiest days of his life, and very uncertain about what was ahead of him.

The stern-wheeler was the *Queen*, the pride of the fleet of the African Lakes Corporation. It was a pudgy little boat which made some considerable fuss about working up and down the great river, with a barge laden with cargo lashed to either side. Every human being on it, irrespective of colour, seemed to be Scots. The African crew spoke English with an extraordinary Scots accent. The captain and the engineer were both Macs, while the passengers consisted of two families of Scots missionaries fresh from home on their way out to a station, a young Scots bank clerk, and a Public Works Department engineer named McKay, both going to Nyasaland to take up appointments.

The accommodation was fair. George was shown to a cabin for himself. By the fusty smell of the bunks it was obvious that they hadn't been disturbed for quite some time. Former occupants may have preferred to sleep on the deck. There was no ventilation. The cabins and community rooms were all stuffy and hot. At night a passenger had to choose between bad air inside, or mosquitoes outside. To complicate matters, the African deck passengers who were accommodated on the tops of the barges were incessantly cooking in braziers and buckets and from whichever side any wind blew, the central accommodation was half-choked with smoke.

Another of the boat's inconveniences was the lavatory—obviously an afterthought on the part of the builders. Being for officers as well as for passengers of both sexes, it served to reduce all to a common denominator. It consisted simply of a hole cut through the deck immediately above one of the paddle-wheels. A partition provided some visual privacy, if only to conceal the alarm of the occupant. The view down the hole was quite startling, with the thrashing paddle-wheel sending up a gush of air, an occasional splash of muddy water, or a glimpse of some hippo or crocodile which had been so unfortunate as to be caught up in the machinery. What the lady missionaries thought of the facility remains unknown. But somebody had attempted to console them by scraping into the partition an interesting notice, probably more a product of wit than veracity.

" Queen Victoria was also here. She had to grin and bear it."

At the first opportunity, George asked the captain how long he expected to take to complete the journey to the terminal river port of Chindio.

" That depends," answered the captain sourly, " on how much time we spend stuck in the muck. The river is like the wages the company pays, terrible low."

George grinned. The African Lakes Corporation was a favourite subject of romantic novelists, but in Africa it had a reputation for being skinflint. It was said that a satisfied employee of the corporation was as rare as the visit of angels.

" We passed that silly bugger, MacIntyre, this morning," the captain went on, " he's been stuck in one place for two days and by what he's trying to do to get off I shouldn't be surprised if he doesn't sink his bloody boat."

George began to feel slightly dismayed. The captain glanced at him quizzically.

" If you are in a hurry you should have walked. Even with the river high, we couldn't do it in less than two days. Add to that every hour we are stuck fast, and you'll know when we'll get there."

The captain nodded, and went on to his duties. George examined his surroundings. The river was certainly at a low ebb. It would be miserable luck to have the *Queen* end the voyage stuck fast on a sandbank for long enough to allow the Portuguese to learn of the shooting and catch up with him. An African bosun at the prow of the *Queen* was doing his best to feel a way for the vessel by prodding about in the water with a pole, but even these efforts failed to prevent an alarming succession of bumps, scraping noises, and urgent reversals of the engines.

The river-boats maintained a service from Chinde, at the mouth of the Zambezi, to a point as near to Nyasaland as the state of the river would allow. In the wet season the flat-bottomed paddle-wheelers went up the Shire tributary as far as Port Herald, about 214 miles by water from Chinde, where a railway took over the transportation of goods and passengers to Nyasaland. In the dry months the river-boats could only go with difficulty as far as a place called Chindio, where an extension of the railway from Port Herald came into operation for the season.

Even in the wet season the journey was a leisurely affair, with frequent stops at river ports for working cargo and passengers or for shipping fuel for the wood-burning engines. A real gaggle of Africans would also storm aboard at each stop, trying to sell scraggy-looking chickens, eggs, papaws, or bananas. The pedlars and passengers came from villages which were mostly completely invisible from the river, built on high ground well away from any flood levels. The stops provided some slight variety for a journey which was otherwise exceedingly dull. At least the passengers could get off the boats, stretch their legs on shore, and climb up the high containing river banks and view the countryside. With the river low, the water level was well under the banks and with the surrounding country being flat grassland from one horizon to the other, with hardly a tree save an occasional wild fig close to the river, the effect from the deck of the boat was as though the vessel was locked in an elongated water gaol with no better view of the world for the duration of its sentence than a glimpse of the curve of the sky.

Dug-out canoes were numerous on the river, while occasionally some other river-boat passed going down stream, or they passed one that was badly stuck. The *Queen* spent at least half of its own time on the mud, with the passengers fretting away the hours playing cards, talking, reading the few books in the library, or just sitting and brooding on chairs on the forepart of the boat. The captain had a sideline selling liquor, tobacco and a few oddments from a little store which he kept very securely locked away in an odd corner of the boat. His stock-in-trade provided slight comfort for the passengers but some good, hard, knock-out drugs would really have been the only things to make the journey completely sufferable.

It took four days before the *Queen* arrived at Chindio, and then George received a final alarm. Tied up at the port there was a Portuguese river gun-boat armed with a few machine guns and manned by some spruce-looking officers who seemed to regard the inelegant approach of the mud-bespattered *Queen* with searching looks. George wondered whether some message had reached them concerning the shooting, but they made no effort to intercept him. He left the river-boat with the rest of the passengers and transferred to the train which left the following morning on the sixty-one-mile run to Port Herald, the entry port for Nyasaland. None of them had any regrets at leaving the river, and George felt no inconsiderable relief when the immigration officer sitting on the railway platform at Port Herald stamped his passport, and he realised that he was well out of Portuguese territory.

To his eye the country immediately had a more cheerful look to it. A low jumble of hills gave promise of higher and cooler country as the train set off on the 113-mile run to the Shire Highlands, where its destination was Blantyre, the capital of Nyasaland. The train itself was a mixed goods and passenger affair, with the passengers accommodated in reasonably comfortable corridor coaches. With the cool breezes and sense of real motion in the train, the passengers soon revived their spirits from the enervation of the river passage. The stops for meals at wayside stations became quite jolly little parties, even though the meals consisted of the same tough breed of chicken, the famed African *kuku,* which had been standard fare on the *Queen.*

George had found McKay, the Public Works Department engineer, to be amiable company on the boat. For want of any other guidance about his future, he resolved to get out of the train with the young Scotsman at Limbe, six miles before Blantyre, in order to be at least in the company of somebody he knew. Like George, McKay had never before been to Nyasaland, so it was all something of an adventure for the two young men.

The train reached Limbe late in the afternoon. In the light of sunset the two young men left the station and walked to the hotel, with porters carrying their bags behind them. It was a pleasant time of the day and the coolness of the air resulting from an altitude of 3,700 feet was quite a tonic. The town was a tiny place, with one street lined by ramshackle little Indian shops, but around it there were some green and well-wooded hills, while the energies of the Imperial Tobacco Company had recently benefited the place with a few well-built houses standing in pretty gardens of flowers. There was a contented and good-natured atmosphere to the town, and the hotel, run by a Jewish host named Easterbrook, was clean and well managed.

George spent ten days at Limbe getting to know something about hunting possibilities in Nyasaland. He soon learned that there was very little game left in the country. Nyasaland was too heavily populated to have much spare room for wild animals. Hippos and crocodiles in the rivers and the lake, and a few surviving specimens of the rare and beautiful Nyala antelope were about all that the southern section of the country could boast.

George visited Blantyre twice and inquiry at the government offices rewarded him with the news that elephants were reported as being numerous at the northern end of Lake Nyasa. The area around Karonga was reputedly much troubled by them and the government interested in a thinning-out of the animals. He secured an introductory letter to the district commissioner at Karonga, and wished his Scots engineering friend in Limbe goodbye.

The journey to the north was made by a combination of road transport and lake steamer. Some enterprising soul had acquired a fleet of old army Hupmobile cars. The back seats were removed to provide freight capacity, and the vehicles also towed small two-wheeled trailers. Passengers, like George, sat in front next to the drivers and the road journey to Lake Nyasa was made in tolerable comfort, providing it wasn't raining and the earth roads churned up into mud.

Fort Johnson was the lake port at the end of the road. A small hotel stood on the beach surveying the rather dismal prospect of a thick mass of sudd which quite choked up the surface of the lake for some distance from the shore. The lake steamer *Gwendoline,* commanded by a red-haired Welshman named Captain George, R.N., lay at anchor beyond the sudd and was serviced by a real fuss-pot of a tug which had to struggle its way with no little blowing-off of steam, towing barges of cargo through the floating weeds.

George went aboard. It was a pleasant little steamer, a perfect miniature of an ocean-going liner with comfortable, if stuffy accommodation. The usual sprinkling of passengers were aboard, a young cadet going to some outpost, the wife of a district commissioner going to join her husband, a couple of missionaries, and two officers of the King's African Rifles returning to their posts from furlough. They were a happy crowd, and the five-day voyage to Karonga passed pleasantly, for Lake Nyasa is a handsome stretch of water, with interesting and varied scenery, and good fishing and swimming at the various lake ports where the inhabitants had built crocodile-proof enclosures around selected lengths of beach. Reed fences planted in the water in a half-moon shape kept the crocodiles from swimming into the bathing areas, while their tracks in the sand would betray them if they attempted to sneak in along the beach.

Karonga was a typical specimen of a lake-side station, with a small huddle of government offices, the inevitable African Lakes Corporation store, and a large and noisy African village. George went ashore in a rowing boat and secured an interview with Abrahams, the district commissioner. For a district commissioner, the man seemed reasonably pleased to see a stranger. It appeared that the elephants were really making some nuisance of themselves, especially around the village of Vua, where they were raiding crops and trampling to death anybody who tried to interfere with them. African hunters had been trying to kill them off for some time and the peppering they had received from muzzle-loading guns had not done their tempers much good.

George secured a permit to shoot as many of the elephants as he liked, and with a few porters to carry his belongings, he set out the next day for the Vua area. The village lay on the lake shore south of Karonga, in flattish country with high grass and clumps of trees. A jumble of mountains in the distance hinted at the possibility of higher and cooler ground.

George camped beneath a tree in front of the village and the local chief came out to meet him. He was a friendly soul, and very glad to see a hunter in his district. With what few words of each other's language they understood, and the aid of an indifferent interpreter, the two men settled down in the shade to talk about elephants. According to the chief the elephants were numerous, enormous, vicious, and outfitted with tusks so large that it would take two men to carry each one. African hunters had killed a few of them, but the rest were particularly aggressive. Recently they had given the district's solitary European settler, a retired planter named Maxwell, something more than a scare when they had pursued him at full tilt down one of the safari paths. He was riding a ramshackle old motor bicycle at the time. As it was not capable of going any faster than an elephant, the man had escaped by little more than a fortunate bump on the path which had thrown him to one side just as his nearest pursuer had lashed at him with its trunk.

George went to sleep that night with some anticipation of a few lively hunts. The next day the chief provided him with guides to the principal area of the elephants, a half-day's walk inland. There were certainly enough signs of elephants, and the tracks he saw seemed uncommonly large. Big elephants of course do not always carry the largest tusks, but the size of the tracks at least bore out the description given by the chief that the animals were large specimens, and made George more hopeful that the account of their tusks would also prove to be true.

Every village they reached showed signs of the elephants. The animals were nothing if not audacious. They simply walked through villages, pulled the grain bins off their stilts, tore them to pieces to steal the contents, and did very much as they pleased in the fields and banana groves. The damage was very considerable.

George saw the elephants for the first time that afternoon. His trackers led him to a small herd drowsing in a wood. He was assured that amongst this herd there were one or two notorious individuals. George viewed them from a distance. They appeared to be very docile and lazy. They were certainly big animals, but their tusks were strangely insignificant. He determined to test their mettle, however, and as a target he singled out the animal with what was comparatively the best looking pair of tusks.

The trackers left him to the hunt. It was a fairly straightforward issue. There was a reliable breeze and reasonable cover. He made his way to a tall tree standing within comfortable range of the herd and waited for his victim to move into a good position. None of the elephants appeared to have winded him. He regarded them with some interest, noticing with surprise that the largest animal had no tusks at all. From its behaviour, however, the lack of tusks was no great disability to its obvious claim of being the leader and general bully of the herd. As George watched, the bull he hoped to shoot was engaged on a leisurely process of stripping the bark off a tree with its tusks. Elephants are partial to chewing the bark of certain trees, notably the miyombo trees, and extracting the juice before they spit out the fibre.

The elephant without tusks was regarding the bark peeling activity very closely. As soon as a nice strip of bark had been peeled, the tuskless elephant gave a sudden squeal. He charged upon the elephant removing the bark, gave him a sharp blow in the flank, pushed him out of way, seized hold of the bark, and started munching at it, looking well pleased with himself.

The tusked elephant was doubly unfortunate. He had lost his delicacy and at the same time been pushed into an excellent target position. George had no time for sympathy. He let the elephant have a bullet straight into the heart, and watched, expecting to see the herd stampede at the sound of the shot. He was shaken at what actually happened. The elephant he had shot staggered around for a few moments as though drunk and then collapsed on its own feet. The rest of the herd, instead of stampeding, milled around in great rage and alarm, smelling the air with their trunks, obviously trying to locate the position of their attacker.

The tuskless bull was the first to locate George. He blasted out a squeal of rage, curved his trunk up out of harm's way on to his chest and charged. George fired, but it was a difficult target. Before he could reload, the elephant was almost on him. He dodged to one side and dropped down on his knees in the concealment of some shrubbery. He hastily reloaded. As he looked up he saw the elephant towering over him. The animal was confused. He had lost sight of George and couldn't find him in the shrub. He moved so close that blood from the wound in his chest dripped on to George's head and shoulders. The animal was a point-blank target but to shoot him would be highly dangerous. Being smothered to death beneath the collapsing weight of a dead elephant would be even less enjoyable than being trampled in any last paroxysm.

George held his breath and waited, hoping that the elephant could not hear the beating of his heart. No-Tusks was now feeling a trifle uneasy. He was wise enough to the ways of men with rifles to sense that a hunter out of sight was dangerous. He whirled around suddenly and made off, holding his trunk and his tail in the air. When he was ten yards away, George put a bullet straight up his backside. It was a pretty grim shot to give an elephant and it certainly made him sit down in a hurry. George could see the perplexity on the animal's face as he tried to turn to see what had happened. George ran to the side and put him out of his troubles with a shot into the heart. No-Tusks collapsed with a mighty groan, while the rest of the herd crashed off for safety through the trees.

The trackers ran up. With George they examined the elephants. No-Tusks had never had tusks. There was not even a sign of rudimentary stumps. The other bull sported a pretty diseased-looking and almost valueless amount of ivory. Altogether, apart from relieving the district of two nuisances, the hunt had been a waste of good bullets. The local villagers would troop up and make a banquet of the carcasses, but so far as George was concerned, all the profit he would get from the encounter would be the experience, and perhaps a couple of juicy slices of elephant's temple. Even in that, however, he was disappointed. Both animals proved extremely tough and painfully indigestible. It was apparent to George, when he considered the hunt that night, that the pursuit of elephants was not necessarily always profitable. Even at best, the hazards of the business must be carefully taken into account when he made up any future balance sheet of the profits and losses of a hunting life.

RUNGWE MOUNTAIN.

CHAPTER THREE

TANGANYIKA

GEORGE shot a total of twenty elephants in the Vua area before he gave up the hunt in disgust. Notwithstanding the most diligent search, there was not a single decent tusker to be found in the locality. Hunting altruistically as a defender of raided African villages might provide some reason for shooting, but it was hardly economic to a private individual of very limited means and the prospect was quite unattractive of going broke in so isolated a situation.

Exactly why the local elephants were so poorly outfitted with ivory provided a problem which George discussed on many a night with his trackers. If Nyasaland had ever been much of a place for elephants, then these animals were the dregs left behind as a result of constant hunting. The dense African peasant population around the verges of the lake had never had any use for elephants. Since the early days of the Arab traders, guns of the gas-pipe or muzzle-loading variety had been used in the area. Before such a barrage of missiles the elephant population had wilted. The big tuskers had been the first to go; then the smaller herd bulls and the cows with tusks.

In the end, as with a nation whose history has been scarred by constant wars, only the runts had been left alive to breed and their progeny had degenerated into a miserable shadow of the former glories of their kind. From eleven mature bulls which he shot, George recovered only a total of 49 lb. of poor quality ivory. One other bull rewarded him with two tusks of 25 lb. each, while the balance of eight elephants were shot purely to rid the district of raiders. George speculated that indiscriminate hunting in Africa might eventually result in an entire tuskless race of elephants bred, as a curious kind of negative defence from hunters, by the freaks who had survived in the first place through being of a tuskless strain.

31

George returned to Karonga when he abandoned the hunt. Although the current world price of ivory was then twenty shillings a pound, the local African Lakes Corporation manager could only offer him twelve shillings a pound for what George had to admit were poor tusks. The whole venture had been a waste of time. George was glad to leave the place in a hired dug-out canoe and, with one overnight camp on the beach, make his way up to the Tanganyika port of Mwaya at the northern end of Lake Nyasa.

The canoe voyage was leisurely, but extremely interesting. As the lake started to narrow towards its northern end, both shores became visible from the same point. The eastern shore was particularly beautiful. The great massif of the Ukinga or Livingstone mountains swept down to the water's edge, crowding so close that for many miles there was no room for even a beach, and great precipices rose sheer from the surface of the lake. The western shore was open, with pleasant beaches of pebbles and sand washed in fine weather by miniature waves which could be lashed to quite a fury by any sudden south-east wind.

Lake Nyasa has always provided its navigators with headaches. It is a deep lake, going down to 2,316 feet, but it is given to extraordinary rises and falls which make it difficult to provide any port facilities. The port of Mwaya had come into use a few years previously when an older port had been submerged. Its few facilities of grass store rooms and passenger shelters were also destined to be flooded before the lake reached an apogee to its cycle of rises and falls, and the waters receded leaving quite a few ports standing high and dry on the land.

The paddlers of his canoe entertained George with some account of the lake and the interesting portion of Tanganyika for which he was bound. They had no explanation for the slow cycle of rises and falls of the lake. When George questioned them on the matter, the head paddler simply stated:

"In the beginning of things, God made the earth, which was then all covered with water. Afterwards he created Mwamfu, the first man, and ordered the water to go back. In some places the water went back and in others it remained in pools like Nyasa and other lakes."

The paddlers were more informative about the place to which George was going. They spoke of it, in fact, with some awe. The verge of the lake, in those parts, was only thinly populated with fishermen for fever was bad. Inland lay a flat alluvial plain, quite uninhabited by man, and teeming with buffalo, puku and other game. At the end of this plain, to the north-west of the lake, there lay a gigantic workshop of the spirit of creation, a vast cluster of dormant volcanoes surrounded by fertile piles of rubble and dominated by the 9,713 feet high mass of the Rungwe mountain.

"Long ago," the paddlers told George, as they pointed out the shape of Rungwe in the distance, "smoke and fire came from the mountain. None has been seen since the time of the first European. It was many years before the first German, Bwana Meyer, came to Mwaya, that any eruption took place. Rungwe sometimes grumbles and the earth trembles when he stirs, but no fire or smoke is seen. The same may be said about the crater of Kyeyo.

" If a man goes up to the craters of those two mountains, it is said that he will hear whispering there. If he approaches too near, the whispers stop. If he goes into the craters, he will find plates and cooking pots of some glittering metal which is not gold. If he tries to take these things they vanish. Just before the war between the English and the Germans, there was a great tremor and rumbling from Rungwe. On two successive days, in broad daylight, many men were seen coming down the mountain side. When people went towards them to see what was happening, the men vanished. It is indeed a magic place to which you go, with many strange scenes and dangers."

George was intrigued at the prospect ahead of him. The great volcanic pile looked very beautiful, dim and almost ghostly in the haze, and the journey towards it from the lake was full of novel scenes and interest. With a few porters picked up from one of the lakeside fishing villages, he set out to walk to the administrative post on the heights at a place named Tukuyu. The path climbed steeply from the plains up the slopes of an intensely green and, at that time, quite uninhabited mass of volcanic hills.

Through these hills there rushed a series of clear and lively streams, fed by the clouds that caressed the tops of the volcanoes, and racing off with leaps and bounds like eager dogs to find a way through the hills to their waiting master, the lake. George loved the country. The streams looked as though they were made for trout, while the greenness and obvious fertility of the place invited human settlement which, through the coldness and dampness of the heights, had not so far attracted any Africans.

Tukuyu was an old German administrative post. It had been built at an altitude of 5,100 feet on the summit of one of the smaller volcanoes. The Germans had built an almost " Beau-Geste " type of fort to act as a *boma* or administrative centre. The officials certainly needed some protection there, if only from the weather, for the great mass of Rungwe acted as something like a magnet for clouds. It rained for eleven months of the year, with only October considered to be reasonably dry. The consequence of all this wet weather was an astonishing greenness and luxuriance in the countryside which made it a fertile mountain oasis in the midst of the wilderness of Africa.

The European inhabitants of Tukuyu were not numerous but very friendly. The administrative officer was Major Wells, whose wife was the only white woman there. Wells, sometimes called " Blow-Hard " Wells, had an assistant named Cheyne, there were two policemen, Hodges and Heard, a postal man, a telegraph linesman, and Doctor Reid. George introduced himself to the officials and Hodges invited him to share his quarters. Most of the men were bachelors living in substantial houses built by the Germans as married quarters and they had plenty of spare room. Hodges took George over to his house and introduced him to another guest already there, a short, tough-looking Yorkshireman named Vivian Lumb who had an odd habit of continuously twisting his forelock as he spoke. He was a trader who had come in for some medical treatment. There was something wrong with his reflexes. When anybody tapped his one knee, the other one jerked, and this became rather upsetting to a man living on his own in the wilds.

"We're having a gay time at the moment," Lumb told George. "There is quite a crowd of officers here from the King's African Rifles. They've all been axed in some economy drive and are going home. They're drowning their sorrows in one long binge while they wait for the *Gwendoline* to pick them up. What are you here for?"

George told him of his past activities and ambitions as a hunter. Lumb seemed interested.

"There is no shortage of elephants in Tanganyika," he said, looking at George reflectively, "as well as other profitable things. This place is the real Cinderella of Africa. How are you off for finance?"

"Just about enough to get myself going."

Lumb nodded and looked thoughtful.

"Come over and meet a partner of mine," he said suddenly. "He's a Scotsman named Bill Cumming. He's pitched a tent in the trees over there. He won't live in a house."

Lumb guided George to the camp. Cumming was sitting on a camp bed in his tent eating a papaw. He seemed so startled at having visitors that he promptly reached under his stretcher, produced two more papaws, and suggested that they join him in his meal. He was a wiry, dark-haired man, about 5 ft. 10 in. in height and with a fairly strong Scots accent when he spoke, which was not too often. He was a man who preferred silence, and made much use in conversation of a non-committal grunt.

"Bill's prospecting here," said Lumb. "The Germans found gold traces in several rivers in this part of Tanganyika. They never found anything payable but where there's traces, there should be gold. Not so, Bill?"

Cumming grunted. George thought that the man was just being like most prospectors, suspicious of possible rivals.

"Prospecting isn't my line," he said hastily. "I'm after ivory."

Cumming at least changed the tone of his grunt.

Lumb took over the conversation.

"I run a store at Ruiwa, down on the Usangu plains on the other side of the mountains. I grubstake Bill on an even share of anything he finds. I could be interested in something like that with you. I've wanted a hunter here for some time. It's not only ivory, there's a big overseas demand for the skins of colobus monkeys and for beeswax. You have to travel around to get things like that, get the tribespeople organised in trapping the monkeys, there are masses of them in the forests here, and gathering the wax. I'm stuck in my store. A man cannot do everything. Bill here is my long-term investment, if you are game for a joint venture, I could grub-stake you as a hunter."

" It sounds like a deal," said George, " but let me think it over tonight. I'll let you know tomorrow."

Lumb nodded. They went on eating their papaws in silence.

" You must come to the party tonight," said Lumb after a while. " It's in Doc Reid's house. Army officers and other chaps. Quite an elegant affair."

Cumming seemed to choke on his papaw. Lumb clapped him on the back so willingly that the prospector's nose and moustache were buried in fruit.

" Do you play poker?" asked Lumb, while Cumming cleaned his face.

" No, never been able to afford to learn," answered George.

" Oh well, there's plenty of booze."

The booze actually lasted five days. Lumb played poker almost continuously. The army officers seemed bent on a marathon session with some pretty wildly-fluctuating fortunes of play. One young subaltern who had talked loudly while he was winning of cleaning the whole country up, ended by asking Lumb to refund him £90, otherwise his projected university training would be jeopardised. Whether he would have reciprocated the favour if he had won, was very uncertain. One or two gratuities changed hands in the course of the play. George couldn't see much sense to the pastime and neither could Cumming. The prospector simply sneaked out one evening in the midst of proceedings, and next morning George noticed that his camp had vanished. When he mentioned the matter to Lumb, the Yorkshireman shrugged without looking up from his cards.

" He always goes like that. He's a funny bugger. Sometimes I don't think he's too sociable. If he ever finds any gold, it will be the death of him. He'd have to mix with people and that he could never stand."

The poker game went on. George always remembered the night after Cumming's departure. It was the one night in his life when he was certain that he had D.T.s. He was sitting in Doc. Reid's house talking to a couple of officers when he noticed the pictures on the wall suddenly seem to float out on their wires, and then fall back with a curiously gentle movement. A cupboard door repeated the same ghostly action.

" By God!" said one of the officers. " I've got the rats. The doc warned me about it long ago, but I never listened."

He crossed himself hurriedly.

George looked around. Even the poker players had stopped. He was slightly reassured. They couldn't all be getting D.T.s, at least not simultaneously. There was a dead silence. Then came the rumble of an earth tremor. They all ran outside. They could hear a few glasses breaking inside and somebody groaned when he heard the crash of a bottle of whisky. The tremor lasted for nearly a minute. Then it was over, and they were aware of a chorus of dogs barking. There was no serious damage. The dormant volcano beneath their feet had simply turned over in its sleep.

The experience had a definitely sobering effect on the party. They all went to bed early. George wondered whether any of them said their prayers. Next day the party broke up. George and Lumb came to an agreement about hunting. Lumb would take all financial risks, while George would do the practical work of organising large scale trapping of the magnificently-furred colobus monkeys, and a trade for beeswax.

Hunting the monkeys gave George the opportunity to explore the gorgeously-forested slopes of the volcanoes. Nature had certainly been in generous mood in the making of this remote part of the world. The high forests were extravagantly wooded with an astonishing congestion of trees, lianes and shrubs waging a struggle for survival on the well-watered, fertile, but quite hopelessly overgrown slopes.

Buffalo, black duiker, and the rare Abbots' duiker, shared the forests with the monkeys. Man was kept out by the dampness and the cold of the high altitude and the only people to penetrate these heights were an occasional hunter or a wood-cutter of the Nyakyusa tribe searching for the handsome red-wooded timber trees, the *Mpegele Lungwe,* whose name has become attached to the dominant volcano in the area in the form of Rungwe.

The monkeys and birds definitely had the best of this world. If, so to speak, the ground floor of their forest home was excessively damp, then the top floor was brilliantly sunlit, it was a roof of green so thick that it seemed as though a man could walk on it while he diverted his eye with stunning views of great heights, and strange volcanic craters whose floors were covered by lakes which, sheltered from any wind or disturbance by the surrounding lava walls, were as still and silent and enchanted as if they were mirrors dropped there by the great god Pan.

The colobus monkeys led a very easy and contented life in this volcanic world. The colobus is the most handsome of all the monkeys, and a curiously solemn character, not given at all to the antics of the rest of its primate relatives. They were numerous in the high forests, and to see them swinging along the deep galleries which bordered the mountain streams was a pleasing sight, with their pitch black backs and heads, the white fringes around their faces, and long white mantles and tails. They were normally very silent creatures but in the early mornings, when the clouds still rested with their cheeks on the mountain slopes, the colobus monkeys sent out a curious throbbing chorus which sounded exceedingly eerie as it rose and fell through the silver mist like a strange hymn in praise of the warming light of the sun.

Hunting the colobus was a specialised business. The animals ranged over too wide an area and were too well supplied with natural food, to be easily trapped. George had to roam around the verges of the forest hoping to catch bands of monkeys feeding in detached clumps of trees. With his African assistants and their tough and curiously silent little shenzi dogs, George would endeavour to work between the monkeys and the main forest. Once they were in the main forest it was impossible to get the monkeys, but in the smaller clumps, they could be picked off by a first class marksman using a small bore rifle. The Africans who hunted them had to manage things the hard way. Their marksmanship was too indifferent to produce profits from such elusive targets. The Africans went to the length of trying to catch the monkeys in clumps of forest so small that a group of hunters could systematically chop every tree down until they brought the monkeys to the ground.

Lumb's store at Ruiwa became George's base camp. It was a primitive little place, just a cluster of thatched bandas, but from it Lumb contrived to do quite a business. The store always seemed to be surrounded by a cheerful crowd of customers from the Sangu tribe who lived in the hot bush where the Ruaha River has its headwaters in the mountain slopes surrounding the Buhoro Flats.

Lumb allocated one banda to house George on his infrequent visits to the store. A second banda acted as home for the uncommunicative Cumming, but he was very seldom there. He lived in the bush and simply sent in runners each month to secure supplies and money to pay his men. George only saw him once again that year, when the prospector came in to Ruiwa with a bad dose of fever. His sickness even seemed to have silenced his grunt so George hardly got to know any more about him.

George's branch of the concern paid handsomely for a few months. Apart from hunting, George traded calico and print-cloth for beeswax and colobus skins. He also shot an occasional elephant and although the ivory was not considerable, it was at least of excellent quality.

What ended the business was a sudden collapse of world prices. It was very dismal when it happened. George returned from a hunting trip with a good load of wax and skins, and found Lumb pouring over a recently arrived batch of letters. The last trip of the *Gwendoline* had taken down a cargo of their skins and wax, and also the hides which Lumb traded in his store. It was the biggest consignment they had ever despatched, but by the time it reached Beira for shipment to the outside world its marketable value had dropped to such an extent that its sale would not even return the freight charges.

It was something of a blow. The isolation of their position made it difficult for them to appreciate what was happening in the outside world. They spent a futile evening being bitter at the rest of mankind for having let them down. There was nothing else they could do about it. Their agent simply advised them to postpone further shipments until better times. The problem to resolve was what to do in the meantime.

George thought it all over when he went to bed. At least the price of ivory was still fair, but the thing was to find elephants, and find them in a place where authority would allow him to shoot them. From what he had heard and seen, Tanganyika was certainly a prodigious treasure house of animals, but the government was not inclined to be over-generous in the matter of hunting-licences. The legal limit was three elephants a year, and unless he turned poacher it was not possible to make a living from such a restricted bag. He had heard attractive accounts of big tuskers and easy hunting controls in the Congo. He admitted to himself that distant hills are always blue. Closer inspection might reveal the Congo to be as sterile a hunting ground as Nyasaland. The descriptions of the place, however, were too interesting not to be investigated.

Before he fell asleep, George made his decision. When he met Lumb at breakfast the next morning he told him that he thought the best thing to do was suspend the partnership until more opportune times. He would go off in search of elephants in the Congo, and return to Tanganyika whenever Lumb found that world prices were on the mend. The partnership had been a friendly affair to both of them and hopes of a revival were mutual.

George talked to his trackers and found twelve men who were prepared to accompany him, at least on the start of his venture to the Congo. The Africans liked elephant hunting. It was a pursuit which not only guaranteed them plenty of meat, but was also exciting and profitable. The only trouble for them was that the white hunters tended to wander too far afield into the territories of foreign tribes who, whilst welcoming the European, could make life disagreeable for any Africans who were not of their own kind.

The trackers told George that the area in Tanganyika around Lake Rukwa sheltered many elephants carrying large tusks. He had heard much from Europeans about the lake and he decided to visit the place on his way to the Congo. Lake Rukwa always had a reputation for game and at least it would be interesting to see the place. There was no great difficulty in reaching it, with the lake itself only a few miles off the route he would normally follow to the Congo.

George set out from the store at Ruiwa early one morning, with Lumb walking a short distance down the path to give him a friendly farewell. From the start the journey led through fascinating scenery. The path climbed out of the Buhoro Flats and over the top of a projecting ridge of the volcanic complex associated with Rungwe. Beyond this ridge the wrinkled old face of earth was scarred with the spectacular gash of the Western Rift Valley, with the Songwe river meandering along through the Mapagoro trees which grow on the hot floor of this prodigious geological fault.

The mighty valley was only scantily inhabited by man. Walking down it, following the course of the Songwe River which flowed into the lake, George had the feeling of finding his way into a lost world. The edges of the rift were fully twenty miles apart and towering up so sheer from the valley floor that more travellers than George have wondered how they would ever find a way out.

Rukwa was essentially the offspring of this rift valley. A number of minor rivers draining the walls of the valley had found themselves imprisoned and been forced to discharge their water into the lowest depression on the valley floor. The resultant lake was a shallow affair, about seven feet at its deepest, and filled with tepid, turgid and such brackish-tasting water that the Mbungu tribespeople who fished from its shores, had simply named it *Rukwa*, which is their word for soda or salt. Notwithstanding the taste and dingy appearance of the water, it teemed with fish, hippopotami, and certainly with one of Africa's greatest concentrations of crocodiles. In the hot and humid climate on the valley floor, the lake seemed a placid languid thing, but beneath its surface there raged a struggle for life between fish and crocodile more vicious even than the battle for existence in the world of mammals in the richly grassed verges around the lake shores.

The tremendous concentration of game in the area was certainly an attraction to George, but on the other hand it was not easy country in which to hunt. The elephants, in particular, favoured the areas where the mateti grass grew twelve feet to sixteen feet high. Short of insects and the smaller creatures, they were, in fact, the only animals capable of forcing a way through so dense a growth. Hunting them in such conditions was almost like hunting whales, you were never certain where they were, whether they were not on the verge of appearing, if not from directly underneath, then in a nerve-shattering crash from the tall grass immediately behind you.

Notwithstanding the difficulties, George hunted in the area with some success. With guides from chief Kivanga's people, he wandered for days through the long grass, following the paths the elephants had made, never quite knowing when he would encounter one of the animals coming around a corner full tilt upon him. Dodging into the grass, taking quick shots at momentary targets certainly made for excitement, but it was a chancy way of securing ivory. Shooting from a tripod, the usual technique in hunting in long grass, was useless in these extraordinary conditions of such high cover.

One morning George and his men came across the fresh track of a single good-sized bull and they followed it. After about three hours tracking they caught up with the elephant. Leaving the rest of his men behind in safety, George and his best tracker ran ahead hoping for a chance of a shot. The animal seemed unconscious of their presence. He moved steadily but unhurriedly along the narrow path, with George and the tracker keeping station a few yards astern.

It was impossible to get in a killing shot. George only had two light rifles with him, a ·303 and a ·318, and taking a chance in the rear with one of them might only speed the elephant on his way. The hunters tried to make the animal turn by imitating with their mouths the curious stomach rumbling sounds which elephants make when greeting each other, but their quarry seemed quite indifferent as to whether he was being overtaken by one of his own kind or not. He simply proceeded on his way, shouldering a path through the long grass with never an attempt to turn round and see what was coming along behind him.

After about half an hour they reached an old path made by some other elephant. This path crossed the route of George's quarry and then swerved almost parallel. It provided George with the opportunity he had been hoping for. With his tracker he darted into the new path and ran up it as quickly as possible in order to get ahead of the elephant. It was stifling hot in the long grass, but at least the absence of any movement of air eliminated any chance of the elephant scenting them.

After running about one hundred yards they reached a place where elephants had trampled down the grass to form what was almost a small clearing. George and the tracker crouched down and waited for their quarry to approach. They could hear the elephant forcing his way through the mateti grass. The animal sounded as though he was advancing directly upon them. He stopped suddenly, and the silence made things even more tense. George wondered whether the animal had scented them, but after a pause of a minute the elephant moved again. From the disturbance of the grass he seemed to have altered his course slightly, but he would still pass very close to them.

The body of the elephant appeared through the grass but he was still protected by the thick canes which were quite capable of deflecting a bullet. George had his rifle ready. He steadied himself and watched closely. The elephant was passing through the grass about three yards away. There was one small gap in the grass and as the elephant passed it, he momentarily offered the heart shot. George seized at the opportunity and fired.

The elephant received the bullet dead on target. At tremendous speed the great animal swerved at right angles and came straight for the hunters. The action was so fast there was nothing they could do. The elephant was over the tracker before the man could even move. Whether the elephant realised what he was doing is unknown. The animal simply crushed the man into the ground and raced on for about forty yards before he fell dead with a tremendous crashing of grass. He was carrying a fair load of ivory but he had certainly claimed a price for it.

The tracker had been killed instantly. George could only look at the man's broken body and think that if he had seen the heart shot a second earlier and the elephant's reactions had been the same, the animal would certainly have been over him, for he had crouched ahead of the tracker in order to protect the man from any charge.

It was a miserable end to the hunt and it was the last time George went after elephants with light-bore rifles in such hazardous conditions. When the rest of his men came up, they carried the man out into the open where they buried him. George sent generous financial compensation to the dependants, but this was scant consolation to anyone for the tragedy. George felt far worse about it than when he had shot the intruder in his tent in Portuguese territory. He abandoned the hunt in the long grass around Lake Rukwa, broke up camp, and left the next day to continue his journey to the Congo.

CHAPTER FOUR

MIGHTY CONGO

FROM Rukwa, George travelled westwards, following the old German track into Northern Rhodesia, and then through Fife, Abercorn, and Mporokoso to Chiengi on the north end of Lake Mweru. It was all thick, green, brachystegia woodland with few landmarks save an occasional bog or marsh where some stream had its source. Game was scarce, with the animals well scattered over a considerable extent of country, while human beings seemed equally rare.

At Chiengi there was a small British administrative settlement on a pleasant site overlooking Lake Mweru. The Europeans, Wickens the district commissioner, and one or two other individuals were all a very agreeable and informative lot. Staying in the settlement at the time there was also the well-known missionary and author, Dan Crawford, a gaunt, wiry sort of man with his head somewhat lost with the angels, but at least he could give George information about the Katanga portion of the Congo which he knew well, having been kept as a slave there for some time by one of the chiefs.

The area around Lake Mweru was excellent elephant country, but as the

Northern Rhodesian Government only allowed three elephants a year to any hunter, it was impossible to consider doing anything there. According to the information given to George, the Belgians allowed a hunter four elephants a year in each province, but their district commissioners were reputedly easy to bribe and a man of enterprise could always effect some suitable arrangement. As all accounts described the Congo as being well stocked with elephants, it seemed to George that the place might turn out to be his best hunting ground.

It was with some anticipation of future profit and excitement, therefore, that he hired a dozen porters, and set out to walk along the north shore of the lake to the Belgian administrative post of Pweto. It was dullish, bush country, with few signs of life save birds and crocodiles. Of the latter creatures there was certainly no shortage. Fording the tributary streams which flowed into the lake was made exceedingly troublesome by their presence. When you are waist deep in water, holding your belongings above your head, it is little consolation to know that crocodiles have a reputation for cowardice, especially if a large specimen who has been regarding you appraisingly for some time, waddles ungracefully down from a sandbank, and quietly submerges.

George reached Pweto, however, without any event. The place was a rather primitive administrative post of the class generally known in Africa as a " two-man " station, that is, of sufficient importance to justify the presence of an assistant to the administrative officer. The place consisted of a collection of wattle and daub buildings standing about half a mile from the lake shore. Its principal inhabitants seemed to be a rather scruffy-looking crowd of African soldiers equipped with antique *Fusil-Gras* rifles, and lounging around without any sign of officers.

George had his papers scrutinised, and then took out a hunting-licence for the district. What he planned to do was move from district to district through the Congo, shooting the legal limit of four elephants in each area as he passed through it. In theory, at any rate, he could collect quite a bag that way and the Congo elephants were reputed to carry excellent ivory.

There was nothing to keep George in Pweto. He secured a new batch of porters and set out down the course of the Luvua River, hunting as he went, and finding the journey diverting, if only because he was travelling through country that was completely wild and untouched by any obvious efforts of mankind. The river, with the path on its banks, simply seemed to wander on interminably through an endless forest of thick, tall bush covering a sandy and flattish landscape. It was hot and sultry, monotonous but very beautiful in parts, with some gorgeous flowers and sweet smelling ground-orchids dropped there by the hand of Pan when he realised that it would be a kindness to present this Cinderella of a land with some slight ornamentation.

By the time he reached Kiambi, the next administrative post down the river, George had shot his four elephants. Their tusks, without being enormous, nevertheless contained good ivory and the price he received from the trader at Kiambi was most encouraging and fully justified his hopes that by obtaining a licence in each district of the Congo, he would be able to enjoy a profitable life as an elephant hunter.

Kiambi lay on a slight rise on the east bank of the river. The track from Elisabethville to Albertville was ferried across the river at this point, and the occasional traffic gave the place a little more life than that usually seen in administrative posts of this nature. Some miles away to the west there was a mining settlement at Manono, a large-scale tin proposition which was a choice example of the unfortunate fact that Providence seldom places minerals in pleasant situations. Manono was murderously hot and sweaty, with men working all night in a great open-cast mine, consoling themselves with some delusion that the years which they wasted there on contract work would be compensated by a life of ease on their savings. The mosquitoes generally had something to say about that.

From Kiambi, the Luvua River flowed onwards as a magnificently broad stretch of water. With a new elephant licence, George continued his journey by canoe, stopping to shoot when opportunity offered, and finding the river journey an agreeable change from tramping through the bush.

The Luvua flowed into the Lualaba at an administrative post named Ankoro, where George once again had a set of tusks to sell, and where he secured a fresh hunting licence. He felt very confident of himself by then. Nothing gives a man a better sense of well-being than profitable occupation. He felt that he was really becoming established as a professional hunter. The Belgians had proved an agreeable crowd, and the general success of his wanderings was reflected in the increasing weight of the money belt he carried around his waist.

From Ankoro, George was recommended to leave the river and go across country to the post at Kabinda, and with another new licence, hunt westwards towards the banks of the Kasai River, selling his ivory and picking up a new permit at every administrative post he visited. The whole idea, in fact, worked capitally, until he reached the junction of the Kasai and the Sankuru Rivers where a tiny administrative post and river port named Basongo became something in the nature of his Waterloo.

Basongo, oddly enough, was one of the smallest of the administrative posts George had visited. There were only two Europeans resident in the place, a trader and an administrative officer, who did not agree with each other. George supposed that this was one of the causes of his trouble. The other cause was the admitted fact that he brought twenty good tusks with him, and only had a licence for eight. Hunting had been particularly good and temptation irresistible.

Protocol should have taken George direct to the administrative officer but commercial interests led him to the trader who gave him an affable welcome. The ivory averaged around forty-five pounds a tusk and the man was very pleased to have such an offer. He invited George to stay in his private guest house and that night entertained him in truly regal Congo manner with the luxury of what was known as palm oil chop. This was a real epicure's delight made from the heart of a young palm tree, cooked with palm oil, ground nuts, and the red liquid from the outer husk of the palm oil nut. The result was a vegetarian's dream of a stew, a dish so rich and superbly flavoured that George spent most of the night in a state of something like bilious ecstasy.

The next morning the administrative officer sent for George. The man had heard of the ivory. He wanted to see such things as licences. George tried to talk himself out of it. He had intended to see the officer first thing in the morning. The after-effects of palm oil chop, however, had only allowed him to fall asleep in the early hours and then, pursued by large numbers of vari-coloured elephants, he had hardly enjoyed a restful time. The result was that he had dozed into the morning and been caught on the wrong foot when the officer had become irate enough to send for him.

Now there was a matter of six pairs of good tusks to account for, and no licence to cover them. George had intended to take out a new licence in Basongo and immediately debit four pairs of tusks to this account. He had hoped to affect some mutual arrangement about the surplus of two pairs but he sensed that it was now somewhat late in the day for any friendly negotiation.

The officer talked around, above and below the issue for some time, taking an increasingly grave view of things as he proceeded. With George moving from one foot to the other, the officer eventually informed him that he would have to stand trial that afternoon for poaching. George went back to the trader in a troubled frame of mind. The man was not quite so hospitable as on the previous night. He sensed trouble.

" Why didn't you give him some dash?" asked the trader. " That's why he talked to you for so long. He was expecting you to make him an offer. The longer you delayed, the graver he sounded, and the more dash he expected."

It was the first time George had encountered the famous African Open Sesame known as " dash ". He explained to the trader that he was scared to make an outright offer of a bribe. The officer might have become offended and charged him with attempted corruption. The trader simply laughed.

" You're very inexperienced."

He looked at the tusks with some regret.

" You'll have to write most of these off as the cost of instruction. Never be afraid to offer dash. Nobody here resents an offer. If it is declined, it is done so courteously, and with regret. Perhaps circumstances may be inopportune, but that is very seldom in the Congo. Now you'll lose nearly everything."

" Is it too late to make him an offer now?"

The trader nodded.

"You have put him on his dignity. You must stand trial."

George reported to the administrative office that afternoon. The trial was a simple affair of standing in front of the officer's desk and being fined one thousand francs, with the confiscation of the surplus tusks and, worst of all, the confiscation of his rifles as punishment for poaching. The loss of the rifles was a particularly sad blow. There was little likelihood of finding replacements in this remote part of the Congo, and even a gas-pipe weapon would be horribly over-priced.

George went back to his quarters with the trader. There was no palm oil chop that night, but at least the man helped him drown his sorrows with a few bottles of wine. The only consolation was the lesson of experience, if he wanted to be a poacher he must be certain of never being caught. It was something which he resolved not to forget.

Five days later a river boat called and George was glad to see the last of Basongo. It was not one of those places to which he ever had any desire to return. Standing in the bow of the paddle-wheeler he signalled the watching administrative officer a poacher's farewell. The man simply spat into the river and turned his back. George laughed, and walked around the ship to meet his fellow passengers.

It was a seven-day voyage down river to Kinshasa, the present day Leopoldville. There was little to see save forest, islands covered with palm trees, and occasional hippos. If he had left in a more cheerful mood, George might have been appreciative of the journey, but as it was, the whole thing was painfully reminiscent of his voyage up the Zambezi, something like an ignominious retreat. The company on the river boat was also dull, two missionaries who kept to themselves, while the European captain and engineer were both secret drinkers, with their off-time spent locked in their cabins.

Even the river ports were uninteresting, but at one solitary little wood post where the boat stopped to pick up fuel, George did see on the bank a tall, gangling, raw-boned looking man with a flop hat, home-made *veldschoen*-type shoes, and a familiar glint to his eye. The stranger also eyed him appraisingly. Intuition drew them together to spend a couple of hours quarrelling about politics. The stranger was an Angola Boer, who had found his way to this odd spot as a timber cutter for the river boats. He was very glad to discover somebody with whom he could enjoy an argument.

"The Belgians here are worse than the bloody English," he said, when George asked him how he was doing. "No wonder the natives call them *Bulamatadi*, the Stone Breakers, they would break anybody's heart."

He launched into some account of the sufferings of his kind, a very favourite source of light conversation amongst Boers. A source of argument can be a reminder that others have had worse troubles and survived. George switched the subject to rugby and from that lead they chatted away amiably enough with a feeling of something in common. When the river boat sounded its whistle and it was time to part, the lonely Boer impulsively gripped George's hand.

" Man," he said, " it was good to meet you here and have a yarn. I'll say this about you English, I went to Europe once, for a holiday. I went to Germany first, and then to Holland. I thought they would be the best parts. But man, I know it will sound crazy to you, but the only place in which I felt at home was in England, even though I still hate the country's guts."

He went off laughing and George watched his odd figure receding into the distance as the boat went down the river. The rest of the journey passed without event. George occupied himself in trying to make up his mind what to do. He was still feeling slightly annoyed about the Congo and inclined to try his luck elsewhere. In the lounge there was a map of this part of Africa and he spent some time in examining its details. There was certainly an awful lot to the continent and he was still certain that somewhere or other he would find a hunting ground for himself. It was intriguing to speculate over the odd place names, lonely-looking lakes, and meandering rivers. He tried to visualise the people and animals who lived in the various parts, strange tribes and solitary Europeans like the Angola Boer. There must be fascinating stories about them all, if only one had the time and opportunity to collect them. He tried to talk to the missionaries again but they were exasperatingly uninterested in their own surroundings. They might just as well have locked themselves up in some rheumaticky monastery in Europe for all they had learned in their years in Africa.

On the map, George noticed the odd little Portuguese enclave of Cabinda, just north of the mouth of the Congo river. By what perversity of fate this pocket colony had been carved out and left to Portugal in the scramble for Africa, George had no idea. But the curious shape of the place, and the mere fact that he had never heard of it before, gave him the whim to visit it, and learn what the position was there about elephants.

When the boat reached Kinshasa, George simply indulged in a day's sight-seeing in the future Leopoldville, and then caught the train to Matadi, the port for ocean-going steamers one hundred miles from its mouth up the Congo river. So far as information about Cabinda was concerned, Matadi proved as sterile as George's erstwhile companions on the river boat. The oppressive atmosphere of heat and humidity stifled all life. People seemed to be uninterested in anything other than making as much money as rapidly as possible from whatever they were doing, and then clearing out back to Belgium. The only advice given to George was that he go on by boat down the river to the port of Boma which had some connection with Cabinda, and where there was a Portuguese consul who would be able to give him all the information he wanted.

Boma was a miserable hole of a place. George landed and booked in to a hotel facing the harbour. It was a mud-walled establishment with a corrugated iron roof covered with palm leaves in an effort to keep it cool and kill the sound of rain. The proprietor was an oily-looking character named Da Silva. His most notable characteristics were a mouth full of gold teeth, an ability to speak snatches of most languages, and the fact that he refrained from ever cutting the nails of his little fingers. He had some notion that long nails were the sure sign of a man of means, well above any indignity of manual labour. The nails were also handy in scratching off any small coin forgotten on the counter of the bar.

The porter was an individual so dirty that he made a point of wiping his hands clean on his trousers before he picked up anybody's luggage. He showed George to a room. It was not particularly cosy. The ceilings were made of mats. The porter giggled when he saw George looking upwards.

" There's not much privacy," said the man, with an accent so good that George was startled to find that he was English. " You can hear everything that goes on." He winked heavily. " Some of the romances are terrific. If you hear any snarls at night, don't worry. We've even got a Russian staying here, room 7, who's married to a chimpanzee."

George was startled.

" Well, at any rate, he lives in the room with her," said the man hastily.

George looked at the room walls. There were numerous smears of blood.

" Looks as though you have plenty of insects," he remarked. " In a place like this a guest could not exactly even call a flea his own."

The porter sniffed.

" They do wander about," he admitted. " It's bugs mainly. Actually this isn't all blood from people from this room. You get some tampans who come in from feeding on the chickens in the yard."

" Oh! Is there any way of telling what blood is your own?"

The porter looked at him.

" You joking, or something?"

" No, no, I just wanted to know in case I felt anaemic. Where's the convenience, anyway?"

The porter was hesitant.

"Actually," he said, " the place didn't use to have one. There were bushes outside until somebody cut them down. So the boss had something made at the end of the passage."

He led George down to a wooden partition. There was a ricketty variety of a throne inside with so little room that any occupant had his knees pressed against the door. There was a peep-hole bored through the door at eye-level, but whether to look in or out was uncertain. Remembering the notice scrawled on the convenience of the *Queen*, George looked at the walls for any sign of wit. There was only one example of this type of humour, however, carved painstakingly deep into the inside of the door at eye-level. It said, sardonically:

" *Cet hotel est infecté.*"

George recoiled and went outside. Somebody guided him to the Portuguese consul, but the interview was not profitable. The man was not interested in visitors to Cabinda, and distinctly hostile to the idea of an elephant hunter. What treasures he was guarding in Cabinda, George never discovered. Not even the hint of a bribe would budge the man into conceding a visa.

George went back to the hotel feeling somewhat depressed. He went into the bar and confided his sorrows to a big, blonde, Flemish barman who responded to the name of Flim-Flam. The man was quite receptive to George's story.

" Why don't you get a job here, while you make up your mind what to do?" He looked at George's build reflectively. " We need a second barman. The other one left."

The suggestion was quite interesting. At least the free living would help George to conserve his resources. He went and saw Da Silva. The hotel man also inspected his build appraisingly. Da Silva's wife was sitting in the office with him. He spoke to her in Portuguese, and she came to the door of the office and subjected George to a long stare. She was a pretty blowsy specimen of a woman. George stared back at her and reflected that she would be safe alone with a regiment of Cossacks. Later he found that she dolled herself up at night to act as a hostess. In her finery she would have been safe even with Turkish cavalrymen, so she was not much fun for the guests.

" You can have the job," said Da Silva. " You get your room, food, tips, and 1,000 francs a month, O.K.?"

The terms were reasonable. George nodded. He went back to his room and before starting work, wrote a letter to Vivian Lumb, telling his erstwhile partner of his present whereabouts and condition, and asking whether times had improved enough to justify a return to the old trade in Tanganyika. He posted the letter, and then reported for duty in the bar.

Flim-Flam showed him around. The bar was surprisingly well stocked with French wines and brandies, Scotch whisky, gin, beer, and the pleasant local fruit drink, grenadine. There were such considerable reserves in a storeroom in the back, that George was surprised.

" It's for the Americans," Flim-Flam explained. " They have prohibition in their own country. The Bull Line run ships straight across to this place. Boma is the first port they reach which has liquor."

George looked at him. He hadn't encountered many Americans in his life.

" What are they like?"

Flim-Flam had views about Americans.

" The kind that come here," he said, " are street sweepings. There's a word they use a lot which perfectly describes them—phoney. Their sentiments, politics and morals are all phoney. They've also got big mouths, and some of them are big fellows. That's why the boss has put triple duckboards on the floor behind the bar, it makes us look bigger.

"One thing you must do is never let Americans get on top of you. It took me some time to learn how to handle them. You can learn by my experience. Let's say that you have a drunk American before you, on the other side of the counter. He insults you. He is like a dog snarling through a fence. He thinks you can do nothing to him. Watch this."

Flim-Flam suddenly placed his hands on the counter and vaulted over it, swinging his boots around in a pile-driving arch as he did so.

"Aim at their jaw with your boots," he said, when he had recovered his balance. "Have no mercy, kick to dislocate their jaw. I've had quite a few of them carried out that way. You must practise as I did, when the place is closed. You can be proficient before the next ship comes in."

He looked at George for a moment.

"You will need such a trick. You're quite a ruggedly built fellow, but a bit short. You'll find that they'll go for you. You'll have to learn all the dirty tricks."

George was slightly bemused.

"Does it pay to have customers like that?"

"Certainly, they throw their money away like idiots. We have them about sized up. There's nothing here which they can break except glasses, and we include the price for them with each drink. The tables are bolted down, and even the photographs of King Albert and his Queen are screwed on to the wall. We have no chairs, only benches that are too heavy to throw. The spittoons and ash-trays are unbreakable. Unfortunately that does make them hurt when they hit you."

"Sounds as though you have some lively times!"

"We do. Last time a ship was in, some fool in the local branch of the Banque du Congo Belge replaced with a red bulb the light they keep burning in the bank at night as a precaution against burglars. The Americans broke the door down to find out where the women were. The best free fight I've ever seen was when the police came to arrest them, and the Americans couldn't make the authorities understand that they were not in the bank looking for money.

"They are quite incomprehensible in their behaviour. As it is, Mr da Silva obliges them by running an establishment in the back of the hotel. Mr da Silva and the girls were quite distressed when the Americans broke into the bank. It seemed as though they were being unfaithful."

George cocked his ears to the sound of a distant siren. Flim-Flam shook his head.

"That's not Yanks. They make more noise. They'll be in next week. Then watch out for your nose. They seem to regard a barman's nose as a bull's-eye, and aim at it all the way from America."

CHAPTER FIVE

GOLD AND IVORY

AFTER three months, George was experienced with Americans. His nose had also been broken into something like the potato and mash of prize-fighters, and the principles of rough-house fighting first taught to him by Jack Gunn, had been perfected to a formidable extent.

Actually, George found the life rather dull. There was a certain monotony to things. A ship would arrive, its crew would stream ashore as soon as they could, and head for the bar. The sight of the rows of bottles would produce a glassy stare to their eyes, like donkeys putting their tongues out at the thought of carrots. They would start drinking with an urgent sense of haste, as though frightened that the supply would run out before they could either get sick, make fools of themselves, or be thrown out after a fight with the barmen. Generally they started off quietly enough, then by degrees they became pally, amorous, lachrymonious, argumentative, and finally obstreperous. It was possible to time the behaviour of most of them. If possible they would be shunted to the establishment in the back of the hotel when they were at the amorous stage. This got shot of them before trouble started, and Da Silva liked it that way. He considered that this allowed the front of his enterprise to preserve its class, and as he made more out of the back of the place anyway, with the young ladies pretty expert at handling drunk Yanks and their dollars, the combination worked admirably.

What ended George's period as a barman, was the arrival of a telegram from Lumb. How the message had contrived to filter its way around Africa from Tanganyika to the wretched hole of Boma was a real credit to international postal arrangements. George was quite flabbergasted to receive the message. He had almost given up hope of ever hearing from Lumb, but now here was the Yorkshireman's reply to his letter brought into the bar by Da Silva just after opening time. The advent of the thing created quite a stir. George opened it, conscious that everybody else was trying to read though the back. It said:

"Come at once. Bill's found it on the Lupa. Johannesburg isn't in it."

It took several moments before George could realise the implications of the message. So Cumming had found gold at last. Claiming a discovery as being richer than Johannesburg was a vainglorious boast in Africa. Still, one never knew. George started to become excited. He showed the telegram to Flim-Flam and Da Silva. He was quite surprised when they failed to respond with any enthusiasm. Da Silva had his own little gold mine in Boma, and Flim-Flam liked the life. They stared blankly at George.

"Are you going to leave?"

"By the next boat."

Da Silva was distressed. Rough-house barmen were hard to find.

"Come and see me in the office before you do anything rash."

He did, in fact, offer quite a substantial increase in wages, but George wasn't interested. A barman's life was not his choice. There was a Belgian ship sailing for Antwerp at the end of the week. George collected his due from Da Silva and bid his friends and colleagues farewell. Even the Russian with the chimpanzee came down to the river bank to see him off. The porter carefully wiped his hands before saying goodbye. Mrs Da Silva shed a tear. One lady on the ship asked George if all the girls were from a mission school. It was the best send-off he ever had, and almost made him sentimental.

From Antwerp, George crossed to England, and spent a few weeks with his family at Jacksdale. Then he sailed on the S.S. *Norman* through the Suez Canal for Dar es Salaam, and landed once more on the shores of East Africa at the end of May, 1923. It was good to be back. When the ship glided past the coconut palms into the placid harbour of the Abode of Peace, George sniffed the warm air of Africa and knew that he was at home. The smells and the noises, the intensity of colours and the very spaciousness of the place, exhilarated him. With gold and ivory somewhere in the distant hills, what more could a man want? He landed and booked himself on to the first train leaving for Kilosa, the usual place for the procuring of porters for any journey by foot into the southern areas of Tanganyika.

George had half-expected to find a general rush of gold seekers in the direction of Cumming's discovery but, although there was much talk about the find, the remoteness of the place tended to make people cautious. There was no superfluity of Europeans in Tanganyika, and, with the Asians, those that were there had specific jobs or a business which they were loath to leave until the discovery really proved itself. The outside world had hardly heard of the Lupa and the Africans were completely disinterested.

At Kilosa, a pretty miserable little whistle stop on the Central Line, George did meet one other man heading for the Lupa goldfield. This was Bill Brearley who, oddly enough, was a cousin of Lumb's. He had been earning a living in Durban as a piano-tuner. Lumb had sent him enough money to pay his fare to Tanganyika and when George met him at Kalageris' Hotel in Kilosa, the two decided to join forces for the journey to the goldfield.

There was one other European staying in the hotel, a gaunt-looking character named R. de la Bere Barker, who was destined to become well known as " Rufiji ", the pen-name which he used in the writing of numerous articles and books. George had an unexpected opportunity of getting to know him. On the day of George's arrival, Barker went down with black-water fever and Kilosa was hardly a place with any comfort for a sick man.

George and Brearley had to delay their departure and act as nurses for Barker, keeping him constantly sipping bicarbonate of soda in water to prevent his kidneys from becoming congested with broken-down blood cells. It was the only medicine they had.

Barker, normally a sallow, bony type of man, looked like death itself. One of the fundamental things about the wilder areas of Africa was that it was all a fine place, until you fell sick. Wandering through the few streets of Kilosa made George think that it would be a pretty miserable village in which to die. Its most notable inhabitant was an old Indian who had discovered that if you let a tap drip, the flow failed to register on the water meter. The man had a big bath under his tap and collected drips night and day. He was said to be the only man making a fortune in Kilosa.

Barker must also have been very reluctant to die in Kilosa. There was certainly very little else to make him get well. He seemed to pull himself up from an open grave by the sheer strength of his little fingers. The attack of blackwater had certainly shaken him. He had originally come out from England in the forces during the 1914-18 East African campaign. With Africa in his blood, he had joined the Uganda administration after the war. Now his ambition was to turn hunter and he had come to Kilosa in search of a licence to shoot elephants from the resident game warden. Blackwater fever had been a very poor substitute.

As soon as Barker was on his feet, George and Brearley left for the goldfield. Apart from Brearley going down with fever for a few days at Malangali, on the fringe of the Buhoro Flats, they had a reasonably pleasant three-weeks walk, shooting for the pot and finding the mountains and hills of the Southern Highlands to be very attractive country.

They struck the Lupa River at what was then called the " Yellow Bend " from the light-coloured gold being found there. The first sign of the gold rush which George and Brearley saw was a couple of grass huts built on the banks of the river with a cloud of dust rising from close behind them. The huts were obviously not of African origin and as the travellers approached they were greeted by two Europeans who were busy with a few tribesmen in excavating the bed of the river. George recognised one of them from Tukuyu. He was an ex-major of the K.A.R. named Micky King. The second digger was C. B. Bird, an elephant hunter. They welcomed the new arrivals in very pleasant manner but when George asked them how they were doing they became evasive. George soon learned that on any diggings, if you ask no questions you hear no lies.

Apart from this reluctance to discuss gold returns, the two diggers were very hospitable. They were obviously living the hard way, using honey instead of sugar, and smoking the venomous native tobacco laced with elephant droppings to take some of the sting out of it. Dar es Salaam was the only point of supply for most things and it was two months before a reply came to even a letter.

According to the diggers, Vivian Lumb was working a claim just up the river, and without much further delay George and Brearley went on. It was very pleasant meeting Lumb again. He and George had quite a reunion and that night Lumb described events on the diggings. At that time there were eight Europeans working alluvial along the Lupa.

"I admit that it's not yet exactly Johannesburg," he said, when George reminded him of his telegram, "but it will be. Where there's alluvial, there should be reef. That's what we are all hoping for, meanwhile we make what we can of alluvial. Everybody is on gold, you don't have to look hard to find colour. There's bound to be a big rush here as soon as news spreads. We all try and keep things quiet at present. No sense in being squeezed out by a stampede before the big discovery is made."

The next day George and Brearley walked on up the river to look for claims for themselves, and to meet the other diggers. Three miles up river from Lumb, an Australian, Danny Maher with a partner named J. F. McDonald were working claims. Further up, Bill Brearley's brother, Charlie, was also busy on a claim with a partner named H. G. "Rope Soles" Jones, a former district officer from Northern Rhodesia whose odd name had come from his enthusiasm for footwear with rope soles. He had once written a letter to some newspaper endorsing such footwear, and would never be allowed to forget it.

Bill Brearley remained with his brother, while George walked up to the last camp, where Bill Cumming was in residence. The Scotsman actually seemed glad to see an old acquaintance and enthusiasm for his find made him slightly more communicative. In the lower camps, George had been told that Cumming had found the gold while following an elephant, but the tale was manifestly untrue. Cumming was no ivory hunter, and in any case the Lupa was not in elephant country.

" What happened," the prospector explained, " was that I heard rumours that a German had once found gold traces in the Songwe River. I tried it, but found nothing to even pay for tobacco. Then I wandered over here to the Lupa. I panned some sand in the lid of my dixie at Manandegi, and there was the gold. Man, I tell you, I felt faint. I could hardly believe it. I had to prove to myself that it was gold. I tested that it was malleable by bending it with the rim of a cartridge. Aye, it was gold all right, and good stuff. I'm glad you're here early. We should all make our fortunes."

He showed George his samples. Most of the gold was astonishingly fine, the diggers had already named it " Fly Speck " gold, while the coarser gold was called " Rice " gold, also from its size. Nothing larger had so far been found, but at least there seemed to be plenty of the fine stuff. The excitement of the prospector and the rest of the diggers was infectious. There is no life in the world more absorbing than working a claim that is rewarding to its owner. Even days of disappointment are compensated by the overnight hope of fortune on the next morning. No lucky dip or sweepstake has more intriguing possibilities, no gamble can be more distracting.

The next day, George pegged a claim for himself just above the camp of Maher and McDonald, and started to build a grass hut for himself. He knew nothing about prospecting, but he liked the look of this stretch of the river. It would certainly be very pleasant searching for gold in such a rugged and sweeping piece of country. The Lupa flowed down a rocky course through a great, rolling expanse of bush, with the Mbeya range of mountains providing a handsome and beautifully wooded backdrop in the south. Lake Rukwa lay within easy reach to the north-west so there was the prospect of hunting or fishing as a diversion from the pursuit of gold.

When evening approached, George walked back to Lumb's camp, where he was staying until he completed his own hut. As he walked, an unaccountable feeling of melancholy overtook him. He tried to shake it off, thinking it simply the reaction from an interesting day. He told Lumb about it when he reached the camp. The Yorkshireman looked at him closely.

" Fever?" he suggested.

George shrugged. He went to bed early and had a restless night with his head full of tensions. At dawn, however, he felt better. He washed, shaved, and then went outside to relieve himself. It was quite a shock to see that his urine was dark red in colour. One in four cases recovered from blackwater fever, and it was a curious feeling to think that he might be dead within a week. He went back to the camp and told Lumb.

The Yorkshireman took his temperature.

" Hell," he said, " what are you doing standing upright? Do you want to be buried that way! Get horizontal."

George lay down and couldn't have stood up again if he had tried. The practical Lumb bustled around concocting a mixture of cold weak tea and bicarbonate. When George relapsed into unconsciousness that afternoon, Lumb sent for the other diggers to see if they had any advice or medicine. The only thing they had was quinine.

George could hear their voices discussing his case while he seemed to be floating in a dark and turbulent sea. He felt so helpless he didn't know whether to try and laugh or cry, and couldn't have managed the strength to do either. The only thing to bring him partly to consciousness was Cumming's voice saying,

"Man, we not only haven't got any medicines for him, we haven't even got any soap boxes to give him decent burial."

George managed to open his eyes enough to give them all a venomous stare. He was lying on the ground and they were standing around looking down at him like doctors at an autopsy table. They looked so melancholy he had a momentary vision of himself being eaten by some scruffy grave-robber of a hyena.

"I'm not going to peg out," he muttered weakly.

Lumb dropped to his knees beside the bed and wiped the perspiration off George's face.

"That's right, laddie," he said, "you're going to be fine."

George was unconscious.

"I think we'd better try and get a doctor," said Danny Maher.

"Rope Soles," Jones agreed. "Somebody had best walk to Tukuyu, it's only about eighty miles away, and ask the doc there to come, or tell us what to do."

"Who will go?" asked Bird.

They discussed the matter. Eventually they managed to send a message through to Tukuyu. Doctor Wilson, who was there at the time, left immediately on a battered old motor-bicycle which he used to ride along the footpath. When the path petered out, he walked. By the time he arrived George was sitting up, well on the way to recovery.

"The troubles I have," said the doctor, "to reach people who are either dead or getting better. There's just no profit to this business. Maybe I'd have better luck as a digger."

He gave George a minute examination.

"It just staggers me how some of you fellows pull through. You know what blackwater fever is? The reward of having malaria too often. So, if you must go on living in places where you get fever, you can only expect blackwater time and again, until it kills you. Booze and bad women admittedly bring a few chaps to grief and those are difficult things for me to treat, but blackwater is still the biggest hazard the European faces in Africa, with nothing better than quinine to combat it."

"So?"

"So, if you don't want to experience it again, go away. If you like it here, you at least know what to expect if you stay."

The doctor shrugged as he saw George's grin.

" This damn continent does get in your blood, doesn't it? Maybe it's something the mosquitoes give us, with fever. Well, don't stretch your luck too much. You've had a very close shave. When you can walk, go somewhere cooler to recuperate, somewhere where you won't be bitten by too many mosquitoes for at least a little while."

George followed the doctor's advice. Micky King had recently taken up some land near Tukuyu and had started to plant coffee. He had built a wattle and daub shack on the farm, and whilst he was trying his luck on the diggings, the place was being cared for by an eighty-year-old retired Indian Army officer, Colonel A. Masters. Micky King offered George the use of the place for his convalescence and the offer was too well-meant to decline.

It was very pleasant going back to the green heights of Tukuyu. King's shack was comfortable and Masters, notwithstanding his age, was a very lively and intelligent man, who made excellent company. George spent a month roaming around the farm, doing some work on the coffee, and refreshing himself in a very congenial manner. He also did some serious thinking about his future.

The dose of blackwater fever had left him with a slightly bitter taste in his mouth about the Lupa. It was probably not a fair prejudice to have about Lumb's idea of a future Johannesburg but, after all, even a man who works in a sweet factory is apt to be put off if he gets bilious on the product.

At the same time George heard that the Tanganyika Government had started a pretty crude form of elephant control. With the possible exception of the Congo, there were more elephants, some 80,000, in Tanganyika than in any other part of Africa. They had no natural enemy save man, and with the numbers of both elephant and man increasing, there was bound to be friction over possession of the more fertile and arable areas, particularly in the southern and eastern parts of Tanganyika where the elephants preferred to congregate.

With some intention of controlling the increase of the elephants the government announced the introduction of what were called " Governors Licences " to be issued free to selected hunters, allowing them to shoot twenty-five elephants on each licence, providing that they adhered to certain conditions. The hunter had no call on the government in any way. One tusk of every elephant shot was to be the property of the government. All elephants shot had to carry tusks of between 50 lb. and 70 lb. If the hunter shot an elephant with tusks of a lesser or greater weight, he had to surrender both tusks to the government.

George applied forthwith for one of the special licences and when this was granted to him, he reverted with some pleasure to his true calling of an elephant hunter. The prospect of action and excitement as well as the profit from ivory quite drove his vapours away. With a handful of porters he made his way in September 1923, through Iringa, over the granite hills of the Southern Highlands, and down into the great elephant country of the Kilombera river where, roaming around in a wilderness of bush covered plain, there was reputed to be an immense concentration of tuskers.

On the Kihanzi river, a tributary of the upper Kilombera, there lived the famous hunting tribe of the Mbunga people. George thought it sensible to visit their chief, Makuwa, before he started hunting and see whether he could obtain guides and trackers from such knowledgeable and expert people. He received a very pleasant welcome. Hunting was a passion with the Mbunga, and a visit from a white man of similar occupation was very acceptable to them. They seemed, in fact, to be as interested in George's techniques as he was in theirs, and quite free in exchanging hunting secrets with him as they tracked the elephants through the bush.

Many of their ideas were plain superstition, and curiously common throughout all the elephant-hunting tribes of Africa. On his first night in the chief's village, George had some absorbing conversation with Makuwa and a party of elders who joined their white visitor at his camp fire.

The women of the village seemed to have discreetly vanished. Their withdrawal was explained by the superstition that no man must sleep with a woman on the night before he went out elephant hunting. In some way the elephants would sense such an indiscretion, and the hunter would certainly be charged. The Mbunga went to such pains in stalking elephants, that they could not conceive of the animals charging without some supernatural cause.

" Should it be that a man did not sleep with a woman on the previous night," said the chief, " but is still charged, then it can mean that his wife is being unfaithful while he is in the act of hunting. Witchcraft can also bring about a charge, if a hunter has an enemy who works magic to do him an ill. You must always carry a charm against such things. Even the elephants carry their own *dowa* (charm)."

George was intrigued.

" What is that? "

They reminded him of the odd temporal gland situated between the eye and ear of elephants of both sexes. It has a slit-like orifice and contains a strong-smelling, cheesy-like substance. Sometimes the gland exudes a fluid and the process has for long been considered by some authorities to have a sexual significance.

The Mbunga hunters pointed out that it was common to find a small piece of wood in this gland. The wood was generally little over one inch in length and slightly thicker than a match. George considered that the wood had its origin when the elephant was pushing its way through a thicket. The tip of some twig probably worked its way into the gland and snapped off leaving the small piece inside. The Mbunga hunters, however, would not hear of such a prosaic explanation.

"This is the magic charm of the elephants," insisted Makuwa. "To possess one for himself, is a great prize even for our own hunters."

He produced one of the fragments of wood from a satchel he carried at his waist.

"I would not hunt without it. It helps the elephants to find their way through the bush, especially at night. It also tells them where to dig for water in the dry river beds. It does the same for us."

George examined the charm curiously. There was no doubt that the African hunters believed in such things so implicitly that possession of such a talisman gave them a very considerable amount of confidence. Periodically, as well, the African elephant hunters had their guns and spears blessed. George was only half amused when Makuwa suggested that he have this experience before he started the hunt. Christian congregations bless quite a variety of objects and deeds. The experience of the pagan god of Africa blessing his own activities might be interesting. He accepted the offer with thanks. It was a ritual which he was destined to undergo on two more occasions in far separated parts of Africa, although the detail in each case was remarkably similar.

The ceremony was conducted on the following morning by the village priest who was entrusted by the tribe with the hereditary right of attending to the mystic needs of hunters. George was led to a shrine consisting of a very small round hut, erected close to the village, but in the seclusion of a clump of bush. The entrance to the place was so low that it forced anybody to go down on his stomach and wriggle through in a position of obeisance to two small wooden idols which stood side by side immediately opposite the doorway.

The hut was so small that it could only contain three or four people in a squatting or kneeling position. Of the two idols, the one on the left was about twenty-four inches high, while the one on the right was slightly over twenty inches in height. They were both dressed in pieces of cloth and beads. A small bowl containing meal stood in front of each one.

George's rifles were laid crossways in front of the idols. The priest squatted next to the smaller idol, whilst George faced them across his rifles. The priest then made several movements with his hands, and prayed for the idols to intercede with God on behalf of the hunter, for whose character the supplicant could vouch. There was no worshipping of the idols, they were simply the intermediaries in the ritual. When the priest was finished, he and George and the few witnesses crawled out of the hut backwards, and of necessity in a humble manner.

With the ceremony over, George commenced his hunting. Whether it was from the efficacy of the pagan blessing, the skill of the trackers, or the number of elephants in the vicinity, he had extraordinary luck. Within a month he had accounted for the twenty-five elephants permitted him by the Governor's

Licence, and all of them had excellent tusks, well within the prescribed limits. George was delighted. He had the tusks carried to Kilosa. There he surrendered the government's share, and sold his own twenty-five tusks for a very satisfactory return. Even more satisfactory was the fact that the local game warden, C. F. M. Swynnerton, granted him a second Governor's Licence and he could return to his hunting ground to find more elephants with the right-sized tusks.

This was far and away the best hunting which George had so far experienced. He was exhilarated by his success, and the Mbunga people were fattening admirably on all the meat. They had quite taken him to their hearts, and it was one night, after a very satisfactory meal on the tender part of an elephant's temple, that Makuwa confided to George that the professional African hunters had their special guilds. These guilds were confined to the real elephant hunters of all the tribes, with almost identical initiations and identification markings throughout the continent. If a first class hunter applied for membership, there was no reason why it should not be granted, even if he was a European.

George took the hint. He made a few enquiries, and gave the necessary presents to the right people. In due course he was informed that a meeting of the local guild leaders had favourably considered his application. He would now be subject to a final test. A leading member of the guild would accompany him on a hunt and watch his skill. He would be expected to do everything himself from tracking to final kill, without any aid or advice.

As it happened, the test hunt passed off perfectly, and the bag was a particularly fine young bull. George cut his trail within two hours of starting the hunt, tracked him down to the complete approval of the observer, and despatched him into the elephant's paradise with the speed of a high velocity bullet straight into the brain.

The following night, George was invited to appear before a meeting of the guild, bringing with him a reasonable amount of trade cloth, a few goats, hoes, and some beer. It was an enjoyable party. The beer was drunk, the goats eaten, and a round of flowery compliments passed. At the end of the meeting he was informed of the date of his initiation into the guild.

The ceremony was held at a secluded spot about one mile from the village. Only guild members were allowed to attend. The ceremony started with a certain amount of mumbo-jumbo, and a form of dance depicting the course of an actual elephant hunt. Whilst this dance was going on, an elder, using a small, sharp knife, made several fine horizontal cuts on the right shoulder, over the right eyebrow, and on the right thumb, of the initiate. In the case of a left-hand shot, these cuts would have been made on the appropriate side.

Into the cuts, the elder rubbed the secret medicine of his trade. This was made from the extreme tip of an elephant's trunk, the tail, and scrapings from the front of its feet. To this was added a piece from the nerve of an elephant's tusk, and powder scraped from the bones of certain snakes and a lion. The nerve from an elephant's tusk was considered to be especially powerful in magic. It could only be safely extracted from a tusk by a full guild member. The operation was done in strict privacy, with the operator keeping his mouth filled with certain leaves. As soon as the nerve was extracted, the man would spit the half-chewed leaves into the cavity of the tusk. The nerve was kept buried. Any man not a member of the guild, or any woman seeing the operation would become impotent or barren.

The various ingredients used in the initiation were mixed as a paste and their effect was considered to make the hunter invincible in the chase. For every elephant killed, a guild member was supposed to have a mark made on his arms. It was common to see African hunters well scarred by these triumphant notches but it was just as well that George never attempted to keep this type of record of his trophies. The number of elephants he was destined to shoot in the course of his eventful life would have left him with far more notches than skin. As it was, he found that membership of the hunter's guild was a pleasant introduction to a far more intimate knowledge of African customs and society than he had so far possessed. The beer drink and dance with which the guild celebrated his membership was alone worth his money, just to see their merriment and satisfaction.

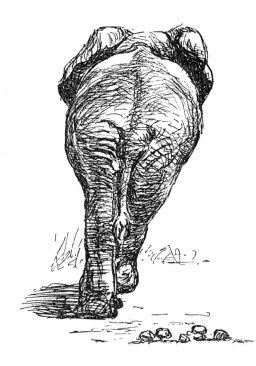

CHAPTER SIX

A POACHER'S LIFE

BY THE time George went back to Kilosa he had shot a total of fifty-three elephants, none of which had tusks less than 50 lb. in weight, with the largest just under 90 lb. The last elephants he shot under the normal Tanganyika licence which allowed a hunter three elephants a year irrespective of size of tusk. The two Governor's Licences had been very profitable to him. He was bitterly disappointed to learn that no more were to be issued. The whole idea of this type of elephant control had been dropped. The folly of the notion had become apparent to the authorities. Destroying what were, in fact, the best breeding stallions of the elephant herds, would affect the quality rather than the quantity of elephants. The runts and the tuskless freaks would simply take over breeding duties from which they were normally excluded by the big bulls by due process of the survival of the fittest. It was also a fact that most of the elephants who raided the *shambas* or small holdings of the country were, in any case, usually the runts who, without tusks to allow them to fossick for delicacies, were tempted to expend their frustrations on the easy pickings found in farmlands.

George sat in the pub in Kalageris' Hotel and considered the matter. Every time he started as an elephant hunter something happened to frustrate him. The only way around the difficulty would be to turn poacher. To do this successfully required careful thought. The whole technique of poaching, like going a-pirating in the olden days, was never to be caught. A poacher in gaol was nearly as much of a failure as a pirate swinging on the gallows. There was just no profit to it.

Of all the elephant areas George had seen, the most attractive to a poacher was undoubtedly along the Northern Rhodesia-Congo border in the vicinity of Lake Mweru. The elephants there were good tuskers who had long been protected. The country was lightly settled. The Congo border could provide a convenient base and, in any case, the few British officials in this area were so widely separated, over-worked, and inexperienced in hunting, that he was pretty certain he would be able to run circles around them if they attempted any pursuit. The whole idea seemed very attractive. In a cheerful frame of mind, he hired porters and set out to walk back to the gold-fields as the first stage on his journey to Northern Rhodesia.

There had been quite a few changes on the Lupa since George had last been there. About twenty more diggers had arrived and pegged claims. They were all at least finding a living, while some of them were reputed to be doing reasonably well. In that year, 1924, in fact, 6,805½ ounces of gold were recovered from the Lupa river, and this was certainly enough to make the diggers eager for more. Although none of them had done as well as George in his brief spell of hunting, at least there were no restrictions on their hopes. Their atmosphere of ebullient optimism, in fact, was very infectious.

George stayed with Danny Maher. He soon had an opportunity of meeting the new diggers as well as his old friends. At Kilosa, before he had set out, he had ordered a couple of cases of whisky from Kalageris. The liquor would make a welcome present to his digger friends. The Greek had been out of stock at the time, but he promised to send the cases on within a few days. The porters arrived with the whisky one afternoon while George was out with Maher, prospecting up the Little Kasanga river.

The two men returned from their outing to find the two cases of whisky safely deposited on the ground at their camp, and surrounded by half a dozen thirsty-looking diggers who were sitting around obviously labouring under great self-restraint. Bill Cumming was there and he actually had his tongue hanging out.

" For God's sake George," he said, " broach open a case and be hospitable to your visitors. You've been an awful long time coming back."

George grinned.

" Talk about vultures at a kill," he said, " how did you all get scent of this?"

It appeared that the porters had arrived on the field that morning with the cases and a letter carrying George's name. They had asked at the first camp for directions to reach George. The diggers there had promptly forgotten their labours in the heat and kindly volunteered to direct the porters to the proper address, even though this involved some five hours of heavy walking. Every other digger they passed on the journey was gathered up, until the porters were at the head of a small procession. Even as George opened the cases, three other diggers arrived. By the time evening came, there was a jolly party on in Danny Maher's camp.

Some of the newcomers to the Lupa were individuals of extraordinary character and background. There was John " Daddy " Park; his partner Charlie Wood, a rather grimy-looking Cockney who had wandered up through Africa after working on the construction of the railway over Sir Lowry's Pass in the Cape; A. G. " Gunga " Dean, who had been chewed up by a lion and only saved himself by pushing his hand down the throat of the big cat and gripping its tongue; A. " Ham " Esterman; W. " Piper " Grant, who, to the delight of Bill Cumming, arrived at the party complete with bagpipes; and a likeable little man with a big name, Estcourt Vernon Herbert Cresswell-George, formerly of Pietermaritzburg and later a Nyasaland tobacco farmer who came to the Lupa to escape the depression. His sister, Doreen, had accompanied him to the diggings. She was the first European woman there, and was married to John Park.

The whisky soon had this diverse company well lubricated. Listening to their yarns and gossip was highly diverting. They were all working under intense difficulties in obtaining suitable mining tools and equipment. The handicap of Tanganyika has always been its communications. The Germans had simply widened a few paths to a width of six feet and these provided safari links between the principal centres. Wheeled traffic over most of the territory was completely impossible, except for an occasional cycle or motor-bike.

Tukuyu, eighty miles away, was still the administrative and postal centre for the diggers. It had at least grown sufficiently to attract its first European trader, J. B. MacFie. The diggers used to despatch their gold to this trader, or to the postmaster of Tukuyu, by means of African messengers who cheerfully tramped along without a worry about the value of their load. Rope Soles Jones had set up a crude blacksmith's hearth where he smelted gold for the diggers, producing small ingots in a mould made from a piece of iron. The ingots he produced were about four inches long by one inch broad and half an inch thick. They were valued at about £100. George found it quite a thrill to handle these little samples of the stupendous wealth of Africa.

Rope Soles had contrived to drive a motor bicycle to the Lupa and with this he maintained some connection with Tukuyu. He entertained the company with an account of his last visit. He had set out with seven of the gold bars owned by various diggers and packed in a haversack on the back carrier. When he reached Tukuyu he found that the murderous bumps of the journey had shaken out all the gold bars. The district commissioner immediately sent a messenger to try and find the bars. About three miles out, the messenger met an African tramping in from the back of beyond to pay his taxes. He had found the gold bars where they had fallen, one after the other, along the path. He had picked up the bars and was carrying them in to show to the district commissioner.

George's return-to-the-Lupa party was made even more joyous as the diggers celebrated the safe recovery of their gold. By the way they handled

the stuff, there was nothing they mined on the Lupa which was more beloved to them than good whisky. Even the four bottles Danny Maher had
slipped aside, had to be re-discovered, broached and downed that night.
Dancing completed the evening, with Bill Cumming providing something of
a climax. He attempted a *pas seul*, tripped, and singed off one eyebrow and
half of his handlebar moustache when he fell into the camp fire with a
shower of sparks, bad language and laughter. Otherwise there was no harm
done in the course of the party.

Leaving the Lupa was quite a wrench to George, even though he had
not gone back to it with any particular intention of remaining. He swap-
ped his claim to Danny Maher for a ·577 double-barrelled rifle and ammunition, collected a tramp of porters, and set out for the port of Kituta near
Abercorn, which then served as the outlet for Northern Rhodesia on Lake
Tanganyika. The poaching life called him, and he had no intention of allowing any further distractions to lure him away from his planned career.

At Kituta, George hired a canoe from the missionaries. He wanted to
travel across the south-western portion of the lake to the Belgian port of
Molira, some sixty miles away. The canoe was a fairly substantial affair
used by the missionaries on their own perambulations. It was a big hollowed-
out tree trunk, with a grass-roofed midships where George sat in a rhookee
chair, while the ten paddlers worked away cheerfully enough, singing their
songs of the lake, and exchanging badinage and ribald jokes with one another.

On the whole, it was a pleasant trip. As a precaution against the sudden
storms which can create a formidable disturbance to this part of the lake,
the paddlers kept close to the shore, with three nights spent camped on the
beach. The scenery was handsome, with a fine jumble of hills rising from
the shore, and superb swimming in water of delightful clarity and coolness.
Occasionally they saw some other canoer, or passed a fishing village on the
shore, but there was no sign of any other European save for the sight of a
large ruined and deserted church standing on the beach at Sumbu and looking as forlorn as a dog whose master had sailed away in some boat and
abandoned it.

Molira, the so-called Place of Fire, was a solitary little Belgian station
looking out over the lake from a plateau a few hundred feet above the level
of the water. It consisted of the usual cluster of wattle and daub shacks
housing one Belgian administrative officer and one trading station run by the
unusual partnership of an Arab and an Indian. George camped on the shore
and walked up to show his passport to the official and secure a licence for
the shooting of four elephants in that part of the Congo.

With these formalities completed he went to see the traders. They were
very friendly. George made no bones about his intention to establish a base
on the border and poach into Northern Rhodesia, especially into the

area of Kipiri, in the Mweru Marsh Game Reserve, which, as George had observed on his last visit, was very good elephant country indeed. The Mweru Marsh was apparently a former lake which had withered up in its bed until it consisted of only a few patches of papyrus swamp mixed up in large areas of mateti and elephant grass. It was the type of place which elephants love, with plenty of food, water, and nothing to disturb them in a range of country some one hundred miles long by twenty miles wide. Hunting them would be almost as tricky a business as it was in the area around Lake Rukwa, with the grass growing up to fourteen feet high. One advantage, however, was that a poacher would be very difficult for any government men to find.

The two traders approved of the whole idea.

" We'll take everything you get," the Indian assured George. "As it is, we receive a trickle of ivory smuggled across the border by African hunters. Have you come to an understanding with the government officer here?"

" Is he amenable?"

" Yes, but with discretion. Perhaps you would like us to handle the arrangement, as your agent?"

George was agreeable. The Indian went back with him to the government officer and they had a very satisfactory discussion. George could make his base on the Congo side of the border. The traders would handle all his ivory, and pay him fifteen shillings a pound. The difference between the fifteen shillings and the prevailing twenty shillings for ivory would cover the costs of the " understanding ". They parted in a very amicable fashion, with the administrator advising George to make his base on some high ground on the border, which directly overlooked the marsh, and was a few miles north west of the village of a petty chief with the simple name of *Tambala*, or Rooster.

Tambala's village had the advantage of being connected to Molira by the old slave path used by the notorious Tippu Tib in the days of the great raids. This path roughly followed the border, but more on the Belgian side, from Molira to the area of the upper tributaries of the Congo river. It had been well tramped into the ground by long and unhappy safaris of slaves with loads of ivory destined to be shipped from Molira up the lake to Ujiji, and thence by porters to Tabora and the distant coast of the Indian Ocean.

Tambala had been one of Tippu Tib's bully-boys in his young days, but he was now an exceedingly fat old man lording it over a tumble-down village of about one dozen huts. He gave George a very hearty welcome.

" It is a long time since I saw anyone here other than missionaries and tax-collectors," he said, offering George a pull of beer from a big pot. " We live in sad times. It seems only yesterday that I was with my true lord and leader, the great Tippu Tib."

He used Tippu Tib's name with a degree of reverence and was full of anecdote about the, to him, halcyon days of the slave trade. He had been with Tippu Tib in his fort at Pweto right up until they had received news of the approach of a British column sent to destroy the place. According to Tambala, this information had reached them at a most embarrassing time. The fort was well stocked with ivory, with insufficient slaves to carry it to Molira. Tippu Tib set the few slaves he had, about fifty, to carrying the ivory to a secret cave and burying it. Even Tambala, perhaps fortunately for himself, had not been told where this cave was. When the last load of ivory was in the cave, Tippu Tib had the slaves shot. When the guards who had executed them returned to Pweto, he had them killed as well, so that nobody knew the hiding place of his ivory other than himself.

Tambala was wounded in the battle for the fort. Tippu Tib's power was broken and his retainers scattered. One of his reputed sons, Sirimani, was living further west along the path, but he had been too young at the time of the disaster to know anything about the whereabouts of his father's ivory. When George met him on a later occasion, he confirmed Tambala's story of the lost ivory, but knew nothing more about the matter.

Buried treasure has proved irresistible lure to many people, and George found it a fascinating distraction. For three months he searched up and down through the bush country along the border, and within one hundred miles of Pweto, but he found nothing. Oddly enough, a trader named Purdue had heard the story at about the same time as George. He conducted a rival search in the same area, with the two parties cloaking their movements in an atmosphere of the heaviest secrecy. Neither of them found anything.

George eventually gave the search up, rather disgusted at allowing himself to be distracted for so long by such an unprofitable pursuit. He went back to Tambala's village and told him that he was going to stick to elephant hunting in future. The old man was contrite.

" What I told you was true," he said, " but I am sorry now that I told it to you."

He hesitated for a moment.

" I brought you ill fortune," he added. "At least allow me to make amends. Do not laugh. I will bless your guns."

George did not laugh. He remembered his experiences with the Mbunga hunters. The next morning he accompanied Tambala to his village shrine, and saw the man go through substantially the same ceremony as the Mbunga priest. When George crawled out of the hut, his trackers were already waiting for him. They set out immediately, crossing the border into Northern Rhodesia, keeping a sharp watch for any government men, and searching for elephants. It turned into quite a day.

The high ground of the north ended sharply on the verge of the former lake. Just before the ground fell away, there was a fine vantage point, about one hundred feet above the withered shore of the marsh. It hardly needed glasses for George to see the elephants. The floor of the lost lake was almost flat. In the last remnants of water there grew thick clumps of papyrus. Where the water had degenerated into mud, the high mateti grass flourished, and where the mud had dried into hard earth, the elephant grass grew. From the vantage point looking directly down on this strange world, George could see the backs of elephants moving about, almost like whales lazing on the surface of a green sea.

Where the grass was too high, or the elephants were too far away, flocks of egrets betrayed their position. The beautiful white birds rose into the air as the elephants moved and then, as gracefully as snowflakes falling, settled again to feed on the insects disturbed in the grass. Even as a spectacle this paradise of elephants would have been remarkable, but to an ivory hunter it represented a fortune. George watched it for a while, spellbound at the possibilites of the place. His trackers were too excited to even talk. When he looked at them, he could see the wonder in their eyes at such a sight.

George had planned his campaign with care. From his experience at Lake Rukwa he had designed a very light ladder which his men had made for him from the fronds of palm trees. The idea was for his men to be able to hold the ladder vertical in the long grass. He could climb to the top, and be elevated at least ten feet above the ground. He calculated that from this height he would be able to look out over the top of the grass and exploit the vantage point to take brain shots at the biggest elephants. Moving about completely concealed in the grass, and using the jack-in-the-box technique to pop up at moments most awkward for the elephants, George anticipated a very interesting hunt. He was confident of being able to lose any pursuing government men in the marsh and the only uncertainty he felt about the whole plan was the general effect the noise of shooting might have on the elephants. They were so lazy, well fed and protected, that when the explosion of his first shot resounded over the grass, this announcement of the advent of a hunter might prove something like a leopard jumping into a flock of gazelles. There could be quite a scatter.

Immediately below the high ground, George observed two bulls, one somewhat larger than the other. They were feeding near the edge of the marsh, and in a very convenient position for hunting, George indicated them to his trackers and the men grinned. They were looking forward to the coming events as eagerly as their master. They picked up the ladder and with George leading the way, dropped down the slope into the marsh and headed for the elephants.

They soon approached the two bulls. They could hear the unsuspecting animals pushing over the mateti grass and munching huge mouthfuls of the tender shoots. The hunters approached as near as they considered prudent and then held up the ladder for George to mount. He was somewhat uncertain about the correct rifle to use from his ladder-top position. For the first experiment he selected a ·450, and cautiously climbed the ladder. When his head was over the level of the grass, he looked around at a unique view. With the grass swaying and billowing with the wind, the effect was the same as if he had raised himself shoulder-high out of the sea. Twenty yards away he could see the backs and heads of the two bulls. The one was obviously much older than the other and a good two feet taller. George watched him for a while, then took careful aim at the animal's brain and pulled the trigger.

The recoil on top of the ladder was murderous. George swayed back and fell with a crash into the grass. The four men who had tried to hold the ladder sprawled on the ground. George scrambled to his feet. The grass had taken the shock of his fall and there was nothing broken. He listened for the elephants. If one of them had charged while the hunters were in such a muddle, the result could have been disastrous. Everything was still, however, save for the interminable rustling of the grass. He signalled to his men to hold the ladder up again. Cautiously he climbed the thing and looked out over the top of the grass. Apart from the fact that the big bull had disappeared, everything was exactly as George had last seen it. In truth, the elephants of Mweru Wantipa were so ingenuous about hunters that the noise of the shot had hardly made them flap their ears. A few had moved on a step or two, but that was all.

The younger of the two bulls seemed to be very preoccupied at something. At best he was too low in the grass to offer a shot, but now he had his head well down and was very busy, puffing and snorting away as though making a considerable effort. There was nothing for George to do except try and approach closer and find out what had happened. He descended the ladder. Leaving the trackers behind, he made his way carefully through the grass. He reached the trampled area where the two elephants had been feeding, and witnessed a curious sight.

The big elephant had collapsed on top of his feet with blood oozing from the hole in his head. The young elephant was making a massive effort to help his friend to stand up again. He had his trunk underneath the older elephant and was heaving and straining to lift the six-ton weight. Suddenly the big elephant gave a groan. A tremor ran through his body and he shook his head, flapping his ears violently. His eyes opened. For a moment he looked around in a very dazed manner. The bullet must have just missed a vital part of his brain. He started to scramble to his feet.

George lifted his rifle, but before he had any chance of finding a target, the big elephant turned on his friendly partner with a harsh trumpet of rage. The smaller elephant was caught completely off-balance and horribly dismayed by the ingratitude and surprise of the attack. He went down with a tremendous thud while his frienzied attacker tore into him with his tusks. The big elephant obviously blamed his companion for the injury and was not interested in discussing the matter.

George watched the struggle from the verge of the clearing and waited for a chance of a target. For the moment all was movement and there was nothing which he could do. The big elephant was worrying and tusking his stricken companion with a heart-chilling ferocity. The ground beneath them was already a soggy mass of blood and entrails as the big elephant ripped great gashes into the flank and stomach of his victim. The smaller elephant was quite dead before his killer wearied of the business. Then the big elephant lifted his head, doubly gory from his own wound and the blood of his one-time friend. He raised his trunk as though in victory, and George shot him straight through the brain, bringing him down in a heap over the carcass of his own victim.

George walked up and examined the two elephants. They both carried good tusks. The drama of what he had seen was overshadowed by mental assessment of the profit of their death. The trackers came up at the same time with the ladder and he told them to hold it upright. He went to the top and viewed the surroundings. There was still no visible disturbance among the elephants. The whole scene was as tranquil as it had been before he started shooting. He breathed a long sigh. This was a real hunter's paradise. He climbed down the ladder and checked his rifles. When he was ready he turned to his trackers.

" Right," he said, " let's start work now, and see what we can do before evening."

By the end of the day George had shot eighteen elephants carrying ivory worth £2,000. Among them was a bull with tusks weighing over eighty pounds each, and a cow, the largest George ever shot, with thirty pounds of ivory in each tusk. Apart from the last three elephants, he shot them all from the top of his ladder, using a light ·318 rifle with a recoil easy enough to leave him on his perch, and a penetrative power capable of blasting a way into the head of the toughest elephant. The last three elephants he found just before sunset. He reached an expanse of water, which the elephants used for drinking. Standing half dreaming on the other side, about sixty feet away, were three fine bulls. Two of them carried good ivory, the third was what the Africans called a *budi,* or tuskless elephant.

George picked off the two tuskers so rapidly that neither of them ever knew what had killed them. He was not interested in the tuskless elephant, but that animal was certainly interested in him. The elephant was in a great state about the death of his companions. He screamed out a shrill trumpet of rage and hate. George stood on the other side of the water and watched him. It was deep water and served as a good barrier between himself and the elephant.

No-Tusks came to the water's edge. His ears were standing out, his eyes were aflame, and his trunk was waving in the air as he smelled the stink of man. He and George looked at each other across the water.

" I wouldn't if I were you," George said to him. " I'd run away."

No-Tusks didn't take the advice. George saw him coiling his trunk against his chest as he made up his mind to take the plunge. He lurched forward into the water. As he did so, George, with some regret, sent a bullet straight into his head. The elephant simply dived into the water with a colossal splash and never emerged from his final bath. Great bubbles of blood rose to the surface above the spot where he had sunk to the mud. The blood spread over the surface, merging insidiously and indistinguishably with the reflected glow of a sky which had turned to fire with the setting of the African sun.

CHAPTER SEVEN

MEN AND ELEPHANTS

IT TOOK five days of hard work to cut the tusks out of the elephants, and this was a tricky time. Vultures had arrived on the scene in great force and their gyrations and descents would be a sure attraction for any government man who happened to be on the move within a radius of thirty miles. George was on tenterhooks throughout the period. Such a prize of ivory would be a very sad loss. The tusks were all of first rate quality, finely grained, cream coloured, easily worked ivory of the very best savannah elephant type. On the world markets it would fetch the top prices, at least thirty per cent higher in value than the brittle, hard, and grainless white ivory of the forest elephants. Even in its own class, this ivory of the Mweru elephants would be considered exceptional; the short, thick, strong stuff, which dealers prized so highly.

As it happened, there was no interference from any government authority. George called on the assistance of the few tribespeople who lived in the vicinity and the ivory was safely carried away to Molira where the traders received it into their store with delight. After the months George had wasted in the search for Tippu Tib's treasure, the traders had almost given him up.

The hazards in getting the ivory out of the marsh had taught George one lesson. It was folly for a poacher to be too greedy. Even if opportunity did allow him to shoot as many as eighteen elephants again in one day, it would be wiser to confine his bag to sufficient tusks to be handled with convenience, so that, even if government men were in the vicinity, there would be little chance of the profits of the chase being lost.

Before returning to his poaching ground, George organised his staff into an essentially mobile group of two dozen porters, two first class trackers, and one cook. He also visited the tribespeople living in the surrounding country, and promised generous rewards for any warnings of the approach of authority. Then he returned to Mweru Wantipa and selected a shady spot on the high ground just over the Congo border as the site of a base camp. While his men were busy making shelters and an enclosure, George walked across the border with one of the trackers and made his way to his original vantage point overlooking the marsh. He had no intention of hunting that day; he simply wanted to make a reconnaissance and see whether the elephants were still present in their original numbers.

George and the tracker reached the vantage point. They were almost paralysed by what they saw. Manoeuvring beneath them through the marsh there was such an assembly of elephants as made George think that he was the victim of some bizarre form of African mirage. Covering an area of some five miles in length and two miles in breadth, there were nearly 700 elephants all moving in the same direction with a curious slow, purposeful walk. None of them were feeding. They seemed intent on executing some special intention and were arranged for that purpose in a curious and regular order.

Leading this assembly, about one mile away from George, was a truly massive bull. Following immediately behind him were four bulls which, in their own right, were sizable animals but compared to the leader were very small fry indeed. Further back there were other big bulls in groups of twos and threes. These old bulls formed the centre of the gathering. Flanking them on both sides, there were younger bulls, and then groups, each of fifteen to thirty cows with their calves. It was a spectacle which George was destined to see only once again in his life, in the Ulanga valley of the Mahenge District in Tanganyika. This gathering also occurred in a marshy area, towards the end of the rainy season in March.* What precisely was the explanation for

---

* These great assemblies of elephants have been reported by other observers in various parts of Africa. The most detailed explanation for them ever offered to the author may be found on pages 74-76 of *The Ivory Trail*. This is the explanation given by the Shangane tribe who live amongst elephants in Mozambique. According to them the purpose of the gatherings is principally to separate adolescent elephants from their mothers and organise them into new herds. Wise old cows show them waterholes, elephant paths, the best feeding places, and otherwise instruct them in matters of interest to elephants. The adults, meanwhile, enjoy the social pleasures of gathering, meeting with old friends and finding new loves. In this pleasant way, nature ensures that there is an annual mixing of blood in the elephant herds, and the newly organised groups are composed of individuals quite unrelated to one another.

these gatherings, he never discovered with any degree of certainty. His tracker was as astonished as he was at the Mweru spectacle. It was obviously some form of social gathering possibly arranged for the purpose of forming new herds. Of all animals save the higher apes, elephants have far and away the most highly developed social sense. Whatever the reason for the gatherings, they are certainly not by chance or for the purpose of wasting time.

George and his tracker watched the spectacle of the gathering for some time. Elephants are such intelligent creatures that there is endless interest and entertainment in observing their habits. They always seem to be up to some activity, with many of their actions curiously expressive of what they are thinking. There are tall elephants, short ones, fat ones, clever elephants, simpletons, aggressive characters, and natural comedians who obviously take great delight in teasing and joking with their fellows.

To see such a variety of elephants together, quite apart from the immense numbers, was in itself remarkable. Normally the elephants practised some form of social segregation, recognising two distinct divisions which produced what hunters knew as bull country and herd country.

In the bull country are to be found the big bulls, either moving about singly, or in twos and threes, and sometimes accompanied by a few younger animals. A herd is very rarely seen in these areas and the boundaries appear to be sharply defined, but not necessarily by any natural feature particularly evident to man.

In the herd country may be found the herds composed of varying numbers of animals, but generally well-balanced collections of cows, calves, and one or two younger bulls. These herds are normally led by an old cow or a no-tusker. Each herd keeps to its own territory. Migrations take place, but these are well-ordered and seasonable, influenced by the ripening of foods in other areas or the drying-up of water supplies. Normally herd country is better watered than bull country as the calves and cows cannot go without water for the long periods that bulls can do in normal life.

Occasionally a big bull leaves his area and goes into the herd country. He joins a herd for a short time or wanders off with one cow for a few days of romance. In his hunting career, George followed quite a few big bulls moving very purposefully towards a rendezvous with a single cow who, by her tracks, had been loitering around at some point waiting for her sweetheart to arrive. The very certainty with which the bulls made their way across miles of rugged country to these trysting places always gave George the distinct impression that the whole thing was a long standing appointment.

George made no effort to disturb the assembly of elephants. It was too overwhelming a sight to spoil by any shooting. He simply watched it until the afternoon waned and the time came for him to return to camp where he spent the evening discussing the matter with his men, and searching his own mind for an explanation for the behaviour of the elephants.

The next day George resumed hunting, but when he led his men to the vantage point of the high ground, the great elephant assembly had dispersed. He must have seen the final phase of the gathering, for the marsh was now back to normal, with the elephants scattered about it engaged on their habitual feeding. There was nothing to be seen of the mighty bull and his attendants George had observed on the previous day. They must have wandered off deep into the marsh, or left the place for the dry surrounding country as the whole elephant community returned to its usual activity.

In his career as a hunter, George was never again to have the experience of shooting eighteen elephants in one day. He did manage ten in one day in after years, and had two days in which he killed nine elephants on each day, but the eighteen he shot on his first day in the Mweru marsh remained his record. Even one tusker a week in the marsh, however, would have been profitable, for he had only to be moderately patient in order to find an animal carrying at least a good 70 lb. of ivory in each of its tusks.

It was inevitable, of course, that authority would sooner or later appear on the scene. George had met Wickens, the District Commissioner at Chiengi, on his first visit to these parts, and he was more amused than alarmed when his spies reported to him that the government man was hard on his trail. Wickens was certainly no fool, but he was too much of a desk-wallah to have much chance of being a serious threat to the activities of any poacher in the marsh. Even a dozen experienced game rangers would have had difficulty in sealing off such an area. George simply ensured that he was hunting in one part of Mweru marsh when Wickens happened to be nosing around in another. When the government man started trying to set spies to locate the scene of George's activities, they were only too obvious in such uninhabited country. A few judicious threats soon sent them off on other business.

George came and went across the Congo border very much as he pleased. With Wickens forced to return periodically to his duties at Chiengi, George developed quite a knack of seeing that he was away at Molira for a week or so disposing of ivory at the time when the district commissioner was doing his best to hunt him down in the swamp. It must have been very frustrating for Wickens.

After a couple of months of this game of hide-and-seek, Wickens called in the aid of the district commissioner of Mporokoso, a tall, rather taut and angry-looking young man named Norton. At least he looked rather taut and angry when George viewed him through a pair of binoculars. George had led him quite a dance through the marsh. He had experienced a good hunt just before Norton arrived, and in order to allow his men an undisturbed opportunity of removing the ivory, George had blazed a clear and humorously-devised trail to lead the district commissioner to distant and muddy parts of the marsh. It had been quite an amusing diversion. George had carefully made tracks to the edge of mud holes, concealed his route around the hole with fresh mud, and resumed the trail on the opposite side. By the appearance of Norton, the man had stumbled into quite a few of these pitfalls.

To keep the pursuit warm, George had also left scraps of paper stuck in forked sticks with messages scrawled on them like:

" Hope you are enjoying your safari."

" Pleasant stay in the area."

A few others were of a more ribald nature. The last one had simply been:

" Have you heard what won the Derby? Leave name here. I will be back in about two weeks time."

George had then made his way out of the swamp, joined his porters with the ivory, and gone to Molira. On his return, he went to his usual vantage point, and was in time to see Norton leaving the swamp. The fellow must have had quite a spell with the mosquitoes. George wondered whether he had been waiting all that time lying in ambush at the site of the Derby note. If he had only known, George would at least have left him the comfort of a bottle of quinine.

Watching the district commissioner and his party trudge wearily off into the bush provided George with food for reflection. His whole poaching venture had been most successful. Notwithstanding the costs of corruption at Molira, he had been able to transmit close on £5,000 to his Dar es Salaam banking account. He could feel well satisfied with himself and he still couldn't see how he could ever be caught. The British Government was hardly likely to deploy an entire army just to catch one poacher and, short of such a reinforcement, he was confident that Wickens and Norton would never catch him. The whole thing, nevertheless, seemed too good to last. Something would happen to end the matter; but even if it did, he had a comfortable little poacher's bank-nest snugly lined with money. This would be consolation for even a gaol sentence.

What did happen was that the British Government sent a stiff note to the Belgians, complaining that some unknown and elusive poacher was working with impunity from the Congo and causing no inconsiderable destruction to the elephant population of Northern Rhodesia. The Belgian administrative officer at Molira was very apologetic when he told George about it.

"A great pity, *mon petit braconnier,* but my superiors are seriously concerned with the matter. It would be discreet if you terminated the activity. Why not enjoy a holiday at the coast? Perhaps you could return another day. The British obviously do not even know your name. They simply say that you are the man known by the Africans as *iNyathi,* or The Buffalo, because you are most dangerous in the long grass. If you come back later, you could perhaps change your identity, and have another spell."

The Belgian sounded hopeful. He had obviously been satisfied with his share of the loot. George grinned. A holiday might not be such a bad idea. For seven months he had been living hard in the bush with never a word with any European other than the exchange of an occasional politeness with the Belgian official. He had shipped out about three tons of ivory from Molira and seventy-five big Northern Rhodesian bull elephants had died in the process. Even without government intervention, it might be desirable to rest the Mweru area for a while. Even a leopard has enough sense to rest a herd of antelope he has been raiding.

George paid off his men with a sizable bonus and had a farewell party with the traders and the Belgian. The lake steamer *Vengeur* happened to be sailing up to Albertville in a couple of days' time. George had come in to Molira to allow the traders to despatch his last batch of ivory. When the little ship sailed, George waved a pleasant farewell to his cronies from its deck, and then settled down to relax during the few days of the journey.

Albertville is one of the pleasantest of all the ports on Lake Tanganyika. It is a busy little place, with a handsome avenue of palm trees shading a line of shops and houses and a couple of tolerable hotels. George booked into Spiro's Hotel du Lac, and looked around him. The first people he met in the bar were two individuals he had last seen on the Lupa, Woollard and Charles Bird, who were sitting at the counter disposing of a bottle of gin and discussing the troubles of a rather unhappy-looking man they introduced as E. H. Bishop.

Woollard and Bird had both abandoned gold digging in order to revert to their original occupation as ivory hunters. Bishop was a newcomer to the scene, and his troubles were complicated.

" I came here to start a fishing industry," he told George bitterly. " I bought a couple of steel boats and arranged with an Indian trader to distribute the catch. I started off all right, then I found that the chap was swindling me. He just wouldn't pay up after selling the fish."

" What did you do?"

Bishop looked sheepish.

" I'm afraid I lost my temper. I never could stand rogues. I've always tried to be honest myself, so why should other people rob me? I gave the Indian a damned good hiding. When he still wouldn't pay I got my boys to carry all the goods from his store out into the bush and just hide them until the Indian paid."

" Did he pay?"

" No."

" It sometimes takes a lot of pressure to make them pay."

" Yes. He went to the police. They arrested me, I've got two months gaol. I'm out on a *proces-verbal* until the sentence is confirmed. If it is, and the Belgians say that they are afraid it will be, I'll have to serve my time. Meanwhile I'm allowed the liberty of the township boundaries."

Discussing somebody else's troubles in a bar is quite a relaxation. After a while two Swedes came into the bar and joined them. The newcomers were

Captain Vorster and an engineer named Alphons Steen, both officers on the ship *Baron Dhanis* which plied between Albertville and the Tanganyika railhead of Kigoma on the opposite shore of the lake. They listened to a repeat of Bishop's troubles. With the gin making everybody lachrymonious, somebody suggested that they should really try and rescue poor old Bishop. There was general acclamation. An atmosphere of heavy secrecy immediately descended upon them.

That evening Woollard, George, and Bird concealed on their persons various items of Bishop's clothing and portable belongings. They walked separately down to the docks and went on board the *Baron Dhanis*. Bishop sneaked out of the hotel later on and joined them in Steen's cabin. There they broached a few bottles and discussed a hiding place for Bishop. Steen did most of the talking in his thick Swedish accent, and by the end of the first bottle he had suggested hiding Bishop in the bilge.

They all trooped down to the bottom of the ship. Steen produced spanners and they spent a good hour loosening the twenty bolts which held in position a manhole cover leading into the false bottom of the ship. With the cover removed, they peered down into the smelly bilge, with a few inches of oily-looking water swilling about. Bishop wasn't too happy about the place, but they found a box for him to sit on, a bottle of drinking water and a bottle of whisky. Then they wished him *bon voyage,* pushed him inside, and screwed him down. With a last few friendly raps on the bottom to wish him well, they returned for a final drink to Steen's cabin.

The ship was to sail at dawn, but by 4 a.m. Bishop had finished his bottle of whisky and the inky-black bilge was starting to give him the creeps. To make it worse he could hear his erstwhile companions in full song in Steen's cabin on the engine deck of the ship. He started to see rats in the dark, whether released from the bottle of whisky or normally resident in the ship, he did not know. He commenced a commotion, banging on the top of the bilge and shouting.

The party sobered up slightly at the thought that Bishop might be suffocating. It took them a long and unsteady time to re-loosen the bolts on the manhole and extricate Bishop, who flatly refused to return to his sanctuary notwithstanding a few stiff shots and a serious lecture. All he would do was hide in an empty cabin, where two police officers found him just before the ship sailed. The officers were very apologetic about it, but they carted Bishop off to gaol and he served his time. When he was eventually released he left Albertville and crossed the lake in an Arab dhow sailing to Kisanga. From there he walked to the Lupa goldfield, sending a rather pathetic little note to the British district commissioner at Kasanga, apologising for not calling on him, the reason being that he had no boots.

By that time, of course, George had made a move himself. With Bird and Woollard he took out the usual licences, allowing them each to hunt four elephants that year in the Albertville province. With his licence Woollard set out to hunt on the Lualaba River. Bird and George went into conference with Spiro, the Greek owner of the hotel. Spiro was a very practical man, and wise in local ways. He agreed to become their agent and arrange matters with his friends among the local authorities. The arrangement cost £60 a month but it allowed unlimited elephant hunting to both George and Bird. They were very happy to have such an opportunity.

Some hundred miles to the north-west of Albertville, in the area of the Kamba hills, there was a renowned resort of bull elephants. It was rugged country, with the slopes covered mainly with dense evergreen forest laced with wild rubber vines. The valleys between the hills were flat and inclined to turn to swamp, with high grass and excellent thicket cover for elephants. It was not easy country in which to hunt, but when George and Bird followed local advice and made their way to the area, they found that it was indeed a magnificent place for ivory. It was pure bull country, and among the bulls there were many first class tuskers.

George and Bird set up separate camps, but near enough to each other to allow them to be sociable. They hunted separately and maintained their own staffs, but it was always pleasant to be able to return to camp after several days of hunting, and stroll over to see each other's ivory and exchange gossip about their various adventures in the chase.

As a hunting ground, the area of the Kamba hills was so different from the Mweru marsh, that it necessitated a change in George's technique. With about fifteen permanent porters carrying food and light camp kit, including the one luxury of an easily dismantled rhookee chair, he would set out on lengthy hunting forays into the surrounding wilderness, heading for some area where information, or his own instinct suggested the presence of elephants. Information was hard to obtain, for there were very few human beings in the area. The only residents were a few widely scattered members of a mongrel pygmy tribe, the Mboti, who wandered about living on the proceeds of hunting or honey and wild fruit gathering. The mere fact that George allowed them to feed off the elephant carcasses ensured their friendship and support. Unfortunately there were too few of them to maintain efficient espionage on the elephants. Hunting in the area always remained something like a lucky dip. Each day contained its own surprises, problems, triumphs or disappointments.

One morning, George left his camp somewhat later than usual and led his men into a new hunting area. About 11 a.m. they cut the tracks of a very big bull, travelling on his own. The tracks were exceptionally large but unfortunately about three days old. The elephant, however, was at least heading in the direction which George intended to take, and he decided to follow it, without much hope of overtaking the animal.

George tramped along, indulging in the usual elephant hunter's day dream about stumbling into some virgin territory, with no elephant carrying less than 100 lb. of ivory a side, and the terrain, nice, open, short grass country with plenty of anthills for cover. Following an old track in bull country can be singularly dull. Bull country is generally not good game country, whether because the bulls choose an isolated area for themselves, or drive other game away, is not known. At all events, there is little to see to divert the mind from the monotony and heat of a pursuit which can have no excitement of its own if the trail is several days stale.

At 4.30 p.m. the hunters found the fresh track of an elephant cutting the old trail they were following. They examined the tracks carefully. The new tracks looked as though they had been made by the same bull who had done a large circuit and then cut his own trail. With heightened excitement the hunters moved into the new trail and followed as fast as they could. All the signs, the distance between steps and frequent meanderings, showed that the elephant was feeding and dawdling as he travelled.

The evening closed in. George stopped his porters at a water-hole and told them to make camp. With one tracker he carried on in order to use the last half-hour of daylight. Twenty minutes later, George heard an elephant in front of him. He left the tracker in safety, and moved forward. The evergreen forest was dense, and the light failing fast. He closed to about ten yards of the elephant and still couldn't see a vital spot as a target. Then he made out a patch of the shoulder and took the opportunity. In the semi-darkness of the forest, the rifle seemed to belch flame.

The elephant crashed off through the dense growth. He suddenly stopped a short distance away, and the forest was completely silent. The elephant was either standing waiting for George to approach, or had moved on with that cat-like silence which they can adopt if they choose.

It was too dark to take any chances. George and his tracker even had trouble finding their way back to the camp. The next morning, however, as soon as it was light, George and his two trackers set out to find the elephant. They continued from the spot where the elephant had been wounded. They soon found a blood trail. From the tracks, it was evident that the elephant was dragging his front leg and travelling very slowly. The hunters would soon catch up with their quarry. One tracker went back to halt the porters who were following in the rear. The second tracker and George moved forward carefully. The tracker kept ahead, his eyes on the trail while George watched the forest, with his rifle at the ready.

Half an hour passed. Then they heard a slight movement ahead of them. George moved into the lead. As he did so, there was a short, shrill blast of an angry elephant just to the left. George whirled around. He saw a real giant of an elephant coming straight at him, weaving a way with his tusks through the wild rubber vines. Never in his life had George seen such ivory. He lifted his gun and took a frontal head shot.

The elephant crashed down but the bullet must have been deflected by a vine. The elephant was hardly stunned. Scrabbling madly, he turned on the ground and rose with his stern towards George. The dense undergrowth temporarily obscured him. George jumped sideways and tried to get in a finishing shot. The bullet tore home somewhere in the animal's hindquarters, but the giant elephant crashed away into the trees. George ran on behind him as quickly as he could through the undergrowth. After about one hundred yards, the tracker caught up with him.

" The elephant is behind," he shouted. " Where you fired at it. It is standing by a big tree. It does not seem able to move."

George was nonplussed. He was certain that he was just behind the big tusker, but the tracker was adamant, and the man was no amateur when it came to elephants. George went reluctantly back with him. Sure enough, there was a big elephant standing very crippled beneath a tree. George dropped him with a brain shot. His tusks were magnificent, around 125 lb. a side, but he still wasn't comparable to the giant who had charged in the forest. What had happened was that the elephant George had wounded on the previous evening had gone a short distance and then been unable to continue. The large tusker had joined him during the night and remained to defend his wounded comrade. It was this newcomer which had charged when George approached in the morning.

Taking his second tracker, George set out to pursue the giant, leaving the porters behind at the dead elephant. They followed the trail until sundown. Then they collected wood, made a fire, and spent the night in the forest. At dawn they were off again. For twelve hours they followed the elephant, but it was a hopeless pursuit. By the trail, the big tusker was a good ten hours ahead of them and obviously had no intention of stopping. There was no sign of the bull being seriously wounded. He had simply had the fright of his life. He had not even halted to relieve himself, his droppings being scattered a good three or four feet apart. He had snatched food from the trees as he passed. An elephant in that state could go on for days.

With no food, it was impossible for the hunters to follow him. George abandoned the pursuit. He was bitterly disappointed. True, the elephant he had shot would reward him with £250 worth of ivory, but he had a feeling that, in the big tusker he had missed something very near to the world's record of 214 lb. and 226½ lb. in a pair of tusks. It was very dismal having to retrace his steps with such a failure to consider. To make matters worse, he and the tracker had a hungry and wet night in the forest before they met some of the porters at 9 a.m. the next day following their trail looking for them, and carrying some welcome food. While he munched at a succulent lump of grilled elephant steak, George visualised another meeting in the near future with the big tusker. It would be a real pleasure to find his trail again and follow it to the bitter end through the shadowy and silent aisles of the primeval forest.

CHAPTER EIGHT

DEATH IN THE FOREST

ELEPHANT hunting has always been a highly specialised profession. The ardours and dangers of the chase have kept it select to the tough and the bold. It was highly profitable. Numbers attempted it but very few graduated into what will always rank as one of the most hazardous and physically demanding of all human occupations. The uncertainties and hardships of the day were enough to provide rapid disillusionment to any heroic notions of the dude or the amateur hunter. The solitude and the menace of the mosquito-haunted nights, were two phantoms which soon drove away all but the most phlegmatic and rugged. In the most impossible and trying conditions, the elephant hunter had to maintain himself in perfect health, for there is no relief and little comfort for the sick or injured in the African bush.

Three weeks after his pursuit of the giant tusker, George was out hunting. He cut the track of a single, good-sized bull. The track was about twenty-four hours old but of sufficient size to be worth following. Late in the next afternoon he caught up with the bull. The elephant was feeding in one of the valley swamps, a rather smelly morass covered with coarse, high, razor grass.

George waded into the swamp. He made his way with great caution to a position where he was about fifteen yards from the elephant, but the density of the growth still partly obscured the view. From what he could see of the elephant, it looked like an excellent tusker. The light, unfortunately, was fading and there seemed no possibility of reaching a better position. George was loath to lose the elephant. He decided to take a chance. He carefully judged the position of the animal's heart and fired through the grass.

The elephant's scream of rage followed so quickly that it was almost like a horribly distorted echo of the gun shot. The animal charged straight at George. The grass and reeds still obscured him but there was no time to wait. George fired the second barrel. The shot checked the elephant slightly but still he came on. George looked back for his second rifle. The bearer had run for it. He cursed and tried to open the ejector of his double-barrelled rifle. The elephant was on him. George was standing knee deep in mud and water some five feet to the left of the elephant's original tracks.

The elephant came hurtling back on his former course. George tried to fall out of his way but the elephant's trunk flashed out at him in a downward movement. The tip of the trunk slashed the skin off his cheek and chest as though it was a lead-weighted whip. If the blow had caught George on his head, he would have been brained.

Without pausing, the elephant seized George around his thigh and snatched him up. By some miracle, George still held on to his open rifle, with the stock lying across his chest. The tip of the elephant's right tusk made a fearsome groove right down the wooden stock. The stock, however, at least prevented the tusk from tearing its way through George's ribs.

It was astonishing how quickly it all happened. In what seemed to be a fraction of a second, the elephant lifted George high above his head.

" I suppose he's going to bash me down on his tusks," George thought, with an almost numbing helplessness. The next thing in normal elephant behaviour would be to throw him down on the ground, to be kneeled on, tusked and trampled.

" I suppose I've bloody well asked for it," George said, quite aloud.

The elephant was travelling at full speed. Suddenly he tossed his victim backwards. George landed on the rear part of the animal's back, bounced, and rolled off into the swamp. He scrambled up, ready to run, but the elephant was disappearing into tall grass growing on higher ground clear of the edge of the swamp.

George became aware that he still held his open rifle. He looked through the barrels. They were clear of mud. He felt in his tunic pocket for ammunition but everything had fallen out whilst the elephant was waving him in the air. Even the six rounds which he carried in a short, open bandolier on his belt, had been lost.

He ran back and grovelled in the mud, trying to find the ammunition. To his delight he noticed three rounds caught up in a low, dense, bush. They were perfectly clean. He loaded his rifle and ran back after the elephant. Thirty yards away, on the rising ground at the edge of the swamp, he saw the animal, facing him, with its ears outstretched as though it was ready to charge. It was a bad moment.

George threw up his rifle, but at the same moment he noticed that something was wrong. He held his fire. It was almost uncanny to realise that the elephant was dead. The animal had turned on his pursuer just before dying. He had collapsed on his stomach and, lying on higher ground with his legs invisible in the grass, it looked as though he was still alive and standing. George's first shot had caught him true in the heart but as usual the great animal had found the will and the strength to crash off for a good sixty yards before the final collapse.

George's trackers came up when he called. They made a camp nearby and he dressed his abrasions with disinfectant. Three of his ribs had been cracked. He strapped them up as best he could and tried to sleep. The next day he was one solid ache. His right foot and ankle were so painful and swollen that he couldn't even hobble. His lungs felt so sore he could hardly curse.

He lay on the ground waiting for the porters to cut out the elephant's tusks. They were sixty-pounders, so there was some slight consolation for the mishap. Then it became a matter of getting back to the base camp. The porters had to tie a blanket to a pole, hammock fashion, and carry him along until they reached the camp late the next afternoon. It was a miserable journey of jolts and anguish. Cursing the porters for their clumsiness only hurt his ribs. By the time they reached their base camp, George felt like a bag of broken bones being taken to a garbage heap. Any further thoughts of hunting had, of necessity, to be postponed.

Bird came into the camp two days later. He had been out hunting and heard through the bush telegraph that George had been killed. He wasn't much of a bonesetter, but at least his company helped to while away days of forced inactivity. Bird moved over to George's camp. He was not averse to taking a short holiday from hunting and acting as a nurse.

"In fact," he said, "I'm thinking of taking a holiday. We've both been pretty successful here. Before I get killed at the game, I'd like to have a good binge in Elisabethville. Why don't you come as well? I know a pretty jolly girl there. She could introduce you to a friend."

George hadn't thought of abandoning the hunt quite so soon. He was inclined to collect ivory while the arrangement lasted with the Belgians.

"You never know when these fellows are going to turn honest," he said. He told Bird about his experience at Molira. "Pressure can also be brought on the local men from their superiors. I'll stick it out until my bank balance is slightly higher. There's also a matter of a big elephant here. He might be a world record. I'd love to get him."

George told Bird about the giant tusker who had led him such a dance. Bird was intrigued. He had not heard of the animal. In well-populated country, the tribespeople knew any individual elephants of note. Particularly big specimens were generally named, with quite a few stories attached to themselves. But in this area of the Congo, the resident Mboti people were too widely scattered to have much real knowledge of the elephant community. The big bull might also have been a visitor to the area. George's porters and trackers had made diligent inquiry about the animal, but could learn nothing of his habits or whereabouts.

" My own bet," said Bird, " is that he still hasn't stopped running. You'll be lucky if you ever see him again. Actually, another reason I'm thinking of taking a holiday is that we are possibly over-shooting this area. Bull elephants aren't exactly fools. I get a distinct impression that quite a few of them are packing up and quitting the place for some quieter climate."

George was inclined to agree with him. He would, however, see the remainder of the elephant population well on their way, and then go off somewhere for a holiday himself. Meanwhile he relaxed in the camp and, while he recuperated, diverted the time with gossiping and yarning with Bird.

Bird, although in his early thirties, was a fairly old hand at ivory hunting. He was full of anecdote of the odd characters of earlier elephant-hunting days. There were certainly some great individualists among the old timers. Mickey Norton, for example, had flourished in Nyasaland in the 1890s, and then moved into Northern Rhodesia, and later to the Rovuma River on the border between Tanganyika and Mozambique. He was a heavily-built man of 6 ft. 2 in., with enormous hands and feet. He had the reputation of being able to kill a bottle of whisky quicker than anybody else in Africa, and in such a dry continent, this was quite something.

One of Mickey's peculiar habits was to remove all his clothing if he happened to be caught by rain while on safari. Wearing only an enormous topee and an equally bulky pair of boots, he would stride along carrying his clothes rolled up in a bundle under his arm. He was a naturally red-complexioned man. After short exposure to the wind and rain he looked like a mobile version of the Union Jack, with parts of him blue and other parts white or red. If the path led him through a village there would be an absolute uproar of laughter, handclapping, and ululating from African ladies seeing him on his way. He was an Irishman, with a prodigious fund of humour. He had abandoned elephant hunting after the 1914-18 war.

On the shores of Lake Nyasa, George had heard some vague stories from the local tribespeople around Mwaya, of an elephant-hunter named Bell who had been trampled to death in those parts towards the end of the last century. Nobody else seemed to have heard of the man, and George and Bird speculated that quite a few of their predecessors must have come to ends just as dismal and forgotten.

In their time and, in the opinion of many, of all time, the doyen of the profession was reckoned to be James Sutherland. He did most of his early hunting in Portuguese territory, in the very wild country east of Lake Nyasa, and in the Southern Province of Tanganyika while that country was still in German hands. No human being had ever hunted elephants with such resolution over so lengthy a period. After twenty-five years of a charmed hunting life, Sutherland was still active somewhere in French Equatorial Africa, the last area on the continent where a man could secure an unlimited licence, known as a *Permis de Chasse Commercial,* and shoot as many elephants as he pleased. George did some serious thinking when Bird gave him this information. French Equatorial Africa was obviously a place which deserved a visit, if only to allow himself the pleasure of meeting Sutherland.

George took nearly three weeks to recuperate from his injuries. Once he was on his feet, Bird left for Elisabethville. George never saw him again. The man spent some time dispersing his hunting profits amongst sundry bars and girl friends. Eventually he died from poison administered by an ingenious technique, novel to science, but well known to young African ladies who wish to rid themselves of stale lovers. It is not a pleasant death. The symptoms include bleeding of the membranes while the eyes become increasingly bloodshot until they are dark pools of red. There is fortunately a very efficient herbal antidote. The only difficulty is to obtain it.

With Bird away on his path of destiny, George resumed hunting. Before the district became too denuded of bulls to be worth any further activity, he hoped that fate would lead him to the giant elephant. It was unthinkable that he should abandon the area without at least another attempt at a meeting with that animal. Accordingly, he instructed his trackers to exert every effort at finding the elephant, and also sent messages to the Mboti requesting their help.

Several of the little hunters came in to see George. He told them about the big elephant but they were frankly puzzled by his description. Not being ivory hunters, they took small notice of tusks. Elephants were not easy creatures to kill with bows and arrows and the Pygmies paid greater attention to smaller game. Periodically, however, they did stage a communal elephant hunt. On these occasions the Pygmies rallied to a pre-selected spot for a mass effort. Usually their society was a very loosely knit affair with their chief acknowledged to have little more authority than that accorded the doyen of a community. For the pursuit of elephants, however, even these natural individualists considered co-operation to be a virtue. As it happened, one of their hunts was imminent. They invited George to participate. His gun would be useful to them and there was always a chance that the great elephant he wanted would be included in the bag.

The hunt was scheduled to take place some miles away, where the bull country verged on an area used by elephant herds. The Mboti told George that they selected the areas for these hunts with great care several months before the actual event. Walking along with them, as they guided him to the site, George questioned them on the technique they used. He was rather thunderstruck at their explanation.

" What we do," said their leader, " is select a piece of country where the elephant grass is good and high. We protect this from all grass fires, and meanwhile burn off the grass in the surrounding country whenever the wind is favourable. In the end, when the dry season comes and food is scarce for the elephants, we have kept for them this special place and we know that they will congregate there to enjoy the grass."

"And then?"

" You shall see," said the little man, with an enigmatic smile. " We always have a great surprise for the elephants."

He stopped suddenly and raised his left arm for silence. They were following a path through a thicket. In the stillness of the forest, George could hear the sound of a crested guinea fowl. In all Africa there is no more pleasant an invitation to dinner, with a vision conjured up of a plump, tender and most piquantly flavoured bird grilled to a juicy turn over the embers of an aromatic wood fire.

The Pygmy hunter moved forward on his own, with an arrow in his bow. The tangle of foliage was so dense that it was difficult for him to find an unobstructed target. He manoeuvred with great caution, trying to get clear of the creepers without disturbing the bird. Watching him move through the shadows, with his ebony body, his primitive costume of a string-bark loin-cloth, and very much of the same intentness and menace of a stalking cat, was seeing mankind unchanged as he was in his most primitive hunting days.

The hunter suddenly released his arrow. Like a glint of light it ripped through the leaves, deflected slightly off a creeper, and half-buried itself in the ground, having missed the bird's head by half an inch. The guinea fowl clucked in a puzzled manner and jumped to one side. The hunter unleashed a second arrow with such speed and silence that even George, let alone the bird, was bemused at the incredible dexterity of the bowman. Once again a creeper deflected the arrow. Once again the bird clucked as the razor-sharp head of the missile whipped into the ground with a sound no louder than that made by a falling twig. The bird moved over curiously to see what had fallen. For a moment it presented a clear target to the hunter standing in the shadows thirty feet away. His third arrow caught the bird a perfect bull's eye. It shot into the air with a convulsive flurry of feathers and then fell back with a thud. The hunter exultantly ran forward. He picked the bird up and grinned back at George.

" Tonight we have a chief's food," he said, and happily commenced plucking the feathers as they walked on down the path.

When they reached the site of the coming elephant hunt, George had another opportunity of watching the Pygmy bowmen at work. There was a pretty substantial gathering of hunters; more men, in fact, than George had thought could possibly be living in that wilderness. It was quite a revelation of the secretive way these people lived, that such a community could lose itself with such ease in an area which he had prided himself on knowing well.

As usual everybody was extremely hungry. The assembly had heard that George was near. They received him with the news that a herd of buffalo was rummaging around in a nearby swamp. The white visitor would certainly oblige his hosts if he went and shot a couple of the animals for them. Buffalo were almost as troublesome as elephants to kill with bows and arrows.

George went down to the swamp with an escort of Pygmies. Sure enough, there was a medium-sized herd of buffalo in the reeds. He singled out a fat-looking bull and fired straight into the high-shoulder, one of the best shots for buffalo. The animal went down with a bellow while the rest of the herd stampeded. A second bull rushed through the reeds out into the open. Before he realised his mistake and could turn back, the Pygmy next to George let fly two arrows at a range of fifty yards. Both arrows hit the buffalo, and both were in the air simultaneously, separated by not more than thirty yards of space, a fabulous example of rapid shooting by a bowman. The buffalo bellowed like a cow as the arrows struck him. He half stumbled in his retreat, and the delay was sufficient to allow George the chance to pick out the heart target and bring the animal to the ground.

The Pygmies were almost delirious with joy. They pounced on the carcasses with a great hacking out of choice bits, and a tremendous chatter and squabbling in their outlandish language. That night the whole forest was redolent with the aroma of grilled buffalo meat. The Mboti steadily and noisily ate their way through the buffaloes until there was nothing left. Even the skin was eaten and the bones broken up for marrow. The Pygmies considered that the best storage for meat was provided in their own stomachs, and by the way those receptacles expanded they were obviously very elastic in their capacity.

The elephant hunt was staged the next day. George attended, still uncertain of the Pygmies' proposed plan of attack. The spectacle he witnessed was something at once fantastic and horrible in its ruthless culmination of early planning, and in its almost frightening demonstration of what the Pygmies were capable of doing once they forgot their individualism and acted in concert.

The Mboti hunters had carefully preserved a block of about twenty square miles of tall grass country. The surrounding area had been systematically burned off. It was now four months since the last rains and the protected area not only provided the best available grazing in the neighbourhood, but it was tinder dry, with the grass having an almost explosive quality once it was fired.

Early in the morning the hunters turned out in full force and moved into position around the edge of the area of long grass. Each man had a torch made from a kind of thin reed, and about five feet long. Each man also carried a length of smouldering tinder made from the plaited dry strands of the inner bark of a miyombo tree.

It took several hours for the hunters to completely encircle the area. At noon the chief in charge of operations finally set fire to a smoke signal. Each man immediately lighted his torch from his smouldering tinder. Then he ran with the burning end trailing behind him along the edge of the high grass. When he reached the line of fire started by the man ahead of him, the incendiary then returned along his tracks, setting fire to any section which might have escaped him on his first run.

Within a matter of minutes there was a complete ring of fire. In the beginning the fire was no more fierce than an ordinary grass fire, but as the smoke and heat met high over the centre of the area, a funnel of forced draught was caused, and the speed and ferocity of the flames became appalling. A terrible roaring noise commenced. So violent was the updraught that clumps of burning grass and fragments of bushes were carried high into the air.

A few buffalo managed to break through the ring of fire before the flames became too vicious. The elephants trapped inside, however, simply panicked. Their frightened screams could be heard above the roaring of the flames. Several small herds had been trapped in the grass. They tried to escape by stampeding into the middle of the inferno. Many of their calves were trampled to death in the stampede, but this was a mercy compared to the fate which befell the others. Every elephant in the trap was burned to death. A few big animals who tried to break through the encircling fire emerged from the flames with most of their hides burned off and their eyesight and sense of smell destroyed. The Pygmies simply tackled them with impunity using spears, while George, feeling physically sick at the spectacle, endeavoured to put out of their misery as many animals as he could by giving them the mercy of a bullet. When it was all over he was very glad to leave the Pygmies to their feasting, and take himself off back towards his camp and away from such a holocaust.

Curiously enough, it was on his way back to his camp that he found the tracks of a very big elephant travelling on his own. If it was not the giant tusker, it was certainly the trail of a large animal. The tracks appeared to be about two days old but George immediately decided to follow them. It developed into an exceptionally fascinating pursuit.

The big elephant was moving in the direction of the Kamba hills. He was obviously an elephant very wise in years, and the prudence he displayed in his movements was doubtless the reason for his long life of immunity from hunters. He certainly knew, and used, all the tricks in the elephant's lore of experience.

Following two days behind the bull allowed George full opportunity to learn the ways of the animal. The elephant had one particularly cunning trick. As with all animals, he travelled into the wind so that he could always be warned by smell of any enemy ahead of him. This was straightforward. It was the elephant's technique in safeguarding himself from any surprisal in the rear that provided George with a real lesson in animal sagacity.

Periodically the elephant changed his course, angling so that the wind lay on his flank. He would dawdle along for a couple of hours, and then suddenly turn down wind and head for any convenient thicket. There he would stop and relax, confident that any pursuer would betray himself with his smell when he followed the angling trail of the elephant and reached a position upwind from the animal's cover in the thicket.

Following an elephant as cautious as this bull, was not easy. Closing with him would obviously be a matter requiring considerable care. At any time the hunter could find himself in the predicament of discovering the elephant behind him just when he was thinking that the animal was almost within range ahead.

George examined many of the thickets where the elephant had rested. The bull liked to doze away the hot hours from 11.30 a.m. till 4 p.m. in the shade of the trees. He not only dozed on his legs, standing, swaying and swinging and fanning himself with his ears, but he also lay down at times, enjoying a good nap with his head resting on an antheap. For some reason cow elephants seldom seem to lie down, but bulls are very fond of such relaxation. The marks of their hides become impressed in the ground while the shape and size of the tusks is also clearly revealed in a manner which can be very tantalising to any hunter. Whoever this bull was, all the signs indicated that he was well outfitted with ivory and the revealing shapes in the ground spurred the hunters on with considerable enthusiasm.

On the third day of the pursuit, George was very close to the elephant. He had not caught an actual glimpse of the bull but all the signs of fresh droppings and broken boughs, indicated that little more than a couple of hours separated them. They were also approaching the actual slopes of the two high, grass-covered Kamba hills, twin summits which quite dominated the surrounding country and were connected together by a low saddle of ground.

After the long pursuit, George was extremely keen to actually see the elephant. The first glimpse would not only allow him to recognise the bull if it was indeed the giant tusker, but by positive location it would be a complete safeguard against the elephant springing any surprise on the hunters from the rear.

George decided, therefore, to leave the elephant's trail and make straight for the hills, which were then about five miles away. From the heights he would be able to search the surrounding country with his glasses and, with reasonable luck, spot the elephant. They were less than half-way up the slope of one of the hills, when a tracker caught George's arm and pointed. The elephant had also made for the hills. He was on the second slope, just beyond the saddle, and feeding leisurely as he made his way through the tall grass.

Through the glasses, George immediately saw that the elephant was not the giant tusker. He was, in fact, what the Africans called an *Ntonda,* or One-Tusker. When the elephant had slept, he must have habitually lain with his tusk side on the ground in order to relieve himself of the weight of the ivory. The relief must have been quite worth having, for the one tusk was certainly the largest George had ever seen. It was a truly superb curve of ivory. Possession of it would certainly be compensation for three days of tracking.

Conditions were ideal for the kill. The wind was right, the elephant was unsuspecting, the hunters knew the exact position of their quarry, and the hills were bathed in brilliant sunshine. Elephants have poor eyesight, especially in bright light. Overcast conditions provide them with a better chance of vision, but even then it is really only sudden movement which alarms an elephant in any visual manner.

George spent twenty minutes in a cautious approach to the animal. The elephant was still feeding happily when his hunter was fifteen yards away. George selected his favourite brain shot, the fastest and most humane of all targets on an elephant. The giant collapsed within a second of the sound of the shot. He simply never knew what had hit him. Fortunately he fell on his tuskless side. There was no chance of his weight breaking the great curved sweep of his one tusk.

George went up and examined the elephant. The tusk was a beauty weighing 165 lb. when it was cut from its socket. The second tusk had apparently been snapped off cleanly at some fairly recent date. Its stump was still in the elephant's head, with no sign or smell of decay. Lightning, which occasionally strikes an elephant's tusks, a fight, or some unusual accident, had broken off the tusk and robbed George of what would have been his lifetime record. It was quite maddening to think of the great piece of ivory lying decaying somewhere in the bush.

The 165-lb. tusk, however, was certainly something of a consolation. With it, George returned to camp and told his porters to prepare for a journey to Albertville. He had done enough hunting for the time being. It would be well to rest the area of the Kamba hills while he and his men enjoyed some relaxation and change of climate. The porters and trackers could return to their families for at least a couple of months. George would go down to the coast at Dar es Salaam, attend to his affairs, divert himself with the novelty of a social life, and then possibly return again for a second hunting spell.

CHAPTER NINE

BACK OF BEYOND

THE trouble, of course, with Dar es Salaam, was that the place was really a terrible bore. The delights of its few sleazy, Greek-run hotels were soon exhausted. In the hot evenings all one could do was promenade for a while beneath the palms and the casuarina trees growing around the harbour. One could listen to the aimless chatter of the Africans, or watch the Asians squatting in their gregarious assemblies on the grass, gambling or conducting interminable business discussions. Occasionally it was possible to encounter some hunting acquaintance, or a visiting sailor with sufficient wit to be interested in anything other than getting drunk, but the majority of European inhabitants were civil servants, and they kept to themselves.

In any community the world over, civil servants are alike. In a developed country, they are submerged by the more diverse and vivacious commercial, financial, or creative population and are not so noticeable. But Dar es Salaam was the capital of a totally undeveloped territory. The civil servants were exposed to view as the majority of the middle and upper-class population, and their special idiosyncrasies were particularly evident. They rotated very much on their own axis in a conversational firmament void of all save dull discussion of past leaves, personalities, future tours of duty, and the possibilities of increment or advance. Anyone not part of this self-absorbed world was completely out of it and considered to be as crushing a bore by the civil servants, as he considered them.

George sat in solitary state at the bar of the one partly presentable hotel in the town and looked vacantly at himself in the mirror. Talking to the Swahili barman was not profitable. From his joint ancestors, the man seemed to have inherited only the Arab's manual dexterity at short-changing and the African's mental characteristic of thinking and working in circles.

George was feeling very dull. He diverted himself by reflecting on his own movements. He had paid off his porters in Albertville, sold the balance of his ivory, and then taken the overnight steamer across Lake Tanganyika to Kigoma. It was late in February 1926 when he entered Tanganyika again, and it had immediately occurred to him that he was entitled to the usual annual licence for three elephants. As these licences expired on the 31st March, the end of the territory's financial year, he would be able to take out a second licence on the 1st April. With six elephants legally within his grasp over a short time, he had made the most of the opportunity to revisit his first and favourite hunting ground on the upper Kilombera River, where the Mbunga people had made him a member of their guild of hunters.

The visit had been very pleasant. He had taken the train from Kigoma to Kilosa, and then safaried with porters to his original hunting ground. He had received quite a welcome from his old friends. They were just about to embark on a hippo hunt in the Kihanzi River when he arrived and they invited him to the affair as an honoured guest. Like all elephant hunters, George disdained shooting other game unless it was to obtain food. Only the elephant could provide the ultimate hunting combination of high profit and dangerous excitement. All other hunting was tame in comparison, although the Mbunga hippopotamus hunt had certainly had its moments.

The Mbunga hunted hippos from small canoes made from light hollowed-out tree trunks each containing two standing men. One of the canoes would be paddled up close to a selected hippo. At the correct moment the hunters would hurl into the animal a harpoon-like spear with a single barbed head attached by a length of rope to the end of a loose haft. When the hippo was speared it invariably dived. The canoe darted away to safety while the haft, now detached from the spear head, floated to the surface as a marker and drag on the hippo. The harpooning process was, in fact, similar to the techniques used in the early days of whaling.

The harpooned animal would make resolute efforts at escape, trying to rush off up or down stream, and only surfacing its head to breathe in hasty gulps of air. Unless the hippo managed to escape into the reeds, its doom was inevitable. The drag of the rope and haft tired it out, while the hunters followed at a safe, but inexorable, distance.

Sometimes the hippos would turn on the attendant canoes, but the little craft were too speedy. They would wheel out of the way. If a hippo chased one canoe, the others would attack the animal by throwing at it more of the loose-headed harpoons. Throughout these initial proceedings there lurked in the background a big canoe with about twelve paddlers aboard. When they judged the hippo to be ready for the kill, the paddlers of this craft moved in, seized hold of some of the floating hafts and applied the weight of their canoe as a final drag. The animal would eventually be forced to surface and proceedings reached a bloody and noisy climax when the hunters closed in with spears and choppers. The Mbunga placed great store on a hippopotamus. Every part of its body had a value to them and they were not inclined to be wanton in their hunts. They arranged everything in definite seasons and restricted their bag to something less than the normal increase of the hippos.

With the hippo hunt completed, George had gone off and shot six elephants, presenting the carcasses to the Mbunga and then taking his ivory in for sale at Kilosa. From there he had caught the train to Dar es Salaam, and ended up sitting in the bar of the hotel, feeling down in the dumps, out of sorts, and pretty blue with himself. He had just decided that he definitely did not like Dar es Salaam, when somebody sat down two stools away from him. George glanced over casually and immediately recognised the man. It was Bill Buckley, the elephant hunter who had given him some well-meant advice when he had first come out from England in 1920. George smiled at the man.

" You don't remember me," he said. " I was on the *Gaika* with you five years ago."

Buckley looked at him closely, and a glint of recognition came to his eyes.

" Good Lord! Yes, of course! You were the youngster coming to Africa in search of adventure. Selous' books, and all that sort of thing."

He eyed George quizzically.

" You've changed a bit since then. Did you find adventure?"

George rubbed his nose, and grinned.

" I've walked into a few Yanks, and a few elephants since I last saw you. By my boyhood standards I suppose it might add up to adventure."

" How have you been doing?"

" I've just come back from a hunting spell in the Congo. I came down, in fact, to see whether all my cash has found its way into the correct banking account. I've not done too badly. I landed with £25, now I've got £4,000."

Buckley opened his eyes at this.

" Lord!" he exclaimed. " That's better than I've done. What are you doing now?"

" Getting bored. I don't think I can hold this bar up much longer. I think I'll go back for another hunting spell. I'd like to go through to French Equatorial Africa and meet Sutherland. He must be quite a hunter."

Buckley nodded.

" It is pretty dull here. I'm just passing through. I'm on the British India liner tomorrow for Mombasa. I don't stay here. This place gives me the jumps. About the only excitement in it comes when the manager of the pub tries to eject somebody from the dining room for not wearing a tie. By the way, did you see that bloke in at dinner with a chimpanzee?"

" No."

" I thought it was a bit beyond the pale, myself, but he had a tie on the thing so the management did nothing. They only kicked him out a little while ago."

" Why?"

" He may have asked for it. The fellow arrived here with a baby elephant and a donkey as well as the chimpanzee. He tethered the donkey and the elephant together in the yard. Then he came in, booked a room, and went in for dinner. Just after he went to sleep, the elephant broke its tether and trooped into the hotel with the donkey tied to its neck. A few of the drunks here thought they had the rats when they felt the elephant's trunk smelling them from behind. It was searching for its master. Eventually the elephant and donkey sniffed him out to his room. They lay down outside the door in the passageway to sleep. You must have come just after the manager bundled them all out, chimpanzee included."

" I missed something."

" Yes."

Buckley considered in silence for a while. Then he said,

" Why don't you sail to Mombasa with me tomorrow? It's just an over-night run, it will give you a change. Then you can have a holiday with me on my coconut plantation, see Mombasa, and make up your mind at leisure about future movements."

" Is Mombasa better or worse than Dar es Salaam?"

" That would be a judgment of Solomon. There is a tale that he and the Queen of Sheba did once come this way."

" What did they do?"

" They went back again."

" Oh."

George thought the matter over. Getting dejected on bad gin, or aggressive on worse brandy, would not amount to much of a holiday. He sailed with Buckley the next day and returned a fortnight later. The short double voyage proved the best part of the holiday. Sailing past the island of Zanzibar in fair weather is always a delight. The island is just a forest of coconut palms, seeming to grow straight from the blue meadow of the Indian Ocean, with the white sails of dhows scattered around it like a flock of grazing sheep. Its clusters of odd little buildings sunbathe on the edge of dazzling coral beaches, while even far out to sea a passing ship sails through air made sensuous by the smell of cloves.

In Dar es Salaam, George arranged his affairs, and then caught the train through to Kigoma. On the ship he had finally decided to visit French Equatorial Africa, have at least one more spell of ivory hunting, and meet the legendary Jim Sutherland. The whole idea of the venture had grown on him during his two weeks with Buckley. Listening to that old adventurer's accounts of past experiences, made it pretty clear that the days of the professional ivory hunters were nearly over. Most of the remaining members of the profession were in French Equatorial Africa, the last area where they could hunt within the law, and it would be both fascinating and profitable to join them.

From Kigoma, George caught the *Baron Dhanis* across Lake Tanganyika to Albertville. He had meant to go on immediately, but when he called in at the Hotel du Lac, Spiro casually mentioned that Woollard was still getting good ivory in the direction of the Lualaba River. The temptation was attractive to see an old friend and account for a few more of the Congo elephants. He had enjoyed hunting around the Kamba hills, and it had certainly been magnificent ivory country, with many tusks above the 100-lb notch.

Information was that there were good elephants south from the railway station of Kignoa, halfway between Albertville and Kabalo on the Lualaba River. It was to this place that George took himself, and then, with his trackers and porters, set out southwards into the country of the Luba tribe.

It was a very wild and isolated portion of the globe. Down towards the Luvuya River, the children up to about the age of twelve had never seen a European and by the way they ran, had little desire to remedy the deficiency. George had noticed before just how easy it was for his fellow ivory hunters as well as himself, to merge with the primitive world around them. Witchcraft becomes much more potent when you live with it. Somewhat to his own amusement he always found himself working up quite a belief in paganism when he was in the bush, and then sloughing the whole idea off as soon as he returned to civilization. He could understand the Africans going through the same process in reverse when they returned to the wilderness from the outside world and were simply sucked back into the quicksands of local custom and belief. No matter how blasé one felt, something inevitably happened to bring one up against the whole rigmarole of superstition and belief.

One such minor incident occurred when George made his base camp near the Luvuya River. Normally he camped well away from any village in order to be clear of insects, stinks, and the constant importuning of starving dogs and fowls. In this area, however, the only good camp site was underneath a magnificent wild fig tree growing in the centre of a village, and convenience induced George to build his camp there.

When his tent was erected and George could look around at leisure, he observed that immediately in front of him there was a circular, well-built hut attached to a half-enclosed compound. In the compound, some fifty feet from George, a middle-aged man was squatting, facing a wooden idol. The man had his back partly towards the camp, and seemed so intent on his supplication as to be quite oblivious of the European observer. The idol was on a small mat, and was surrounded by the usual dishes of offerings.

George was seated in his rhookee chair drinking tea and relaxing at the time. He was watching the man with some casual interest when he noticed the idol move its head to the left. About half a minute later the idol faced front again. George leaned forward in his chair and intently watched the thing. On two further occasions it repeated the movement. The light was bright, there were no shadows, and certainly no cause for any optical illusion.

George was puzzled. He thought that possibly the head of the idol was loose, and manoeuvred by means of some attachment, although there was no sign of any strings and the man seemed to be perfectly immobile, with his hands on the ground in front of him.

For a quarter of an hour the man continued with his supplications. Then he stood up. He rolled up his own mat, walked over to the idol and picked it up, together with its mat and offerings. George went over and greeted the man.

" Is there anything wrong?"

" Yes, my wife is very ill and I have been asking my idol to ask God to make her better."

" I hope that he will. May I look at your idol?"

With a smile the man handed the figure to George. It was made of solid wood. No part of it could possibly have moved, although George would have been prepared to swear before any court of law that he had clearly seen the head turn on several occasions. He went back to his camp slightly shaken. His eyes were excellent, he had no fever at the time, and the strongest drink which he had in camp was tea. He spent the evening trying to make up his mind whether he had been affected by the sun, or whether paganism produced indisputable results.

The next day George commenced hunting. He found the area to be fair elephant country, but nothing like his old hunting ground around the Kamba hills. He shot seven bulls carrying profitable quantities of ivory, but there was nothing in the area remotely approaching the giant tusker whose memory so often tantalized his dreams. The Luba tribesmen knew their homeland well. Their assessment of its elephant population and the size of the animals' tusks did not provide George with much enthusiasm for the future. In any case, his ambitions were increasingly inclined towards French Equatorial Africa.

After a few weeks of roaming around, George packed up and went north in search of Woollard. On the way he crossed the railway line from Albertville to Kabalo and heard from some gangers that there was another European camped a short distance down the track. Camping next to the line was quite a good idea. There were very few trains to disturb anybody's sleep, and at least such a camp was out of the bush and in a clearing. George, accordingly, made his camp at a convenient spot and sent one of his men along the line to inform the other European of his presence.

The man actually came in to see him the next morning. He was a Greek elephant hunter who seemed somewhat disconcerted and suspicious at the arrival in his area of a possible rival. George reassured him that he was only passing through, and the Greek, in a more friendly mood, went off after an elephant reputed to be in the vicinity. He suggested that George remain that day. They could have a convivial evening and exchange gossip of their trade. George was agreeable. Unfortunately the Greek's hunt went the wrong way. Four hours after he had set off, his porters carried him back to the camp. George had a look at him but there was nothing he could do save write a note to the Belgian authorities confirming the manner of the hunter's death. The Greek had wounded an elephant and then been surprised when he attempted to pursue it in dense bush. The annoyed animal had tusked him clean through the chest. At least death must have been instantaneous, and better that than a lingering agony of gangrene with no help or comfort.

The next day George moved on and made his way to Woollard's reputed hunting ground. He actually found his old acquaintance encamped on the Lukuga River. Woollard seemed to be very well established there. He had an African wife, was busy raising a family, and his camp was a substantial affair of grass bandas and huts with some attempt made to start a plantation in the fertile ground along the river. He greeted George with pleasure, but also with some bad news. He had a note from Spiro. The Belgian Government had started a campaign against corruption in the Congo service, and the local officials were in some flurry of alarm. At least for the time being, the elephant hunters would have to conform to the law. Otherwise there could be serious trouble.

George had more or less expected the news for some time. The whole arrangement had simply been too good to last.

" In any case," he told Woollard, " I had decided to get out of the Congo and try the north. The French areas still seem to be so much in the back of beyond that you can do more or less what you please there. Sutherland seems to be doing well in those parts. Why don't you come up with me?"

Woollard looked around him.

" Strangely enough, I like it here. I think I'll settle down and have a go at planting. I've done fairly well from ivory but we cannot keep on hunting all our lives. We'd all end up by going the same way as the Greek. When are you going to settle down?"

The idea had never even suggested itself to George. He supposed that he would have to stop some day. It was certainly a restless, exciting sort of life. So far he had flourished on it. On the other hand he had to admit that it was a solitary and inordinately rugged way of making a living. Injury, fever, or blackwater, were as much a part of the elephant hunter's day as movement and tension. The nights were the worst part of the life. You couldn't even keep a dog for companionship, as tsetse or leopards would soon dispose of it. Apart from an occasional encounter with some head-man who might be able to exchange very limited gossip, the companionship of the porters and trackers was almost non-existent. There was always the temptation of getting an African woman, but in the long run that simply meant a rather dull and not very romantic relationship, for their minds worked in even tighter circles than their men and there was literally nothing they could talk about other than the most trivial and pointless things.

George shrugged his shoulders. He was still young.

" I'll go on," he said to Woollard, " I suppose something will happen in the end to either kill me off, or make me change. I'll wait until then."

He left a few days later on the start of the journey to French Equatorial Africa. He never saw Woollard again. Woollard remained on the Lukuga River until he died of fever a few years later. His little plantation, and the ruins of his home, were simply swallowed up by the insatiable thirst of the forest to take back that which it never recognised to be anything other than its own.

George made his way in some comfort, by means of train and river steamer, right across the Congo to Coquilhatville, and then up the Ubangi River in a small rear paddle-wheeler which maintained a service as far as the French administrative post of Banqui. The enforced inactivity of being a passenger on the little river ships was restful, even if it was inclined to be dull. The food, however, was at least good, and certainly a pleasant change from elephant meat. One could while away as much time as possible by loitering over the meal, and then withdrawing to a deck-chair for a doze. The slow passage of the riverine scenery would lull anybody to sleep in the heat. The great river bored its way through an interminable thickness of silent trees, with the only break coming from the blocks of land on the banks and the islands where firms like Lever Brothers grew oil palm trees for their soap-making. The passengers were equally uninteresting. The usual mixture of administrative officers on furlough, and a cadaverous-look-ing lady missionary who exercised herself around the deck with such resolu-tion that she carried a pedometer to ensure that she walked at least five miles a day. George reflected sourly that it was just as well that her charms were negative. If she had possessed anything at all notable she might have provided terrible distraction to the males each time she strode around the deck. As it was, the Belgian trader who slept in the chair next to George, simply spat into the river when she passed, and he looked like a man who could have seen charm in a female hippopotamus.

Bangui, the terminal of the paddle-wheelers, was a small post of the semi-military administration of French Equatorial Africa. George regarded the place with interest as the ship tied up to the bank on the 20th November, 1926. It was the first he had seen of the French. There was at least some novelty in the sight of the tricolour lazing in the humid air, and the red and blue uniforms of the Senegalese troops who garrisoned the place. He had been told that the French administration was superior to that of the Belgians and in this he was certainly not disappointed.

He went ashore and saw the local administrative officer. The man knew no English, and George's French was bad enough to provide some hilarity to the office staff, but at least everybody was very friendly. A *Permis de Chasse Commercial* cost £90 a year. George paid over his money with alacrity. It was the first time in his hunting career that he had received unrestricted licence for elephants. The Frenchman assured him that the territory was still swarming with tuskers. There was sufficient advertisement of this in the mere fact that a hunter with the reputation of Sutherland was content to live in the area permanently. George became increasingly impatient to get out into the wilderness with his guns and find the trail of a really big elephant. It would be a pleasure to have some action again.

It was useless attempting to use Bangui as a hunting base. The elephant country was well to the north-west. The best base for organising porters and starting a venture would be Fort Crampel, some 250 miles away in the Ubangui-Shari area. The immediate problem was to reach this place.

George moved his belongings from the ship to the guest house maintained by the administration in Bangui. There were three other guests already in residence. Two of them were young Estonians, Karl Nurk and one Marx, who had wandered out from their northern home and travelled right across the Sahara desert earning fifteen francs a day, together with the use of a guide and a camel, while they examined and repaired the telegraph line for the French authorities. Only Marx knew a few words of any language at all comprehensible to the local residents. How they had contrived to travel as far as they had was an advertisement for the tolerance of savage people, and the kindliness of Providence.

The third occupant of the guest house was an American missionary. He was returning to his station in Fort Crampel after furlough in the United States. If the passage through the Sahara of the Estonians was something in the nature of a miracle, then the fact that this particular example of the genus Americana was still at large was a reflection on the laxity of his country's lunacy laws. He was quite off his head.

The Estonians were sleeping in the kitchen. There was only one bedroom in the guest house and they were nervous of being left in the dark with the missionary. Marx described the man's state with the internationally understood gesture of circling a finger around his head, and then raising his hands in horror. George took the hint. He dumped his belongings in the dining room before tapping on the door of the bedroom and walking in to meet the missionary. He backed out again hurriedly. The man was in the process of giving himself an enema.

George considered the matter outside. The fellow might at least have locked the door if he wanted any privacy. Now he might understandably feel so embarrassed that it would be awkward talking to him. It was annoying. If the Yank was returning to Fort Crampel he might be expected to have made some arrangement about transport, and a lift would be very acceptable to George. Meeting the missionary, however, would now require some delicacy in approach.

The bedroom door suddenly opened. The Yank came out carrying his health impedimenta in his hand.

" Would you care to try a colonic irrigation?" he asked. " I guess there's nothing like it in the tropics. It really purges you of all your internal miasmas."

He went on outside without waiting for a reply. When he had cleaned up his appliances he came back.

" Come on inside," he said.

He led the way into the bedroom. The place had a faint resemblance to a gymnasium. There were bar-bells for weightlifting on the floor, a device to simulate the exercise of rowing, and another expensive looking contrivance to develop the leg muscles without the necessity of the athlete having to do any walking.

" I take these all over the place," the American said, when he noticed George's interest. " They really keep me fit."

George glanced at his build. He was a husky enough looking man, with wide shoulders tapering off surprisingly to almost non-existent buttocks. Fetching the fellow a kick in the pants would be difficult. There was nothing at which to aim.

" I understand that you are heading for Fort Crampel," said George, after he had introduced himself.

" Mm, that's where I'm aiming to go."

" How?"

George had been told that there was a fair track to the place. It was used occasionally by transport lorries which ran on charcoal-burning suction-gas plants, and carried supplies up for the traders. There was nothing due to depart for another week. The American pursed his lips.

" Well," he said slowly, " there is a French trader here who has a model T Ford. He wants somebody to deliver it for him at Fort Crampel. I've been thinking of offering to take it for him."

George's eyes lit up. This would be something like luxury travel.

" Could I have a lift?"

" Why sure. I guess we could both stack our things in it. What are you carrying?"

George told him. The American carried far more than he did, and had also picked up a young African servant. There would still be ample room, however, for all their belongings.

"Just fine," said the American. "Will you go and tell the man we'll deliver the thing for him. I'm feeling a bit tired. I guess I lifted the weights a bit too much today. I like to rest at this time."

George took the hint and moved towards the door.

"Who's the trader?"

The missionary told him. He went outside. He was already in the street when the American put his head out of the window.

"Say, can you drive?"

"No."

The American giggled.

"Well, don't tell the man that. Let it be a delicate omission. We should have quite a ride. We might establish a record for the Bangui-Fort Crampel run. I've never been allowed to try to drive before. It must be fun."

CHAPTER TEN

HUNTER'S PARADISE

GEORGE and the American set out the next morning for Fort Crampel. The American drove. On the strength of the fact that he came from the same country as the car, people were inclined to bow to his superior mechanical knowledge. The Ford was new, but by the time it reached Fort Crampel it had experienced strain. Fortunately they encountered no traffic in the 250-mile stretch of road, while any animal or human life which normally frequented the verges was driven to take shelter by the mere noise of their approach. Their right-of-way was never disputed.

They spent two nights on the road. This was not so much the result of the mileage, but of the number of times they stuck in sand, or became entangled in bushes when they ran over the verges. It was always a problem to get started again. The missionary's African servant was at first delegated the duty of cranking the engine. He declined further services after being pursued down the road when his master left the car in gear while it was being started. George had to do the job after that. He had several very narrow escapes, for the American was no great respecter of persons when the vehicle was mobile. Once started, he would decline to stop. On such occasions when George and the African had to push the vehicle out of sand, the American simply roared away with a bronco-busting cheer as soon as the wheels were on firm ground, and left the others to sprint along behind until some slope slowed the Ford down enough to allow them an opportunity to tumble in from the back.

The two evenings on the roadside were also fairly nerve-racking. The American insisted on the African unloading all his physical culture equipment. He would then spend some time in exercising himself, meanwhile recommending the other two to join him in order to keep fit. George shared the African's opinion that all his energy was expended in the process of earning a living. The American argued that certain muscles would be developed by exercise. So far as George could see, these were not muscles for which he had much use, so they could remain undeveloped. The American always ended his activities with a colonic irrigation. Listening to the gurgling water in the dark was a very disturbing experience. It was quite a relief to reach Fort Crampel and see the American off to his mission, with the African struggling along behind him carrying the equipment. The man went completely off his head a few months later and was returned to America for treatment.

Fort Crampel consisted of very little save a few wattle and daub administrative buildings, the usual Senegalese garrison, and a Hausa trading community. The only Europeans were a couple of pleasant French officials. George had the little guest-house to himself while he organised his hunting project. He wanted porters, trackers, and all possible information about the distribution of elephants. In this connection the Hausa traders were the most informative. They wandered around the country peddling goods and their interest in ivory gave them a close regard for elephants and hunters. They treated George, in fact, to quite a welcome, inviting him along to their quarters for a dinner, and entertaining him with a dance and a serenade played on their national instruments, odd affairs which sounded something like out-of-tune bagpipes.

The information supplied by the Hausas indicated that the best elephant country lay to the north-east of Fort Crampel. It was semi-arid country, and very sparsely populated. Sleeping sickness and squabbles with the French authorities had driven most of the population away. On the subject of the political troubles, the Hausas were somewhat cautious. One entire tribe, the Kresh, had packed up and removed bodily across the border into the Sudan. They were a hunting tribe, very expert with elephants.

" They still come back hunting," warned the Hausa leader. " They are well armed, so be careful."

When George told him that politics and hunting didn't mix, the Hausa shrugged.

" The trouble," he said in parting, " is that you are the same colour as the French. It's a pity you cannot darken yourself up slightly. Then you would be all right."

George set off the next day. His immediate objective was to conduct a reconnaissance of the area, find the best hunting ground, and then erect a permanent base. For this purpose he went north as far as the Auk River, and then turned south through Wada Jellab to the lonely little trading posts of Muka and Bria. It was all good bull elephant territory, almost uninhabited by human beings and very desolate. The elephants wandered at will over a prodigious range of flattish tall grass country, with few scenic features save clumps of evergreen forest, thick in the south, but petering out as the country grew more arid in the north. Buffalo were very numerous in the area, while bongo, eland, saddle-back duikers, and a considerable number of chimpanzees, provided diversity to the animal population.

It was inevitable, of course, that in such a splendid hunting ground there had to be competition. The first time George encountered any rivals, he was following the tracks of a small herd of elephants. The tracks suddenly broke up, as though the elephants had been disturbed. George was trying to interpret the signs when his tracker, who was standing behind him, clicked his fingers as though he had spotted an elephant. George whirled around to find his rifle. The tracker simply pointed ahead. Scattered among the trees, and looking very menacing, were a party of Kresh hunters.

The Kresh had their rifles half-ready. They looked what they were, extremely tough customers, and not inclined to allow any liberties. George's trackers ran towards them, shouting in Arabic that the white man was all right, and not a tax-gatherer. George heard the description with a grin. He walked up to the Kresh, and greeted them. They seemed perfectly affable.

Their headman came forward, and George presented him with some tobacco. They introduced themselves as belonging to the same elephant-hunting trade. This broke any ice in a very satisfactory manner. They settled down to examine each other's rifles, the Kresh being very knowledgeable in the finer points of the gunsmith's art. The headman possessed a French army rifle of excellent workmanship, but it would have been indiscreet to enquire where and how he had obtained it. He told George that he would encounter quite a few similar Kresh hunting parties in the area but providing he approached them openly, there would be no hostility. Their principal dislike of the French lay over the question of taxes, and the behaviour of the Senegalese troops, who were notorious bullies.

So far as other European hunters were concerned, there were quite a few operating profitably in the area. From information gathered from various sources, George was aware that the famous Jim Sutherland was somewhere in the northern districts. Near him there was a hunter named A. Anderson. A French-Canadian hunter named Verkerni and a Swiss named Christanger were working in the west, with an Englishman, Dr FitzWilliams still further away in the same direction. To the east, a hunter named Simpson was also busy, while an Italian named Rossi, an elderly Greek, a man named Kespars, and another Italian, a trader named Stagni, were at large somewhere to the north-west. Bands of the Kresh roamed more or less at will over the whole area. At first consideration, this seemed as though the last hunter's paradise was slightly congested. It was, however, a large block of wilderness, some 200 miles by 200 miles in French Equatorial Africa alone, with lesser elephant areas stretching far to the west, to Lake Chad and the Cameroons. It would also be a wonderful base for poaching into the Sudan and the Congo. It was the latter consideration which finally influenced George in his choice of a base for operations.

8—T.H.I.D.

From what he had heard, and from its appearance on the map, he rather fancied the south-east tip of French Equatorial Africa. Elephants were reputedly very numerous in those parts. The adjoining portion of the Congo across the Mbomu River was also renowned for its tuskers. Poaching into it would be particularly easy, as sleeping sickness had caused the complete evacuation of the area by its original human population. No other hunter was working the area, so George would have it entirely to himself.

George set out for the south to reach the Mbomu River, hunting as he travelled. From the very nature of his trade, hardly a day passed without incident, and it would have been expecting too much if these events had all been pleasant.

One day he was following a small herd of six elephants. The porters had been left well behind and George was accompanied by two gun-bearers and an extra man. The country was open with grass shoulder to head high and well trampled with elephants' paths. They reached the herd without difficulty and George killed the best tusker with his first shot. As usual the rest of the animals stampeded, keeping together in an alarmed huddle. George sprinted after them. In country such as this, it often paid to follow stampeding elephants. With the hunter concealed in the grass, the elephants were so confused they were quite uncertain as to what had attacked them. They generally stopped after running for about 200 yards, and faced around in order to find out what had happened.

George had only covered about fifty yards when it was his turn to stop in a hurry. The five elephants were coming at full speed back along their own tracks. George had to move fast. At forty yards he dropped the leader. The rest swerved to the left. As they did so, he put down another animal with a bullet in the brain. The three survivors stampeded off, angling away from the hunters as fast as they could go.

George watched them over the grass to see if they would stop but they gave him no further chance. Only one of them seemed to be held up for a short while at some little gully. He paused, hesitated, bobbed down as he crossed the obstruction, and then rushed on for safety.

George went to examine the fallen elephants. They were all dead, and carried excellent ivory. While he was assessing the weight, one of his gun-bearers remarked that the extra man was missing. Nobody had noticed him run off. They called out for him and heard a faint reply from the direction where George had thought he had seen the elephant crossing the gully.

They ran to the place. They found the man lying on the ground. He was covered in blood and dirt, with several bad abrasions, and holding in a double handful of his entrails which were protruding from a gash in his stomach. The elephant had tusked him before it had stampeded on, and made quite a job of it. The man looked in pretty poor shape. He had panicked and tried to run when he saw the elephants coming. Unfortunately for him, he had run in the wrong direction.

George sent one of the trackers back along their trail to bring up the porters as fast as possible. When the men arrived, he unloaded his small first aid outfit. He mixed a solution of permanganate of potash and carefully washed the dirt off the entrails. Then, with the help of one of the trackers, he stowed the things back where they belonged.

There was a surgical needle and thread in the first aid outfit. With some effort George managed to close the wound. The gash was so long, he ran out of surgical thread before he was half-way, and had to resort to a normal reel of cotton. At the end he fixed a pad over the wound and bound the man up around the body with bandages made from strips of calico reinforced with a buckle belt. The man was then cleaned up generally, with his minor abrasions bathed in iodine. They made him comfortable on a grass bed, and pitched their camp close to the fallen elephants, generally expecting the patient to have a painful death from peritonitis.

The only person who didn't expect the patient to die, was the man himself. When George visited him about two hours after sundown, he was tucking in to huge hunks of grilled elephant meat and declined to be cautioned off his feed. He was perfectly cheerful, and quite relished the attention and privileges awarded him by his comrades.

George remained in camp at that spot for two days in order to allow the patient a chance to recover. Then they made a stretcher from bush poles tied together with bark rope and carried the injured man on with them. He withstood the rigours of travelling extremely well. After three weeks he had completely recovered, with nothing to show of the experience other than a slight bulge in his stomach on the site of the wound.

The hunters eventually reached the Mbomu River at Rafai, the seat of the *hetman,* or sultan, of the Azande tribe who lived in this not particularly salubrious portion of the globe. The sultan was a resolute character of about sixty-five years of age. He ruled his people with such complete authority that he was not only their administrator, judge, benefactor and castigator, but even acted as auctioneer at a sale of produce held as a variety of quarterly fair in his capital.

George was actually attracted to Rafai by news of the imminence of one of these fairs. Traders came up by canoe from Bangui to attend the fairs, and this would provide him with an opportunity to unburden his porters of a load of ivory.

Attending the fair was quite an entertaining distraction after the weeks of hunting. The town lay in tropical country, close to the river. It was well crowded with visitors for the occasion. Large numbers of Hausa peddlers always gathered for such fairs, while French, Greek and Syrian traders were also present.

The auctions were conducted in a large open-sided banda roofed with palm leaves. The principal produce of the country was ivory, beeswax, and wild rubber. Stocks were displayed in the building, the ivory leaning against racks while the wild rubber looked like huge coils of home made sausages festooned over the floor. The hetman conducted the auction with no little aplomb. He was not exactly an amateur at his business and the visiting dealers had to have their wits about them if they wished to strike anything like a bargain. The auction lasted a morning, and then there was a great bustle of traders organising canoes to carry their goods downstream to Bangui. Meanwhile there was a considerable traffic by the Hausa peddlers who dealt in cloth, beads, ornaments, sweets, and a mixture of minor essentials and luxuries.

George sold his ivory without any difficulty. Once his men had enjoyed some relaxation and gambled away their pay with the sharps who attended the fair, he planned to move up river until he found a suitable place in which to build his permanent camp. All available information indicated that he would be moving into an excellent hunting area. The renowned Sutherland was said to be very partial to that part of French Equatorial Africa, and George would certainly have the opportunity of meeting him there sooner or later.

The track leading eastwards from Rafai followed the course of the Mbomu to the post of Zemio about one hundred miles away. This little place had quite a reputation. It had for some years been the farthest outpost of the French Foreign Legion. Most of the garrison of legionaires had by this time been replaced by the usual Senegalese troops, but several of their bad habits remained, along with a handful of N.C.O.s who were clearing up affairs.

George arrived in Zemio in time to be invited to the annual Bastille Day celebrations. This was always a very jolly occasion among the French. Even in isolated outposts of empire such as Zemio, they contrived to stage something of an entertainment, with a few bottles of good wine produced from a hidden cellar, and at least something more tasty to eat than George's habitual fare of elephant meat. Securing a change from that diet always made him welcome an invitation to Thanksgiving Day dinners on American missions, Christmas dinners on British stations, and now Bastille Day celebrations with the French.

The banquet was staged in an open-walled storeroom. All the Europeans in the community attended, except for a few American missionaries from a station nearby who kept their distance. The local French administrative officer presided over a long table running down the centre of the room. A very good spread of food was provided, along with more than generous quantities of liquor. After the usual grace, the courses were carried in by young African girls, all well polished and spruced up for the occasion. It was really a pleasant assembly, at least at the beginning of the celebrations, of a pretty rugged-looking crowd of legionaires and administrative men. The party only became hectic towards the end of the meal when the menu called for a dessert known to legionaires as *Le Baiser de l'Ange,* or The Kiss of an Angel. By then, however, George had enjoyed his fill and could sneak quietly back to camp. The girls were already disappearing under the tables and their activity was producing far-away looks to the eyes of the seated assembly.

From Zemio, George went on to the last French outpost of Obo. This little place acted as the seat for a solitary French official, living in the company of a small Senegalese garrison and a few African traders. The Sudanese frontier lay fifty miles east, while the Belgian Congo was about twenty-five miles south. Altogether, George liked the look of the area. The Frenchman was very agreeable, elephants were certainly present in substantial numbers, and although their tusks were not record breaking, they seemed to maintain a remarkably high average weight and be of an excellent quality of ivory.

George camped a short day's walk from Obo towards the Congo border and started to look around for a site for his permanent camp. On the second day he was there, two of his porters brought him the news that they had seen a European travelling with his men along a path about a quarter of a mile away. He had informed the porters that he proposed camping a couple of miles further on, and sent his greetings to the other white man, whoever he was. The Africans could never remember a European's name correctly. They knew George as *Tibugera,* or the Buffalo. It was the same name, in the local language, which he had been called in the south. All they could tell him of the traveller was that he was an *Ngresa,* or Englishman.

George walked after the newcomer. He had a curious feeling that the man was Sutherland and, after all he had heard and read about the hunter, he wondered what impression they would make on each other. He walked rather diffidently up to the camp. There was an odd-looking man with a curiously flattish face, sitting at ease drinking tea in front of a tent. He was only about five feet seven inches in height, slim, clean shaven, in his late fifties, and as tough-looking as an African thorn tree. He greeted George with a pleasant grin, and introduced himself. It was Jim Sutherland.

They sat down and had a good yarn. Sutherland was glad to receive recent news of Tanganyika, of the Lupa Gold Field, and of mutual friends. He had been in French Equatorial Africa for some years with no better contact with the outside world than the postal facilities offered by the British sleeping-sickness post of Yubo which lay just across the Sudanese border. He was on his way back from a visit to this place, and recommended George to make use of it, for it was certainly a great convenience to any hunter to have some reliable line of communication.

It would have been expecting too much for Sutherland to provide any information about elephants. Ivory hunters were as cautious as prospectors when in the presence of possible rivals. But Sutherland did allow that he had done very well in his life. George had read his book, *The Adventures of an Elephant Hunter,* and although it had been published as early as 1912, it had provided some inkling of a highly profitable profession. Sutherland had gone to French Equatorial Africa in company with a well-to-do friend of his, Major G. H. *Miguu* Anderson, in order to exploit the opportunity of the unrestricted hunting licences. Anderson had subsequently gone off to Kenya, but Sutherland was obviously having a thoroughly enjoyable time. He did not seem perturbed at George's advent as a possible rival.

" There's room for all of us," Sutherland assured him. " So long as we don't actually try and work the same tracts of country at the same time, we should manage without friction. There are quite a few other hunters in the area, as you know. So far we have got along without exactly having to dodge one another's bullets."

From Sutherland's descriptions, and from what he had heard from the Africans, George gathered that the rest of the hunters were a reasonable crowd of men. The one possible exception was an individual named Marcus Daly, who occasionally visited the area and had a somewhat offensive reputation for personal aggressiveness and unscrupulousness, especially with the tribespeople. The man was a first class hunter, but very tough indeed, and inclined to be over-free with other people's food, women, and liquor.

When Sutherland had gone, George resumed his search for a site for his permanent camp. He eventually found a pleasant spot on high ground about midway between Obo and the Mbomu River. There was a fine stand of shady trees growing there, with a cluster of permanent springs of sweet water bubbling to life in the shadows. Over the next few weeks, George erected for himself a wattle and daub room with a large, open veranda, an ivory store and a cluster of huts for his porters and their women. The place soon had the appearance of a farmyard, with hens clucking, and the women cultivating patches of maize and vegetables.

George was particularly satisfied with his base. It was an ideal centre for the pursuit of the local elephants, and also for raids across the Congo border. Following on Sutherland's advice, he arranged for his postal matter to be addressed to him through the kind offices of the doctors at Yubo, while supplies were relatively easy to obtain from the Greek traders at the Sudanese provincial administrative centre of Wau. The same traders, C. Yiaimanis and G. Diplas, also shipped his ivory out to Gilliats, who sold it for him on the London auctions. Altogether it was something of an ideal professional hunting arrangement and he made the most of the opportunity.

The first foray George made across the Congo border was also, in one curious respect, his most profitable. He had established excellent relations with the resident Azande tribe on the French side of the border, and was gratified when their chief suggested that George allow his rifles to be blessed by the local wise man. It was the third time George's rifles had experienced the pagan ceremony. From the success which had followed on the previous occasions, he was interested to discover what results would follow the third blessing. The raid across the border was his first hunt after the ceremony.

Immediately after crossing the border, the trackers found the fresh trail of an elephant. They followed eagerly through a dense evergreen thicket. Ahead of them, they were surprised to hear a curious sound. At first they thought it came from some chimpanzee, for there were many in the area, but it had a very unusual note to it. They stopped and looked at one another in puzzled fashion. George moved forward cautiously. In the midst of the thicket he found an African, quite naked, digging with a sharp pointed stick in order to excavate a yam. He had his back to George, and was crooning softly to himself.

It was an embarrassing discovery. George had banked on the country being quite unpopulated. If the man, whoever he was, carried news to the Belgians of the operations of a poacher, it could bring authority on the scene in a hurry. George signalled to his trackers, and they took the man with a rush. The fellow was so wild looking, he would certainly have run away if they had simply attempted to talk to him.

The yam digger was surprisingly tough. He swung the two trackers around almost at will while they tried to seize hold of his body. A naked man is never easy to hold. He even managed to slip loose from their grasp, but this was his undoing. It forced George to intervene. He settled the matter with a round-house right to the man's temple which sent him down like an elephant with a brain shot. The trackers tied him up, and they sat down to wait for the yam digger to recover his wits.

George imagined that the prisoner would be in some state of alarm when consciousness returned, but even he was startled at the blank look of sheer animal terror when the man opened his eyes. It was easy to see that the prisoner was a completely wild man of the forest. Even when the porters came up and tried him with words from half a dozen different tribal languages, he was completely unresponsive. There was little likelihood of him carrying any tales to the Belgians, but he was too interesting a find to immediately release. They tied a vine round his waist and, with three porters handling him, they continued with the hunt.

About mid-afternoon they caught up with the elephants. George killed two good bulls, and they made their camp close to the carcasses. The wild man watched proceedings with the most intense interest. George took a lump of the best piece of elephant meat, skewered portions on green wands, and jabbed them into the ground at angles to grill over his fire. He could see the astonishment in the man's face as he watched this simple operation of cooking.

While the meat grilled, George rolled out his blankets and pitched his mosquito net under a bush. The wild man watched his every move. It was very curious to think that such simple things were being seen for the first time by this strange human being.

With his bed ready, and the meat grilled, George brought the wild man to the fire and made him squat down. He gave him one of the skewers of cooked meat, and also a handful of salt, traditionally a symbolic gesture in Africa. The wild man was immediately relieved by the gesture. His fear manifestly disappeared. George untied him. They squatted down on opposite sides of the fire and ate their dinner. When it was over, they looked at each other and grinned. The grin of the yam-digger was that of a sane man, and no lunatic.

George tried him with words from various languages. He was surprised to find that the man could understand something of the Ngala language which was spoken around Stanleyville, some 400 miles south of their present position. The few words in common produced a feeling of confidence between them in a manner which was hard to define. When George wandered off around the camp, watching the tusks being cut from the fallen elephants and generally seeing that everything was in order for the night, the wild man simply crouched near the fire and made no effort to run away, although he was now at complete liberty.

When George awoke the next morning, he found the wild man still beside the fire. By dint of gesture and the few words they had in common, George explained to him that he was at liberty to go. The wild man indicated that he would like to stay. George thought the matter over. Using the wild man as a tracker might have interesting results. George indicated his agreement to the man remaining, and actually kept him in front when they went out to hunt. The result was phenomenal. The wild man soon realised what was required of him. He proved the finest tracker George ever employed. Not only did he possess extraordinary understanding of animal behaviour, but he was also absolutely fearless, and the only African George ever encountered who would stand even in the face of a charge from a bull elephant.

George named the man, Kinanda. He presented him with some cloth to cover his nakedness, but this the man simply wound around his head like a turban. A pair of cast-off trousers made a more acceptable gift a few weeks later. By that time the wild man had become aware of his nakedness. He received the ragged trousers as a great honour, and from that time on became daily more civilised and settled in his ways. George found him to be the most devoted of assistants and a hunting asset of such value that, if he was, in fact, the reward of the third blessing of the rifles, then the pagan ceremony had certainly produced a remarkable result. Just how much happiness the wild man, on his part enjoyed as a consequence of his civilisation was another question entirely, for he soon linked up with a woman who thoroughly nagged him.

CHAPTER ELEVEN

THE LAST OF THE IVORY HUNTERS

FOR two-and-a-half years George hunted from his base near Obo, and the results of his activity were extremely satisfying. The area seemed to have an inexhaustible supply of elephants. It lay directly across one of the main migratory routes used by the animals in this part of Africa. As such, no matter how much it was hunted, it was constantly being replenished by influxes of new animals from the south. The wet season was an especially profitable hunting period, for the elephants tended to abandon the forest country of the Congo. They migrated northwards in order to escape the consequences of damp ground, the ceaseless dripping from wet trees, and the activities of siafu ants and blind flies which were active in the wet season. The cluster of professional hunters in French territory provided the elephants with a warm reception, but this seemed to have little effect on the number of bulls who annually crossed the border in search of the sun.

The hunters all did very well in the area. With such a concentration of elephants, rivalry between them was simply on a friendly basis. At the end of each year, in fact, it amused them to compare their figures and see who had been able to obtain the most ivory. Sutherland, notwithstanding his years—for he was approaching sixty—invariably managed to have the edge

113

on his younger rivals. He was certainly a most extraordinary hunter, and it pleased George immensely to become firm friends with the man, especially when Sutherland moved his camp to within a couple of days' walking distance north of Obo. The mere fact that their hunting grounds now abutted made it inevitable that they meet each other periodically. Whether these encounters were by accident or design, they were always very agreeable affairs.

For the Christmas of 1927, George also had the happy idea of inviting the hunting community to his camp for a relaxed spell of yarning, feeding and drinking. George had experienced the most profitable year of hunting in his career. Even Sutherland had been hard pressed to surpass him in weight of ivory, and the success of the year had suggested that its conclusion be marked by some celebration. The project of bringing the hunters together for a general exchange of reminiscence had always appealed to George. These men were the last of the long and romantic line of professional ivory hunters. When the day came for the French to end the privilege of unrestricted licence, the breed would inevitably die out. A few of the profession might linger on as poachers or salaried hunters on some government elephant control, but such activities could never rank as anything more than a shadow of the adventurous years when a man could do as he pleased and wander at will anywhere in Africa on the trail of bull elephants.

George's camp took on something of the appearance of one of the local trade fairs for the four-day duration of the party. Each hunter brought with him his camp-following of African porters, trackers and servants. These individuals entered into the spirit of the holiday with great gusto. While their masters settled down to serious discussions of hunting techniques and adventures, the African staffs made merry on huge pots of beer carried in for sale by women from the nearby villages, and staged an uproarious confabulation in a general exchange of accounts of their own activities.

To add to the entertainment, George had attached to his staff a variety of combined troubadour and camp jester. This man was named Bakuyu. He had simply wandered in to George's camp one day, bringing with him a lute-like instrument made from a calabash attached to a flat piece of wood. Four or five strings were stretched along the length of the wood and over the open side of the calabash. The instrument produced a most agreeable sound, and Bakuyu was a very skilled performer, with an entertaining knack of improvisation.

The troubadour always accompanied the hunters on their forays. After the evening meal he would play to the men. He would compose a verse on each day's happenings, using all the licence allowed to a poet. Some of the verses were humorous, others full of ridicule, with exaggerated descriptions of some very minor incident. A truly exciting hunting episode was suitably glamorised, praise was awarded where due, while any skit on George was always included to the great delight of the men. A short, repetitive chorus linked the verses together.

At the start of any hunt there would be only a single verse to the saga, and Bakuyu would make up his programme with sundry tribal songs. But by the end of a hunt, the song would be from ten to twenty or more verses in length. No matter how often it was repeated, it always delighted the men. Even George joined in the choruses, and Bakuyu's wit passed many an otherwise dull evening in camp. The troubadour, of course, was in his element at the time of the Christmas gathering. He produced what one could call an omnibus edition of his best works and was the star performer each evening for everybody in the party.

Among the Europeans, the conversation, no matter how it started, inevitably worked back to that interminable argument of all hunters, the choice of rifles. Rifles are so vital, and yet such matters of personal choice, with so large a range from which to make a selection, that there is no surer way of raising dissension than to drop some pertinent opinion about them in a hunting community.

Sutherland used a ·577 double-barrelled ejector, a pretty murderous weapon for a lightly built man to handle. George shared his opinion that this was, in fact, the most effective of all rifles to use on elephants.

"After all," Sutherland said, " we are in the business to kill elephants and the more efficiently and humanely we do it the better. All the hunters I know, particularly the young and the cocky ones, who use small-bore weapons and consider themselves such stylish shots that they cannot possibly miss a vital point, invariably litter the bush with wounded animals, or get themselves killed before they learn any better. Common humanity demands that if we are to kill, we at least do so with maximum despatch.

" I remember using a ·318 rifle on an elephant once. It was really a most extraordinary affair. I shot one of a group of bulls and brought him down without trouble. His companions ran off. I went up to him. He was lying on his side groaning. I thought I would put him out of any pain. I placed the muzzle of the ·318 within a foot of his head, at the correct angle to reach his brain, and fired. As soon as the bullet struck him, his huge body was convulsed with the usual tremors. His tail stiffened, and all the signs indicated that he was dead.

" My tracker actually mounted the body to secure a better view of the surrounding bush. I sat for five minutes having a breather on the elephant's head. Then we set out after the rest of the elephants. We never caught them. The wind turned variable and no matter what we did, they scented us.

" I thought we'd rest for a while and make some tea, hoping that the wind would settle. While we waited I sent one of my trackers to cut off the tail of the dead elephant. He came back looking quite astonished. He told me that the elephant had vanished. I couldn't believe it. At first I thought the tracker must have lost his way. He was very offended when I told him this. I went back with him. He was right. The elephant was gone.

" From the tracks we could see how the elephant had struggled to regain his feet. He had lurched against the trunks of trees in an effort to steady himself. We followed his trail. From the impressions of his toes in the ground, and the way in which the grass had been brushed aside, we could see how his manner of progression had gradually changed from staggering to a firm gait, and then to a good steady pace. Incredibly enough, there was no blood trail. We followed him for six hours before night forced us to camp on his trail. Next morning we found that he had met with a couple of other bulls, then joined a herd of females, and his track was lost with those of a dozen other animals.

" My trackers all swore that the elephant was a wizard. The real moral of the tale, however, is that a small-bore rifle has admitted accuracy and penetrative power, but, no matter how near the miss, unless it actually strikes a really vital spot, the animal has the chance to recover, either completely, in which case good luck to him, or to escape in a very sorry state of pain or disablement."

" The only trouble with the heavy rifles," George said, " is their recoil. I don't find the recoil of a ·577 too bad, providing I fire not more than six rounds in rapid succession. If you fire more than that number of rounds, the barrels become hot and you can be pretty severely punished. The most I ever fired rapidly from a ·577 was twenty-six rounds, and it took me three days to recover the use of my shoulder."

The rest of the company laughed.

"Actually," said Simpson, " it's really only the dudes who use the light rifle, and most of them do it because they're too lazy to carry anything more serviceable. Mickey Norton used a ·577, and so did Miguu Anderson. Karamoja Bell is about the only one of the professionals who swore by a light rifle, and he didn't do too well with it when he was in these parts."

" Of course," said Anderson, " you have to use a light rifle if you're shooting from a tripod or antheap or any precarious perch."

George told them of his first attempt to shoot from the top of a ladder in the Mweru marsh.

" The only thing is to carry two rifles with you, then you're ready to take any opportunity. I used to place some store on light rifles, but I soon learned better. I remember shooting a big bull through the lower region of the heart late one evening. I used a ·303 calibre rifle. It was so dark that I could not follow the elephant in the long grass. I went back to camp, five miles away. I searched for him the next morning. I found him standing in the open about one mile away from the place where I had shot him. He moved off as we approached. We lost sight of him for a while. Then we found him dead. He had lived for over twelve hours, and walked a full mile with a ·303 bullet clean through his heart.

" On another occasion I found a round muzzle-loader bullet grown over and embedded in the heart of an elephant I had shot. Nothing like that could have happened with large-bore rifles. I must say that I like a ·318 if I am in open country. I agree with Karamoja Bell that a light rifle is more handy to use in such conditions."

" They also make you more accurate in your aim," said Verkerni. " If only because you have to, you wait for the best target. A bullet in the right place from a light rifle will drop an elephant as quickly as a shell from a cannon."

" True," said Anderson, " but you cannot always wait for the ideal target. What happens when you are in thick country? You seldom have a clear chance of a shot. And what do you do with a light rifle if you have to face a charge, with an elephant coming at a rush head-on, probably pushing a wall of grass or bush in front of him on to the hunter? For the professional, a large-bore rifle is the only weapon."

The others agreed.

" You can only indulge in the luxury of a light rifle in the most ideal conditions," Sutherland summed up. " In any case, the hunter must know exactly what he is doing. Anybody who advises a novice to start off with anything light should be guilty of culpable homicide when the fellow gets himself killed. In this game all of us have had some narrow shaves. As it is, most of us who haven't been thrown at least once have just been fortunate. Stretching your luck by taking foolish chances is a sure way to die."

" How do you want to die?" asked Christanger.

" Following an elephant, not in front of him," replied Sutherland, without hesitation. " I cannot imagine a better death for the likes of us. Don't tell me that anybody here has dreams of an old men's home? God forbid! Let's get on the trail and stay there. Did I ever tell you fellows about Watkinson?

" Watkinson was an elephant hunter in the Portuguese country between Lake Nyasa and the sea. Somewhere deep in the forest there he lies buried. Exactly where, no white man knows, and perhaps that is as he would like it. All I know is that in 1903 he left the lake, intending to follow the Rovuma River to the sea, hunting as he went.

" Four months later three of his men, diseased and emaciated, came back to the lake. They reached Matengula bringing back their master's guns, a few personal belongings, and his diary. In Watkinson's diary you could read the story of what had happened. Most of his carriers had deserted for they were frightened at the desolation of the country. It was the wet season and Watkinson soon went down with fever.

" Leaving his heavy kit in trees where it would be safe from animals, he attempted to go on. It poured with rain, with hardly a blink of sunshine to allow anybody to dry their clothes. Their food ran out and Watkinson developed sores in his mouth which made him incapable of chewing meat.

" When he was quite done in, his men built him a small grass shelter. They tried to keep him alive on the roots of a wild plant called aka, quite nutritious stuff, but, like tapioca, it has to be boiled in several changes of water to remove poisonous matter.

"Watkinson was half-delirious. He crawled out of his hut one evening and found a pot of the stuff steaming over the fire. There was only one of his men present at the time, and he couldn't dissuade Watkinson from helping himself to the pot. I suppose that he would have died even without that meal, poor fellow, but it made him die in great agony. Even then, he was game to the last. The final entry in his diary read—

"'Feel like dying, but must get right. Nothing to eat for seven days. Elephant here, if only I could get after them'."

Sutherland grinned sardonically, and shook his head.

"Elephant here, if only I could get after them," he repeated. "If that's not engraven on the tombstones of all hunters who die in the bush, then surely it must be written in the dust from their hearts! What makes this game get such a hold on us?"

The others were silent for a while.

"I wonder which of us will be the first to die?" asked Simpson. "Speaking for myself, I'm going to stick it out for another two seasons, and then go somewhere for a holiday. If I stay here too long, I'll end up by marrying a gorilla, or turning into a cannibal king. Let's have a last toast, for good luck, bull elephants, and all our tomorrows!"

The party broke up the following day. The next time George saw Simpson was when his bearers carried his corpse in to Obo for burial. An elephant had caught him a full blow with its trunk and broken his neck. It was not a particularly glamorous way of dying, but certainly quite painless. The Africans had carried his body in to Obo in order to prove that there had been no dirty work on their part. They always found it embarrassing to have a white man killed off by some violence while in an isolated part of the country. The authorities could also see that no part of the corpse had been mutilated for any purpose of black magic.

Marcus Daly also made an exit from the local scene at this time. His departure was long expected and hardly noble. The French simply ran him out as a result of sundry misdemeanours. Mangin, the new commandant of Zemio, raided his camp, surprised him with his rifles packed away, and arrested him in no particularly gentle manner. Guarded by a bullying crowd of Senegalese troops, he was bundled off to Zemio where he was tried by his prosecutor and fined almost everything he possessed in money, rifles and ivory. He appealed to the senior administrator at Bangui, only to have the sentence confirmed. He left French Equatorial Africa in a very disgruntled mood, swearing vengeance, but the consensus of opinion behind him was that the handling he had received was no rougher than that which he normally awarded to others.

The end of 1928 saw George for the first time actually surpass Sutherland in the amount of ivory the hunters obtained. The difference was only a few pounds but George was highly gratified. Admittedly, there was always a large measure of varying fortune in hunting, and he was a virile twenty-seven, in magnificent physical condition, while Sutherland was nearly sixty. But still it was something to have more than equalled the acknowledged master.

The hunters did not gather for Christmas that year. The elephants were on the move right through December, and there was no time to spare for any relaxation. They agreed to postpone the party until a more opportune time but, as it happened, this never came.

George was hard on the trail of an elephant, in the second half of January 1929 when a messenger caught up with him carrying a letter from Sutherland. He opened the page and had to struggle to read the writing. Sutherland at the best of times was a poor hand at letter-writing, but this particular effort was a most dreadful scrawl. It was dated the 16th January.

" My Dear Rushby,

Those damn niggers almost got me on the 8th. Poison, blast them. As soon as I thought it was poison, I vomited like hell . . ."

The rest of the letter was practically indecipherable. George questioned the messenger. The man told him that Sutherland had recently taken on a crowd of men from the Azande tribe to act as porters. This tribe had been at odds with the French for some time over political troubles. Sutherland had nothing to do with these quarrels, but it was given to him to discover too late that the Azande had formulated a scheme to poison all persons with a white skin. They had slipped into his tea a tasteless poison named bhanga, which they extracted from the tips of the flame tree. Fortunately Sutherland had eaten a full lunch before he sipped his tea. As soon as a feeling of paralysis in his legs warned him that something was wrong, he forced himself to disgorge the entire meal. This at least relieved him of most of the poison, but his muscular system had already suffered damage, hence the distorted nature of his writing.

George immediately abandoned the pursuit of the elephant. He set out for Sutherland's camp as fast as he could. He found the hunter in a dismal state of shock, and partly paralysed. His loyal assistants had arrested the four men responsible for the poisoning. They had also secured an antidote known as bakalanga. This certainly saved Sutherland's life, but it was doubtful whether he would ever recover the complete use of his leg muscles.

Sutherland always kept a pair of riding mules in his camp. With an African supporting the sick man on each side, George managed to induce one of the mules to carry Sutherland in to Obo where there was at least some crude medical relief in the form of a small clinic run by one of the missions. The four poisoners were also tried for their effort. They quite openly admitted that they had nothing against Sutherland. He was simply to be the first on the list in a general killing of all foreigners. Their only regret was that they had failed in their object. The French punished them with a lengthy term of imprisonment. The Senegalese guard would certainly ensure that they enjoyed no rest cure in gaol, but this was hardly much compensation for Sutherland.

From an active and restlessly vigorous man, the great hunter was reduced to a miserable state. He never entirely recovered the use of his right leg. He resumed hunting, not even poison would ever take him off the trail of elephants, but all his subsequent activity was effected from the backs of mules, and this was a serious limitation. He was also forced to change his firing position to his left shoulder, as his right eye was affected by the poison. Only a fellow hunter would appreciate how difficult such a change would be, even to a man just learning to shoot, let alone one set in his ways after years of experience as a marksman. It was a sorry culmination to such a renowned career. If hunting was not so much in his blood, Sutherland could easily have afforded to retire, for the proceeds of his adventures had made him a well-to-do man. But when George suggested that Sutherland at least join him in a holiday to Europe, the hunter was completely disinterested.

" I probably haven't too much time left," he told George with a grin. " I rather imagine that dollop of poison will be the end of me yet. To waste my last days in jaunting around Europe when I could be here in the bush! Good Heavens! I suppose everybody to his taste. As for me, I am too old to ever again accommodate myself to the stuffiness of a city. Whatever happens to me, I will never regret the life I have led. I've had weary days and restless nights, fever, solitude, bad food and poor water. But in exchange I've had sunlight and air, the freedom to move in vast spaces, and all the excitement of the chase. If you want to exchange the stars for the lights of a city street, or the sigh of the forest at night for the tramp of thousands of feet, then you go off on your own, my boy, and good luck to you."

George rubbed his nose. To tell the truth, he was also increasingly reluctant to return to civilisation. But his broken nose always rankled with him. Whenever he met anybody, their eyes always seemed to focus on that squashed potato of a proboscis, and he was still young enough to feel self-conscious about it. Now that he had the money, nearly £15,000 from his ivory hunting, he could easily afford the attentions of a plastic surgeon. Seeing his mother again might also be something in the line of duty. For the past few years he had been roaming around in such desolate areas that he had seldom been able to exchange letters with her without at least one of them being lost.

After no little vacillation, George eventually decided to take his holiday in the second half of 1929. News of his coming departure brought consternation to his men. His base camp had grown almost to the size of a village in the last couple of years, with most of the men married and the owners of snug huts and cultivated lands. George explained to them that they could remain in the place. If he failed to return, his own house would act as an admirable residence for their headman. In time their descendants might grow into something of a clan. With the bonus and presents which he would leave it the little community would at least be launched into independence more comfortably endowed than quite a few others in Africa.

Kinanda was particularly upset at the idea of a change from his new way of life. He spent most of the time during the walk to Zemio trying to persuade George into taking him to Europe. By the time they were actually stowing George's goods into the canoe he had hired to take him down the river from Zemio to Bangui, Kinanda had almost won his point. George would take the former wild man at least as far as Bangui. That would get him some 600 miles away from the tongue of his wife. Even such an experienced nagger would have difficulty in throwing her voice so far.

The canoe was a commodious affair, cut from a huge mahogany tree. Eight paddlers and a captain navigated it down river while George was housed in some style in a grass-covered canopy amidships. The upper reaches of the river were too shallow, with several rapids, to be accessible to the paddle-wheel steamers. All traffic up stream from Bangui was conducted by canoes. With a heavy trade in wild rubber, beeswax and ivory, there was quite a collection of such craft working the various river ports. They gave the whole river route an air of animation and interest. The scenery was also handsome, with a lush green riverine forest on the banks, full of monkeys and chimpanzees and many extraordinary birds. Hippos, crocodiles and otters were in considerable profusion, while elephants could quite often be seen coming down to water. A few tuskers paid for their thirst with their lives, for George was not averse to keeping his rifles in use. The convenience of hunting from a mobile river house-boat, in fact, rather intrigued George. It was quite a dream to think of finding some stretch of river flowing through really good elephant country. After the hundreds of miles he had tramped pursuing elephants, what a life it would be to simply pick out good ivory from the comfort of a rhookee chair, with no trouble in porting the tusks or carrying camp kit over difficult country. It was, of course, too good to be true. Hunting in such comfort would soon have the profession overcrowded with amateurs. At least the hardships of the business kept ivory hunting for the select.

When they eventually reached Bangui, George asked the first European he met on the banks for news of the paddle-wheelers' departure down river. The information was depressing. Some chapter of accidents had so dislocated the service that there was not expected to be any passenger-carrying vessel for three weeks. This was quite a blow. Bangui was a pleasant enough spot, but having nothing to do there for three weeks would try anybody's patience. Getting drunk was about the only available entertainment, and this would certainly turn into something more than a headache after such an amount of time, in such a climate.

George had his belongings carried up to the guest house. The place was already occupied by what at first appeared to be a veritable young giant, and an exceedingly good-looking one at that. He came out of the building to welcome George, and had to stoop very low to clear the doorway. He was somewhere in his twenties and, apart from his six feet five inches of height, he was a sturdily built and rugged-looking individual, although somewhat pale in complexion. He introduced himself as John Molteno. George trusted that he was shaking off a dose of fever rather than about to have one. Occupying three weeks as a nurse to a man of such proportions, or burying him from blackwater fever, would not be particularly amusing. Molteno noticed his scrutiny, and smiled.

" I'm just out of dock," he said, " I had something of an accident."

George sniffed, and started to set up his bed. There was a smell of ointment and medicine to the place. It reminded him of the lunatic American with his health fads. At least, however, Molteno looked and spoke as though he was sensible.

" What hit you?" asked George.

"A buffalo."

" They usually hit hard."

" This one certainly did. Perhaps I asked for it."

George grinned.

" Most people who get hit by buffaloes ask for it."

Molteno winced slightly. Later on he told George about his experience. He was a member of a well-known Cape family. He had wandered up to French Equatorial Africa in search of hunting opportunities and had received far more than he had bargained for on what was almost his first day out.

With a couple of trackers he had gone in search of the vicious little red forest buffaloes which frequented the vicinity of the rivers. They had disturbed a herd, and Molteno fired at a bull. The bullet caught the animal in a spot more tender than vital. The buffalo immediately charged. Molteno tried to stop him with a second shot, but the buffalo simply swept forward in the usual nose-first fashion. With Molteno being tall, and the buffalo short, the animal's horns had caught the hunter high up in the thigh. The animal tossed him. Molteno sailed through the air and came down on the ground with a bruising thud. He rolled down on to his back as the buffalo came at him a second time.

" I suppose you'll say that I should have lain still," Molteno said ruefully. " Obviously that is what I should have done. But when he came nosing at me, I couldn't resist the chance. I was so annoyed at the blasted thing. I drew my legs back, kicked at his snout, and he simply tore into me again; caught me between the legs, threw me over his head, then raced on in to the bush and dropped dead about thirty yards away."

" What happened to your trackers?"

Molteno snorted.

" They'd run for it. They came back when they realised that the buffalo was dead. They simply went to the animal, made a fire and started to cut up meat. I called to them to come and help me. They laughed at me. One of them did come and look at me about an hour later. I was covered in blood. He simply said, ' Have patience, white man, you'll be dead soon,' and then went back to his eating. I lay there all night. Next day I crawled to a village. The people there helped me into a Belgian post on the river. The Belgian there put me in to a canoe and sent me to Bangui. I had a pretty narrow shave from loss of blood and all the usual complications of tetanus and gangrene. Now I'm nearly well."

" What are you going to do?"

" Go hunting again, of course; that's what I came here for."

George looked at him. The man was inexperienced, but he obviously had spirit. Knocking about with him would be far more fun than just sitting in Bangui.

" We might do a trip together," said George. " I've a feeling to try what they call the *Moyen* or Middle Congo. It's said to be good elephant country, providing you can avoid gorillas and cannibals. I'd like to do a reconnaissance before I leave for Europe. If the country is any good I could come back to it after I have my nose patched up."

CHAPTER TWELVE

MIDDLE CONGO

THE administrative centre for the Middle Congo was Impfondo, about 250 miles down river from Bangui. A small river-boat used for collecting cargo at minor ports took the hunters to this place. There they secured the necessary licence and collected information about the territory to the west. Nobody seemed to know much about it. There were the usual tales of wild men and wilder animals which are inevitably told about most remote parts of the earth. George could not find anybody who had done any actual travelling in the area. The French administrative officer simply did not seem to consider it a particularly desirable part of his nation's possessions.

" Our flag flies over it," he admitted with a grin, " but rather limply. If you would care to pay double your hunting licence fee I might recommend to our government that you keep the place. Personally, I do not think that it's worth more than that. So far as I am concerned, you could have it for less."

The prospects did not seem too hopeful. At least, however, it was new territory. There was always a chance of making some discovery. If it turned out to be a disappointment, then at least it couldn't be worse than it was generally made out to be.

The hunters started the journey into the interior from a small wood-fuel post named Bétou which lay on the west bank of the Ubangi River, about

124

midway between Impfondo and Bangui. It was a sparsely-inhabited portion of the river and, if only through the difficulty of obtaining porters, the hunters travelled light, with a minimum of baggage and comforts.

From the beginning the journey led them into miserable country. All the way through to the border of the Cameroons, the landscape seemed to consist of a vast, flat expanse of soggy swamp and dense evergreen forest. It was a rare event to catch a glimpse of the sky, and even then the most one saw was a low overcast of sickly-looking mist. To find a clearing in which the sun was shining was so unusual that they would stand in the place, looking upwards, as though they were sun-worshippers, and allow the warming rays to saturate their damp clothing. If they were lucky, this happened once or twice a week.

The atmosphere of the place was completely oppressive. The fact that elephants were scarce was hardly to be wondered at. Any creature capable of motion and remaining voluntarily in such an area would be singularly stupid. A few wild pigs and yellow-backed duikers were about the only animals to be found on the ground. The rest of the inhabitants, monkeys, chimpanzees and birds, kept to the tops of the trees. There they were away from the drip and the damp and the rotten vegetation of the surface. They could feed on the wild fruits and nuts which turned the tree-tops into something curiously like a garden cultivated by some lost spirits using this eerie wild as a refuge.

The nights were particularly depressing. On the fifth night out from Bétou, the hunters were rolled up in their sleeping bags trying to doze off after a disappointing pursuit of a few elephants. Dinner had consisted of little more than arrowroot washed down with coffee made from swamp water. George was thinking that even the mosquitoes sounded as though they were half-starved when he heard the sound of something approaching. It was a peculiar sound, just an occasional rather dull and furtive "crack" as the visitor trod on a half-rotten twig.

There had been some conversation among the porters, but their voices died away as they became aware of the sound. The surrounding forest was absolutely quiet. Listening to the approaching noise produced a curious feeling of dread, as though death itself was the expected visitor.

Whatever it was that wandered through the forest at night was taking its own time in approaching. The sounds drew nearer with an agonisingly slow, menacing regularity. The porters poked the camp fire into a blaze. The last "crack" came from the undergrowth only fifteen yards away. Then there was complete silence. The hunters were all tense and mute. Not one of them realised how they knew that the creature of the night had withdrawn. They simply became aware that the whispering of the wind in the trees had crept back again into their consciousness. Their tension had vanished. They relaxed, chuckling at one another's nervousness, and within ten minutes were all asleep. The next morning they looked for signs of their visitor. It had been a gorilla, and a large one, what the Belgians called a *Grand Garçon,* or Big Boy. From his tracks, he had stood watching them for some time from behind a shrub, and then silently moved off on whatever business was taking him wandering through the darkness away from his sleeping place that night.

They encountered gorillas quite often after that. There was never any friction with the giant apes. Notwithstanding a few stupid stories told about them, gorillas are reasonable creatures. They are strict vegetarians. With no appetite for man, they attend to their own affairs and leave the human race alone. There is, unfortunately, little reciprocity in this commendable habit. The local tribes regard gorillas as being excellent eating. They call them *mabubu* or fools, and hunt and slaughter the creatures with no little cruelty. Why they should behave to gorillas with such particular barbarism is unknown. Perhaps some feeling of spite is aroused by an inverted realisation that the giant apes are so closely related to man. Such a realisation would hardly make the tribespeople fastidious about eating gorillas. Most of them were full-blooded cannibals, with gorillas regarded as second-best fare for weekday nights.

Local relations between man and chimpanzee were on a much happier footing. For some reason there was not much eating of chimpanzees. George had even heard odd tales of man and chimpanzee finding each other's company so agreeable that on occasions they even attended joint functions, such as the funeral rites of important individuals. Admittedly, this may sound absurd, but the way of life in this sweltering forest was so primitive, with man so close to animal, that nothing was impossible. When George questioned the Mbinga Pygmies about the story, they simply became evasive without confirmation or denial. They seemed, in fact, to be slightly embarrassed about the idea.

The Pygmies were the most numerous human inhabitants of this forest. They were true Pygmies, about four feet six inches in height, and smaller than the people with whom George had hunted in the Kamba hills. They were a very pleasant and interesting little people, phenomenally good as trackers, with an almost infallible sense of direction, and an ability to move with complete silence through the densest cover. The only trouble about them was that they had absolutely no inclination to work. Occasionally one of them would join the hunters as a tracker, but no matter how well treated, he would become bored after a few days and then just vanish into the forest without a word of farewell.

According to their lights, they lived very comfortably. They hunted and their womenfolk collected quite a tasty variety of wild fruits and honey. Kola nuts also grew in great profusion on vines which festooned most of the trees. The dark-green nuts contained a white kernel, rather bitter to chew but with a stimulating and tonic effect. They provided sustenance for all forest dwellers, while another vine produced a very palatable variety of butter bean, rich enough in calories to make anyone eating them keep sharp watch on the girth of his stomach.

One very distinctive thing about the Pygmies was their body odour. This immediately marked them as a people apart from the Negro and Bantu tribes of Africa. Pygmy body odour has a curiously sweetish tang to it, as opposed to the more repellent sour acid smell of the Negroes. The Shangane people of Mozambique are generally reputed to have the most powerful of all human body odours. A trading station filled with them on a busy and hot Saturday morning would be enough to bring tears to the eyes of a potato. But even Shanganes pale into insignificance when compared to a gorilla. Once smelled, the body odour of a gorilla is unforgettable. It has the same sourness to it as the odour of a Negro, but in so pungent and concentrated a form as to be quite overwhelming and an infallible indication of the presence up wind of one of the giant apes.

The whole chemistry of stinks deserves careful scientific study, with field research extensively conducted in Africa, essentially the continent of powerful odours. It can be truly said that smell, in Africa, is at least as important as vision. The subtle chemistry of odours allows, not only of positive identification of an individual, but in some intangible way it also reveals his nervous state. What is particularly remarkable is the speed with which chemical changes in odour can betray changes in the emotions of the individual.

Fear produces its own smell. Man or beast in mortal terror emits a distinctive odour. Sexual change also has a pronounced effect on body odour. Animals in season, and even man to a lesser degree, emit special odours capable of attracting the attention of the opposite sex from a considerable distance. A menstruating woman also emits a peculiar odour so easy to discern that primitive Africans, who in general taboo a woman in that state, have no difficulty in detecting the smell several days before the actual commencement of the menstrual flow. They turn aside in order to avoid her on a path. The odour has nothing to do with personal hygiene. It emanates from chemical changes deep seated in the human body and is most difficult, if not impossible, to conceal.

The Pygmies, when they hunted, attempted to conceal their own body odour by smearing themselves with the droppings of the animals they were pursuing. It was always a dream of most hunters that they find some way of eliminating or camouflaging body odour. In hunting elephants such a change would be particularly desirable, for the animals are so highly sensitive to smell, and so sagacious in interpreting the slightest scent. The Pygmies swore that their device was at least a partly effective camouflage, but George saw little signs of any special success to their hunting which might have been expected from any immunity from odour.

Apart from the experience of penetrating such an untrodden wild, the hunting venture of George and Molteno was a failure. There were some elephants, but their tusks were small and of poor quality. To make matters worse the price of ivory on the depressed world market of 1929 had dropped sharply from twenty shillings to fourteen shillings a pound even for tusks of the finest quality. Hunting in such miserable conditions for inferior ivory was obviously a waste of time. Presumably the dismal environment had affected the elephants by stunting them. They had certainly not been over-shot. Several herds which the hunters disturbed consisted of what the local Africans knew as *bakri* or pygmy elephants. They had the reputation of being particularly fierce and dangerous, but whether they belonged to an authentic sub-species of the race of elephant is uncertain. George was more inclined to regard them as herds of runts bred and formed by immature beasts, but there has always been controversy about these creatures.

Much disappointed with their venture, George and Molteno made their way back to Bangui and broke up their party. Molteno proposed hunting in a westerly direction, where the country was drier, more open and better populated than the area inland from Bétou. George still intended to make his way down river and then go off to Europe. With some regret, therefore, he transferred the faithful Kinanda to the employ of Molteno, and helped them to prepare for an adventure of their own.

The hunters were camped on a very pleasant site where a White Russian trader named Konus had a store a short way down stream from Bangui. The place was the centre for quite a considerable trade with river people. George hoped to be able to obtain there a canoe large enough to carry him in comfort all the way down the river, and allow him to thoroughly explore the idea of using a house-boat as a hunting base for shooting elephants. There was certainly no doubt that elephants resorted in great numbers to the banks of the river. Marcus Daly, who had hunted down that way since his expulsion by the French, was talking very largely about shooting a giant bull carrying 207 lb. of ivory in one tusk and 203 lb. in the other. Even allowing for exaggeration, for such an elephant would have been phenomenal, the man had obviously had some interesting results in river-bank hunting, and the whole idea remained very attractive.

It was not easy to secure a suitable canoe. Eventually Konus produced a very well made dug-out mahogany canoe, about seventeen feet long and equipped with an ancient outboard motor. He offered to trade the craft for a Westley-Richards double-barrelled 400/450 rifle which George possessed. It was a high price, for such a second-hand rifle is worth well over £50, but the canoe was certainly an excellent craft, very stable on the water and perfectly suitable for the navigation of the lower Ubangi and Congo Rivers where sudden storms can make the water treacherous.

George took the canoe. He spent a few days tinkering around with the engine, laying in supplies, and engaging a crew of two men experienced in river travel. When all was ready he set out on the thousand-mile river voyage early one evening, with a full moon glinting on the waters. Travelling down the river at night would be pleasantly cool, with a refreshing breeze coming up the stream, and the light of the moon providing ample illumination for the journey. Saying goodbye in the shadows to his friends was quite affecting. Kinanda made George promise faithfully that if he ever returned to this part of the world he would find a place among his hunters for the former wild man. It was a promise, unfortunately, which George was never able to keep. When Molteno ended his own hunt, he transferred Kinanda to the employ of Konus, who set him off hunting the forest buffaloes. Kinanda faced the charge of a wounded bull. His strange life-story ended when the animal gored him to death against the trunk of one of the great trees of the forest which the wild man always regarded as his special home.

The outboard motor on George's canoe only lasted for half an hour. Then it choked, and simply petered out. Fiddling around with the thing in the moonlight was frustrating. The three men took to the paddles. With the aid of the current they made good progress. After the pestilential buzz of the motor, it was certainly a relatively peaceful and pleasant way of travelling down river. With an occasional pause for a rest, they glided on until the false dawn gave a sheen of light to the surface of the water. Then they tied up on the river bank and slept until the hippos were grunting with lazy pleasure as they felt the warmth of the noonday sun on their backs.

While the two Africans prepared a meal, George tinkered with the engine. It was a crochety piece of mechanism which obviously considered that it should have been pensioned off some years ago to a comfortable junk yard. Konus had included a few pieces of wire with the deal. At the time, George had wondered what the wire was for. Now he realised that it was intended to hold the motor together. He soon began to wonder whether Konus had given him enough.

The second camp was made at a village on the Belgian side of the river. The headman strongly pressed George to remain and hunt, for there were many elephants in the area. Unfortunately it was not a convenient time for poaching. A Belgian doctor was expected almost daily on a routine visit to treat victims of sleeping sickness. He would certainly report the activities of any hunter.

The third camp was made at the village of Mongumba on the French side of the river. This place was the seat of a petty chief who was particularly impressive in his account of the numbers of elephants waiting to be hunted in the immediate hinterland. George found it very difficult to resist the man. The chief pressed home his arguments by sending off a messenger to the local Pygmy headman, requiring his immediate presence in the village.

The traditional political pattern in this part of the world was for the Pygmies to acknowledge allegiance to the Negro tribes by bringing in tribute of wild fruits, honey, palm wine, kola nuts, ivory and meat. In exchange the Pygmies received salt, tobacco and some cloth. The Pygmies were expected to join in any local celebrations, for they were renowned dancers. Occasionally a Negro married one of their women, but unions between Pygmy males and females of other tribes were very rare.

The local Pygmy headman came in to the village on the afternoon of George's arrival. He was a cheerful little soul, and amply supported the accounts of elephants in the interior. The animals were said to be fine tuskers and never before hunted. Everybody in the locality was so hungry for meat that men tumbled over themselves to volunteer as porters. The whole thing was too tempting to ignore. George set out the next morning with a substantial following of porters who would carry back to the village the meat and ivory of any elephants he shot. Just before he left, the village chief warned him that there had been a recent rising in the Mbayiki area. A few armed bands were still wandering around near the Lobayi River. They were all cannibals but, so far, had not been known to eat Europeans. This was at least some assurance, but George was advised to be prudent.

They were not very many miles on the journey before George realised that the country was just as bad, if not worse, than the lost world inland from Bétou. It was the same swampland with the mud full of voracious leeches, and the forest haunted by enormous bats with wingspans of four feet, flitting silently down the dark aisles in the trees in a manner so sinister as hardly to provide a cheerful sight to any traveller.

For consolation, there were some elephants. The third day out, the hunters found a herd feeding in a swamp. George had to half-wade, half-swim to reach a position from where he managed to shoot two fairly good bulls. Very muddy and wet, and covered with leeches, he then made camp on a dry rising some 300 yards away. There were no tell-tale vultures to indicate the kill, but within a couple of hours he was astonished to see over thirty Pygmies busy hacking the two elephant carcasses to pieces and spreading the meat on racks for smoking.

Later in the afternoon a pretty tough-looking party of twelve Negro men and four women arrived. They were armed with muzzle loaders as well as bows, poisoned arrows and spears. George didn't like the look of them, but their leader, an elderly man, came up and politely asked if his people could have some of the elephant meat. George nodded.

" Yes, there is plenty of meat for everybody, but if there is any fighting, I'll shoot the whole damn lot of you."

The man gave George a very tolerant smile, thanked him, and led his people to the meat feast. Towards evening he came back to the camp, seated himself on his haunches and became sociable. It appeared that his party belonged to a local tribe who were in a chronic state of rebellion against the French. They spent most of their time lurking in the forest hoping to catch some detachment of Senegalese troops in an unfavourable position.

"You are a provider of meat," added the man. "You are not a tax collector. You have nothing to fear in this country."

"What about cannibals?"

The man grinned.

"I am one," he said frankly. "What is wrong with it?"

George considered the matter.

"Would it be pleasant to be eaten yourself?"

"It is not pleasant for animals to be eaten. But we eat them. The elephants do not like you to shoot them, but see what you do. Are we not all made of the same meat? The only difference is the flavour."

"Which do you prefer, human or game meat?"

The cannibal sucked at his teeth reflectively.

"Well, there are streaks of fat running through human meat, almost like zebra meat. Also, there is a remarkable thing about human meat. As you know, when you place a piece of elephant meat in a pot to boil, it just sinks to the bottom and lies there like a stone while it is being cooked. It is quite dead. But boil a lump of human meat and see what it does. It is much lighter. It bumps and bounces around and jigs in the pot as though it has life. Yes, I would also say that human meat tastes better and is much sweeter than any other meat."

"Is it tender?"

The cannibal viewed him appraisingly.

"With some it is. With others the meat is tough."

"You must give some to me. I have given you much elephant meat."

"Certainly, we have some drying on the racks in our camp. I will send you a nice piece as soon as we return."

"Don't worry. I am told that there are elephants near your camp. I will hunt that way. When I visit your camp I will choose a piece."

The man nodded.

"You will be very welcome. I will select something special for you."

The next day the hunters moved to the area occupied by the cannibals. The elephant carcasses were left to be carried away piecemeal by the Pygmies and the Negroes, whose combined efforts ensured that not a scrap of the precious meat was wasted.

The Pygmy guides led the hunters towards a camp site in a small, treeless glade on dry ground. On the way they passed through the encampment of the cannibals. The leader hospitably indicated a number of smoke racks well laden with meat.

"Take all you want," he said.

George inspected the offering. There was no doubt at all that the meat was human, and not gorilla or chimpanzee. The cannibal, in fact, seemed quite hurt at the suggestion that his supply came from any second-grade source. George selected a juicy-looking piece, thanked the cannibal, and went on to his camp site. He would examine the meat at leisure and then quietly bury it.

All the signs confirmed the Pygmy's reports that there were elephants in the vicinity. George decided to start an intensive hunting programme from the next morning, using the camp as a centre and going out in a different direction each day. He went into the porters' section of the camp in order to warn the men for the hunt, and immediately noticed a woman. Women in a hunting camp were always a nuisance. Sooner or later the men would fight over them and the consequences could be bloody. It was also a serious breach of discipline, for George always made it clear to his men when he hired them that women were forbidden.

He called the headman and asked him about the woman. The man looked uneasy, but admitted that the woman had been with them ever since they had left the river. She belonged to one of the porters. George summoned the man and told him that he would be paid off. He must leave the camp immediately and take the woman away with him. The man was greatly upset. Nobody in the entire district had ever had a better time than the porters. They were being well fed and paid for the first time in their lives, and for work which was considered to be little more than sport.

" I have done wrong," admitted the man, " but do not pay me my money now. I will take the woman back to the village and then return to work."

George was agreeable. The couple left within the hour and the hunters soon forgot about them in the excitement of the pursuit of elephants. There certainly were elephants in the area, and with fair-sized tusks, but the technical difficulties of hunting were immense. The elephants seemed to be almost as much at home in the swamps as prehistoric animals. They waded in to the most appalling slush, sometimes with little more than their trunks held above the mud for air. The sight of these appendages moving above the surface of the swamps was certainly very curious, but they did not offer any profitable target for a hunter. Even shooting an elephant on dry land was hazardous. Unless the animal fell dead immediately, it could always stumble off and sink in some deep part of the swamp where recovery could be difficult even when the body floated.

Gorillas of the lowland variety were very numerous. They seemed to be partial to a type of wild celery which grew around the verges of the swamps. Normally they were very docile, feeding in family groups, with little noise save an occasional grunt. The trouble was that the hunters inevitably stumbled into them when they were hot on the trail of an elephant. The old men gorillas would invariably scream at them with that heart-chilling, maniacal yell which has to be heard to be really appreciated. Even if the hunters grew hardened to the noise, it always served as a warning to the elephants and stampeded them in to the swamp. The chimpanzees, fortunately, kept to the trees. They were almost as noisy as the gorillas, but they at least confined their shouting to their own affairs and the rest of the animal world ignored them.

On the third day of hunting, George noticed the husband of the woman back in the company of porters. As the village was at least one week's travelling away, this certainly seemed like a speedy return. George remarked on the matter to the headman, but that individual just seemed surprised at the question.

" The man didn't take his woman anywhere at all," he said. " He killed her as soon as he had spoken to you. We've been eating her for the last two days. Did you think we had gorilla meat?"

George felt his stomach turn. Curiosity had prompted him to ask the cannibals for the cut of human meat. He had simply inspected it. Now he was obviously regarded as one of the crowd. Living in such a primitive environment would soon taint even an angel. He could understand the cannibals. If the human being has to live in such a wretched environment, with hardly any game animals, and the tsetse fly so rampant that no domestic livestock can survive, then the lack of proteins stimulated the dreadful hunger for meat which can only be satisfied by eating people.

George thought things over that night. He could make a point about cooking his own food in future, and have separate meat-drying racks in order to avoid any possible mixture with the delicacies of his porters, but the whole atmosphere of this part of the world was depressing. He was certainly securing some worthwhile elephants, but there were many more congenial places in Africa where elephants could still be found. He was also not feeling too well, and this was alarming. Despite large daily doses of quinine he was unable to shake off a general feeling of lassitude and lethargy. Going down with sleeping sickness in such an isolated area would be suicidal.

After one more week of hunting, George led his porters back to Mongumba. It was very pleasant emerging from the forest and reaching the broad river once again. At least the clear breezes could blow unobstructed up its length without taint from rotting vegetation and swamp. His canoe and belongings were all intact. He paid off the disappointed porters and explained to the chief that he considered it prudent to abandon the hunt and try to reach a doctor. The chief was as full of regrets as the men. He had hoped for profitable and lengthy employment for his people, with a good tribute paid to himself. He agreed with George, however, that no sensible person would stay in the swamps if he felt that sleeping sickness was in his system. A few miles down river, on the Belgian side, there was an American mission station with a small clinic. He directed George towards this place, and saw him off on the journey with many pressing requests for an early return as soon as he felt well enough to try another hunt.

CHAPTER THIRTEEN

ELEANOR

THE American mission at Kaka was a diminutive one-man affair, run by an extraordinarily pleasant and efficient individual named Wallen. The missionary was no doctor but, realising the great local need for medical facilities, he ran a small amateur clinic. He knew enough about sleeping sickness to put George on a precautionary course of injections and advised him to go on down river as soon as possible in order to have a thorough medical checkup in some place like Brazzaville.

George remained at the mission for five days before he felt well enough to continue with his journey. It had been a real pleasure to sleep in a clean bed and be able to talk to an intelligent and cultured person. If Wallen had his head with the angels, then at least his feet were well on the ground. He had no delusions about the people with whom he worked, consoling himself with the thought that even if what he was doing was very little, at least in such a miserable environment of brutish human beings, the slightest kindness or sympathy might be the means of aiding some soul lost in the degraded wilderness of a land without hope.

The last George saw of Wallen was the dapper figure of the missionary standing waving goodbye from the bank. There was not much time to indulge in any exchange of farewells. The American had warned George that a short distance down stream he would find an island which divided the Ubangi River into two channels. The channel on the Belgian side was never used by river traffic as it was narrow and the current extremely swift. The broader channel on the French side provided the safe route for canoes and paddle-wheelers.

Unfortunately the cantankerous outboard motor on the canoe had the final say in the choice of channels. Just when the current was speeding up to shoulder its way into the narrow channel, the engine decided to become difficult. It fell into a spasm of gasping and then choked off. There was nothing which three paddlers could do to steer the heavily laden canoe into quieter water. The current simply swept them off and they shot down the narrow channel, with George doing his best to keep the craft out of trouble by steering with a paddle from the rear.

It was certainly an exhilarating ride. The banks swept past them at a fine rate. A major hazard was a flexible vine-like plant which grew in great quantities along the high banks. The finger-thick canes drooped down to the water. Every few inches along their length they had large hook-like thorns with a devilish ability to fasten themselves into the persons or clothing of any passers-by. With the canoe travelling at speed, the occupants had to be pretty lively in ducking. The thorns were quite capable of tearing them right out of the canoe, and a tumble into the water could be fatal. In such a current the canoe could never turn. A man would be swept away down stream. At the first calm eddy there was sure to be some crocodile waiting with the patience of a spider in his web for chance to bring a dinner floating down the river.

It was only after dark that they reached the end of the island. Where the two channels re-united into one broad and tranquil flow, they were able to make their way to the bank and camp. The tension of passing through the channel had made them tired and hungry. They enjoyed a meal, and then slept until the moon was low in the early hours of the morning. Then they went on down the river, while the hippos feeding on the banks harrumphed in surprise at the sight of the dark canoe silently gliding with the current over a water surface shining in the moonlight as though it was made of quicksilver.

On the evening of the eighth day they reached the confluence of the Congo and the Ubangi. Three days later they were at the English mission station of Bolobo on the left bank of the river. There one of the missionaries, a Mr Daws, took blood smears from George's neck glands and tested them for sleeping sickness. To his relief the tests proved negative. His lassitude probably came simply from the past few years of cumulative fever, and the effects on his liver of the daily doses of quinine.

The last stretch of the river journey was reputed to be the trickiest. This part of the Congo River was notorious for its sudden storms. The river was wide and winds could whip up short, choppy waves. It was easy for canoes to ship water and founder. At noon the day after leaving Bolobo they were caught in the midst of a wide stretch by such a storm. Fortunately this was one time when the outboard motor condescended to work. With the two Africans using cooking pots to bale as fast as they could and George nursing the engine, they managed to reach shelter with no worse effect than a thorough drenching.

Below the confluence of the Kasai and the Congo, the river entered a gorge compressed by high, cliff-like banks. This stretch had an evil reputation with river navigators. The wrecks of two river-boats were piled up on the rocks as a warning to travellers. The crew of one large canoe, battling its way up stream, also shouted out a cheerful opinion that so small a craft would certainly founder if its occupants were sufficiently injudicious as to persist with the journey.

Half an hour later the opinion was almost proved correct. A sharp storm swept up the full length of the gorge. The effect it had on the current was quite frightening. Within minutes the canoe was tossed by substantial waves. Fortunately there was a good-sized cove close by, with trees growing on the banks and the branches touching the water. They ran for shelter underneath the branches. There they unloaded the canoe and dragged it on to the bank while they waited for the storm to pass them.

Sixteen days after leaving the American mission at Kaka, they entered the great Stanley Pool. It was night, and the lights of Brazzaville and Kinshasa (Leopoldville) facing each other from opposite banks made a handsome sight to people at the end of a thousand miles of travel down so dark and savage a river.

They were not to be allowed to complete the journey without one final misadventure. It was nearly midnight when they first glimpsed the lights of the towns. There was no sense in attempting to land at the Brazzaville docks at such an hour. Also, they were tired. They found a convenient sandbank, offloaded the canoe and dragged it up the miniature beach where they planned to sleep. They had hardly made their meal and tried to sleep when another tropical storm blew upon them. The sandbank was miserable shelter on such an occasion. There were no trees and the wind blew the water so high over the sand that they had to spend the time holding the canoe in order to prevent it from being washed away. The wind was followed by two hours of torrential rain which thoroughly soaked them. It was a very bedraggled-looking trio which tied up at the Brazzaville customs depot as soon as it was light that morning.

George cleared his party through the customs as soon as possible. Now that he was at the end of the river journey, he wanted to be off to Europe by the first available ship. He sold his canoe, paid off his two-man crew and booked them on a paddle-wheeler back to their homes up the river. Then he sold his ivory. He received something of a shock in this transaction. The value of ivory was down to eleven shillings a pound. At this rate the profit had almost vanished from elephant hunting. Any hunter continuing to work on such a marginal return would definitely have to add his own enthusiasm for the chase in order to secure a credit in the balance sheet. Apart from the irrepressible Sutherland, there were not many of the fraternity who would be prepared to do that.

George was interested to receive a letter from Sutherland in the poste restante at Brazzaville. The news was pretty dismal. The man was still hunting, using his mules for transport, but the poison in his system had obviously affected him very generally. Dysentery was also giving him constant trouble. He was a shadow of his former self. In that condition, Marcus Daly had taken a shoddy advantage of him. The swashbuckler had been raiding for elephants in French territory for some time, using a base in the Sudan for his poaching operations. His treatment of the tribespeople remained as rough as ever and his relations with Europeans in the area were very strained. He strode into Sutherland's camp while the hunter was away, took what he wanted and left his mark on the persons of the African women there. Then he went off and, fortunately for that part of the world, it saw him no more. The Government of the Sudan considered him as undesirable as had the French, and he found it politic to remove to Kenya.

The rest of the hunting community were trying to make up their minds what to do about the fall in the price of ivory. A few of them, like Anderson, were inclined to try coffee planting or transport riding in an effort to tide themselves through the depression. Others, like Fitzwilliams, were talking of going home. So far as Sutherland was concerned, the African wilderness was home, there was nowhere else where he wished to go and no other occupation than elephant hunting to which he had the slightest inclination to turn his hand. He would stay where he was. He would try to relieve the women from the taint of their contact with Daly. His own favourite, Powina or Chatterbox, was the worst sufferer. At least he could be kind to her.

" Better to have tried to play the game of life decently," he wrote at the end of his letter, " even if one feels a damn idiot in not having played it with more acumen.

The best to you,

Jim Sutherland."

It was the last George heard directly from the hunter. When Fitzwilliams eventually packed up in 1932 and left for England, he called at Sutherland's camp on his way to Yubo, intending to leave some of his surplus kit there. He found Sutherland dying from blood poisoning picked up through a scratch on one of his legs. He did what he could for his friend, but Sutherland was finished. They carried him in to Yubo and there he was buried on the 26th June, in a place where, as Fitzwilliams later wrote to George, " an elephant may yet walk over his grave." He was the last of the great professional ivory hunters and his death marked the end of a most adventurous epoch in the history of Africa.

By that time George's life had undergone a very radical and, to him, quite astonishing change. From Brazzaville he had crossed to Leopoldville and then gone by train to catch the Belgium-bound mailship at Matadi. Watching the sweltering hole of Boma pass him as they went down river gave George quite a few memories. After all, one of the reasons for his visit to Europe was to eliminate the effects on his nose of his spell as barman in that tough little place. It was a pleasure to see the last of it as the brown waters of the Congo merged with the blue of the ocean.

Brussels and Paris provided a couple of months of distraction. Then he crossed to London and one of the leading plastic surgeons straightened out his nose and generally smoothed over a few scars and bumps on his face. The results were so artistic that he felt almost a stranger when he looked at himself in a mirror as he shaved.

He went to show off his rehabilitated features to his mother at Jacksdale and immediately went down with what he knew was blackwater fever. As the village doctor could hardly be expected to comprehend so outlandish a tropical disease, it was certainly an awkward time and place in which to get sick. Before he lapsed into unconsciousness, George called the doctor in. He gave him a detailed account of the disease, its symptoms, the course it could be expected to take, and what was normally done about it in Africa. All he could do then was trust in the doctor's common sense and hope for the best. The hot winds of fever allowed him no alternative. Whether he resisted or not, he was whirled off into the nightmare-ridden sea of unconsciousness and for five days had no further knowledge of the world.

It was a very bad dose indeed. Just how he managed to survive was something of a mystery. The old doctor had referred to his medical books and found little in them save the bald confirmation of George's information that at least a quarter of the victims of blackwater died. All the doctor could do was follow the patient's technical advice, feed him bicarbonate, and leave the real battle to be fought between the disease and the strength of George's system.

George awoke, half expecting to see the faces above him of the gold-diggers of the Lupa, for the delirium seemed to have carried him back in years to the time of his first experience of blackwater. Instead he recognised the kindly faces of his mother, his half-sister and the village doctor. It took him some time to realise that he was in a clean bed in England, that Africa was far away and the angel of death in the guise of the mosquito had once again touched him, but moved on.

Convalescence was a tedious business. George was still unsteady on his feet when he decided that he would really have to get out of England. He accepted the fact that he had become something of a foreigner to both its atmosphere and its climate. He could understand the making of the British Empire. Strong men had made it so that they could get away from the English climate. He would certainly have to go back to Africa. He would feel more at home there, and although he had no set ideas about his future, he was at least certain that whatever he did he would do it away from Europe.

As soon as he could move about, George went to London and booked a passage for Cape Town on the *Armadale Castle*. While he waited for the ship to sail he roamed around London and stayed in the Overseas Club. The place was filled with a friendly crowd of colonial visitors mainly bent on sightseeing or study in Britain. They made very congenial company.

Among the crowd, George met Eileen Graham, who had come to England from Cape Town in order to study music. She was a practical soul and highly intrigued at his account of the past few years of his life.

"You'll find Cape Town pretty dull compared to your kind of Africa," she said reflectively at dinner one evening. "If a lion is ever seen in the place, it's in a circus, and every old fogy writes letters to the newspapers complaining if the creature sneezes. I'll really have to see you introduced to somebody lively."

George tried to sidestep the issue by changing the conversation. He hated being organised. Somebody had told him that the people of Cape Town lived in the shadow of their mountain with an insularity from the rest of Africa which could be likened to fleas feeding on a dog's tail, all absolutely certain that the tail wagged the dog. But even if that was the case, he had liked the look of the place when he had passed it on his first voyage to Africa. All he wanted now was a salubrious climate and the opportunity to make up his own mind about his future.

He hoped that the well-meaning Eileen would forget the introduction. But two days before he sailed she reminded him of it.

"I've thought of exactly the right person," she said brightly. "I've already written to her and asked her to meet your ship. She's as smart as paint, a keen mountaineer, and a very good school teacher. She's also very attractive. I'll give you her name and address now."

George groaned inwardly. An athletic mountain-climbing type with the bossy disposition of a school teacher might ruin his holiday. Eileen saw his face and laughed at him.

"You certainly don't appear grateful," she said. "But I've already written to her. Watch out for her on the docks. I specially asked her to be there."

George forgot the whole matter on the ship. There was a particularly jolly crowd on board. The intermediate liners on the Cape run were generally rather informal, but this particular voyage was almost bohemian.

There was certainly no need for George to make any effort to get up before dawn in order to view the famous landfall of Table Mountain. It was Monday, the 16th June 1930, when they arrived. He had still to go to bed from the final night's party when one of the crowd suggested that if anybody was expecting friends he had best go on deck as the ship was in process of docking. There was a general run on peppermints. George remembered the arrangement made for him. He went to his cabin and hastily searched for the piece of paper given him in London. It was still in his coat pocket. The name on it was Eleanor Dunbar Leslie, with an address marked as somewhere in the suburb of Plumstead. He winced when he noticed that Eileen Graham had added a line to the effect that if he missed the girl her father would be easy to find as he was a well-known magistrate.

George went on deck. He saw her almost immediately. At least he hoped it was the girl. He looked hastily over the rest of the quayside crowd. There were one or two other solitary young females. He breathed a sigh of relief when he noticed that they all seemed busy waving at some friend. He looked back at the girl. She was definitely cute. She was twenty-four with auburn hair, a pretty face, and a neatly balanced figure. He caught her eye and half-waved. She smiled and somewhat hesitantly waved back. George cursed the all-night party. He must look a wreck. He'd have to tell her that he had been down with fever on the voyage. He thought of his breath, and tried to gulp good clean sea air. At least her father wasn't with her. The old man might have thought that he had been running an illicit still in his cabin.

When the gangway was in place, George elbowed his way down as far as an officious old fusspot of a ship's guard would allow, and introduced himself to the girl. Standing mouthing at someone from the aloofness of a ship's deck is always a hopeless way of starting an acquaintance. George also wanted a closer view of her, in case she turned out to have squint eyes, or boils on any visible part of her anatomy. Before the ship's guard drove him back up the gangway he was highly satisfied. If this was the type of female bred in South Africa then the country had at least found the answer to one problem of human relations—how to produce pretty girls.

He collected his bags and cleared through immigration and customs as quickly as possible. Then he was free and they were together in the crowd.

" My father should be here any moment," she said immediately, to his dismay. " He'll take you home. I have to go and teach."

" What do you mean, take me home?"

It appeared that the family often had some friend staying with them. George was very welcome to be their guest for as long as he pleased. While they were talking the father arrived. He looked a dour, conservative type, with shaggy red eyebrows and a bristling moustache. He gave George a firm handshake, but immediately wrinkled his nose slightly. George hoped that the magistrate could at least judge good whisky when he smelled it.

They called a cab and drove off to the railway station. The presence of the old man had a somewhat dampening effect. Conversation became the usual questions and answers about the voyage. At the station, Mr Leslie went to buy the tickets.

" I'll have to get off the train at Rondebosch," Eleanor said hurriedly. " I teach in the Rustenburg Girls' High School. Daddy will go home with you." She hesitated slightly. " If you like, come and meet me after school. We can have a talk."

He nodded.

" I'll be there."

" I don't think you had better come to the actual school," she added rather diffidently. " The girls are dreadful chatterboxes. They always imagine things if they see a mistress meeting anybody. Perhaps, if you met me in Claremont, we could have tea together."

She gave him the name of a tearoom. He spent the morning waiting for the time to pass until the meeting. The old man and Mrs Leslie, fortunately, thought that he would be tired after the excitement of landing. They left him to unpack, take a hot bath, and catch up on some sleep.

School finished shortly after lunch. George was waiting outside the tea-room when Eleanor arrived.

" How did you get on?" she asked, rather breathlessly.

" All right. I had a bath and a sleep. Your parents were extremely nice."

She seemed vastly relieved.

" I've been on tenterhooks all day," she said. " I forgot to tell you that I'd told daddy we'd met before, years ago. It doesn't make any difference, really. But you know how conservative old people are. They always like to think that everybody has been formally introduced."

George grinned.

" Perhaps they are right. You certainly don't know anything about me. We'd better have a talk."

She nodded.

" There's a very beautiful public garden here. It was presented to the city by a Mr Arderne. He collected trees and shrubs from all over the world. They make quite a show. It's very pleasant walking there. We can take some monkey-nuts to feed the squirrels."

They went to the garden. They strolled along the paths beneath the trees and told each other the story of their lives. It was amazing how quickly the afternoon passed. There seemed to be so many questions and answers. It was all very pleasant and peaceful. The only distractions were a few nursemaids with their charges, a wedding party which came to be photographed against a background of flowers, and a cough-drop of a caretaker who had the task of enforcing some stupid regulation that people could walk, but not sit, on the lawn planted by the estimable Mr Arderne.

Towards evening they went home for supper. Eleanor's two sisters were there, Marjorie who was the oldest and Sylvia who was still in school. A married brother lived in another part of Cape Town. After supper George entertained them with some account of himself. The female side of the family all appeared to find him very agreeable company and quite a romantic figure. It was more difficult to discover what the father was thinking. George hoped to have some opportunity of a manly discussion with him over a couple of bottles of beer. The mother, however, had signed the pledge as a girl. The only liquor in the house was a medical reserve. The old man allowed himself a carefully measured nip each evening when everybody else had gone to sleep, but that was all. If anything this night-cap tended to make him slightly grumpy as the evening wore on and he waited for the family to retire to their rooms.

George went to bed and did some thinking. It was strange how these things happened. Until that morning, Eleanor had been nothing other than a possible threat to the pleasures of his Cape Town holiday. Now the whole voyage seemed to have taken place years ago. It was difficult to think that he had only landed that morning. He felt as though he had known Eleanor all his life. The chemistry behind human attraction would certainly repay study. Before he fell asleep, he decided that he must have Eleanor, even if it meant changing his entire way of life to allow for a wife.

The next day, after Eleanor had left for school, he went into the city and spent the morning attending to various affairs. When school ended, George was waiting at the entrance. He was quite oblivious to the glances of the outpouring school girls. When Eleanor appeared they took a tram direct to the Claremont park. He had never in his life felt such a feeling of pleasure and contentment as he felt in her company. He took her hand and they walked to an ornamental Japanese pool, spanned by a pretty little bridge beneath which goldfish and waterfowl caused the only ripples on an otherwise mirror-like surface.

For a moment he lost confidence and wondered whether she would think him impertinent, or a lunatic. He glanced at her. The obvious happiness in her face reassured him. He had rehearsed quite a speech for the occasion, but all he could say was something which weighed heavily on his mind.

" When are we going to tell your father?"

She gave him an odd look, and asked in a small voice,

" Tell daddy what?"

" That we are going to get married."

" Oh, George," she said, with a funny little laugh, " what a way to ask me."

He didn't give her more time to talk. It was very romantic kissing her on the bridge. They hardly knew how the rest of the afternoon passed. When they tried to leave their paradise garden, the caretaker had already locked up the gate and gone home. They had to clamber over the fence with a great deal of laughing, and not a few suspicious glances directed at them from passers-by. Then they had to wedge themselves into standing room in the train to Plumstead. The homeward business rush-hour was on. There was little further opportunity of talking to each other. George spent the time of the journey wondering how Eleanor's father would take the news. The day could end up with quite a lively evening. It would be difficult not to admit that he had known Eleanor for something less than thirty-six hours.

CHAPTER FOURTEEN

MBEYA

BY THE time they reached home, George was feeling increasingly bashful. Eleanor, on the other hand, was only too obviously thoroughly excited. She held his hand with complete indifference to the glances of passers-by and the moment she saw her mother standing on the front veranda she blurted out the news. The old lady seemed quite overwhelmed. George slipped off hurriedly to his room on the excuse of fetching something. Through the window he heard the old lady's voice.

"He has a nice smile and gentle manners," she said rather plaintively. "His hands are nice but, oh dear, Eleanor, you are such a harum-scarum. Why does he have to be an elephant hunter?"

Her voice ended in something of a wail. George started to see the funny part about the business. He went out again and encountered Eleanor in the passage.

"I suppose you heard that?" she accused him. When he started laughing, she put her arms around him.

"Isn't it peculiar? All mothers want their daughters to marry somebody settled, like a bank clerk or a lawyer, or preferably a millionaire. But not me! Whoever heard of anybody marrying someone as exciting as an elephant hunter? I'm thrilled to bits."

She hugged him, and then bustled off down the passage.

"I must tell Marjorie."

George was left severely alone until supper time. Just before he went in for the meal, Eleanor appeared again.

"I've talked it over with mother," she said. "She suggests that we go off to the cinema this evening. That will give her an opportunity to talk to daddy. She can prepare him for the news. Then you can see him tomorrow. She feels that it might make him think that we've known each other for a little while longer."

George was dubious, but he accepted the postponement with some relief. The meal passed with the old man casting an occasional suspicious glance at Eleanor. She was obviously in quite a state of nerves and as pleased as George when they eventually slipped out with her younger sister, and went off to waste a good evening in watching some tasteless rubbish.

It was an earlier show than they had expected. When they returned home they found the old man sitting in his chair with an expression on his face that indicated that he would still have been there even if the show had lasted until midnight. Sylvia scuttled off to the safety of the kitchen with the muttered excuse that she would make tea. The old man fixed a cold eye on Eleanor.

" Your mother tells me that you have become engaged to George Rushby. You had best sit down and we'll talk this over."

Eleanor sat down on the piano stool.

" Well," continued her father, " I suppose that you are of age now, so I could not forbid this marriage even if I wanted to do so."

He switched his attention to George.

" I have nothing against you. How could I? After all, I know absolutely nothing about you."

George tried to say something, but the old man went on.

" I confess that as a magistrate I am possibly more than normally suspicious." He smiled very slightly with his eyes. " If you were standing before me on some charge, I would certainly be inclined to deal seriously with you. Instead of that, you want my daughter. Tell me, how do you propose to live?"

George had thought it all out during the previous evening. Eleanor had also apparently been doing some thinking.

" But he's a hunter, daddy, and I'm going with him," she blurted out.

Her father recoiled visibly.

" You'll soon fill up a hunter's tent with babies," he said. " Then what will you do?"

George chuckled.

" The hunter's life is not exactly the idea, Eleanor," he said hastily. "Actually, ivory hunting is finished, at least for the time being. I see that the price of ivory is now down to five shillings a pound. At that rate it would be a complete waste of effort. I was lucky to make some money just at the end of the good times."

"A very destructive way of making money," interjected the old man.

George thought it necessary to correct a few evident misconceptions.

" Look here," he said, " hunting elephants is no more destructive a way of making money than, say, mining for gold. The gold-miner simply exhausts the earth of its treasures and puts nothing back other than the profit into his bank balance. I confess that I've shot about 600 bull elephants, but providing that the numbers shot are balanced to the natural increase, what is wrong with it? Gold and ivory have always been the great exports of Africa. Quite an international industry has been built up from the ivory. The tips, what are known as the scribellos, are sent mainly to the Far East for carving purposes. The centre, or billiard ball section, goes to Europe and America for manufacturers, while the hollow base goes to India and is used for inlaid work, carving and ornament. Nothing is wasted. No genuine ivory hunter has ever been a butcher. I soon grew out of any adolescent pleasure I ever found in killing small game. An adult man has to be something of a moron to consider it sport to kill an antelope with a high-velocity rifle. I've shot for the pot but I find no more pleasure in the act than I trust the butcher found in slaughtering the ox which provided you with your beef tonight. There is certainly nothing heroic in it, and anybody who claims that there is, is just being foolish."

The old man pursed his lips thoughtfully and looked at him.

" What do you intend doing now?"

" I have a reasonable amount of capital," George reminded him. " I've certainly saved far more in the past ten years than I would likely have done if I had spent the time working in a bank or sitting in an office. I plan to go back to Tanganyika and take up some land. The country is just being opened up to the settler. There is good land available, and it is cheap. I'm going to become a planter, sisal or coffee or any of the other crops."

" Do you know anything about farming?"

" No, but I'll soon learn."

" H'm. Many others have said that as well. Some of them have learnt, of course, but the hard way. Are there any agricultural colleges or experimental farms in Tanganyika?"

George shook his head.

" You know," warned the old man, " farming is an occupation fraught with technicalities and uncertainties. It is a tragedy that so many people, army officers, retired people and others like them, suddenly plunge into it as though agriculture was simply a rather genteel pastime. None of them would dream of plunging into a new profession or trade without intensive preliminary study. If you even suggested it to them, they would laugh and say that they would go bankrupt. But they jump into farming. Quite naturally, they go bankrupt."

George shrugged.

" Perhaps some of them are too old to learn," he suggested, " or too lazy, or they start off with insufficient capital. I like work, I'm still young enough to learn, and even if we had bad luck in the beginning, I have enough money to support us for quite a time."

" When do you want to get married? "

"As soon as possible. Then we can go up to Tanganyika together."

" But Eleanor has just signed a new teaching contract."

Eleanor broke her silence rather reluctantly. She explained that with the ending of the current school term on the coming Friday, she was leaving Rustenburg High School. She had accepted a post in the Eastern Cape Province, in the Queenstown Girls' High School. The contract had already been signed and she was bound to give the new school at least a full term's notice. Her father immediately reminded her of something else.

" If I know anything about you, you are also up to your eyes in debt."

Eleanor became visibly embarrassed.

" It would be an excellent idea," her father added, " if you at least settled your dress bills. If you cannot offer a dowry to your future husband, you might as well join him without being pursued by any debt collectors. We'll talk about it all again."

This ended the discussion. They left Mr Leslie to his night-cap. When George glanced into the medical chest the next morning, he was intrigued to see that the bottle was empty. Apparently the old boy had needed something more than his usual nip to brace him up after the shock of the previous evening.

Actually, it wasn't difficult to understand the parents' point of view. It was such an eminently respectable household, with the father always sober in dress and habit as befitted a person in the public position of a magistrate. He obviously regarded George as being something of a man of the world. In fact, he hinted strongly to Eleanor that he was absolutely certain that George had a past. It needed discretion to handle him, and make him realise that ivory hunters could be just as solid in character as any professional man, and that there was no greater proportion of scoundrels to the occupation than one found in, for example, the legal profession.

George bought the engagement ring in time for Eleanor to wear on the last day of her school term. There was quite a sensation among the girls. For the prettiest mistress in the school to have so whirlwind a romance with so rugged a character as an ivory hunter gave them all a fine tale to carry home to their parents. The news soon spread. The local newspapers made the most of the matter, with photographs and accounts of George's hunting experiences. Even the Cape Town radio station drew him in to its studios for a talk on his adventures. The publicity put Eleanor in quite a tither. Apart from becoming a public figure, she had a large circle of friends. They were all on to her for details of the romance, and pressing invitations that she display George to them at tea.

The holiday period did allow the couple an amiable opportunity of really getting to know each other. It was winter, but the weather was superb. Cape Town normally has about one coldish winter in every five, but as its inhabitants spend most of their time talking about it, they have given the place a reputation for a harder climate than it really possesses. In a very green and pleasant world, George and Eleanor made the rounds of the beauty spots. He even participated in one of Eleanor's habitual weekend climbs on Table Mountain. This was his first, and last, attempt to climb a mountain for pleasure.

The climbing party was highly experienced. George spent a good part of his time hanging on the end of a rope having an alarmingly spectacular view of the suburb of Camps Bay a few thousand feet below him. It was not a particularly dignified position for a young man in the presence of his beloved. To add to his chagrin, a tiny silver Cornish lucky pixy which he had carried in his pocket for some years apparently considered that fortune was running somewhat on the thin side. It found a hole in its owner's pocket and slipped out. Oddly enough, when George eventually reached the summit, Eleanor suggested that he pin a notice on the wall of the Mountain Club hut reporting the loss and requesting any finder to return the charm to him through the address of her parents. Two years later a climber discovered the pixy sheltering on a narrow ledge. It found its way through the post safely back to its proper place in George's pocket. There it provided him with some company on the dark nights when he faced the man-eaters of the Njombe district.

Eleanor had reserved her passage to East London on the *Ubena*, a German ship which also continued its way up the east coast to Dar es Salaam. George booked himself on the same ship. With the three weeks of holiday passing very rapidly, the few extra days together on the voyage would be particularly acceptable. They could make their final plans at leisure and when the time came for them to part on the riverside docks of East London the period to elapse before they were to meet again would not seem to be quite so long.

George was very keen, now that he had made up his mind about the future, to return to Tanganyika and find a farm. It would be pleasant meeting his old acquaintances again, discovering what was happening on the Lupa goldfield, and, if possible, settling somewhere in the Southern Highlands. That was the part of Tanganyika which he knew best. He had always liked it, and he was drawn back to scenes which were familiar to him.

George landed in Dar es Salaam on the 25th July 1930. It was four years since his last visit to the harbour but there seemed to have been few visible changes. At least, however, it was the cool season and he was sorry that Eleanor would be destined to arrive near Christmas time, when the East African coast can be really sweltering.

A few enquiries around the town soon elicited news of developments in the Southern Highlands. The Lupa was still growing. In the previous year, 11,100 ounces of gold had been recovered there as a result of the activity of about 300 diggers who were now busy along the banks of the river and its tributaries. To facilitate government administration of the field, a new centre had been established in 1926 on the southern slopes of the mountains known to the local Safwa tribe as *Mbeye,* from the mineral rock salt which was found there by animals and man. George knew this area well. He had walked over the site of the new centre on his first journey to Lake Rukwa, when he had made his way down the Western Rift Valley, and the boldness of the scenery and romantic nature of the atmosphere of the mighty geological fault had enthralled him. Now there was great talk about the future of Mbeya, as the administrative centre was called. The Great North Road which led through it from the Rhodesian border up across the middle of Tanganyika to Kenya was being improved for the use of motor traffic, there were surveys under way for a railway line and, most intriguing of all, an aerodrome was being developed at Mbeya for the projected Imperial Airways' London to Cape Town air service.

Settlement schemes were afoot all over the Southern Highlands. In the Iringa district, Lord Delamere had founded the enterprise known as Colonists Ltd to stimulate settlement in that area. He had built a bacon factory at Uleti, and a pleasant hotel, known as the Colonist, in Iringa itself. Further south, close to the Rhodesian border, an advisory board sent out by the British Government had recently selected the fertile, high-lying area around the Mbozi River as being ideal for European settlement. Excellent land was being offered at most reasonable terms, along with pro-mises of undying Government support for any pioneers and bold empire builders who would settle there in the virgin wilderness and work towards a noble future for a splendid new territory. It all sounded most exciting, stimulating and thoroughly worthwhile.

George went south as soon as he could, hoping that he wasn't too late to share in such an excellent thing. At Iringa he booked in at the Colonist and found himself in the company of quite a gathering of new settlers and immigrants, all happily talking of their projects and the rumours of coming developments. Among the crowd there was a transport rider named Evelyn Hickson-Wood who had started a truck service between Mbeya and Dodoma on the Central Railway. George introduced himself to the man and im-mediately received some unexpected news. Hickson-Wood was married to the widow of the amiable Vivian Lumb. This was the first George had heard of the death of his old partner and the information distressed him.

It appeared that Lumb had done reasonably well on the Lupa. He had gone over to England on a holiday, married, and brought his bride back to Tanganyika. Not wishing to make a permanent home on the Lupa, he had joined Rope Soles Jones and another digger named B. L. Waizeneker in the purchase of a block of three farms situated on the slopes of the 9,272-foot-high Mbeya Mountain. The three men had planned to develop the farms on the profits of their gold digging. Unfortunately, Lumb had gone down with blackwater and had died on the farm. Hickson-Wood, a former district commissioner, had married the widow and was now working the farm as well as running a transport business. He was a lively, nice-looking, temperamental type of Irishman about ten years older than George and very opinionated about most subjects, but especially the future of Tanganyika.

George discussed his own ambitions with the man, and Hickson-Wood made a suggestion. The three farms originally acquired by Lumb and his friends were beautifully situated and very convenient to Mbeya. Lumb and Rope Soles Jones had built houses and developed their lands, but Waizeneker had never done anything. Eventually he had given his farm to Lumb's widow as a wedding present on her second marriage. If George liked, he could buy this undeveloped farm. It was about one hundred acres in extent and this would be ample for him to start a coffee plantation. Hickson-Wood offered a free lift to Mbeya in order to allow of an inspection of the farm.

They left at dawn the next morning. Hickson-Wood's transport service consisted of one International truck with the sign " M.O.B. Transport Co. " painted in large letters on the door. The letters, explained Hickson-Wood when George asked him, stood for My Own Bloody Transport Company, and he was very proud of it. He hoped to develop the service into a fleet of trucks, although the roughness of the road literally shook pieces off any vehicle. The Great North Road, especially around a place called Sao Hill, was sprinkled with broken shock-absorbers, springs, and odd nuts and bolts. A life of 30,000 miles would be considered excellent for a car, while a truck lasted only as long as the mechanical ingenuity of its operator could bolster up its resistance to harsh service and persistent overloading.

The last time George had travelled south from Iringa, he had done the journey by foot on proper safari. No matter how rough the road, therefore, it was still a novel experience to cover the 249 miles on four wheels, and be entertained all the way by a loquacious account of local news and gossip. It was soon apparent that the Lupa goldfield was even more productive of scandal than it was of gold. It appeared to have developed into something of a real roaring camp. Excessive doses of sunshine, strong liquor and hard living had generally loosened up morals and values. There was quite a sprinkling of women on the field. Most of them were pretty blowsy old battle-axes, their complexions, hair and figures well mauled by the weather, drunken husbands and rowdy children, but they were still very willing, and a great deal of rather heavy-handed romance was the order not only of the night but also of any hour of the day.

By the time they reached Mbeya, George felt himself to be reasonably knowledgeable, at least about current affairs, and his companion's yarning had certainly passed the time of an otherwise dusty and wretchedly rough journey. Hicky-Wood (as the transport man preferred to be called) brought his vehicle to a sudden halt outside the door of what was one of the newer amenities of Mbeya, its first hotel, a collection of thatched huts arranged behind a sign which read " The Sluice Box."

" I think we could do with it," said Hicky-Wood, looking at George with a grin. They were both so covered in the red dust of the Great North Road that their faces seemed to be concealed behind masks of the filthy stuff.

George nodded. They clambered stiffly off the vehicle. George felt sorry for the thing. It looked as though it could do with a stiff bracer itself. The radiator was steaming, there was a drip of oil from the innards, and an odd moaning noise persisted from the works even though the ignition was switched off.

" It'll survive," Hicky-Wood said reassuringly. " Come on in."

The largest part of the establishment seemed to be the bar. It was both well patronised and well stocked. Painted in large letters above the door leading to the residential quarters there was a sign—

Diggers are requested to please take their boots off before going to bed. Accommodation nine shillings.

The proprietor of the establishment also served as chief barman. He noticed George reading the sign and gave him a quick smile.

" It's very necessary, I assure you."

Hicky-Wood introduced them. The host was a friendly man named Ken Menzies whose wife, May, whom George met later on in the dining-room, was a quite remarkable personality, a thoroughly trained and most conscientious nurse from the famous Guys Hospital, in London. She was considered to be one of the major assets of the district and was never sparing in her readiness to tramp a hundred miles, if need be, to reach anybody sick in some lonely mining camp or trading outpost in the bush. She was known to all as Auntie May. In the habitual costume of khaki shirt and stout riding breeches, she looked as competent, sturdy and resolute as a frontierswoman could be. The couple had originally emigrated from Britain to Nyasaland in 1925. In Blantyre they had met a Lupa digger named Laurence Zotta who was displaying a nice little pile of alluvial gold in the local pub. The sight had stimulated the Menzies to turn digger themselves. They pegged claims, had reasonable luck, and with part of the proceeds built the Sluice Box Hotel in Mbeya.

The diggers in the bar were all strangers to George. But from them he learned that most of his old friends were still busy on the Lupa, and enjoying the usual varying luck. They were all well, although Bill Cumming seemed to be growing into something of a recluse, with an increasing tendency to keep to himself on some isolated claim. His discovery had not so far rewarded him with much fortune.

Apart from the hotel, the rest of Mbeya, four years after its foundation, consisted simply of the boma, a house for the district commissioner, Callaghan, a one-room post office managed by an African, and three small Indian stores of the *duka* type, with the largest run by Yussuf Mia, who sat cross-legged on his counter all day whiling away the time in between customers by picking his nose and considering methods of reducing his income tax.

From Mbeya a track had been made to the Lupa goldfield. It followed the southern slopes of the Mbeya range until the mountains petered out. Then it twisted round in a U bend and went back on the northern slopes until it reached the area of the diggings. Hicky-Wood's farm lay twenty-three miles out of Mbeya along the first section of this road. George liked the place as soon as he saw it. The situation was high enough to be cool, the soil looked good, there was perennial water from the mountain streams, and the outlook was spacious and handsome. He would also have some most jolly neighbours.

Kathleen, Lumb's widow, was an attractive, curly-haired Irish woman, with big brown eyes and a capacity to enjoy life. Lumb had left her with a baby daughter, while she had presented her second husband with a son. Lumb was buried in the garden outside the farmhouse. Looking down on the little mound of earth it was hard to think that it marked the end of the road for so mercurial and enterprising a character. Mosquitoes were certainly the only things which had ever got the better of Lumb, and the thought warned George that if he was to bring a young bride to this part of the world he would have to look sharp if he didn't want her to end the same way.

George concluded his deal with Hicky-Wood that night. For £100 in cash he bought Waizeneker's original farm. It was separated from the Hicky-Woods' property by the Mntshewe stream. Rope Soles Jones, who had walked over from his own adjoining farm as soon as he heard that George had arrived, heartily endorsed the transaction and the occasion was a very pleasant party. The Hicky-Woods had a nice snug little farmhouse and, by the light of a lamp, they sat and yarned until the early hours. George was sure that Eleanor would like them all. Kathleen would make an excellent friend for her, while old Rope Soles was quite a fabulous character, with his almost bald head, his monocle screwed into one nearly blind eye, and his skinny, slight build. He was a cultured man for all his rather odd appearance and name, a mine of information and gossip about local goings-on, and one of the few in the district to keep in touch with world news by means of a radio.

George started to lay out his farm the next day. If he was to have anything like a home ready before Eleanor arrived he would have to work hard, hire labour, secure the materials for building and make a branch track to the site of his homestead. He wrote to Eleanor immediately, sending her a description of her future home and assuring her by his own enthusiasm that her family's prediction was quite groundless that he would lose interest and

simply wander off elephant-hunting again as soon as he was back in East
Africa.

The months passed with alarming speed to George. He hardly seemed to
have arrived in the area before it was time to drive off in company with the
Hicky-Woods in order to meet Eleanor in Dar es Salaam. She was booked
to arrive there on the Italian steamer *Timavo* early in November and he
found that he had so many preparations to make that he was almost glad
when the ship was a few days late. It was eventually announced as due
first thing on the morning of Friday the 7th November.

At least Dar es Salaam was looking its best at the time. Summer rains
had turned it even greener than the normal verdant shade, while the streets
were quite aglow with the scarlet flowers of the flamboyant acacia trees.
Arriving in Tanganyika at such a time would leave nobody the slightest
doubt but that Dar es Salaam was the gateway to a real tropical garden
where a truly remarkable variety of wild game and some 120 different tribes,
each with its own customs and language, lived in a wilderness at once romantic and beautiful.

When the great day eventually dawned for George, he was down on
Gymkhana Beach in time to watch the trim Italian ship enter the harbour.
Dar es Salaam, The Abode of Peace, was not so-called by the Arabs without
excellent reason. It is a most beautifully landlocked harbour, with only a
narrow but deep channel leading to the sea. Inevitably Eleanor was standing
watching the islands and coral beaches slipping past on the side of the ship
opposite to where George was standing. He had a horrible feeling that she
had missed the ship. The Hicky-Woods, who were standing on the beach
with him, reminded him cynically of his own account of his all-night party
before he arrived in Cape Town, but this memory was not particularly funny
at such a time.

They hired a small boat and had themselves rowed out to the anchored
ship as soon as possible. Eleanor of course was immediately discovered looking over the rails, as pretty and as feminine as ever, waiting to be reassured
that George had not forgotten her in preference for elephants. The Hicky-
Woods discreetly withdrew into the saloon while George made his assurances.
When they gathered again, Mrs Hicky-Wood was busy kicking her husband's
shins to make him stop giggling. He had requested refreshment from the
first uniformed individual visible in the saloon, only to learn from the man's
pained expression that he was the ship's captain.

After that it was a bustle of collecting Eleanor's belongings and rowing
ashore to the customs jetty. Her suitcases were bulging enough, and she had
armfuls of the usual wedding present bric-a-brac. George bundled most of
them up into her blanket roll, but inevitably the wretched strap snapped just
after they had completed the customs declaration, and provided the officer
with some embarrassing evidence of a mild case of perjury.

The wedding was arranged for that morning. George was never a man to waste time, and having Eleanor dawdling around being chaperoned for days was not his idea of good sense. He simply rushed her off to the Splendid Hotel, left her with the news that he would see her in church in an hour's time and that everything was arranged for her to be fetched and attended. It was all delightfully exciting to her. She had to dive into her cases to retrieve her wedding dress, be tempted to a quick dash out on to the balcony in order to catch a sight and sound of the smart King's African Rifles band swinging down Acacia Avenue for some parade, and then just manage to be ready in time to open the door to a sharp rap and find a police officer immaculate in a starched white uniform, who introduced himself as McCallum, come to escort her to church.

Just how George and the Hicky-Woods had organised the whole affair she never knew. But downstairs waiting for her was a big man dressed in a tussore silk suit. He was the local Director of Medical Services, Dr Shircore, who was to give her away, while the policeman had a dark blue government car decorated with white ribbons to carry her to church, with a tall African police askari standing to attention holding the door open for a formal entrance. Eleanor felt almost as bemused as Alice in Wonderland. If the white rabbit had been waiting to act as her page he would hardly have seemed out of place.

The wedding was held in the tall church built on the waterfront by the Lutherans in the days when Tanganyika was a German colony. The ceremony went off very quickly and easily. They hardly realised that it had started before they were being congratulated by Mrs Hicky-Wood, looking very ravishing in mushroom-coloured georgette and lace, by a few shipboard acquaintances of Eleanor, including an old lady with a lily-of-the-valley corsage who shed tears, the ship's captain and chief engineer who stood at the entrance slightly embarrassed in their rather plain uniforms because someone had thought they were taxi-men, and a few total strangers who exploited the general confusion in order to treat Eleanor to a series of hearty kisses. A final touch was provided by George's cook boy, Lamek. He had accompanied his master all the way from Mbeya. He viewed the wedding, squatting on his haunches in the back of the church. When the bridal pair walked out he greeted them by clapping his hands and producing a wedding gift for Eleanor, a faded mauve straw toque of the kind worn by old Queen Mary. With his splayed feet, kindly old face, receding forehead, flat nose and enormous mouth, he looked almost like a happy chimpanzee as he watched them walk to the car.

Then there was the reception in Dr Shircore's house, with champagne corks popping, "Happy Days Are Here Again" being sung with increasing merriment, and the old lady with the lily-of-the-valley sprouting mysteriously into a red carnation while one of the total strangers took over her original corsage. At the height of the merriment George and Eleanor slipped away. They changed, collected their belongings and went down to the harbour. A motor launch chugged them off across the calm waters, with the complex panorama of shipping and movement and colour unfolding itself all around them as they sailed out to Honeymoon Island. Beneath the coconut palms on that gentle little place there stood a cottage. The bridegroom had to carry his bride ashore because the surrounding waters, translucent green and alive with tiny tropical fish, were too shallow to allow any boat to approach the coral beach, just as troubles, thoughts about the future, and the worries of the outside world were never allowed the remotest chance of landing in such an atmosphere of languid tropicality and carefree romance. The only snag about the place, in fact, was that nobody had warned the honeymooners that they had to take mattresses with them as well as bedding. Sleeping on springs is cool but not comfortable, even when you are on honeymoon.

CHAPTER FIFTEEN

MCHEWE ESTATE

THE honeymoon ended with George giving a man a black eye. During their weekend on the island, Eleanor had confided to him her experiences of the voyage. One concerned a masculine pest who had been overpushful in his intentions, indulged in some peeping-Tom activity, and even tried to pull her through a cabin window in her nightdress with lecherous intent. The *Timavo* had not sailed when the honeymoon was over and George happened to encounter the Romeo in the shipping agent's office. George's two Sunday-best punches and a good uppercut sent him sailing over the counter where he landed in a waste-paper box with a nice black eye and a nose all bloody and sore.

"I don't mind anybody window-shopping at you," explained George to Eleanor, "but where you are going there's a pretty rugged digger community. If any of them reach out and grab, they will have to be pretty firmly dealt with, and this booby gave me some practice."

It sounded to Eleanor as though the future could have its moments. She was looking forward very keenly, in fact, to her new life. George had described with such enthusiasm the whole environment of what he had named the *Mchewe Estate* at the foot of the Mbeya Mountain that she longed to be there to see what he had done, while the journey through the heart of Tanganyika would be far and away the most novel adventure she had ever experienced.

They were booked on the train for Dodoma, which left after lunch on the

156

Monday afternoon. They almost missed it. The taxi came late, and then they found that the vehicle was nearly too small to carry all their impedimenta, with old Lamek precariously perched somewhere in the back holding his bedding roll and cooking pot. Just as they set off, as well, Mrs Hicky-Wood ran out with the unwrapped bottom layer of their wedding cake and dumped it on George's knees with the information that it was unlucky to throw away such ceremonial confectionery. George had to nurse the confounded thing all the way through the crush on the station, and it was a nuisance to him until they were safe on the farm in Mbeya. For a man who never ate cake, it was a sad trial.

The train was comfortable but tediously slow. The wood-burning engines could never work up much of a head of steam. They puffed and fussed to haul their load up through the lush green coastal terrace and on to the higher plateau where the great sisal estates around Morogoro looked very melancholy, the usually well-tended rows of plants half-overgrown with weeds owing to the world slump in prices.

The further the train travelled the more arid became the landscape, with Dodoma, 285 miles from Dar es Salaam, lying in the centre of a hot and drought-stricken saucer-shaped plain. They actually reached the place in the early hours of the morning, and Eleanor was as startled at the experience as everybody else who has ever used the train in Tanganyika, as a transition from the comparative veneer of civilisation on the coast to the quite wild and undeveloped interior of the country. Dodoma railway station in the dark hours is always a remarkable sight. The imposing German colonial-type station building dominates a long platform crowded with some of the most elementary forms of humanity to be seen anywhere on earth.

Dodoma, you should know, is the centre for the Gogo tribe. These happy primitives, who like to ape the Masai in costume and habit although there is not much real relationship between them, habitually use the railway station as a variety of combined overnight hotel, when business brings them to Dodoma, and as an entertainment for themselves and families simply in watching the trains go by. They sleep on the hard surface of the platform, wedged together in such numbers that it is often difficult to find a way to step over them. When a train steams in and the floodlights give the scene a garish illumination, Dodoma station might almost be a whistle stop somewhere betwixt and between the world and the nether regions.

Important-looking Sikh railway officials in their smart uniforms, turbans and beards, bustle around on their duties. Passengers appear from and disappear into the surrounding gloom, with African porters struggling to manoeuvre suitcases through the throng. Other passengers in transit exercise themselves in the night air: White Father missionaries who sometimes look as though the presence of a few women around their house might smarten them up a bit, a couple of Japanese commercial travellers, the usual Government officials returning to or leaving their posts. All these people wander about for a little while through the watching crowd of Gogo tribespeople who observe the romance of transport, standing in their curious costumes, the men holding long sticks or spears, the women suckling frightened-looking children, the whole company silent, wondering and subdued. Then the train steams off again. Its red light vanishes with a final glitter, and the primitive watchers sink back to the ground to sleep until some other train wanders in from an outside world of which they can have not the slightest knowledge or comprehension.

Eleanor really realised for the first time that she had travelled a good distance from Cape Town. She picked her way through the crowd, trying to keep up with George. There were a few other passengers leaving the train at Dodoma. They all made their way outside the station and across the road to the hotel. The place was dark and well locked up, the host apparently not being much interested in obliging early-morning passengers. While somebody went in search of the night watchman, the others sat on the veranda amidst a litter of broken glass. There must have been quite a party the night before and it had apparently spread to the bedrooms. The beds were in something of a pickle when the new arrivals eventually reached them and there was a bucket of vomit beside one of the old-fashioned washstands. A certain amount of bad language in Swahili from George was required before the place was put to rights, and everybody tried to sleep.

At breakfast the place was astir, with George already up and eager to show Eleanor his recent acquisition of a car. It was a box-body Chevrolet, a variety of automobile with sides, roof and doors hammered on to the maker's chassis by a local carpenter. George was very proud of it. It was the first car he had ever owned. He was still in the happy stage when he could see no fault to the thing.

Lamek occupied himself in loading their belongings into the back of the vehicle. It was just as well that the box body was reasonably commodious. Besides suitcases, bedrolls, cooking utensils, boxes of provisions for the journey, and tins of petrol and water, there was also Lamek's impedimenta, which now included amongst the bits and pieces, three chickens in a wicker cage, as well as an enormous bunch of bananas, about three feet long, which he coyly admitted to having won in a gambling game on the train.

When everything was packed in there was no room for Lamek. Considerable rearrangement was necessary. Eventually the cook squeezed himself into a small space between goods and ceiling. There he lay on his back for the whole 400 miles of the journey over bumpy earth roads and crude pole bridges, with his horny feet slightly less than an inch from the back of Eleanor's head. For all that he appeared serenely content at what was his idea of luxury travel. Whenever his master stopped for a roadside meal he wiggled out like Aladdin's genie, but much more cheerfully, and conjured up some excellent food in no time at all.

The road from Dodoma to Iringa had not been open very long. The large bridge being built over the Great Ruvaha (or Ruaha) River was still in process of completion and vehicles half-swam their way over a rough fording place. To Eleanor, sitting with large eyes next to George, the whole area was a real howling wilderness. The bush seemed to be bone dry and horribly dusty, with giant baobab trees looming out of an evil-looking tangle of thorn shrubs. She was longing to see game, but as usual the animals, offended by the noise and dust of traffic, avoided the road in the daylight hours and all George could show her was an occasional dainty little dikdik darting across the road, or a litter of elephant droppings where one of the big fellows had crossed their route during the previous evening.

The principal events of the journey were punctures and an awkward occasion when the wooden spokes of one of the wheels worked loose and the whole affair collapsed in a cloud of dust. Wooden wheel spokes were always wonderful devices for motoring in Africa. They could always be depended upon to contract and work loose in dry weather. Inevitably this happened on the driest and most shadeless stretches of road where the process was particularly trying of hammering together and moistening the spokes to make them expand again into a tight fit. So far as Eleanor was concerned, the periodic hold-ups at least allowed her some opportunity to talk. In transit, the car made such a noisy botheration of roars, rattles and bangs that conversation could only be shouted in monosyllables, which was terribly trying to a young woman with questions on her mind. There was so much in this new land which she found remarkable or puzzling, and so much which she wanted to say about it all.

The primitive character of the Gogo people and the arid harshness of the land in which they lived had particularly disturbed her. George could only shrug when she asked him if he thought they would always be that way. It was easy to answer " For their sake, I hope not." But on the other hand, it was not easy to explain exactly why and how they should change. The Gogo homeland was certainly a hellish stretch of country and not one in which it was easy to imagine a developing culture or a flourishing community. It was part of the great *nyika* or wilderness of acacia thorn trees which had given the territory the name by which Europeans knew it, suggested probably by some early description of the place by the Arabs in Zanzibar— *Tanganyika*—Where You Travel Through the Wilderness.

The Gogo happened to like their wilderness. They had wandered into it at an early date, dispossessed a few even more primitive residents, and, as always with the human being, found charms in their new possession which few others could see. They roamed around in the bush with their cattle, levied heavy toll from passing caravans in the days of the Arab safari trade from the coast to the lakes, and generally considered themselves to be a very fortunate and happy people. If the scope of their lives was simple, then so were their worries, so why change if they were satisfied?

The Ruvaha River marked the end of the Gogo country and the commencement of the lands of the Hehe tribe. Eleanor remarked sagely to George, while he was repairing another puncture, that for the Hehe to name a river Ruvaha was surely enough to make a cat laugh, but he did not see the point. He was seldom in a humorous mood when he had to patch punctures. Eleanor discreetly left him to the chore and brooded on the information already given to her, that the Hehe were a martial tribe of some reputation, with a long history of warfare with their neighbours, and a record of stubborn resistance to German conquest. Their last great chief, Mkwawa, had eventually shot himself to avoid capture, and his head was removed to a museum in Germany where it remained until very recent times, when a British governor secured its return to the Hehe tribe.

The Hehe had the advantage of the Gogo of living in a higher and better-watered part of the country. Across the river, the road set out to climb this highland, with many a view behind of the great plain of the Gogo people. By nightfall, George and Eleanor were well up in the heights. After dinner served by Lamek beside a camp fire and a yarn about the sights and experiences of the day, they opened their bedrolls and enjoyed a sound sleep, with nothing to disturb them more threatening than the moan of a hyena and the hearty snoring of the cook.

Before lunch the next day, they arrived in Iringa and booked in to the Colonist Hotel so that they could enjoy a dinner, overnight rest, and a hot bath in a portable, galvanised tub which the bedroom boy carried in for them on request. The bar of the hotel, as usual, seemed to be full of rather hearty settlers who wasted much of the day and most of the evening in exchanging ill-founded opinions and talking the usual rubbish which passes for conversation when people are in an alcoholic glow. Eleanor was closely inspected, handsomely complimented, and George well warned to keep close watch on his new acquistion, something which he fully intended to do.

The next day they continued with the journey. *Iringa,* whose name indicates a fortified stronghold, was the capital of the redoubtable Mkwawa and it lies on a height which might have provided a fitting site for the medieval castle of a feudal baron. Immediately south of the place, the road dropped down steeply to the valley of the Little Ruvaha River and then wandered off through green and pleasant country where Lord Delamere had established his settlers, and George was tempted to turn aside in order to see how some of them were coping with their building and agricultural problems.

By evening they were down on the Buhoro Flats. They halted for the night by the banks of a stream, and while George and Lamek unpacked the car, by the light of the moon, Eleanor went off to wash in the cool water. She had hardly settled down to wash her feet when she shot into the air with a feeling of red-hot pins being sunk into her tender parts. She started to claw off her clothes. George rushed to the rescue expecting at least a lion by the noises she was making. He appreciated the scene with a grin.

"Only siafu ants," he reassured her calmly. "Peel off your clothes and jump right into the water."

Eleanor splashed off with the grace of a hippo at sport, while George fetched a lamp and searched her clothes for the ants. Old Lamek was giggling while he busied himself cooking dinner. It became one of his favourite anecdotes. If Eleanor heard any chuckling in her kitchen for some months after the event, she could be certain it was Lamek retelling to some friend the story of the night the memsahib had ants in her pants.

There was only one other remarkable thing in an otherwise warm and still night. In the distance, far away in the early hours of the morning, Eleanor heard a lion roaring, his rumbling voice just rising above the fundamental background level of the rustlings, sighings and insect noises of the African night. George simply rolled over on his other side when she touched him and asked him to listen.

"It's just a lion, somewhere towards the Njombe district," he said sleepily. "He's quite harmless, I assure you."

Old Lamek chuckled from his side of the fire.

"Do you know what the lion says?" he asked, "Listen, carefully, he says, '*Hi ni inchi ya nani? Yangu! yangu! yangu!*' Do you know what it means? It means 'Whose country is this? Mine! mine! mine!'"

Eleanor shuddered slightly, and the cook chuckled again in the dark. The coughing grunt with which the distant lion ended his roar, the "mine! mine! mine!" sounded infinitely more sinister than the challenge about "whose country is this?" She snuggled into George's back for some protection, but he was fast asleep. The rest of the night passed in peace.

They had a final long and hot day's drive, and then rumbled through Mbeya after dark, with George trying to drive as fast as possible in order to reach home. The last stretch of road was the bumpiest. They ploughed their way through long grass growing from the central ridge of the road, with all manner of odd little eyes winking back a reflection of their head-lamps. At last George turned into a side road and said,

"This is our place."

Eleanor strained her eyes to see her future home. In the dark, all she could see were the half-built walls of a house, with a tent pitched beside it. A smiling crowd of Africans bundled out of their huts to welcome the new mistress. Lamek conjured up supper from tinned foods, and scalding hot tea with a nice tang of wood smoke to it. Then there was hot water in old paraffin tins for a bath, and a comforable enough camp bed, with no lions in the night to make any counter-claim to the ownership of the Rushbys' Mchewe Estate.

With the dawn there was a great chattering of African workmen. Eleanor followed George outside as soon as she could in order to inspect her surroundings. George watched her mounting excitement with the pleasure that always comes from showing something worthwhile to one's fellow man. It was a superb morning, with the dew still heavy on the long grass. Away from their tent on the hillside, the landscape swept off in a majestic view across the mighty fault of the Western Rift Valley. Wisps of mist and smoke from distant African villages twisted lazily through the still air. In the trees on the estate, huge wild figs and acacias with flat tops like Japanese sun-shades, some lovely birds moved and sang. There were louries with bright plumage and crested heads, and blue rollers, while in the grasslands the widow birds fluttered heavily with their long black and unwieldy-looking tail feathers seeming to act as so great a handicap to their flight. Monkeys gambolled in the branches, while tree lizards with blue bodies and orange-coloured heads scuttled for safety across the ground as George escorted Eleanor around on a grand morning tour of inspection.

Apart from work on the house, he had obviously been extremely busy. By the banks of the river he had made a vegetable garden and a nursery for coffee. The growing of coffee is a tedious process. George had bought his seeds, of the variety known as Blue Mountain, from a neighbouring farmer, I. G. Stewart. He had planted them in beds, with the rows carefully covered in grass until the seeds showed signs of shooting. Then the grass had to be lifted and the seedlings protected with low straw roofs. Every day the seedlings had to be watered and tended. After eighteen months they would be ready for transplanting into lands cleaned of all natural growth save selected trees left standing to provide shade for the delicate young plants. Additional protection from tent-like piles of grass would have to be provided, while wind-breaks and additional shade trees must be established between the rows of coffee. After four years, if the planter was fortunate, if the rains had been dependable, and parasitic insects reasonably kind-hearted, the planter might harvest his first crop. That was always an eagerly anticipated day for any beginner. With most settlers, their capital was carefully calculated to last just until then, and the first crop would re-establish some shaky finances in the eyes of bankers and traders.

Eleanor soon discovered that in this planter's world there was very little which she could do. In fact, the only thing she was really expected to do was nothing save sit in the tent and read or write. Lamek, like all cooks, not only East African, resented any intrusion into his kitchen affairs by the mistress. Housekeeping in a tent is essentially a life of limited activity and opportunities of participating in the building of the house were very restricted. Walking on her own around the hills through the long grass was rather dull, and in any case she lost enthusiasm after the first day when she encountered a large-size monitor lizard, a good four feet long, like an adolescent crocodile. Then, when she returned home, it was just in time to watch the workmen killing a fine fat puff-adder. After that she preferred to wait for George to accompany her on a stroll in the evening.

Watching the house being built was at least interesting. Practically all its materials, save steel window casements, were made on the site. For bricks, the workmen collected piles of mud which they trampled with their feet until it was of the correct consistency. Then they filled wooden moulds with the clayey mixture, pressed it well down, and turned out beautiful dark-brown bricks which were laid out in rows and covered with grass to bake slowly in the sun. For the chimneys and floors, George was busy building a kiln in order to produce burnt bricks and tiles.

There was a local white clay which yielded an excellent whitewash, while poles for the roof were cut in the hills. Every day, as well, African women carried in large bundles of thatching grass balanced on their heads, and this would provide excellent roofing. As for the actual construction, it was all done by George and an experienced African bricklayer named Pedro who had come from Northern Rhodesia wearing a heavy overcoat and had never been seen without it, even at noon on the hottest day.

Apart from the activities on the estate, there were no other distractions or entertainments. The neighbours were all away, the Hickson-Woods being still at the coast, and Rope Soles Jones busy constructing the new aerodrome at Mbeya, he being a versatile individual who often occupied himself profitably on public works.

Going shopping in Mbeya did provide occasional relaxation. There was not much in the little Indian stores save expensive tinned foods and cheap Japanese textiles, but at least one always encountered somebody for an exchange of news, and there was the treat of a meal in the hotel. Lamek's home-cooking was really very good, but his menus were understandably restricted by the fact that the only ingredients available were one or two vegetables and the inevitable partridge-sized African *kuku*. Eleanor had still to become jaundiced about these tough little fowls, but George had a permanent aversion to them and a great hunger for good red meat.

The hotel was always full of diggers from the Lupa. Eleanor was somewhat bashful at first for she and Mrs Menzies were generally the only women present in such a rough-and-ready company, and the conversation was inclined to be robust. The diggers were a kindly crowd of men, however, mostly of better than average education, even though they generally looked unshaven and their clothes revealed unmistakable evidence that they were habitually used as pyjamas. The famous sign requesting them to take their boots off before going to bed was obviously very necessary. Watching them arrive from the Lupa was always fascinating. They went straight in to the bar, placed a tobacco tin or Kruschen salts jar of gold dust and small nuggets on the counter, asked Menzies to weigh the contents on the scale he kept for that purpose, and then tell them when they had spent the lot. When they had the gold they seemed only too keen to be rid of it. The food, drink and good companionship in the hotel, as well as the comfort of being nursed by Mrs Menzies if they went down with fever, was their idea of value for money.

Fever was the normal background to life in Tanganyika. It was a miserable handicap to an otherwise highly diverting and lovable country. Everybody went down with it sooner or later. The anopheles mosquito was a basic part of local life. If you escaped it under a net at night, it reached you in the daylight hours. Whether you were black or white, a newcomer or a member of one of the most ancient tribes, it was your destiny to lose a substantial portion of your life in feeling miserable, in being wretchedly sick, and having your whole time-table of living completely disrupted, often at the most awkward occasions.

Eleanor inevitably went down with fever. She took ill one evening with a splitting headache and fits of shivering, symptoms all too familiar to George. He put her to bed immediately and dosed her with the vile-tasting quinine. Then he piled a massive collection of blankets over her, with a few hot-water bottles packed into the sides for extra heating. Eleanor complained in a small voice that she would blow up but George reassured her. It was the usual counter-measure. If all went well she would start perspiring and her temperature would drop. Unfortunately nothing went according to plan. By next morning her temperature was up to 105 degrees and she was in an alarmingly cheerful and chatty state of half-delirium.

There were no women within easy call, and conditions in the tent were miserably stuffy and hot. The Hicky-Woods were still down at the coast so George decided to move in to their empty house. They wouldn't mind and it would certainly be far more comfortable for Eleanor. As she could not walk, and the shaking while being taken in the car would hardly do her weakened digestive system much good, he borrowed a *machilla,* or canopied canvas hammock slung from a bamboo pole and carried by four bearers. In this contrivance Eleanor was carried over to the neighbouring farmhouse and put to bed in a large, cool, and restfully dark bedroom. At the same time George sent a runner to Tukuyu, where the district's only medical man, Dr Theis, was stationed. Two days later the doctor arrived in an understandably battered-looking car and brought Eleanor's temperature down sharply with two injections of quinine. She was left feeling like a dehydrated vegetable trying to recover its life blood for the next few days, while George laboured from dawn to dusk with redoubled energy trying to complete their own house before the Hickson-Woods returned.

With the approach of Christmas, Eleanor had recovered her spirits well

enough to be moving around again under her own power. It was nice seeing
her up and looking slightly more cheerful. Spending Christmas in bed with
fever would have been completely dismal. Once she could travel comfortably, George moved her in to Mbeya. Some company from her own sex
might make convalescence more cheerful and he arranged that she stay with
Mrs Harmer, the wife of the newly appointed mines officer who was away on
official business. As it happened, it was not a particularly fortunate convalescence for Eleanor. Mrs Harmer was also nursing a digger down with
blackwater fever. He was dying, and the thin walls of the house allowed the
pathetic babble of his delirium to drift in to every room. Even after he was
dead the sound still seemed to linger on and Eleanor was so distressed that
her own fever returned in a sharp relapse.

George was away at the time. In Mbeya he had met the newly appointed game ranger, Colonel Sherwood-Kelly, V.C. Notwithstanding a
lingering poacher's suspicion of such officials of government, George liked
the man. He was a big, burly South African of Irish descent. Apart from
the Victoria Cross, he seemed to have gathered to his person nearly every
decoration for valour and distinguished service possible in the British Army.
He was also a very human type of man who had eventually been thrown out
of the Army for writing letters to newspapers criticising the ill-conceived
Allied intervention in Russia after the 1917 revolution. Now he was game
ranger of the Southern Highlands of Tanganyika with the immediate task
of controlling elephants who were raiding peasant crops in the Lupembe
area. Never having hunted before, he asked George to accompany him for a
week on his first outing and teach him some of the skills of shooting
elephants.

They returned on Christmas Eve. Eleanor was just sitting up again after
her second dose of fever. She had experienced a short but wretched relapse,
with her head full of nightmares that George had been trampled to death
by a giant elephant. The safe return was a better tonic for her than medicine.
The two men sat on her bed and cheered her up with an account of their
experiences.

Sherwood-Kelly was obviously quite an admirer of George. The whole
hunt had gone with the smoothness which only comes to any human activity
when it is backed by long experience. The hunters had reached the area
devastated by the raiders. They had tracked the elephants down without
great difficulty, and found them in good open country, with just enough cover
to make an approach easy. George had done the shooting, using his ·577
with its usual devastating effect. The three rogues were despatched with minimum trouble or pain, and the whole police action successfully concluded in
time for the hunters to be home for a community Christmas dinner.

" Your George should have been made game ranger of this area," the
Colonel told Eleanor. " With his background he would make a far better

job of it than a run-down Army man like myself. Why don't you try for a post in the game department, George?"

"With my past!" exclaimed George. "The game department would spend half of its time wondering if I had reverted to poaching."

"Perhaps they would be interested in setting a poacher to catch poachers," said Eleanor. "You certainly know all the tricks."

"The most important thing about the job," added the Colonel, "is to understand men and animals, and particularly elephants, without becoming maudlin or sentimental about them. The emotional animal lover would never make a good game ranger. The animals would simply take as much advantage of his sentiment as cats and dogs do of some doting old maid. To conserve you must control. To control you must be fair but firm. It is a perhaps unfortunate fact that the basic tool of the game ranger's trade is his rifle, and one of the best skills he can have is the ability to use it with maximum efficiency when the judicious occasion demands. And that, my friend, is your great talent. You are just wasting it on a farm."

George simply smiled.

"Don't tempt me. I'm a farmer now, with vested interests. I've had my hunting days."

They all enjoyed a pleasant Christmas dinner together the next day. The Harmers, the Colonel, and the assistant district commissioner made very lively company on such an occasion, even though the room temperature was well up to the hundreds and hardly a time or place for Father Christmas and any reindeers.

When it was over, George drove Eleanor back to their new farmhouse. The house was almost finished. George had left the thatchers at work on the roof before he went off on the hunt. Now the roof only needed a few more bundles of grass and their home would be ready for them. It looked a very charming little cottage. There was a living-room with a large ingle-nook fireplace on the one end and a bedroom leading off the opposite side. A smaller guest room stood at the end of a cool and sheltered-looking veranda from which one could enjoy a glorious view far out over the Rift Valley to a jumble of mountains, all blue and hazy and romantic in the distance. Behind the house there was a bath and storeroom, while the kitchen was some distance away to minimise fire risks with the thatched roof.

Wandering through the empty rooms selecting positions for furniture and planning cupboards and shelves gave them both some pleasant hours, while visualising a garden of flowers in front of the cottage was very delightful. High up on the mountain slopes, the climate was ideal for such things as roses. To have the foreground aglow with flowers, setting off the stupendous view to the distance, would place the cottage in a setting close to a dreamworld. Eleanor could hardly wait to move in. The future looked so exciting and inviting that it was impossible to visualise any troubles or problems.

CHAPTER SIXTEEN

ANN

GEORGE and Eleanor moved into their cottage on the 1st January 1931. It was certainly an auspicious day on which to take up residence in a new home. They both hoped that such a move on New Year's Day would be an omen for a happy future. They were full of good resolutions. They had even arranged a special dinner. The Hickson-Woods had arrived back from the coast in time to see them off to their new home, and presented them with a sucking-pig for their first meal. Lamek served it up in style that evening. Unfortunately the heat had reached it in the few hours since its death and it stank. That was always the great problem of keeping meat in the tropics. The banquet had to be continued on bully-beef.

There were still a thousand things to do in the cottage and in the garden. The rainy season had also started and George was busy planting out coffee seedlings. When the showers came he would run up to the house and spend the wet hours in hanging doors and fitting shelves, while Eleanor left her curtaining or gardening and held the tools for him. The showers came in distinct waves separated by periods of dazzlingly clear sunshine. One could hear the downpours approaching with a curious rushing noise along the range of mountains. The border-line between sunshine and storm and sunshine again was as sharply delineated as if the rain was a falling curtain of water suddenly dropped down over a stage to allow the scene-changers of nature to transform the dusty brown grass of the dry season into something new and clean, and all beautifully green again.

It was really amazing how quickly the time passed. Perhaps it was the very sameness of the days which made them slide so rapidly together. But before they knew where they were, the rains were over, and the dry winter months of May, June and July were on them, with the evenings cold enough for a crackling log fire in the ingle-nook, and supper to seem particularly cosy when they sat together in the soft glow of the lamp and toasted cheese before the glowing embers, or read, or played some records on the gramophone.

Everything was so quiet and peaceful that it was hard to realise their home was isolated in the heart of Africa. The Safwa tribe who lived around them was as primitive as the Gogo without the more picturesque habits and costumes of the latter people. They had never been a large or martial tribe. By nature they were a peaceful and amiable crowd, doing as little work as they possibly could on their hillside patches of maize and bananas, and only offering their labours to a European if they were particularly keen on earning ready cash to buy some luxury or pay their tax. Apart from her domestic servants, and the running of a small clinic on the farm where the women brought their infants to be dosed for worms or sore eyes, or ulcers on their legs, the only regular contact Eleanor had with the tribespeople was with three little *totos,* or children. The trio came to the house each morning carrying for sale a bottle of milk balanced neatly on top of each of their heads. They habitually greeted her with a broad smile, which immediately revealed the one repellent tribal characteristic of the Safwa. They filed their teeth to sharp points, giving them a real " all ready to eat you " look, like little sharks.

As for the wild-animal world of Africa, very little was ever seen on the farm other than the cheeky little black-faced monkeys who liked the trees outside the bedroom window, or the big baboons who sneaked down from the mountains at times, and put Kelly, Eleanor's Irish wolfhound puppy, into paroxysms of rage and fear when he tried to drive them away, and the old males showed him their fearsome-looking long and yellow fangs.

Occasionally some European neighbour would call in to see them. In this part of the world there was no knocking or ringing on doorbells. The front door was always open, for life was secure and safe. The home owner would simply hear some cheerful voice call out, " *Hodi?* " that standard Swahili visitors' cry, meaning " May I come in?" It hardly needed the host's welcome of " *Karibu!*" (" Come in!"), to bring the guest to a comfortable seat, with a cup of tea produced in minutes from a pot of water always kept boiling in the kitchen. Perhaps it was a party of diggers on their way to or from the Lupa, and full of gossip about who was " on gold," or whose wife was living with who. Perhaps it was Kathleen Hickson-Wood, looking very trim and right in her corduroy slacks and khaki shirt, or Rope Soles Jones, carrying over some news picked up on his weird-looking wireless, or just strolling across for a chat accompanied by his even weirder-looking brother, Llewyllen, who had come to stay with him, and resembled exactly the portrait of Trader Horn, with the same emaciated features, burning eyes and long white beard. His health had broken down, but he was still an excellent conversationalist, and proud of a fine Welsh tenor voice, which he often raised in song.

Very occasionally, as well, there would be a dance or party in Mbeya or Tukuyu. Everybody would dress in formal clothes and the handful of women would be half-shunted off their feet by relays of awkward partners who knew little more of dancing than one step forward, one back, and then a quick retreat to rejoin the huddle of surplus males in the bar. For mild flirtations, or serious breaking of marital vows, there was a very pleasant botanical garden in Tukuyu, laid out by Major Wells during the war years, and including a large pond with islands in it, reputedly designed to resemble in miniature one of the lakes of Killarney. A few Romeos, and one or two Juliets, ended up in the thing when their raptures were disturbed by irate husbands.

The really big change for George and Eleanor was heralded in August. Eleanor was listlessly poking her food around at lunch one day when George quite brightly asked her,

" When are you going to tell me about the baby?"

This was distinctly not according to the book. Eleanor had actually looked it all up already. Apart from reckoning out with remarkable accuracy the birthday to be on the 8th February of the following year, the book also recommended something in the nature of soft lights and sweet music as the correct background to breaking the news to a husband.

After some enquiry on Eleanor's part as to how he knew, they fell to discussing the problem of where she would have it. There were just no conveniences for babies in their part of the world. February was also always a wet month, with the roads so slippery that the doctor in Tukuyu could never be relied on in any emergency. The hard-pressed man had made it generally known that so far as he was concerned, babies were distinctly unwelcome little treasures in the muddy months. Would-be parents were recommended to look sharp to a suggested time-table which avoided complications with the weather, but babies can be very awkward about such and other matters, as many people know.

The logical decision was for Eleanor to go back to her parents in Cape Town and have the baby in comfort. Naturally she protested the matter. She had grown to love the life on the farm in Tanganyika. Its quiet progression of days might have seemed dull to others but it had all been a great adventure to her. George had to secure the doctor's opinion before she was finally convinced that her old home was the best place, and resigned herself to preparation and packing.

The Imperial Airways service was, unfortunately, not due to start until the beginning of the next year. With luck, she would be able to return to Mbeya in some comfort, but leaving it, George would have to thrash the box-body Chevrolet into tackling the long and bumpy stretch of the Great North Road linking Mbeya to the railway town of Broken Hill in Northern Rhodesia. Such a journey today is simply 640 miles of flat and dusty monotony, but in the early 1930s it was a purgatory of ruts, sand traps, and puncture hazards for tyres. However, they would do the journey by stages, camping out each night by the roadside, and the instalment system of travelling might make it all slightly more agreeable.

There was a great stir among the servants when news spread of Eleanor's departure. Old Lamek cooked all his best dishes so that fond memories of him would be taken down to Cape Town. His hopes of remembrance were certainly fulfilled, if only because his chef's specialities were so queer it was impossible to forget them. He loved to cook up such wonders as stuffed *kuku* made by carefully removing an entire inside of a chicken from its skin and mincing the meat with onions and potatoes. The minced mixture was then re-stuffed into the chicken skin. The skin was sewn up and the whole affair roasted and served looking something like a football, but with bloated legs pathetically raised in the air as a last supplication. The dish really tasted very well. Lamek had the better of Eleanor with another speciality, a surprise dish served with a great flourish, and revealed to be a tortoise roasted minus its shell. Eleanor couldn't face that one, although George reckoned it was tasty. The following day Lamek routed even George by serving up a real *pièce de résistance,* a skinned baby monkey roasted whole, lying flat on its back with its hands folded peacefully across its breast. This brought back certain memories to George of the Middle Congo, and he hastily joined Eleanor in the garden until the corpse was removed and replaced with a boiled egg.

Just before they left for the south, Llewyllen Jones died, very suddenly. It was a sad shock to poor old Rope Soles. All the neighbours went across for the burial. There was no minister available. The body was simply wrapped in a blanket, bound to some boards and lowered into a grave dug on Rope Soles' farm. There was no service. The men present simply said, " Goodbye

Llew " or " Sleep well, Llew," and Rope Soles, with his brother-in-law, a Swedish geologist named Max Coster, shovelled the first soil over the body. It was a beautiful afternoon, and Llew probably liked it that way, with the sunshine far too bright and cheerful to allow anybody to shed tears for long.

George and Eleanor left for the south soon afterwards. The journey occupied the best part of the last week of August 1931, with numerous punctures, and the wretched wooden spokes becoming so loose in the hot and dry weather that wet rags had to be bound around them in order to keep the wheels together.

There was very little other traffic on the road. The stream of odd characters, hitch-hikers, freaks and adventurers, who frequent the road today in a constant movement between the Cape and Cairo had still to start their wanderings. A few transport trucks rattled and lurched along the road while the silent forest of brachystegia hemmed it in on either side even more closely than it does today. Only occasionally a family of greater kudu would leap gracefully across the road ahead of the car, but for the rest of the journey even Africans were a rarity on the long and lonely reaches of the road.

At the administrative post of Mpika there was some activity in the building of a refuelling point for the projected air service. A rest house for the convenience of passengers was also being built there by an enterprising man named Ronald Smith. This subsequently developed into the Crested Crane Hotel, one of the best known of all the landmarks and staging posts along the trail from the Cape to Cairo.

Further down the road, at Kanona, an Australian named Digger Mills had built a tiny wayside hostelry which he used as a base for hunting parties he conducted out around the verges of the great swamp and lake of Bangweulu. George and Eleanor stopped there for a meal on the way south and the host pressed them to stay the night so that he could discuss a joint hunting proposition. It appeared that his clients occasionally wished to continue their expeditions to Tanganyika and for some time he had been hoping to find some resident of that territory who could take them over at the border point.

George had never before considered becoming a white hunter. The prospect had always seemed rather unpleasant to him. The type of trigger-itchy client who came out to Africa with something like a shopping-list of animals to shoot always seemed to be dreadful bores when he had met them in the past. There was not even the consolation of the big money in the occupation which there is today. With Hollywood still to glamorise the white hunter and deck him out with the leopard-skin hat-bands, bowie knives and other trappings of its wardrobe department, clients were just not prepared to pay excessively for any invisible overheads. With the four-wheel drive vehicle still to be fabricated, clients were also of a tougher and more athletic and demanding breed, while their wives remained at home, and had not yet been lured out to the wilds with the notion that white hunters were strong and silent men, with service and discretion written into their code.

George promised Mills that he would think the proposition over. On his way back, after seeing Eleanor safely aboard a south-bound train at Broken Hill, he did call in and agree to experiment with any clients Mills passed on to him. With the farm not likely to be remunerative for some years, a source of income would certainly be an advantage. Unfortunately, Mills explained, with the world in depression, clients were not very numerous and naturally he tried to keep the few he had to his side of the border until they exhausted their finances.

Back on the farm, George kept himself busy digging a long furrow to lead one of the mountain streams to irrigate his lands. There was always something to do on the estate or in improving the house in honour of its anticipated new occupant. It was actually nine months before he saw Eleanor again. The baby, a girl named Ann, was born exactly on the date Eleanor had calculated from her book, but the doctor was not enthusiastic about the idea of flying back to Mbeya before she was at least four months old. Commercial flying was still very much of a novelty and its effect on a baby was an unknown factor. Returning to Tanganyika by sea would subject the infant to the miserable overland journey to Mbeya, and in any case the box-body Chevrolet had limped its way home from Broken Hill in a manner which indicated that it had not the slightest intention of ever leaving again.

When Eleanor eventually did arrive back at Mbeya aerodrome in the middle of June 1932, it was Ken Menzies who met her, and not a proud father. The Chevrolet had refused to even leave the farm, so George was waiting for Menzies to drive Eleanor and the baby home. In the circumstances, Eleanor was quite glad that George was not on the aerodrome to meet her. She was no picture of radiant motherhood. It had been a horribly wretched flight in a rickety three-engined aircraft of the " Hercules " type which Imperial Airways used to open their weekly London to Cape service in January of that year. Eleanor had joined the thing at Broken Hill after a train journey up from Cape Town. She had been assured that her baby was the first of its tender age to do a flight, and after completing the journey she was not surprised that others had avoided it.

The aircraft had no ventilation, sound-proofing or pressurisation. It was only capable of lurching and bumping along at one hundred miles an hour at an altitude just about sufficient to clear the trees. Everybody save individuals with stomachs made of corrugated iron was violently sick. The baby brought up what seemed to be her twelve previous bottles of milk all over her mother's brand-new coat and dress. The stop at Mpika saw very few indeed enjoying Mr Ronald Smith's offering of lunch, while the evening landing at Mbeya found the adult passengers pale green and the infant as white as a ghost. It took a good night's sleep in the Sluice Box to bring the roses back to anybody's cheeks. Eleanor heard the aircraft take off in the early morning on the next leg of its journey to the north. She could lie in bed and anticipate not only a decent breakfast, but the stability to retain it, and then be driven out to a joyous reunion with her George. What the rest of the passengers were doing in the aircraft she could imagine, with a sigh of relief that she was no longer with them.

Of course she noticed numerous changes. Mbeya was definitely growing. Even the hotel had been rebuilt, with electric light and accommodation for the transit aeroplane passengers, while new buildings were in evidence all over the once vacant areas of the embryonic town. As for the farm, it was full of surprises. George had occupied the nine months on quite a few projects. His domestication was remarkable. With his firstborn proudly held in his arms, he treated Eleanor to a conducted tour of all new additions to their home and property. In the lands there were now forty acres planted with coffee seedlings, and there was also a vigorous grove of assorted fruit trees. In the house there was a new reed ceiling to the living-room, a dresser gay with willow-pattern plates specially imported from Britain, such comforts as a writing-table, a stand for visitors' hats, and a huge double bed made from strips of tyres taken from the box-body Chevrolet, nailed to a frame so that they made a fine, springy support for a kapok mattress. As a final virtuous touch there was a complicated model ship painstakingly assembled from a hobbies kit during the course of many solitary evenings.

Eleanor was partly concerned and partly gratified to find George looking slightly on the thin side. Wives always like to think of husbands as having pined during their absence. The merest suggestion of this, however, was promptly quashed by George informing her that Lamek had made his departure to rejoin his family in Northern Rhodesia, and only after several indigestible experiments had a satisfactory new cook been found, a domestic treasure named Abel who had few faults other than an unfortunate disinclination to wash himself.

News of Eleanor's return soon spread among the neighbours. The local tribeswomen started to troop in with their children to view the new baby, bringing small gifts of eggs or bananas or the inevitable half-starved fowl. Eleanor would exchange compliments with them about one another's infants, and be well lectured by experienced African matrons on techniques of child care. They were always quite shocked to see the elaborate activity in washing napkins. They used no napkins at all on their infants, and as they carried them on their backs they had obviously found a pretty fool-proof method of baby care. They tried to persuade Eleanor to adopt their techniques but her head was too filled with the current European vogue for the rigid methods of Dr Truby King. It might have been an idea to inform the distinguished doctor of older African methods certainly more tried than his own. His opinion would have been interesting. The African mother knew the times of her baby's calls to nature with great dependability. A short while before the event, the infant was removed from its place, held in a sitting position, and its stomach massaged to induce a motion. In particularly recalcitrant cases, a length of thong was placed around the belly and tightened by twisting a piece of stick attached to the ends. After final hygiene from a tuft of grass the baby was returned to its mother's back where it was warm and comfortable without expensive blankets and certainly well out of the way without feeling itself to be at all neglected.

The European neighbours also came to view the baby. Rope Soles peered at it through his monocle; his sister, Marion, who had now settled on a portion of his farm with her husband, Max Coster, made some flattering comments, rather spoilt, unfortunately, by the Hicky-Woods' two children who rode over at the same time, sitting one behind the other astride a fat old white donkey. They made a diplomatic remark that all infants looked like monkeys.

Eleanor liked to think that even the animal world paid its compliments. She and George were at supper one night just after her return when the back veranda of their house was suddenly invaded by a crowd of African women and children all yelling " *Simba! Simba!* ". The cook half-tumbled into the room with the breathless news that there were lions in the servant's quarters. George dived for a rifle and ammunition and went off to investigate, with the trembling house-boy behind him carrying a lantern. Eleanor tried to complete her meal like an ice-cool frontier wife. She only managed this until there was a shattering crash behind her. Something big and hairy hurtled through the back window. She never afterwards doubted anybody's ability to have their hair stand on end. Fortunately it was only Kelly, the Irish wolfhound, taking cover in a hurry.

The lions had already cleared. The commotion raised by the Africans would have frightened off a steam-roller. The big cats, after playfully tearing open a bag of maize, moved on to the Hickson-Woods' farm, where they killed and ate the children's two white riding donkeys before wandering back to the wilderness from whence they had come. Hicky-Wood sat up all the next night with a rifle hoping for a chance of vengeance, but the lions weren't interested in making his acquaintance. They never returned.

Eleanor had brought one interesting piece of news back from Cape Town. She had met John Molteno down there. He had returned from his hunting adventures after enjoying reasonable luck and was looking around for something fresh to do. In one of the Cape Town newspapers he noticed some mention of Eleanor's arrival and the fact that she was married to George. He went to see her, listened to an enthusiastic account of life in Tanganyika, and half made up his mind to go there. He wrote to George immediately and in reply received a detailed account of farming opportunities, as well as some description of the Lupa goldfield. This was the last George heard of him by post.

Late one afternoon in the middle of November 1932, just when the farm labourers were going home, a battered-looking Baby Austin, making some noise about itself through a broken silencer, came to a dead stop half-way up the hill to the farmhouse. Molteno, all six feet five inches of him, managed to uncoil himself from the inside and emerge to discover what was wrong. How a man of his size could have driven all the way up from Cape Town in such a tiny vehicle was a credit to his own compressibility and the surprising strength of what was certainly one of the most remarkable cars ever built. The farm labourers simply stood around and gaped, like Sindbads watching a genie emerge from a bottle. The Baby Austin and its driver eventually reached the top of the hill in some style, pushed by a dozen Africans all laughing at the tops of their voices.

Fitting the welcome guest into a bed was a problem, although it was hardly necessary on the first night. He and George sat up until almost daybreak reminiscing about their past adventures. Eleanor could only listen to them in silence, and marvel that George had been able to settle down so well, after so rough and masculine a past.

The idea of a farm next to George was very appealing to the newcomer. He had a notion to turn himself into a married man, with a pretty girl waiting in Cape Town for him to establish a home in the new land. George took him over two days later to meet Hickson-Wood and see if the Irishman would sell another one hundred acres of his estate. After some wavering, however, Hicky-Wood declined. He had plans for further developments on his coffee plantation, and he had no spare acreage for sale.

This disappointment turned Molteno's thoughts to the Lupa goldfield. All accounts of the place painted it in most romantic colours. To add to its attraction, in 1932 the idea of a gold premium had been introduced in the country in order to stimulate production from low-grade mines, and the output of the Lupa alluvial diggers reached a new record of 15,843 ounces for the year. This, of course, was still far from Lumb's hope of a new Johannesburg, but at least on the Lupa, every man was his own master. There were no share-pushers, or pretentious company promoters, and the gaudy criminal element which infested Johannesburg was just not attracted by such a comparatively tiny field. It happily remained the preserve of the small man, who, relieved of the ruthless exploitation he experienced as a working miner on larger gold fields like the Witwatersrand, could there feel himself to be a potential millionaire, certain that if he starved today it was only because his luck had been postponed until tomorrow.

Even George was often half-tempted to return to the Lupa. It did not take much persuasion from Molteno to lure him into a week's visit to the field in order to show his friend around and introduce him to some of the diggers. They did the journey in the long-suffering Baby Austin. How it contained both of them was almost as much of a mystery as was its ability to survive the bone-shaking roads. The little vehicle simply seemed to grit its teeth, tackle anything, and ignore the normal British automobile designer's faults of weak suspension, low ground clearance, and half of a car's brake cables, petrol tank and other rusty-looking innards hanging underneath as untidily as a well-dressed woman showing a dirty petticoat.

Molteno liked the Lupa as soon as he saw the place. There was certainly quite an air to it and the diggers were so obviously a chronically optimistic happy-go-lucky, slightly sun-touched crowd of strong drinkers, strong lovers and downright noisy men, that it was impossible not to like them. They were all certain of big things on the Lupa and its tributaries, and their only complaint was lack of water in the dry season. Gold recovery was all effected in sluice boxes and when the streams dried up in the winter months there was just nothing anybody could do. Water became even more valuable than gold, for it was certainly harder to find, and men turned to liquor to while away months of frustration until the rains came again.

Most of the digging activity was on the Kasanga tributary at that time, for gold had been found there in some quantity. George introduced Molteno to the diggers. Well before it was time for the two men to return to the farm, Molteno had decided to join in the search for fortune on the Lupa field, and also establish himself as a gold buyer. Life on the Lupa would suit his temperament to perfection. All the way back along the vile road to Mbeya he talked about the prospects with such enthusiasm that George was on the point of joining him in a venture. Coffee growing was a tedious business. With tumbling prices on the depressed world markets and the much-talked-about railway to Mbeya now no longer heard of, things would have to improve substantially before it would be even worthwhile reaping his first coffee crop in a couple of years' time. Already several of his older, established neighbours were talking of abandoning their farms and moving to the Lupa. At current prices they could hardly recover the costs of trucking their crops to the railway at Dodoma, let alone pay for their farms or show a profit.

It was not a question of any of them losing interest in their farms. Like George, they had all found the process of land ownership to be completely fascinating. Creating a farm from a stretch of wilderness was a patient but most absorbing labour. If only the years of planning and work could be rewarded by even moderate success, then life in the exhilarating spaces and sunshine of Tanganyika would be very delightful. It was the continuing, long-drawn-out world depression which was the real worry.

To George, the great consideration about returning to the Lupa was Eleanor. She was going to have another baby in May of the coming year. But even without the addition to the family, the idea was not attractive of taking her to the diggings with a little girl to look after in that rough-and-ready society. Before he reached home he had resolved to remain a coffee planter and just hope for the best. Life was always full of changes and surprises. There was no knowing what world conditions would be like in two years' time. For all he knew they might be in the midst of a tremendous boom within six months, with coffee worth more than Lupa gold.

He returned home in a more cheerful mood, and was greeted by an excited Eleanor, full of an odd story about how the garden boy had unearthed a large, heavy, earthenware cooking pot, carefully sealed at the top. In an atmosphere of considerable tension the object had been carefully carried on to the veranda. It was opened, with Eleanor absolutely certain that it contained a treasure large enough to solve all their economic worries.

" Well," enquired George, when she paused theatrically in her account of proceedings, " what was in it?"

She sighed.

"A real treat for a pregnant female. Nothing but a grinning skull, not even a copper coin buried with it."

" Who on earth do you suppose it was?" enquired the interested Molteno.

" The fact that the fellow was buried without a penny tells us that," said the disgruntled George. " It was a prehistoric coffee farmer."

They went into the farmhouse for a good bath, a meal and a comfortable sleep.

CHAPTER SEVENTEEN

WHITE HUNTER

LITTLE George was born on the 29th April 1933. He was a funny little character with a shock of hair like a gollywog and a slight black moustache. Big George had the giggles as soon as he looked at him. Eleanor joined in the amusement, while the doctor, a rather prim German by the name of Eckhardt, looked completely shocked at such hilarity so soon after a confinement.

Dr Eckhardt was a welcome newcomer to Mbeya. He was established in a neat little hospital, and the convenience was much appreciated by everybody in that part of Tanganyika. Eleanor had been delighted at being able to have her baby so close to home. The prospect of repeating her plane journey to the south had not been at all pleasant. Instead of that, when she had felt her time approaching she had simply been carried in from the farm to a point on the road to Mbeya where it was comfortable for the doctor's car to pick her up. It had actually been quite an amusing journey. Four farm labourers carried the *machilla,* while eight reliefs walked along on either side of the litter, singing something that sounded like a sea shanty, with one man giving the verses and the rest picking up the chorus. The words were improvised as they went, sly complaints about Eleanor's weight, hopes that she would have a son, and that they would all be handsomely rewarded by George.

George and Kelly the dog followed the *machilla,* with the cook's wife carrying little Ann, and the cook just behind, togged out for some reason in

178

a Palm Beach suit, large Terai hat, sunglasses and two-tone shoes. At a very respectful distance behind this personage followed the rag-tag and bobtail of the farm staff who joined the procession just for fun. Being carried at the head of such an entourage made Eleanor think of herself as the Queen of Sheba returning in the family way from her visit to Solomon.

The confinement was unremarkable. Almost before she knew where she was, Eleanor was home again, absolutely certain that the rash on her infant, and the fact that his moustache was falling off, was due to the German nurse insisting on feeding him strong tea every time he cried. It was good to be home again, even after so short an absence, and find everybody well, the house decorated with sprays of bougainvillea to welcome her, and even a special sponge-cake prepared as a surprise by Abel, the gentlemanly cook.

George, at the time, was very busy hammering together a hatching box for brown trout ova which were due to be flown up from the Jonkershoek hatchery in South Africa by the next week's plane. Since his first visit to Tukuyu, George had been certain that the beautiful streams flowing from the Rungwe and Mbeya mountains would be ideal for trout. His enthusiasm had induced a number of the local residents to club together to buy ova. On George's farm there was a small stream quite ideal for a trout hatchery. When the fingerlings were old enough they could be transferred to the various streams in the Mbeya and Tukuyu districts.

The ova duly arrived, almost to Eleanor's chagrin, for the process of hatching the fry commanded as much attention in the household as her own clamorous family. The little fish had to be fed on ants' eggs collected by the farm labourers, and their dead had to be carefully removed by sucking them up in a glass tube in order to avoid contamination of the water.

In the midst of all this intensive infant care, John Molteno arrived very gaily one night on his way back to the Lupa with his pretty new bride, Angeline, from the Cape, and a boisterous escort of diggers who had welcomed her to Mbeya with what had obviously been quite a party. One of them had only half of his beard and moustache left, the other side of his face having been forcibly shaved on the counter of the bar in the Sluice Box. They spent a noisy night in the farmhouse, sleeping all over the place, and then leaving for the Lupa the next morning, with the bride looking slightly bemused at such a retinue and rather uncertain about the prospect of having to do some substantial walking in order to reach her husband's claim.

While the household was still recovering from this visitation, two army officers arrived in Mbeya on furlough from India. With them they had a letter to George from Philip Teare, the game warden of Tanganyika. They wanted a white hunter to take them on a month's hunting safari, and were prepared to pay the prevailing rates of expenses, together with a salary of £100 a month for the hunter. They were strongly recommended by Philip Teare.

George was slightly disconcerted about the matter. He had hardly thought about turning white hunter since he had first discussed the idea with Digger Mills. And now there was also the matter of the trout. Looking after two babies, as well as several thousand voracious little fish, would keep Eleanor somewhat occupied. The fish required feeding every four hours, just like little George, but at least they were not so noisy.

The officers were a pleasant enough pair named Tuck and Hayter, and the financial side of the safari was certainly attractive. George discussed it with Eleanor. She was quite willing to allow him to go.

" It's just one month. I'll manage all right. Every time little George bellows for his bottle, it will at least remind me to feed the fish. But, of course, it's up to you. Do you want to go?"

George allowed that at least the business might be worth trying. There could possibly be some novelty to it on the first occasion. After the years of waiting for coffee to grow it would certainly be refreshing to earn some money. But the idea of sharing the enthusiasm of trigger-itchy amateurs, with their heads full of some adolescent nonsense about the mystique between hunter and hunted as justification for the slaughter of some harmless little antelope, was just not attractive. With such moral qualms, Eleanor could not help him. He thought the matter over for some time and then decided to accept the offer. At least the safari would be short, and an experience. One month would soon pass and the amount of damage the two clients could do in that time would of necessity be limited.

The clients were desirous of securing a mixed bag of game, so George decided to take them down to the area around Lake Rukwa. There was always a considerable concentration of animals there, and they could blaze away to their heart's content for a couple of weeks. Then they could move to the Usangu Flats for a change of scenery and end the safari at Igawa on the Great North Road, where George arranged for a truck to pick them up on the last day of the hunt and take the two officers off to the railway at Dodoma. The whole outing would at least be good exercise. The officers had no funds for expensive trucks and light four-wheel drive vehicles were non-existent. It would be a proper foot safari. Arranging the business of porters, trackers and suppliers gave George quite a few memories of his past.

They started off cheerfully enough in a hired truck which took them from Mbeya to Lake Rukwa. The actual process of hunting soon taught George the practical duties of the white hunter's life. By day he escorted his clients in what seemed to him to be a rather dull ambuscade or pursuit of various antelope. Puku were particularly numerous and very tame. It was easy to crawl the clients up to within ten yards of a good ram but even then they were very inexperienced shots. George usually occupied an hour in the afternoon in the necessity of straightforward shooting for the pot. In the evenings the clients expected to be entertained by hunting stories and accounts of any colourful episodes in the white hunter's life. Such accounts could be very colourful indeed. A really successful white hunter, in fact, requires something of the creative ability of the professional story-teller, along with the knack of acting the part.

The client's contribution to the evening round consisted largely of accounts of pig-sticking for some cup in India. Pig-sticking, it must be allowed, is not everybody's idea of pleasure, but at least one of the officers appeared to be very expert at it. There was not much drinking on this safari. One client had brought a bottle of whisky with which to celebrate any successes. This was very carefully treasured. Any thirsty white hunter was obviously intended by nature to drink water. In Africa, after all, that is the liquid which makes lions roar, and grows hair on their chests.

At the end of the Rukwa section of the hunt, George led his clients to the salt pans at Ivuna, where C. R. Sargeant had a concession to extract salt from some saline springs in the tribal area of the Mbungu people. From this place a track led off to Mbeya, and George hired a truck to take the party to Marere's village on the Usangu Flats for the second stage of the hunt. The clients were keen on bagging a greater kudu, a lion and an elephant, so this stage of the safari promised to be more lively than plain antelope shooting.

The greater kudu ended up without particular trouble as a rather doleful-looking pair of horns. The lion was more recalcitrant, although George was reasonably glad to hear, if not see, the last of this particular animal. He was a nice black-maned specimen who spent two nights keeping everybody awake by roaring around the camp. Eventually George tracked him down to a nice cover and the beaters flushed him into a convenient twenty-yard range. One of the clients hit the animal in the foot with a ·318 Westley Richards, the other missed with a ·375 magnum Holland and Holland. The two manufacturers promptly received on their heads a considerable tirade for the inaccuracy of their weapons. George promised to zero the rifles that afternoon. The lion, meanwhile, had understandably bolted. The clients had to be established in a tree, the wounded lion re-flushed after some search, and despatched. George took the skin back to the clients with some feeling of relief that he would at least be able to sleep that night.

The elephant was likely to put up stouter resistance than the lion. Lions really make a poor show against high-velocity rifles. Elephants, however, quite often kill people, as they are creatures capable of some resentment at any pot-shotting. When his trackers had located a suitable animal, a nice bull with seventy-pounder tusks, George went so far as to lecture his clients on the anatomy of the elephant and draw a diagram showing the best targets. After only a month in the bush, however, it was doubtful if they would produce accurate shooting. Then the hunt started. The elephant received one bullet in the belly and another in the backside, both dismal shots for such an animal. George sprinted after the elephant and put him out of his misery.

He collapsed in a heap, looking rather pathetic with his front legs stretched under his chin as though he was a child saying his prayers. George felt sorry for him. He had killed elephants for profit, never for pleasure. This type of hunting seemed futile, but the clients obviously liked it. When they emerged from the bush at Igawa and boarded the truck for Dodoma they were in very high spirits from the success of their outing.

George simply went home. On the way he stopped in Mbeya long enough to buy a new six-foot-long galvanised bath. At least the proceeds of the hunt could provide the family with that luxury. Their old bath leaked so badly one had to fill the thing to the brim and then scrub away as quickly as possible in order to avoid being left high and dry. Another thing he bought for the children was a grey riding donkey from some wandering Masai. He also noticed that Dare was in Mbeya. Eleanor could travel in and have her teeth tinkered up. Dare was an itinerant Australian dentist who roamed around in an old Rugby car with a few rather tarnished instruments and a tent which he usually erected on the Lupa with a sign " Have your Teeth Filled With your Own Gold." A few diggers stored some of their gold in that interesting way and at least for some months had considerable difficulty in being able to close their mouths properly. For an extraction, Dare was more expert. He generally placed two bottles of beer in front of a patient, said, " Don't get mad at me if it hurts. We'll have a drink afterwards," and out would come the tooth in pretty smart fashion. There was no anaesthetic and the same forceps were used to remove the bottle tops with even greater skill immediately after the operation.

Back on the farm all seemed well, except that little Ann appeared to have malaria, cut worms were killing off the seedlings in the nursery, and borer beetles were at work on the coffee in the plantation. Otherwise, everybody was happy including the fish. Eleanor had even thought that she was going to have another baby, but this proved a false alarm. When George had recovered, she asked him how he had enjoyed his hunting safari. He was about to say " Never again," when he thought better of it. He would be lucky if he secured his first bags of coffee in 1935. Even then the beans might hardly be worth the picking unless world prices improved. He might have to resort to something worse than white hunting if the family were to survive.

George's second hunting client, in fact, came to him in the following season. A letter from Digger Mills appeared in the mail-bag one day with the information that an American client by the name of Daub wanted to visit Tanganyika after hunting in Northern Rhodesia. The man was a wealthy fish canner from the American west coast. He wanted to spend at least two months hunting in Tanganyika and would pay the usual rates, together with expenses, for a well-mounted safari with all possible conveniences and luxuries. Mills took it for granted that George would accept the commission. He simply asked him to meet the party at the Abercorn Arms Hotel, in the Northern Rhodesia border town of Abercorn.

George thought the matter over. There was certainly nothing to prevent him leaving the farm for this safari. The fish, by this time, had all been distributed among various streams. Everybody at home was well. The coffee was struggling, but there was nothing which he could do about it. If beetles were going to masticate the crop, staying at home to listen to their jaws working at night was not likely to be profitable. There was no technical guidance available, no chemicals completely suited to local conditions, and his neighbours were all just as inexperienced as himself. At least Mr Daub's £200 for the two months would provide something of an income.

Daub apparently had his own transport, but expected his white hunter to provide a second vehicle. Menzies occasionally hired out a box-body Ford, and it was in this vehicle that George made his way to the rendezvous. He arrived in Abercorn on the same day as the hunting party. They met one another on the veranda of the little pub. This was the first moneyed American he had encountered. The client was actually an elderly and very hard-boiled business man. He had shouldered and gouged his way up through the scramble for wealth in his native land and, emerging on the top of the pile of corpses of those who had fallen by the way, found himself the possessor of a mobile cash register for a mind, and flat feet, for the relief of which he wore steel arches as supports in his boots. On the hot soil of Africa these arches unfortunately became hot. He carried bottles of water which he poured over them for the sake of coolness.

As soon as opportunity allowed, George asked Mills for a report on the client. Mills shrugged.

" He's a fair shot, very well equipped with all possible gadgets, including photographic gear, but he is a slow thinker in everything except money. He needs plenty of time to get his shot and you'll find that he is apt to blame you if the animal moves. He is also as mean as they come."

Mills sounded slightly disgruntled.

"Anyway, I've had worse, at least I'll say that for him. The only real trouble about him is that his conversation is pretty limited. He gets dull-going at night."

The client wanted a mixed bag of game, and he was also interested in seeing something of the famous Serengeti Plain and the Ngorongoro Crater. As George had not so far had the opportunity of visiting either of these renowned natural wonders of Tanganyika, the travelling part of the hunt would at least be novel.

For a start, he took the client directly to Lake Rukwa. There was a rough track leading down from Abercorn into the Western Rift Valley. On the way they turned aside along an even viler route which led to the remarkable waterfall of the Kalambo River. At this place, a prodigious and eerie gorge leading down to Lake Tanganyika, the Kalambo River which acts as

the frontier line between Northern Rhodesia and Tanganyika takes a spectacular 726-foot leap. It provides a scene both beautiful and curiously haunting in such a setting of wild solitude.

Unfortunately, the day was overcast while they were at the waterfall.
George soon learned that, so far as the client was concerned, scenery was to
be photographed and animals to be shot. There was no other interest in
such natural features of the country. The client simply regarded the waterfall for a moment, expressed an opinion that the light was useless, and suggested that they go on. For the rest of the safari it was the camera and the
rifle, rather than the man, which were taken on tour, and providing that the
escort realised this basic fact, everything went splendidly.

In the Rukwa area the client shot his mixed bag of puku, impala, sita-
tunga, Defassa waterbuck and a few other varieties of antelope. He showed
little interest in keeping trophies. A photograph of himself with rifle, seated
on top of some corpse, was perfectly satisfactory. If he was larger than the
corpse, as with such antelope as Sharpe's steinbuck, then he liked to hold
the creature up by its hoofs, or drape it over his knees. Game birds, and
water-fowl, of which Lake Rukwa is a fabulous nursery, were elegantly
arranged around his feet as though they were offerings to Zeus. The final collection of photographs must have added to a very varied and happy record
of a tour through one of the most fascinating countries on earth.

There was only one mishap during the Rukwa portion of the hunt. Menzies' Ford broke its chassis negotiating an awkward gully. It had to be
patched up with wooden poles wired to its innards like splints on a broken
limb, and then sent limping back to its owner to be doctored by a man with
an acetylene welder. The rest of the safari was completed on the client's
one-and-a-half-ton Ford truck, which vehicle upheld the manufacturer's reputation with admirable fortitude.

At the end of the Rukwa hunt the party made its way to Mbeya, paid a
visit to the farm so that George could be assured that all was well, and then
set out for the north. The journey was without event, other than that the
client felt poorly before they reached Dodoma and was forced to bed down
there in the hotel for two nights. This unexpected addition to his bill, for
some curious reason, made him miserable for several days afterwards.

The journey north from Dodoma went through entirely new country for
George. It was arid, open bush land, rising beyond Kondoa to a ridge of hills
from whose wooded heights there was a long and hazy view out to the east
over the prodigious flatness of the Masai Steppe. Then the road dropped
sharply to the pretty little lake of Babati, with its thick grove of fever trees,
and at this stage in its journey entered the verges of one of the most extraordinary landscapes to be found anywhere on earth.

To understand this landscape you must know that the road has now
entered the Great Rift Valley and here the volcano is king. Babati itself is

dominated by the extinct cinder pile of Ufiyome, with a silent lake now resting in its crater. All around there are smaller lava piles, cinder cones and sunken craters. The road makes a troublesome corrugated way along the floor of the valley whose alkaline soil, dreadfully arid and sterile, is a place more for dust devils and heat mirages than for human beings, although the small Mbugwe tribe cling to the place with misguided affection for a homeland which can never yield them more than the most wretched of livings.

Further north the road starts to climb. Ahead of it the traveller sees looming towards him the prodigious 14,979-foot-high relic of the exploded volcanic cone of Meru, on whose fertile slopes, watered by the streams and rainfall of the clouds which caress the shattered summit, lies the pleasant little town of Arusha. This is the real hunting capital of the world for the organised commerce of shooting animals. With Tanganyika possessing the most varied and numerous concentration of game still surviving in Africa, it is a magnet for predatory individuals from many distant nations. Arusha is the base from which they commence their forays into the adjoining areas of the Masai Steppe, the great plains where the Selenget (or Serengeti) section of the Masai still wander, and down further south to Singida and Tabora where that prince of game conservationists, the tsetse fly, has prevented man from settling, and thus preserved the wilderness for the animals.

At Arusha, George and his client booked in to Ray Ulyatt's Arusha Hotel and busied themselves, like so many others of their kind, in arranging their coming safari, in hiring an extra truck to carry petrol and water for them, and securing provisions. George also had the pleasure of meeting Philip Teare, the game warden of Tanganyika, whose headquarters were then at Arusha. They enjoyed a pleasant afternoon's discussion while the client was enjoying a post-lunch nap. The American, really, was quite an astonishing character.

" He looks," said Philip Teare, " as though at his age he should be more concerned with the comfort of his slippers and the late delivery of his evening paper. And yet his head seems stuffed with small-boy nonsense about telescopic sights, gadgets, and the virtues of different rifles. How you white hunter fellows digest that sort of thing for so long I really have no idea. Do you like it?"

" No more than you do. The tragedy is that there is so much of interest in Africa to study and observe. If only half the money that is normally squandered on these hunting safaris and phony expeditions organised by film people and others of their kind was put into anything worthwhile, what a difference it would make to this place. At least we might start to understand it."

Teare looked at him.

" If you only knew how I've longed for some wealthy fellow or institution to endow a thorough research on game," he said. " Just imagine, if one of the Lupa diggers would strike it rich and bequeath his fortune to a university in Tanganyika with the finest chair in zoology in the world, as befits a country with such an astonishing concentration of animals."

George sniffed.

"If any of them do make a fortune, they'll probably leave it to a barman or a dancing girl, or die without a will and have the fortune claimed by some old dears running a cats' home in Wapping."

Teare nodded.

"You know, I've always wished I could have you in the game department. We could do with you on elephant study and control, but what could I offer you? With this blasted depression on we are even forced to retrench good men like Sherwood-Kelly in Mbeya. There is just no money left in the country. But it cannot last for ever. Would you be interested in joining us some day?"

"I am a farmer now," George reminded him. "The only reason I'm crawling around the country with this chap is that, to be quite candid, I haven't earned any money for nearly five years. It's just been expenditure. I've enough to last until my crops are ready, but unless prices improve I'll simply go bankrupt and clear out. If prices do improve, then I suppose I'll be a successful farmer. I certainly won't waste my life as a hired help for pot-shotters."

Teare laughed.

"Anyway, remember us. We like to think that we are doing something of value for this Cinderella of a country. We may not get much money or recognition for what we do but none of us feels that we are wasting our time. We happen to love this country and its wild life." He paused a moment. "I am glad you are taking your client out to the Serengeti," he added. "You'll see one of the real natural wonders of the world. And unless we guard it properly, it can be lost to mankind, simply by being wasted into a few farm lands for a handful of European settlers, as a grazing ground for a parcel of nomadic Masai and their scrub cattle who would be much better off somewhere else, or just ruined by parasitic hunting parties. Have a good look at it and see what you think. I'll be interested to hear your opinion."

George left with his client the next day. They retraced their steps for the first sixty miles on the road up which they had come and then branched off westwards along a track which led them into a landscape, not only justifying Philip Teare's description of it as a natural wonder of this earth, but, in its very strangeness and eerie mystery, a place so out of this world as to make one think that by some monstrous trick of fate a wrong turning on the road has led by magic into another planet. This, in fact, is the landscape one would half expect to find beneath the cloud cover of Venus.

At first the track made its way into a forest of remarkable lushness which lay around the shores, and particularly on the western side, of a lake known as Manyara. The lake is just a shallow surface accumulation of rain-water caught on the floor of the Rift Valley and heavily impregnated with soda from the adjoining volcanic craters and cones. The place is baked in heat, with a nightmare quality to its beach where soda and the moulted feathers of countless birds provide a deceptively thin white layer over an evil black slime of mud. Flamingoes in prodigious quantities frequent the place, while the green forest on its shores has always been full of game—zebra, buffalo, elephant and rhino. In a final curious enchantment, these animals are often duplicated in the mirages which may be seen shimmering over the water, and are a famous feature of the place.

Immediately beyond the lake, the track climbed steeply up the wall of the Rift Valley. Just beyond the top, on the high point known as *Kilima ya Tembo* or The Hill of the Elephants, the travellers stopped to make their evening camp. It was from there, just before sunset at the end of a beautifully clear day, that they saw in the distance, over one hundred miles away, the snow-covered dome of Kilimanjaro. Even the client was interested. In all the world there is no scene more dream-like than this almost god-like mountain looming up over the African landscape with a brooding contradictory atmosphere, at once utterly remote and overpoweringly dominant. At Arusha, George had suggested that they drive twenty miles along the Moshi road in order to catch a glimpse of the mountain from the other side of the obscuring bulk of Meru. But through some quirk in his nature the client would never agree to the expenditure of even ten shillings in petrol for anything not strictly on his planned itinerary. He was not so much mean, as very systematic in his accountancy and rigidly set in routine.

The next day the travellers went on to reach the great cluster of volcanic blow holes and cones which provide this landscape with its most remarkable feature. In the centre of them all is the gigantic *Ngorongoro* or Crater, a scene so stunning that even without its animal population it would be one of the most awe-inspiring sights of the world. From a luxuriant forest growing on its rim, the visitor looks 2,000 feet down into what was once an enormous volcanic blow-hole. The trapdoor of this entrance to the earth's core has now been closed. The flat surface floor is covered with grass, with a dry *Magadi* or Soda Lake in the centre, a handsome grove of fever trees, and one pleasant little lakelet where a laze of hippos have found a sanctuary for themselves. Beyond these features there are antelope, wildebeeste, zebra, Grant's and Thomson's gazelle, eland, and kongoni, to the total of about 15,000 assorted animals who, finding their way originally by chance down some precarious crater rim path, discovered the place to be a paradise, and have remained there with little desire to ever make their way out.

Elephant and rhino frequent the forest on the crater summit, while all around may be seen the companion volcanoes, *Oldeani*, with the bamboo-covered summit which has given it the name, the gigantic pile of *Loolma-*

lasin, and that ancient and most perfect crater of especial enchantment, *Ela Nairobi,* The Place of Coldness, whose purple lake, Lake Embagayi, in a setting of silent forest, is the home for so many thousands of flamingoes, both greater and lesser, that from a distance it seems as though some wounded warrior god rested there and the vivid scarlet of his blood still stains the waters.

Both George and his client had a day of absorbing interest in this wonderland. The client was especially busy in taking notes of the game varieties he had seen. That evening he discussed the coming journey with George.

" I've listed all the animals I've seen here which I've still to shoot," he said, producing his notebook. " I reckon my licence is only about a third through. There's plenty of good hunting ahead, and remember, I want to shoot two lions and two leopards myself. I want the skins for home and I don't want to have to bluff my friends about who shot them. O.K.? "

George nodded.

"And another thing," added the client, with a touch of suspicion in his voice, " you didn't tell me that baboons were on the open list."

" I didn't think that you would be interested."

" Why, sure I am. They make terrific practice with a ·22 rifle. I just love to see them jump every time I hit them. It's funnier than a slapstick movie. You must have a wonderful life living right here. Boy, do I envy you. You could shoot all day; birds, monkeys and things. Never a dull moment, hey? "

George looked at him. A two months' hunt was definitely far worse than a one month's hunt when it came to being friendly with the client. Please God that the coffee price would rise in time for his first crop and he could leave the hunting business to those individuals who had nothing better to do with their time.

The next day the party went on to the Serengeti, down Olbalbal, past Whispering Sands, where the dunes make a sighing noise in the wind, and then off across the vast and spacious flatness of the plains.

The client was in his element. Shooting was easy. With an estimated antelope population of one million animals, it was very difficult to miss. Lions were so numerous that when the client wanted to photograph a pride, George lured thirty-six of them into close focus, simply by using a few hunks of zebra meat as a bait.

Securing the two lion-skin trophies was also easy. On the open plains any animal was a sitting target. The two leopards, however, appeared more reluctant to oblige the client. Quite a considerable amount of hunting was necessary before they found one animal incautiously stretched out along the bough of a tree and offering an easy target. The client had his wish and fired. The startled leopard was wounded, but it managed to claw its way down the tree-trunk. It vanished in the thick waist-high scrub. George cursed. A wounded leopard is no plaything. He waved the client back. With the two trackers he moved carefully towards the place where the leopard had disappeared.

There was no need to search for the animal. With a rumbling snarl it hurtled out of its cover and was on to one of the trackers, springing straight at his face, and raking his body with the ruthless power of its back legs. The unfortunate tracker was completely disembowelled. George shot the leopard through the head. It died on top of its victim, the two bodies seeming to be locked in a dreadful embrace from which it was a very dismal process to separate them.

George and the second tracker looked down at the mess in horror. Even the client was out-of-sorts at the very suddenness of the tragedy. Almost involuntarily he managed to take a few photographs of the scene. George and the tracker watched him in silence. Thoughts among the three men were very conflicting. After a little while the rest of the party came up. Their arrival relieved the tension slightly. The dead tracker was rolled up in a pair of blankets. The client, with some concern, watched the leopard being skinned. He remarked that it was a pity that the head had been so damaged by the closeness of the shot. They went back to the camp and he and George spent an evening being awkward with each other.

CHAPTER EIGHTEEN

THE PLANTER'S LIFE

THE hunt ended on schedule at Engaruka. The client considered that he had had his money's worth. He even talked wistfully, in fact, of extending the safari for a second helping but George received the proposal coldly. For two months he had fulfilled his contract to the letter and wanted no more. He rounded up the safari by taking the client down from the plains back into the Great Rift Valley at the place where Lake Natron lies in a stark landscape of lava, with the still surface of its waters crystallised as though covered by pink and scarlet ice from the heavy impregnation of carbonate of soda and saltpetre. In this strange lake there live nearly 200,000 flamingoes, while looming over them is the menacing black shape of the volcanic cone of *Oldonyo Lengayi,* the Mountain of God, from whose crater a wisp of smoke speaks of fires raging far below.

George wished his client a hunter's farewell and they separated at Arusha. It was nice to have it all over and be heading for home. He was longing to see how the coffee looked, and the welcome he received from the family made the absence seem quite worthwhile. They were all well and it was certainly a very sunburnt and jolly company of Rushbys who celebrated his return with a special dinner and a close hearing to a detailed account of his travels and adventures. At the end of it all, he gave them some special news.

" We can't go on like this. You people never get off the farm. We'll simply have to buy a car."

The family seemd to erupt like Oldonyo Lengayi.

" Get a car, daddy?" asked little Ann, jumping in her chair until her plaits bounced.

" Get a car, daddy!" echoed little George, with his brown eyes sparkling.

" Get a car, George?" enquired Eleanor, looking very startled. " However can we afford one?"

" Well," said George, " I earned £200 from the client. He even wanted to tip me a couple of pounds. Somebody must have told him that white hunters expect tips if they have been polite. I told him to add it to the compensation for the tracker's wife. Anyway, it was while I was on the way back from the safari that I heard that a car is to be sold in two days' time at Tukuyu court. It's a deceased estate or bankruptcy or something. Anyway, it will probably go cheap and," he paused importantly, " it's an A.C."

This didn't mean much to the family, so he explained that an A.C. was considered to be a first cousin to a Rolls Royce. What such a vehicle was doing roughing it in the backblocks was uncertain. Eleanor wondered whether it might not have been there on some variety of remittance.

" It may have been a dud and the manufacturers paid to get it out of the country," she suggested in some alarm. " The same sort of thing that sent a few of our neighbours out here."

George wouldn't hear of any criticism. He went off on the following day to attend the sale and the family spent thirty-six hours listening for the sound of an approaching motor-car. Eventually, towards evening on the second day, they were rewarded with what appeared to be the roar of an aeroplane. They all ran outside in time to view the A.C. battling its way up the steep hill to the farmhouse, with a long plume of steam waving gaily above the radiator.

George was absolutely beaming. He displayed the points of his purchase with pride. It was really a very elegant-looking car, albeit slightly worn, with a radiator leaking like a sieve, the exhaust pipe broken off, the tyres worn down to the canvas, and no windscreen. George had bought it for £5. He didn't like to admit that he could have had it for less, but he had started off the bidding at that figure as a joke, only to find that nobody else was prepared to increase it.

"Anyway," he said, " it brought me home without any trouble. I'll find a second-hand engine for it, and a new radiator, and it will be fine."

The next day he took the family for a drive along the road while Eleanor carried a shot-gun on her lap so that they could shoot a guinea-fowl for supper. The A.C. managed grandly until they had to turn for home. Then it simply petered out and left them to walk, with George carrying both children and Eleanor trooping along behind with the shot-gun, just as though it was a hill-billy wedding procession. Even the A.C. must have had a giggle about the spectacle. When George returned with some of his labourers to push the vehicle, it simply started up with a roar on the first touch of the button, and made its way home literally under its own steam.

At Christmas time George was still tinkering with the vehicle. It was quite a relief when the Moltenos arrived for the Christmas season, with their arms full of presents for the children, together with chocolates and beer for the parents and an entertaining mass of gossip and news about the Lupa and its people. It had been a good year on the diggings, with a new record output of 31,644 ounces of alluvial gold and 1,752 ounces of reef gold. Molteno had established himself there as a gold buyer and digger with reasonable success and he was very confident of the future. Compared to the depression in the rest of Tanganyika, the Lupa was certainly a bright spot.

While the two women busied themselves in making good things for the festive season, George and Molteno went down to the salt springs at Ivuna in order to shoot some guinea fowl and perhaps a wild goose for Christmas dinner. It was an amiable arrangement, as everybody had specialised things to talk about. The two wives were both expecting babies and somewhat absorbed in the details, while their men were engrossed with the problems and possibilities of making anything worthwhile of their lives in Tanganyika.

The actual Christmas dinner, however, proved a fiasco. The men failed to return until the evening of Boxing Day, when they trudged wearily in and faced two irate wives who were certain that they must have been caught up somwhere in a diggers' party. What had actually caught them was mud. Molteno's Baby Austin had its limits when the going became really slithery. It tended to subside in the muck with the sigh of a rhino sinking in its mud-bath, and remain there for a period of contemplation. To add to the general mortification, their bag of game birds had turned high in the bogged car over Christmas and they could practically consume them by taking a deep breath. The only reason they had clung to the birds was to prove to the wives that they had, in fact, gone on a hunt.

Festivities were postponed until New Year's Day, when Eleanor also expected to have her sister for company, Marjorie braving the air journey up from Cape Town in order to spend a holiday on the farm. The air trip was actually much improved since Eleanor's experience. The Hercules-type aircraft had gone to the scrap heap in March 1933. Their departure had not been regretted. Any relationship they might have had to the strong man of that name was definitely to the phase of his life when, like Samson, he was shorn of his locks. Their successors, high-wing four-engined monoplanes of the Atalanta class, were a considerable improvement in speed and comfort.

Whether Marjorie enjoyed her holiday was a point which George and Eleanor discussed for some time after her departure. She arrived just in time to see Eleanor taken off to the Mbeya Hospital with a dose of pernicious vomiting. This postponed the projected New Year's Day celebrations for an indefinite period and left her alone on the farm to look after the children. George had planned to return from Mbeya as soon as possible, but a diggers' New Year party in the Sluice Box detained him for the night.

When he returned to the farm the next morning he found Marjorie just recovering from a rough night. Little Ann had been reasonably co-operative, but little George was what she described shortly as "a really wild child." On top of these troubles, with the children at last asleep, she had gone out with a sigh of relief at midnight to visit the earth-pit convenience, carrying a hurricane lamp and some newspapers to brush around the seat in order to chase away spiders. She looked at George rather stonily when she informed him of this. He remembered belatedly that he had forgotten to warn her that Joseph, the Masai donkey, slept in the convenience at night.

It must have been rather a shock for Marjorie. She had arrived expecting to see lions around every corner. She was still looking tense when George drove her in to Mbeya to catch her return plane ten days later. He wondered if she had become constipated. To complicate the journey, it was pouring with rain. The A.C. still had no windshield or side flaps and the radiator was stuffed with a piece of cloth which blew out every time steam built up pressure. Notwithstanding its aeroplane-like roar, the conveyance also had to rely on manpower prudently stationed by George at all steep slopes, and it only completed the journey after the consumption of numerous spare four-gallon tins of water kept on the back seat. Eleanor saw her sister off from the airport with the fond hope that she would soon return again. Marjorie simply nodded.

George returned to the farm determined to do something about the convenience and the A.C. For the latter he had recently bought a second-hand Chevrolet engine which was reputed as still containing some life. Providing that he could fit it into the A.C. it might have a rejuvenating effect. So far as the convenience was concerned he would either have to eject the donkey or advise guests to regularity of habits in daylight hours. Both solutions would require delicate handling, and he had problems enough at the moment.

The rainy season was more than well under way, with a succession of violent downpours and hailstorms which seemed sent by some malevolent sprite to strip the coffee bushes of their first berries. To add to these losses there was a sudden plague of snails, and nobody seemed to know what to do about them apart from tediously picking them off by hand and crushing them underfoot. The wretched things made a point of ring-barking all the best bearing little coffee bushes, and this was heart-breaking. It meant that the bushes had to be cut right back to allow them to grow again. The Africans had also lost their bean crops to the same pests, while locusts had consumed their maize. There was not much cheer for anybody in the first months of 1935.

"The only negative consolation," George remarked bitterly to Eleanor, "is that if prices for coffee remain where they are, the snails might as well have the berries. In fact, if the pests realised just how cheap coffee was, they'd probably turn their attention to eating something else. Every planter is in the same mess. If I want to do any picking this year I'll have to go to the expense of building a curing shed, with trays of wire and calico to hold the beans. The point is, is it worth it?"

Like most of the others, he continued work simply because he couldn't bring himself to think of giving up. There was just nothing else to do. The Hicky-Woods had been fortunate. They had found a deposit of bat guano in a cave in the hills and this gave them a profitable sideline in selling fertiliser; but no others had made so fortunate a discovery. George found himself thinking more and more of the Lupa, but the farm now seemed as much a part of him as the children. Simply abandoning all his work would be a serious personal defeat. On top of it, Eleanor's third baby was due in August and George's mother had written expressing her determination to fly out from England and be with them for the event. He could hardly move them all out to the noisy life on the diggings. The old lady would have a seizure on the spot if she even walked into Meyer's new Queen's Hotel, just built in Mbeya, and read the large sign painted up in the bar as competition to the famous notice in Menzies' establishment about guests going to bed with their boots on. The rival sign advertised:

Diggers welcome, boots and all. Accommodation eight shillings a night.

As it was, the old lady would have to accustom herself to quite a few changes from English village life. Eleanor was trying to spring-clean the place in her honour, but it would still seem pretty rough. Also, he would definitely have to get the donkey away from the convenience, and little George would have to be hammered out of a disgusting habit he had picked up from visiting diggers, of spitting on the floor with an accuracy which spoke of practice, like good shooting.

The visitor from England arrived in some style on the 17th of June. The district commissioner's car brought her out to the farm, as the A.C. was indisposed. Eleanor viewed her arrival with diffidence, conscious that she must look something like a circus tent, while her mother-in-law was smartly finished in well-set tinted hair, an ankle-length afternoon frock and some very good rings. She had obviously been quite a killer in her young days.

George watched the two women embrace and silently prayed that they would get on all right. Actually, apart from very minor skirmishing, the two managed most agreeably. The donkey had been put out to distant grazing; he was, in any case, too bone lazy to be much good as a riding animal for the children, and the house really was looking its best, to the owner's eyes at least.

Mother, of course, inevitably found many things strange which they accepted as normal. She had come out expecting to make herself useful in the kitchen, but the current cook, a rugged-looking character of very distant Somali descent named Alfani, who affected a grimy turban and brass earrings, made her feel distinctly unwelcome in his domain. What little she was allowed to see of the place, in fact, put her off her food. Not that the kitchen was dirty. Primitive Africans simply worked to different standards. On the second day of her visit she discovered the house servant scrubbing the box lavatory seat with a brush dipped into Eleanor's best saucepan. From then on she did little other than peck at her food, and the consequences were remarkable. When the time came for her return to England in the middle of August, the smart frock she had worn on her arrival dragged on the floor. She had lost at least a stone from her dieting and did not seem quite as pleased about the matter as most women would be.

By that time, of course, Eleanor had also lost weight. Her third baby was born in the Mbeya hospital on the 30th of July. It was a girl, a cuddly little thing with golden-syrup-coloured hair. They named her Margery Kate and her advent was remarkable only for the fact that she came unexpectedly early, just before dawn on a windy morning, and in the general tither of Eleanor waking the nurse, and the nurse sending for the doctor, a black cat contrived to sneak into the room and produce kittens under the confinement bed. This annoyed the doctor, but gave everybody else the hope that it was an omen of good luck.

Good luck was certainly something which George felt he needed. He just did not know what to do. He had always looked forward to 1935 as the year of his first crop and the real start of his fortune as a planter. He had worked costs out carefully with his neighbours and their figures agreed with his own. They had to allow for the fact that they were four hundred miles from the railway, that road motor transport was highly expensive, and even when the coffee reached the railhead, there was no local marketing organisation in Tanganyika. The individual farmer had to ship his coffee all the way to Europe in order to find a sale. With all these expenses added to normal farming hazards, coffee would have to fetch at least £90 a ton to even pay to grow it. When he had started planting, coffee prices had been around £115 a ton. In 1935 the ruling price was around £50 a ton and there seemed no sign of any increase.

Talking things over with other planters made George even more depressed. They had all been such a cheerful, happy, slightly sun-touched crowd, that it was miserable hearing them talk of bankruptcy, of offering their farms for sale at pathetically low prices, of trying to find employment, or going off to the Lupa. Rope Soles had already taken on a job as a road-maker, while his brother-in-law, Max Coster, was planning to return to his profession as a geologist. The Hickson-Woods were also on the verge of departure. These would be the last of their once happy neighbours. The same dismal story was being told of all the other settlement areas in the Southern Highlands. Whether it was in the Mbozi area, at Mbeya, or Sao Hill near Iringa, all that was to be seen of the once optimistic little settlements was a melancholy wreck.

It was hard even to be cheerful as George and Eleanor drove back to the farm after seeing his mother off. They both loved the farm and every disadvantage of isolation and improvisation could be accepted with humour by them, if not by their guests, providing that the justification was a worthwhile future. Remembering the warnings of Eleanor's father was not entirely relevant to their present difficulties. Borer beetles, snails and hailstorms apart, the general economic mess in the outside world had simply destroyed the whole economic foundation of coffee-growing. The problem was what to do about it.

"The thing is," George told Eleanor above the roar of the A.C., "that we may not be entirely broke yet, but is there any sense in just waiting here until our cheques start to bounce? If we are going to be forced to start something else, we had better do it while we still have some money left."

They had tried to thrash this question out on a number of occasions and never reached a conclusion. The wishful hope that conditions would improve always effectively stilted their reasoning. Or something provided them with the excuse to postpone the decision for a later time. The A.C., in fact, obligingly broke down at this stage, but they continued the discussion while George tinkered with the engine.

"Well, what shall we do?" asked Eleanor.

"Get a new connecting hose for this blasted radiator, that will at least get us home."

George had mounted a truck radiator in the front end of the A.C., hoping this replacement might eliminate the steaming troubles. It looked something like an oversize patch on a pirate's eye, but it certainly did keep the engine cooler. What was gained in steam, however, was lost in leaks at the connecting points.

"I'll really have to go to the Lupa," George added from the depths of the engine. "You know, I haven't earned a sixpence for the past six years other than £300 from the hunting safaris. We just cannot go on like this, and there's a great boom developing on the Lupa. Some chap by the name of Gerry de Jager has found a way of recovering alluvial gold without the aid of water. It's a machine called a dry blower. Quite a revolutionary idea on a diggings."

Eleanor had to admit that the Lupa diggers were the only people who seemed to have any money. Whenever there was any noise in the Sluice Box it always emanated from some diggers' party. A sure sign of a settler was a certain nimbleness of step and slimness of figure which came from dodging pursuing creditors.

But life was so pleasant on the farm, and really they lived there so cheaply. Their vegetable garden was flourishing, and there was plenty of milk and fruit. As for meat, when George overcame his own distaste he could always go out and shoot a nice fat bushbuck or other antelope. And there were so many pleasant little habits and conventions they had devised around their lives. She sighed.

" The longer one stays in a place, the more it grows around you," she said wistfully. " Personally, I don't ever want to leave. Let's at least try another season. You never know what might happen. We'd feel foolish if we gave up now, and coffee rose sharply in price because of this trouble in Abyssinia with the Italians. Maybe the Nazis in Germany might do something useful for the world, like taking to drinking coffee instead of beer. Our good blend might make even Mr Hitler sound less hysterical and more contemplative."

George sniffed, but it was easy to persuade him to do something which he wanted to do.

" We'll try it until the beginning of next year," he agreed. " But that will definitely be the limit."

Oddly enough, having such a sword of Damocles suspended over their heads on the slender thread of economics gave the following months on the farm a peculiarly poignant atmosphere. It was almost as though a balmy autumn was trying its best to stave off winter from overwhelming what had been a wonderful summer. In some way, all the pleasant habits of their lives came into sharper focus simply because these things were in such danger of being lost. The particular charms of their land, and the spaciousness of its views. The friendliness of their home, and the pleasant relations with their workers. The clatter and chatter of the house servants, and the amiable habit of the old gardener who, each morning before breakfast in the fruit season, came to the house with two large leaves from a wild fig tree, pinned into cones with a thorn and filled with luscious-looking wineberries, to be presented to the children who waited eagerly for the daily ceremony.

It was an exceptionally dry winter. The rains only came in the middle of November, and when they did come they started with a bang. A violent succession of thunderstorms swept through the hills, with hail falling thick and fast, and the children dancing and yelping with excitement, slipping out to get wet in the showers and play with the globules of ice under the eaves every time Eleanor took her eyes off them and half-cried as she wondered what was happening to the tiny coffee berries.

By December the countryside was almost unbelievably green and lovely, with the rain still pelting down in such tropical storms as few of the local residents could ever remember from their past. The roads were turned into muddy bogs with odd vehicles sunk down below their axles, and simply abandoned by their owners until sunnier days would allow them to be rescued from their plight.

The A.C. was among the vehicles to stick fast by the way. George had waited some weeks for an opportunity to drive in to Mbeya to attend to business and Christmas shopping. When the weather eventually seemed to lift he took little Ann off with him on her first journey to town without her mother. She looked in a blissful state as she drove off, dressed in a new blue frock with her tiny plaits tied with matching blue ribbons, and importantly clutching a little basket containing her lunch of sandwiches and half a bottle of milk. At mid-day a veritable cloud-burst occurred in the hills. The water-courses flooded with tremendous torrents, with a full-scale cascade suddenly materialising only thirty yards from the farmhouse, and George and Ann forced to tramp home looking very wet, muddy and bedraggled, while the A.C. remained in a mud-bath until the new year.

With the roads in such a state, it was understandable that most people had a quiet Christmas, with everybody staying in their own homes. In any case, there were no longer any neighbours, and visitors were a rarity. When two diggers from the Lupa did call in just before the holidays, the children found the novelty of a visit so great that they practically stared the men out of countenance and Ann eventually routed one of them by loudly remarking that she could see wax in his ears.

For Christmas, George had the farmhouse whitewashed throughout, so that it looked beautifully cool and fresh inside. The children selected a young cypress as a Christmas tree and decorated it with weird and wonderful paper figures, while George made himself a revolting set of false teeth out of plasticine, and a moustache and beard of paper straw from a chocolate box, so that he could look like a rather decrepit version of a particularly senile Santa Claus.

There was a nice mailbag of presents for everybody from the various relatives, with home-made Christmas pudding and cake from England, toys, crackers and candles from Cape Town, while Tanganyika partridges were shot by George on the farm to provide a more tasty meal than the plumpest turkey of Europe.

It all went splendidly. The only disappointment was for little Ann. Her favourite doll, Barbara, was bedridden with a broken head which had been pieced together a few times too often and had finally come unstuck. Eleanor staved off any tears by promising to write to Cape Town immediately for a new head to arrive by air in time for Ann's birthday in February. The party proceeded to a lively finish when George killed a large black snake in the bathroom, and Eleanor developed toothache which kept her awake all night, and made her aware for the first time that George's own worries about the future had effectively prevented him from enjoying a good sleep for some time.

Lying in bed thinking of troubles is always a futile way of trying to sleep. It is better to be up and doing something than simply indulging in depressing mental rumination, regurgitating old thoughts about what might have been, and why one's hopes have been broken.

" It's just been what the Africans call *kazi buri* (wasted effort)," George said, " and now the snails look as though they are coming back with the wet weather to eat what the floods have left. The greybeards in the village have some tale that there is a curse on this country lingering on from some ancient time. Everything anyone starts in it always seems to go wrong, no matter how bold the beginning."

He tossed about restlessly in his bed.

" Perhaps it's because everybody has tried to do something against the natural grain of the place," Eleanor said. " I suppose we've tried to do that as well. I suppose that is why so many settlers in new lands do go broke. They try to fight nature and lose. They break their hearts wondering what went wrong, and all the time the real key is not to struggle against such self-appointed odds, but rather to do something in harmony with the world around us. Perhaps its because we try to graft new crops and livestock on an unnatural base that we all make the same mistake. Anyway, I don't believe in such childish things as curses. That would be too unjust on such a lovely land. I don't believe Nature is unjust. It is completely impartial. We usually make things difficult for ourselves by being stubborn or foolish or ignorant. Our vanity makes us expect Nature or God to help us when there is not the slightest reason why we should be entitled to anything at all apart from what is our natural birthright, a chance to live and do a worth-while work in so wonderful a world."

George listened to her in the dark. For some reason he was reminded of Hill 60 and Durban beach, with Green's voice and the background of the music and the sea. He had almost reached the bottom of hope then, living with that crowd of unfortunates and tramps. Being young and on his own had not made it quite so bad. Now he had a family who would go down with him if he allowed himself to sink. There could be no Hill 60 for them. He would have to start again from very close to the bottom. He would have to find a new way of living. The only consolation for the wastage of the past few years was that they had certainly been pleasant. He could not find it in him to regret a moment of them. If destiny had, in fact, any use for him and was trying to guide him from some false start, then he prayed that at least the God of Africa would make it a worthwhile task, for he would be a very willing worker.

CHAPTER NINETEEN

THE RIVER OF GOLD

GEORGE remained on the farm until little Ann's birthday on the 8th February 1936. It was useless lingering on after that, hoping for a change in the economics of the whole world simply because his own finances were nearly bankrupt. Even remaining until the birthday was a concession to sentiment and his own reluctance to abandon a way of life to which he had become so pleasantly attached.

The actual birthday was not quite the gay occasion for which he had hoped. The previous day was mail day and he sent a runner for the post, hoping that the bag would include a parcel from Eleanor's father, who had promised to obtain a replacement head for the broken doll. The runner left for Mbeya at dawn but, as it was a very wet day, he did not return until well after dark, when the children were fast asleep. Eleanor and George sat up waiting, hardly expecting the man to come at all, for the overcast sky made the night especially black. The tropical darkness outside seemed to press thickly against the trellis-work enclosing the veranda, spilling inside whenever the faltering light of their lamp allowed it. The little circle of light, in its way, was symbolic of their own state. So long as the paraffin lasted, the lamp could hold the night at bay. If it failed, the darkness would envelope them, and it seemed a lonely night, full of the insistent drone of the circadas, and no other sound save the occasional plaintive cry of a bush-baby.

The postman came in with a sudden bustle and a flash of the white of his teeth in the light. George took him into the kitchen for something hot to drink, while Eleanor opened the mailbag on the table next to the lamp. The parcel containing the new head for the doll was squashed flat. She shed a few tears over that broken little toy, and even George's heart sank when he came in and found it battered beyond repair. It was a small matter, really; there were other toys in the same mailbag which had survived the usual hammering of the post. The only thing was that the doll's head had been so keenly anticipated. When it arrived broken, it reminded them of all their hopes in the past that the same mailbag would bring them good news of a rise in the coffee price, and the disappointment they had so often felt but never mentioned to each other.

They went to bed feeling very miserable. Curiously enough, it was Ann who aroused them and cheered them up. She woke early the next morning and began to open her parcels. Almost immediately she said:

" But mummy, didn't Barbara's new head come?"

So they had to show her the fragments. She didn't cry. She simply lifted the glass eyes in her hand and said, in a tight little voice,

" Oh, poor Barbara."

George saved the situation by saying, with a forced cheerfulness,

" Come on, Ann, get up and let's play your new records."

So they had music and sweets before breakfast, and later Eleanor removed the doll's faded old blonde wig and gummed on the glossy new brown one. Ann seemed quite satisfied, so the day ended better than they could have expected. The simple resignation of the child in the face of disappointment was actually something of a tonic. Life was certainly not lost. They were at least better off then a few other unfortunate settlers who had gone completely bankrupt. They still had enough money to keep themselves in food, the house was snug, the servants were faithful, and Eleanor would be perfectly safe there even if George left her alone and went off in search of work.

That night they had one final discussion about their future. They found that they could regard their problems with greater composure. George would have to go to the Lupa. He would have a look around, see John Molteno and some of his old friends, and try to find a claim. If he pegged anything worthwhile, he would put up a wattle and daub shack, and then Eleanor could join him with the children.

George left in the A.C. two mornings later. Eleanor listened to the roar of his departure until the sound dwindled into the sigh of the wind in the hills. She was left wondering how long it would be before she would be able to run outside at the noise of his return. At least, she thought with a smile, there could never be any surprise about George's return. The A.C. would betray his approach from several miles away. In the days that followed she always had one ear hopefully tuned for that welcome medley of splutters and bangs.

Of course, when he did come she was not only unprepared but horribly embarrassed. At 2 a.m. on the last Saturday in March she woke up to the sound of someone whispering her name. She started up in bed, still half asleep, and flashed on a torch. There was George at the window. He was thin and unshaven and the tiredest-looking man she had ever seen. He was staring at her as though she was a ghost. She realised that she must certainly look like one. While he was away she had read a silly piece entitled " Are You the Girl He Married?" in a woman's magazine. A cursory inspection in a mirror had decided her she wasn't. The article recommended certain exercises to restore a figure and investment in some proprietary concoction of pink-coloured mud to be daubed over the face at night in order to counteract dry skin, wrinkles, and the hint of a shadow on the upper lip.

" It is me," she said reassuringly, if ungrammatically.

" Oh! Well, let me in and get me something to eat. You can take off what you have on your face later on." He smiled in the dim light. " I suppose that you can get it off? Or have you lost the directions?"

He gave her a rather cautious kiss when she opened the door. Then she went off to the kitchen while he lit a lamp and slumped into a chair. She had hardly any ready food in the house. She had even given the remaining milk to the dog before she had gone to bed. All he could have was the heel of a loaf, a tin of bully-beef, and a box of crustless cheese washed down by what seemed like dozens of cups of black tea. He was too hungry, however, to have any aversions as to what he ate. While he fed, she sat at the table and told him about such events as had occurred during his absence.

There was really not much to tell. At least, however, by talking she managed to contain her impatience to hear what had happened to him. The days of his absence had passed very quickly. Most of the time it had simply rained. The farm was already half-overgrown with weeds. George had been forced to pay off most of the labourers before he left and Nature soon reclaims its own in tropical countries, if man relaxes his efforts at cultivation. The road to the place would soon be impassable unless something was done to it quickly. The only visitors to the farm had been assorted troops of monkeys who, seeming to sense the absence of any disciplinarian on the premises, came and played the fool with impunity all around the house. They pulled faces through the windows at the children and raided the maize *shamba*, with Eleanor not having the heart to do anything other than fire an occasional shot over their heads, which hardly worried them.

A couple of snakes of the *boomslang* variety had also made the most of George's absence by taking up residence in the roof. They had come to grief, however, when they tumbled through the flimsy reed ceiling and practically landed on Eleanor's head. This was slightly too much and they had to be despatched by the house boy. For the rest, the remaining labourers and servants had been most attentive, trooping in to touch her hand and say " *poli,*

memsahib," or " sorry, madam," when they heard she had been frightened
by the snakes, and at all times being most courteous and kind. The nursemaid, Janey, even insisted on acting as a bodyguard by spending each night
sleeping on her mats before the fire in the living-room. She was lying there
now, a few inches from George's chair, snoring gently all through proceedings
and not aware of her master's homecoming until she awoke in the morning.

With his last cup of black tea, George started his own story. It was very
eventful. He had left the farm taking with him for company Kiyanda, one
of his workmen. They had reached the goldfields safely and the first thing
George had heard was that there had been a new find of gold near the capital
of the chief of the Fipa country, a place with the outlandish name of
Sumbawanga (Abandon your Witchcraft). There was a considerable amount
of talk about this discovery. It had been found by a Belgian and rumour
made it extremely rich.

George discussed the matter with Molteno. That individual was by then
one of the biggest men on the Lupa in more ways than just his height. His
numerous enterprises in mining, prospecting and gold buying made him the
fount of a very considerable activity. He was always interested in new finds
and opportunities and financed, with varying success, quite a few searches
for supposed El Dorados. He and George soon came to an agreement.
Molteno would supply porters, prospecting tools and supplies. If George
found anything worthwhile he would peg claims in both their names.

The trouble, of course, was the rains. The countryside was largely under
water and all roads were closed. A wise man stayed at home in such conditions. Gold-seekers, however, have seldom been notably wise. If they were,
in fact, there would be precious few discoveries made. George was aware of
what he would be attempting, but the mud seemed to offer a chance of a
good head start on any other Lupa prospectors who might be waiting
for dry weather before they attempted the journey.

The whole thing turned into a real nightmare of a trip. Four of the sixteen porters deserted on the second day out. Five others went down with
malaria. They waded through water for a good part of the journey up the
Rukwa Valley. Rough pole rafts took them across swollen rivers. Rations
were scarce and they lived on rice and ground-nut oil. The only consoling
thought for George was what a marvellous holiday he and the family could
have on dry land if only he had any decent luck.

When they reached Sumbawanga, of course, they found that the strike
was further on at a river known as the Mpanda. And then, when he reached
the place, it was not only a washout, with its Belgian discoverer a very
secretive individual indeed about the site of his find, but there were already
several other Lupa diggers there, including such an unlikely individual as a
perky and erudite little insurance agent named Phillip Fuller whose persist-
ency after gold would cheerfully have carried him twice the distance to

Mpanda through four times the difficulties of flood and wild animals.

The only thing for everybody to do was to go home again. By this time the floods had reduced even the Indian-trading *dukas* to empty shelves through lack of supplies. A couple of mission stations of the White Fathers did treat George to a few dinners on the way, but he arrived back on the Lupa a thinner and wiser man. Altogether it had been a waste of time, and carrying heavy prospecting kit on such a useless round trip of six hundred miles really dripped bitter aloes into any gold-seeker's wounds.

To add to his troubles, George decided to return to the farm for a short rest and to find out the state of his family. Of course, he expected the worst of the road by this time, so really he had no surprises. In alternate patches the road was either under water, the grass in the central ridge head high, or the top surface quite washed away leaving what seemed to be a rocky river bed for the use of traffic. After several preliminary bogs, the A.C. eventually settled down in a morass like a wart-hog in a mud-bath and showed no signs of budging.

They were twenty miles from home with night already near. Kiyanda declined flatly to do the walk, so George left him to sleep in the vehicle and defend it against all-comers by means of a shot-gun. The thought of remaining alone in a lion-infested area obviously disturbed Kiyanda mightily. But as he was even more reluctant to move, there was nothing for it but for him to remain while George set off in search of help.

The twenty-mile walk, actually, went reasonably well. It didn't rain, the moon came out, and the only lions George saw were in one large pride he encountered strolling down the road towards him. He was unarmed, so he avoided them by a detour. The shadowy figures eyed him in the dark, but did not deign to wet their paws by leaving the road for the verges of damp grass. They strolled on down the track. He watched their departure in the direction of the bogged car and imagined that Kiyanda would not have much sleep that night. Then he went on and reached home with no further alarm than the sight of Eleanor's mud-packed face.

The next day George walked back with his farm labourers to retrieve the car. Kiyanda had experienced a rough night. He had kept himself well barricaded in the car. When his rescuers arrived, he simply projected a woebegone face out of one of the windows and complained that " the lions roamed around the car all night, just like cattle waiting to be fed ". There were certainly enough tracks of the big cats in the mud. After the car had been extricated and George had driven it home with Kiyanda, the farm labourers failed to return. The following morning George set out to find them. He met them half-way along the road. They had encountered what appeared to be the same pride of lions which he had seen, and all been treed for the night. They returned home under his escort looking very stiff and jumpy.

George spent two weeks putting the farm into order. Apart from the weeds, it was in a reasonable state and the garden was aglow with the colour of hollyhocks, snapdragons, marigolds and phlox, with roses and carnations all blooming to perfection. The whole place had the appearance rather of an English country cottage than a farmhouse in Africa. The general atmosphere of peace and security allowed him to return to the goldfields confident that the family was safe and content, notwithstanding his absence.

The problem on the goldfields, of course, was to decide what to do, and where. He could always work for some established digger, but such activity was hardly likely to bring him fortune, particularly if he remained honest. Prospecting for a claim of his own was a gamble on luck. However, it offered the chance of success, and the man who complains of failing to win a prize in a lottery has little substance to his wailing if he has neglected to invest in a ticket.

The goldfields along the banks of the Lupa River, in that year, 1936, were at the zenith of their activity. One thousand Europeans and an increasing number of Africans and Asians were busily engaged on the winning of what proved to be the all-time record of gold recovered from the area in any single year, 46,058 ounces of alluvial and 9,969 ounces of reef gold.

The key to this whole climax of activity along the river of gold was undoubtedly Gerry de Jager's invention of the dry blower. It was an appliance at once ingenious and simple which made the Lupa quite unique among all the goldfields of the world. Simply put, it consisted of a motor-driven fan with its forced draught concentrated along a funnel. Well-crushed gold-bearing soil was poured down through this draught, the wind blowing away the lighter earth and allowing the heavier gold to be gathered in a receptacle at the bottom. The success of this device on the Lupa depended on the fact that the local soil was loose while the gold content was extremely coarse.

The basic idea of the dry blower completely released the diggers from dependence on water for the recovery of gold. With its aid men found it possible to work in the most arid portions of what was essentially an area of heat and drought, with the Lupa and its tributaries less often running than reduced to the state of a succession of pools or completely dry watercourses.

A whole variety of developments were effected on Gerry de Jager's basic idea. Diggers are always individualists, and each man was certain that he had a patent improvement. One mining engineer by the name of Andre Moraitinis, managing the African Mineral Company, had whole batteries of dry blowers going with bulldozers, 2,500 Africans and thirty-two Europeans employed on feeding them with the gold-bearing earth. The cloud of dust rising to the heavens from this mass activity would have been enough to give miners' phthisis to the angels.

Single dry blowers constructed from the most ingenious of components could be found scattered throughout the area. They were either noisily at work, or being tinkered-up by some hopeful operator who, covered in grease and dust, with an oversize pith helmet resting on his ears and long shorts cut from worn-out khaki slacks, looked anything but a schoolgirl's dream of romance.

There were reputed to be men of some thirty different nationalities working on the Lupa. In the course of his own fossicking George met most of them. They all had at least one thing in common, hospitality. A man could be down to his last handful of *posho* (maize-meal), but he would still share it with a visitor. Diggers' homes were open to all-comers and some of the consequences of this largesse were certainly evident in the children. A good few families presented so striking a type difference that cuckoos in the nest were very obvious.

The fortune of the diggers was as varied as their origin. Most of them had tales of really tear-jerking bad luck, while others had literally tumbled into what seemed to be veritable jewellers' shops. The very hazard of the diggers' life gave it a peculiar fascination.

Molteno was a particular fund of assorted experiences and not all of them were fortunate. One of his bitterest memories was connected with the finding of Golden Hill. He had found some gold at the foot of the hill, but the discovery had been slight and made at the end of the wet season, with water supplies dwindling and the soil not dry enough for De Jager's machine to be used. He decided to take a short holiday before a new season's work. The claims were safely in his name and he instructed his labourers to simply carry on with fossicking and not attempt to work any gold. A digger named Lennox Stretch, who was recovering from fever, stayed in Molteno's camp in order to care for the place.

One of the fossickers unearthed a handsome nugget in an area just out of Molteno's claims, well up the hill. He took it to Stretch and asked the man to keep it. Stretch showed it to his wife. She talked to friends that evening. By 3 a.m. over one hundred diggers had rushed to the area. The whole of Golden Hill was thoroughly pegged leaving Molteno with only his original claims on the fringe of what became one of the richest fields on the Lupa.

Golden Hill, in its day, rewarded its diggers with some handsome returns. Nuggets weighing up to fifty-two ounces were not uncommon, while one of the diggers, Sandy Kerr, recovered over £7,000 worth of gold in seventy-two days of excited work. Everything depended upon the luck of the location of your claim. Nicolas Lagopoulas, a member of the substantial Greek community, participated in the rush to Golden Hill but had no luck on the place. When he moved, an Indian re-pegged his claims and took over the house. The new owner dug a fresh pit for the earth closet and discovered excellent gold at the bottom of the hole.

Listening to such accounts of the caprice of fate could be both amusing and alarming. Some of the diggers were such born story-tellers that they could have made their mark in life as novelists, for they embroidered their tales most skilfully with humour, pathos and the most extraordinary of misadventures. One of the most outstanding of these raconteurs was a lean, sunbronzed, leather-tough character, always spruce no matter his circumstances, and affecting in that wild part of the world a Captain Kettle beard and the incongruity of a monocle. The monocle was worn because he really needed it. It said much for his physical condition that in so rugged a community he was allowed to wear it. His name was Herbert Faram. With a partner named Jock Edmundson, he had wandered up to the Lupa in 1930 from the Northern Rhodesia copperbelt. On the goldfields they found a batch of diggers busy around the Itewe Itawa, a pair of hills which emerge from the bush with the shape of a well-rounded pair of breasts. These prominences had attracted the attention of diggers for some time, but only recently had any gold been found there.

Bert Faram and his partner pegged claims, prospected for two weeks and then returned to Mbeya to celebrate Christmas. An excuse for celebration was always very welcome to Bert. He was a man with a formidable capacity to enjoy life. After a week in Mbeya, his partner decided to walk to Beira, a couple of thousand miles away. Bert returned to the claim and found that his labourers had produced forty-two ounces of gold. This really started him off as a digger. His wife, Hilda, flew up from Northern Rhodesia to join him and the two remained to be numbered among the greatest characters of Tanganyika. Of all the women George met on the Lupa, Hilda was the ideal of a frontierswoman. Tough, generously proportioned, bighearted, with a mass of beetroot-coloured hair, she was a real human rock on which Bert's often storm-tossed boat of life could tie a painter and come home for shelter.

Meeting all these characters of the goldfields at least provided some evenings' entertainment in an otherwise strenuous life. For most of the hot days George tramped about searching for signs of payable gold, and in this activity a man worked essentially on his own intuition. To expect advice from the amiable companion of the previous night would be absurd, if only from the obvious fact that if anybody knew of the whereabouts of gold he would naturally be working it himself.

Occasionally George managed to visit the farm and see Eleanor. Sometimes, if he was prospecting in the vicinity of the Mbeya range, he would walk across the mountains for a few days at home. At other times some digger would give him a lift along the hair-raising mountain road which had recently been built to connect the goldfields with Mbeya town. Travelling along the road was always a pleasure, not only because it led home, but because of the stunning scenery and the wonderful wild flowers. The road actually climbed to a point 8,050 feet high, the highest altitude reached by any road in Tanganyika, and the change of climate from the heat-prostrated bush of the Lupa to a temperate green watershed on the mountain top was very refreshing. An evergreen forest made the summit a place of delightful shadows, while numerous springs provided water by the roadside to cool steaming radiators and diggers' dusty throats.

Eleanor remained well, with little more disturbance to her rustic life than that provided by one obstreperous leopard which, developing a taste for dogs, made a practice of roaming around the farmhouse at night hoping that one of the canine defenders of the place would be so unwise as to venture out for a bark.

There was also a problem about little Ann. She seemed to be pining. Watching her grow increasingly listless was a depressing business. Eventually Eleanor accepted an invitation from Mrs Pollock, the wife of the district commissioner of Mbeya, to stay in her home in the town for a change and for the opportunity of having the children medically overhauled.

The stay at least confirmed the fears about Ann. Dr Eckhardt, once he could disabuse his head of the prevailing vapours of Nazism in the German community, was an excellent medical man. He stated flatly that Ann would have to leave the tropics until she passed adolescence. Dr Aitken, the Government doctor for the Lupa, also confirmed this opinion when he happened to visit Mbeya. There was just nothing they could do about it. Eleanor travelled up to Tukuyu so that Ann could have a spell of really cool weather and the benefit of the opinion of a third doctor, but this was simply a respite. Trooping around from one doctor to another hoping to hear a more favourable opinion was too much like going to a succession of dentists wanting to be told that you aren't suffering from toothache. Sooner or later the tooth must come out, and obviously little Ann would have to go to a less oppressive climate.

Eleanor returned to the farm in a very dejected mood. There was certainly no joy in the prospect of breaking up the family. Even the news that Laza, the local African hunter, had, in her absence, treated the leopard to a full charge from a muzzle loader of formidable proportions, failed to cheer her. The skin on the living-room floor simply made her feel that another old acquaintance had gone. She was still wandering listlessly about the house that evening when she heard a car arrive outside. It was not the A.C., but nevertheless, when she ran outside with a storm lamp, there was George, beaming cheerfully and presenting her with a hearty kiss, and the offering of a heavy lump of something wrapped up in a knotted handkerchief.

"A present for you at last, my love," he said with a bow, and some attempt at gallantry.

She opened the little bundle on the table. Inside there was a fine nugget of the bright gold of the Lupa. Turning it over in her hand while the lamp-light reflected from it with a glow quite drove away her depression. While

George stoked up the fire to make tea, he told her about it. It was his first good find on a claim of his own. Of course it wasn't a fortune, and the hazards of digging gave no guarantee that he would ever find another remotely like it. But at least it was valuable enough to wipe out some of their debts.

Even more cheering was the news that John Molteno was off to Cape Town to visit his family for a few months. George was to look after his claims in his absence and would have the use of the most comfortable camp on the field, and also of a first-class motor-car. Eleanor could start packing immediately. George would leave a headman in charge of the farm, and take the whole family back with him to the goldfields. Perhaps the finding of the nugget would mark the end of their miserable run of bad luck. But even if it didn't, the family would be together for a while in a home on the banks of the river of gold, and they would have the chance of deciding on the future in an atmosphere where at least hope was most infectious.

CHAPTER TWENTY

LUPA DAYS

MOLTENO'S camp was extremely comfortable. It consisted of two wattle and daub buildings erected end to end in a clearing in the miyombo bush. The main building was a combination of large living-room, a store, and office. The second building contained a large and a small bedroom separated by a room for bathing. Both buildings were thatched. They had no doors or windows. The place of doors was taken by curved grass screens which gave a degree of privacy at the same time allowing the very welcome visit to the interior of the slightest breeze or draught. As an additional aid to coolness, one wall of each building was only built up a couple of feet, leaving a six-foot gap below the steeply slanted roof to allow space for light and air.

To the children, the camp was particularly exciting. It was entirely surrounded by old prospecting trenches. The children spent hours each day grubbing around for gold in the piles of gravel. There was always some piece of rock to be found containing a glittering fragment of mica and the enthusiasm of the children survived endless disappointments when they carried their finds to George for identification.

The camp stood about three miles from the town of Chunya which had been founded in 1934 as the shopping and administrative centre of the goldfields. Eleanor had heard so much of the roaring nature of the place that inevitably she was disappointed when George drove her in one afternoon to see it. There was one dusty street lined with shops and buildings built of sun-dried brick. The two pivots of the whole place seemed to be John MacFie's bottle store and the Goldfields Hotel, from which establishment a very considerable noise could be heard emanating at all hours of the day.

The stores were reasonably stocked. Vegetables and fresh butter were brought in regularly by truck. Tinned foods were plentiful, if expensive. Butchers sold fresh meat every day. Drinking water was supplied in empty kerosene tins, clothing was serviceable, if lacking in variety, and the only missing thing was fresh milk. This was unobtainable. Tsetse fly prevented the keeping of cows, and trucking milk along such hot and dusty roads was impracticable.

One result of her visit to the town was to satisfy any curiosity Eleanor had about the female inhabitants of the goldfields. They were as mixed a batch as their men. Some of them were hard-working, resolute individuals like Christina Nel, widow of a Nyasaland tobacco farmer. She had moved up to the Lupa in an old truck in 1934, pegged a claim at Mawogas, and then opened Nel's Boarding House in Chunya, a renowned diggers' home where many a lame dog found a generous hand-out when times were bad. Other females were completely different, real ladies of leisure dressed to the nines in smart frocks, silk stockings, high-heeled shoes, with handbags, make-up and whatnot to match. They included in their armament what they considered to be a smart line in conversation, a few topsy-turvy views about life and a vocabulary which made Eleanor's hair curl. Tripping about among them were also quite a number of African tarts who attempted to out-vie the European members of their profession in absurdly lip-sticked mouths and shoes with heels like stilts.

The men, notwithstanding their odd, and sometimes comic, improvisation of clothing, generally seemed to be a trifle more cultured than the females. At least some of them had more sense to their conversation than the ludicrous rubbish spouted by the women, most of it based on half-read articles published in junk magazines. The men were, of course, nearly all hard drinkers, and some pretty flaming rows took place between them when liquor mixed itself in discussions, particularly the interminable debate and uncertainty about the future of Tanganyika, with the Nazi Government of Germany currently making some claim for its return as a colony. Some of the men were eccentric, especially old bachelor diggers like Bill Cumming, the discoverer of the field, who seemed to have withdrawn entirely to himself, living in the loneliest parts of the bush. Others had the curiously contagious habit of spitting, which they did with almost a disconcerting old-world elegance, aiming their projectiles most accurately to the right and to the left, according to the wind, while the persons to whom they were talking momentarily expected a shower, and suffered nervous frustration when they found themselves left high and dry. Among the most renowned of these spitters was Bishop, George's old crony of the Congo days. He was earning a living of sorts by doing signwriting on the goldfields. Whatever signs he painted could certainly never have prohibited expectorating. Talking to a lady he would simply raise his hat, say " Excuse me, Ma'am," and let drive with what appeared to be an aerial bomb. Another expert was an elderly French-man who had his shack near Molteno's. He was often stricken with rheu-matism. He had removed one brick from the wall opposite his bed and could expectorate from a recumbent position, twelve feet unerringly through the gap.

At that part of the year, November of 1936, there was generally more time for leisure on the diggings. The rains had just started. The ground was too wet for dry blowing while there was still insufficient water in the streams for the traditional type of panning. Men tended to frequent the bars and find relaxation in parties. George, who always enjoyed being among the boys, used to slip off periodically for an evening at the pub. It was perfectly safe for him to leave Eleanor alone. There was remarkably little crime on the goldfields. As a gold buyer, Molteno invariably kept several thousand pounds in a cash-box under his bed, but nobody ever worried him. The only security he took was to chain the box to his waist when he slept. If anybody took the cash they would have to take him as well, which he considered fair enough. Periodically he sent his gold in to the bank at Mbeya. A guard of African spearmen would tramp in overnight carrying the gold across the mountains. They would sleep on the pavement outside the bank, dump the box on the counter as soon as the place opened for business and then walk back to the camp, carrying any ready cash which their master needed. The only time he ever lost anything was when an old Scotsman he employed did the disap-pearing trick one night and took a few shillings with him for pocket money.

Eleanor preferred to stay at home with her children and a book when George was on his outings. One of the local girls once asked her,

" George is such a handsome devil, aren't you scared to let him run around on his own?"

She almost blurted out,

" No, he's the type of man who prefers his women to bath rather than use perfume."

Instead she simply shrugged. She was quite happy. He always came home, and the walk back in the evening air evaporated any bad tempers or hot spirits. She always had sandwiches and something warm for him to drink, and she could be sure of hearing all his gossip red hot before they went to bed. He certainly picked up some entertaining tales. The great romance of the Lupa was on at the time, with Eleanor very partisan and so eager for news she would happily wait all night to hear an instalment.

The hero of this romance was a handsome young Swede named Pete

Pettersen, a useful all-in wrestler, who had wandered on to the Lupa in company with a rugged one-time amateur heavyweight boxer of Sweden, Thorsten " Swede " Peirson. On the goldfields there was living a dumpy little Austrian woman named Mrs Hunke who had something of a carefully guarded treasure in an eighteen-year-old daughter.

Pettersen pegged a claim next to the Hunkes near the Little Kasanga River. He met the girl and they fell in love. Mrs Hunke, however, wouldn't hear of any romance. She removed with her treasure to Chunya and took in a gentleman lodger, a Belgian auctioneer named Bertrand, to provide masculine support against any intrusion. Pettersen and the girl were forced to resort to ruses in order to meet, and it was the ingenuity of the lovers, and the counter-scheming of Mrs Hunke, that kept the diggings interested.

The current rendezvous was the quietest corner of the veranda of the Goldfields Hotel. Each Saturday Pettersen went in to Chunya to sell his gold and buy stores and rations for his men. He would then stay in the hotel for the night. His sweetheart always ostensibly retired to bed early on Saturday nights, slipped out of the window and went up to the hotel for a spell of holding hands.

George was sitting on the same hotel veranda on the Saturday night when Mrs Hunke discovered the rendezvous. She and Bertrand had rigged up a girl trap underneath the daughter's window. The trap consisted of a pile of tin cans attached to a trip wire. When the girl slipped out that evening she made a noise like a traffic accident. She ran off to the hotel, too befuddled to reason that the best scheme would be to clamber back into her room and blame burglars for the noise.

In full pursuit came Mrs Hunke and the gentleman lodger. They found the girl with her sweetheart on the hotel veranda. Bertrand set upon Pettersen with a sjambok. The subsequent sequence of events carried George's memory all the way back to his halcyon days as a bouncer in Da Silva's pub at the mouth of the Congo River.

The shock of the onslaught sent Pettersen down to the floor. Diggers poured out of the bar at the vibration to the building. The two men grappled on the floor, side by side. Mrs Hunke brandished a large-sized six-cell flashlight. Seeing Pettersen's head exposed she let swing with this illuminated missile. Pettersen saw the light arching down. He wasn't a wrestler for nothing. He relaxed sharply and allowed the gratified Bertrand to wriggle on top of him. The torch caught the gentleman lodger a full bullseye on the head. It exploded with a shower of lens glass, reflector and bulb. Bertrand went out with the light. He was carried home feet first by a party of diggers inevitably trying to sing something about poor Cock Robin.

While Bertrand was recovering, Mrs Hunke wrestled with the problem about what to do with her daughter. She was uncomfortably aware that popular sympathy on the goldfields lay with the lovers. She had talked too loudly about never allowing any dirty digger to lay hands on her treasure. Eventually she resolved to pack the tearful girl off to relatives in Austria. Bertrand drove her off to Dar es Salaam as soon as he recovered from his wound.

Eleanor's particular interest in the affair came because Pettersen was one of their own special friends. The young man used to discuss his problems with them. With an air of heavy secrecy seated around a lamp in Molteno's camp, they devised counter-strategy to Mrs Hunke's latest move. It was really very simple. Pettersen cabled money to the girl and told her to leave the ship at Mombasa and take the train to Nairobi. He would meet her there and they could be married. Pete actually passed Bertrand on the Great North Road. As their two cars edged past each other on the narrow road, Bertrand treated him to a leer and cocked a snook. The gentleman lodger had seen the girl sail. He could report her to her mother as being well out of reach. Pettersen kept a straight face and drove on to Nairobi. The marriage proved most happy and lasting.

There was one newspaper, the *Lupa Herald,* published on the goldfields by Rufus Naylor. An old booze-artist from Fleet Street, George Leighton, edited the sheet, until he came to grief over the catholicy of his drinking. Firewater distilled from such ingredients as rotten pineapples, bamboo, papaws, bananas, and sundry wild fruits of the bush which fermented to a liquid capable of anaesthetising an elephant, could only have one possible effect on the human system. While the newspaper lasted, however, it provided George with many a chortle. He contributed a column under the name of "Aunt Flo". There was no money to it, but the stimulus of collecting diggers' stories forced him to keep his ear even closer to the ground than was normal in a community which habitually awoke each morning wondering what rumours were afoot of somebody else's gold finds.

Just how valuable such rumours could be was beautifully displayed by the career of Lambert Lock. He was a character as restless as most of the men on the goldfields. In February 1912 he had travelled from England to join his brother Alfred, who ran a butcher's shop in Elisabethville, in the Belgian Congo. From there Lambert wandered down to Cape Town and stowed away on the old immigrant ship *Armadale Castle* to seek his fortune in Australia.

In 1914 he was back in the Congo. When war broke out he served in Northern Rhodesia and then France. After the war he was drawn back to Africa, first to the Congo and then, in 1921, to Tanganyika where he worked on road construction. In March 1924 he reached the Lupa and, with a partner named Gordon Griffiths, pegged a claim on the Golden Bend. There was enough gold in it to keep them in spending money, but little more. Then, in 1926, Lock stumbled on what became known as Lock's Reef. It was almost typical of a good find on the Lupa. It was a small reef and deceptively pockety. Just when you considered it to be exhausted you could find a jewellery box. In one explosive charge Lock blew open a pocket, six feet by four feet by six feet and carrying eight per cent pure gold. He extracted £900 worth of gold from this find, with some really beautiful lumps of sparkling quartz. The hot African sun never looked down on a happier digger than Lambert Lock working his mine.

"Unfortunately," he said cynically to George, when he described the event, "I was no sooner into the jewellery shop than I was out of it by the back door, and into the pawnbroker's shop."

The rest of the reef simply petered out. Lock was left with one real treasure, a wife, Asha bint Lusinde, a particularly handsome and versatile daughter of a Hehe chief. When times were bad she opened an hotel and kept her husband going on her enterprise. It was in this establishment that it really paid to listen to rumour. Men have always talked in their cups and it was in Asha's pub that Lambert Lock in due course found the lead to one of the greatest discoveries on the Lupa goldfields and was rewarded at last with a comfortable fortune.

While Bert was still working his Lock's Reef, an Australian digger named Phillip Thomas came in to his camp once and over drinks showed him a cigarette box filled with wonderful quartz containing gold. Bert naturally asked "where?" Thomas told him that he was going off to Chunya but on his return he would reveal the site of the gold. He never did return.

Bert commenced diligent enquiry among the tribespeople to retrace Thomas's steps. All they could tell him was that Thomas had been fossicking along the course of the Mbilwa stream. Bert prospected the stream but found nothing payable. It was all very puzzling. He gave up and Jewboy Bayliss took over. Bayliss worked an indifferent alluvial claim for some while and then also gave up. A third prospector, Lew de Jager, moved in. He found some gold, worked a claim to exhaustion and pulled his pegs out.

Lock still had a feeling about the area, but hunches are frustrating unless they prove themselves with gold. Occasionally he prospected there but found nothing. When he went off to England on holiday he even raised £50 to grubstake Major H. B. Dunman to continue the search, but nothing came of it. The whole riddle of the area, in fact, was destined to remain a secret until March 1938. Then an African digger, John Tusakarege, started supporting Asha's pub by banking good gold in the till of her bar at Sinyela village.

Asha kept her ears and eyes open and carried the story to her husband. John Tusakarege had originally learned his trade as a headman for Lew de Jager. He had lingered on in the area of his former employer's claim and seemed to share Lock's feelings about the place. But he was very secretive. Eventually Asha's best brew loosened his tongue. He was working an alluvial claim on a small stream which ran into what was known as Bayliss

Creek. Lock went off and examined the place. The claim looked good but the man had covered the whole area with his pegs. The only available adjoining ground was on an ironstone hill. It did not look too promising but Lock took a chance. He pegged Kizumbe Hill. On it he found the reef, Lock's Luck, one of the most phenomenal finds on the Lupa.

This reef not only rewarded its fortunate owner with over £50,000 in gold and, within the three-year period in which Lock worked it, made him the most successful of all the alluvial diggers, but it produced the greatest sensation on the Lupa. In February 1939 Lock was sitting in his shack eating when he heard a great shouting and singing from his African mine workers. He looked out and saw the whole crowd coming down the hill carrying something in a *machilla*. He thought that it was an injured man being carried in and opened his first-aid box. Instead, the men were carrying down the greatest nugget ever found on the Lupa goldfields, a real giant, eighteen inches by nine inches by four inches, weighing a total of 127 lb. and yielding 1,025 ounces of smelted gold.

Living in such a phrenetic world could certainly never be dull even if, to the great majority of diggers, it really wasn't particularly profitable. There was so much pure luck involved in the place that any geologist would be reduced to tears by the very contradictions of the field, and a mining engineer would have apoplexy at the improvisations of machinery which worked many of the discoveries. In this respect Bert Faram was particularly ingenious. It was said that he could build an ore crusher out of his wife's sewing machine, and by the long-suffering appearance of both wife and machine this was perfectly feasible. At the time George and Eleanor were staying in Molteno's camp, the Farams were working a small reef nearby and using a most extraordinary type of home-made recovery plant based on a device known as an arrastra, first introduced by the Spaniards in Mexico 400 years ago. In appearance it resembled a medieval torture machine, with a revolving wooden spider dragging heavy stones around to crush ore on a pavement in the ground. Mercury was then poured into the pool to form an amalgam with the liberated gold. This contraption, notwithstanding its antiquity, appeared to be producing sufficient gold to provide the Farams with a very snug camp, with proper doors and windows to a brick building and attractive furnishings contrived from petrol boxes. Periodically, if their returns were good, they went on a prodigious binge of shopping and celebration in the pub. If times were hard, Hilda simply shrugged it off and took the rough with the smooth.

"My dear," she confided to Eleanor, "when we're broke we just live on tea and cigarettes."

The diet at least seemed to keep them happy.

Another family of diggers who were living well at the time was that of the Cresswell-Georges. They also had a permanent camp with a brick house, a large wireless set, and all the usual status symbols of the successful mining man, including champagne and boundless hospitality. For Christmas of 1936 they staged a very pleasant party, with a gaily decorated living-room full of garlands, streamers and balloons, and an excellent dinner of turkey and plum pudding cooked by George's one-time *chef de cuisine*, Abel, who had found his way to the diggings not so much in search of gold as to get away from his wife.

The party passed off very well, although Eleanor was by no means the first mother to be glad when Christmas was over. Janey, the nursemaid, had gone to bed complaining of fever, and the three children all had minor troubles which demanded love and attention, Kate with a cold, Ann with sore eyes, and little George well off his food, even though it was plum pudding. On top of it all, it was raining and everybody had to be entertained indoors.

By the new year things were worse, with Janey and little George well on the boil with temperatures which no amount of quinine seemed able to reduce. For malaria, this was something beyond a joke. The local medical man, Dr Spears, eventually put the nursemaid in his car and drove her off to hospital. When he returned the next morning he knew the worst. It was typhoid.

Something better than amateur nursing was needed for little George but there was no way of obtaining it. The only suitable hospital for children was at Mbeya, and a fifty-mile drive in the mud over that hair-raising route would do more harm than any good at the end of it. The boy would just have to stay in the camp. What had previously appeared as a comfortable, well-ventilated residence now seemed very crude, with the rain streaming down outside, with the doctor near but separated by three miles of mud, with the roof leaking and the water-saturated wind wandering through the place at will, keeping everything damp and musty.

Before he recovered, little George looked as though he was made of hair, eyes, teeth and ribs. On the rainy days, George kept him alive with an interminable serial account of past adventures and present doings, like Scheherazade telling her tales of the Arabian nights. He would sit in a chair next to the boy's bed and meticulously clean a rifle, yarning away until he reached some climax to the tale where the suspense would be guaranteed to keep the boy alive until he could hear the denouement in the next day's instalment.

By the time little George was up and about, his parents had reached a decision about the future. A long holiday out of the tropics for Eleanor and the children was imperative. This was an order from the doctor. George would have to remain on his own while the family went down to the coolness of the Cape. Eleanor's parents had already suggested that she send Ann to them. And George's mother had offered to sail out to Cape Town later in the year and take Ann and little George back to England with her until such time as their parents had found their feet, with George established in some more regular way of life.

They all felt sad at the breaking up of the family. But the children's health came before sentiment. At least Eleanor would be back with Kate, who was so plump and rosy that it did not appear that any temperate climate would suit her better than the tropics. And there was always the hope that George might have a change of luck. Something might turn up to allow them to bring the children back to a proper home built in a cooler part of a country which they all loved as their own.

As it happened, John Molteno returned by plane on the same morning, the 10th February 1937, that Eleanor flew off with the children. He actually presented her with his spare air-sickness tablets when they met at Mbeya airport and sympathetically told her that she would need them. She said "Thanks," rather sourly. The last George saw of the family for, in the case of the two children, the long period of eight years, were their faces peeping at him through one of the port-holes. Eleanor was crying, but the children were obviously too excited for sorrow. Molteno simply smiled at him understandingly. He was having some domestic troubles himself.

"They'll feel some grief as soon as they take off," he said. "It was like a bucking bronco flying up here, thunderstorms all over the place. Come and have a drink. It will brace you up."

They drove in to the Sluice Box as the aircraft took off, like an over-gorged marabou stork, and climbed heavily to the cloud world of the southern sky.

CHAPTER TWENTY-ONE

THE GUANO RUSH

WITH Molteno back, George was released from any immediate commitments on the goldfields. He had worked his own claims simultaneously with Molteno's without, however, finding anything even fractionally as valuable as the nugget he had carried to Eleanor that night on the farm. If he continued as a gold-digger he would have to base his future simply on the hazards of fortune. It was really not much security to offer a family.

While he tried to make up his mind what to do, he went off fishing in the streams he had stocked with trout around the slopes of the Rungwe volcano. For a few days it was pleasant to relax. There are few occupations more amiably diverting than wandering along the banks searching for trout in a rippling stream. After the relentless heat and dust of the Lupa, the cool air of the mountain country was a real tonic. And the pleasure was rich of a night without the curse of mosquitoes, with the wind brisk enough for the luxury of blankets, with the contentment of a stomach well filled on a fat, grilled trout, and a long sleep lulled by the murmuring music of the cleanest of waters.

He had as many pleasant memories of the Lupa to consider as he had of his farm. The rugged masculinity of the community of gold-seekers had certainly given him great pleasure. The uproarious pranks, the varied rumours and scandals, and the remarkable personalities of the diggers, were all quite unforgettable things. There were wild nights to remember; when George the Greek, notwithstanding his claims to being an all-in wrestler, was thrown bodily out of his own pub at Kunguta's with a crash which permanently cracked the wall; the evening in Menzies' hotel at Piccadilly Circus when Bob Sutherland, the gold buyer, became the first man to throw five aces in one on the Lupa; the time at Mwawogo's when bushy-bearded Charlie Wood's chickens gobbled up a good day's gold recovery left to dry in a pan. Castor oil and scrupulous cleaning of the floor of the poultry run provided a hitherto unknown 100 per cent method of gold recovery.

And then there was the great afternoon in the square outside the Goldfields Hotel in Chunya, when Swede Pierson fought Piet van Dyk for the heavyweight title of all Tanganyika. The whole diggings had seemed to be

there that day, in a swirling mass of half-frenzied punters, drunks, and individuals whose inflamed feelings made them less intent on watching the
contest than on settling personal scores in a series of free fights on the fringe
of the crowd. Fupi Jordan, an ex-bantamweight professional boxer, refereed
the main bout, with the men boxing for a £50 purse together with side-bets
and the championship. The end was a draw, after a rattling good ten-round
fight.

The temptation was certainly strong to go back to the Lupa. On the
other hand, the place had its troubles. The heat and climate made permanent
living there unthinkable, especially for a family. At best, a man could only
have the ambition for a quick fortune and a rapid departure from the place.
Not many achieved this happy ending to their search. Even those diggers
considered to be successful seemed to linger on, always hoping for more,
and hardly living a life which could be described as either constructive or
useful. Apart from buying larger radios, newer motor-cars and more expensive liquor, the affluent mining man seldom knows what to do with his
money. He is too used to living without it. Most of the breed eventually
vanish from the scene of their fortune leaving nothing behind save a hole in
the ground. All the real pleasure they could afford themselves is completely
denied, of doing something in return for the often poverty-stricken country
which had yielded them their wealth.

George switched his thoughts back to his farm. The economic doldrums
which had beset the world for so long were largely over, but coffee was still
in a slump. Brazil was dumping the bean on the markets of the world at
such a cut-rate price that it was quite useless even thinking of shipping a
crop from Mbeya. Wherever he looked he seemed to encounter some
frustration.

More and more his heart was set on going back to the elephants and the
game, this time as a protector and friend. One of the great pleasures of his
life had come from stocking the mountain streams with fish. The whole venture had been a complete success. And what was particularly pleasant was
to see that the resident tribespeople had become as interested as the European settlers in the fish, thoroughly appreciating the pleasures and advan-
tages of eating and conserving them. If man could only be taught the same
lesson that the wild life of Africa was the continent's greatest natural asset,
the most varied and numerous of all the earth's natural population of mammals, and surely intended by Nature for some better fate than plain
destruction.

The whole vision of conservation and scientific cropping was enthralling
to George. The thorn wilderness of Tanganyika which made the country
appear to some as a shabby badland could be transformed by man's understanding into the greatest ranchland in the world, with its incredible variety
and numbers of livestock maintained and selectively bred, not only for the

aesthetic pleasure of their display, but for their ability to provide the entire world with a massive and ever-increasing contribution to its wealth in the form of foodstuffs, leather and skins.

From the goldfields, George had already written to Philip Teare enquiring whether there was any prospect of a vacancy in the game department. The answer had been negative for the present. Of all government departments, the game department was the most ill-founded in finance and establishment. In the depression years it had suffered most in retrenchment and economies. And now that things were improving, it would certainly be the last department to be restored to anything remotely like its working strength.

Governors succeeding one another in short terms of office and fresh from Britain could hardly be expected to think of a game department as being anything other than a body of keepers so employed that gentlemen with licences would have the opportunity to shoot. It would be relatively easy to convince such governors on schemes to squander fortunes of money in clearing bush and wiping out game in order to make way for some totally unsuitable European crop or livestock. To talk to them of the selective breeding of heavy-meated antelopes like the eland, of the domestication of buffalo in the tsetse areas, of the planned cropping of elephants so that their numbers might be controlled and their enormous weights of meat be available at regular times for organised distribution, such arguments could only end in game rangers being quietly certified on grounds of insanity. It would not be much consolation for them to remember that the human race has invariably awarded this accolade to those of its kind who have proposed anything at once revolutionary or progressive and not destructive.

Whatever he did in the long run, it was necessary for George to return to the farm for at least a short while in order to attend to its affairs. And here he had a rather unusual piece of good luck. Examining the coffee plants with his foreman, it was very evident that if they were to survive at all they would have to have some fertiliser. The problem was to finance such an expenditure when the result would simply produce an unsaleable crop. On the other hand, it was not only sentiment, but the perennial hope that prices would improve, which prevented him from simply abandoning the farm.

He remembered the good fortune of his former neighbours, the Hickson-Woods, in finding a cave of bat guano in the heights above their farm. This was the ideal fertiliser for coffee, and to have one's own supply was obviously very advantageous. For the next few days he tramped around the Mbeya range, probing in the odd crevices and caves, but all he found was something definitely not much to his liking.

He was returning to the farmhouse one sunset when he heard guinea-fowl calling, as they usually do towards evening. The sound was very tempting for anyone hungry for a good dinner. He turned aside from his path and soon found the birds settling down for the night in a tree. He selected a juicy-looking dinner, took aim at leisure and shot it. The bird crashed to the ground while its fellows took off in a flurry of alarm. Simultaneously there was a scurry through the grass with an entirely different sound. Out of the base of the tree there came a big and resolute-looking mamba. The snake came straight at him like a black whip-lash. There was no time to reload his rifle. Nature simply intervened and protected him by freezing his muscles. He stood dead still and the startled snake failed to even notice him. It shot straight between his legs and vanished into the bush, quite unaware of his existence. Some hours passed before George recovered his appetite for guinea-fowl.

Oddly enough, it was partly through the snake that George, in fact, did find a guano cave. Looking back at his farm from the other side of the Songwe Valley, there was a bald-headed hill known to the tribespeople as Panda. The obvious limestone nature of the hill had often attracted George's attention. He had several times resolved to pay the hill a visit but never found the opportunity. Now, with his ardour for exploring the Mbeya range temporarily dampened by the encounter with the mamba, he walked across to the bald-headed hill, camped at its foot, and next day found a spacious cave well stocked with guano. It was also well stocked with bats. The shower of guano and urine with which they received him, the foul stench and the skeletons of bats littered over the floor, all made the cave a retreat of death in its most putrid and repugnant form. He backed out of it as quickly as he could after making an assessment of the amount of guano contained in the place. Returning to the camp he celebrated his success with little more than a sniff from an empty brandy bottle and considered his next move.

The first thing to do was to peg the discovery, and then commence an experimental working in order to test the purity of both limestone and guano. The next day, accordingly, he went in to Mbeya to register his claim. A week later he was back on the hill with a party of labourers and the tools necessary for commencing operations.

Recovering guano from a bat cave is filthy work, although once the regular inhabitants of the place have been ejected it does become slightly more hygienic. At least it was cool inside the cave, while the camp site on the floor of the valley was baking hot, with water never in entirely sufficient supply to allow the labourers to wash the last stench of guano from their persons before they went to bed. To George, however, there was consolation in working on the production of something with a definite marketable value. Guano and limestone were always in demand. Even if times were still not the best, there were builders and farmers who needed such essentials for their industry. The only immediate problem was to carry the product to the consumers. Starting any industry without capital is a heart-breaking struggle.

George's activity on Panda Hill soon attracted attention. Robert Sargeant was the established lime and guano producer in the district. He came around to George's camp one afternoon and examined the product. George was glad of the visit. He had something more than a nodding acquaintance with Sargeant, and professional advice on his discovery was desirable. The limestone he was burning had a brownish-coloured adulteration which lowered its marketing value. The problem was to discover the nature of this adulteration and, if possible, find a method of eliminating it.

Sargeant was obviously puzzled at the appearance of the limestone.

"It's quite a deposit," he agreed, after examining the cave, "and the guano looks all right. But the limestone is beyond me. You'll have to send a sample off for analysis."

He regard George quizzically.

"You're obviously battling. There's not much fun to things when you're short of capital, especially if you have a working problem like this."

George agreed with him. Sargeant produced a half-jack.

"I tell you what," he said, "I'll give you £100 for it."

They spent the next hour in bargaining, and then suspended discussion until George could have the limestone analysed. This took time, with samples posted away, and an inspection of the site by the government geologist. The result was a rather puzzling report that the adulteration was a pyrochlore-bearing carbonatite containing niobium oxide, a very rare heat-resistant metal, not currently in great demand, although there was no knowing what the future might hold in the line of its use in such things as aeroplane engines or armaments. There was no cheap method of removing the adulteration from limestone.

By this time George also had the idea that the guano wasn't quite as good as he hoped. Its effect on his own coffee plants was something short of electrifying, and he guessed that the pyrochlore adulteration had somehow or other debased the chemical potency of the guano as fertiliser. Accordingly, when Sargeant visited him again he was more inclined to sell. They eventually reached agreement on £100 in cash and a second-hand model B two-seater Ford, guaranteed to at least move away under its own power from its parking place. It would be a replacement for the A.C. whose bones were rusting on the side of the road to the farm.

It was in this stylish vehicle, painted bright red, that George eventually met Eleanor when she returned by air from her Cape holiday in the beginning of June 1937. She had enjoyed a pleasant change. A family friend had given her the use of a cottage at Hout Bay, and the fresh winds of that pleasant place had soon blown away most of the children's moods and ailments. Invigorated by the change, little George and Ann were now with Eleanor's parents in Cape Town, and would remain there until George's mother took them to England at the end of the year. Kate returned to Tanganyika to keep her mother company.

George drove them back to the farm and told them all the local news. His small success with the guano had acted as his own special tonic. The £100 had slightly rehabilitated family fortunes while the little Ford seemed to ride like the wind compared to the rattle-traps they had owned in the past. At home he had quite renovated the farmhouse, driven away a few unwelcome reptiles and insects which had moved in when they had moved to the goldfields, and arranged for a nice little dinner of welcome. He had also been able to telegraph a few pounds to Eleanor to allow her to buy a new dress for herself and some toys for the children before she left Cape Town. Altogether it was very pleasant to return to the little farmhouse. Everything there looked fresh and tidy and the garden as usual was full of flowers. The only sad note was to find little George's favourite pair of boots, forgotten in the rush of departure and still standing by the side of his empty bed.

George, for once, was also full of optimism. There was obviously money to be made from guano. He had been busy looking for a new deposit and had heard very definite news that down on the coast, near the old trading port of Kilwa, there was one enormous deposit in a hidden cave. The information was reliable, and he had already tried to raise support on the gold-fields for a venture in pegging and testing the cave.

Eleanor was slightly alarmed at this news.

"Aren't you afraid that somebody will get there before you?"

George wasn't worried.

" I only asked men I could trust, but they were all too set on gold. As soon as you have had a rest we'll drive down and visit Sargeant. I'll tell him about it and see if he will back me."

They drove down to Sargeant's camp two days later. The lime worker had his base where the Great North Road crossed the Songwe River on its journey from the Rhodesian border to Mbeya. They found him in a very agreeable mood. Guano was bringing him a comfortable living and new sources of supply were always interesting. He offered to advance £25 to cover the cost of George's trip to Kilwa, the pegging of a claim and the taking of samples for analysis. If the deposit proved really worthwhile, he and George could form a partnership and ship the guano out from Kilwa to a ready demand all along the coast. Sitting around Sargeant's campfire planning it all out was a very absorbing way of building castles in the air, if not in Spain at least in Africa.

George set out a few days later, accompanied by Kiyanda. The little two-seater had originally been used by Sargeant to carry salt from the saline springs he worked near Lake Rukwa, and for this purpose he had converted the dicky seat into an odd-shaped box in which George could pack his camp kit and provisions. Kiyanda elected to spend most of the journey reclining on the top of this impedimenta in order to secure a position for himself which would provide both a vantage point for greeting women and friends, and a comfortable bed for sleeping during the journey.

They left Mbeya after a last drink at the Sluice Box, and immediately found that they were being followed. A burly-looking Ford V8 truck dogged their trail in such an obvious manner that if George slowed to allow it to pass it simply dropped behind into the dust; while if he tried to speed up, it had no difficulty in maintaining station at any distance its driver chose to keep.

By the time they had covered two hundred miles George was certain that he had a rival for the guano cave. Just before sunset he stopped at the bottom of a sharp gully and waited for the truck to catch up. The vehicle actually came bowling along the road at such a pace it almost landed in his dicky box before the startled driver could stop. George was confident that his shadowers had speeded up simply because they could no longer see him. He walked to the truck and looked in. He was intrigued to find two Lupa diggers sitting in the front seat. They were both men he had approached for support in his search for guano. They regarded him rather sheepishly, but when he asked where were they going they simply looked innocent and said:

" Down to the coast to fish."

There was certainly nothing illegal about going down to the coast to fish. Real courtesy could also be the reason for their refusal to travel ahead of George. The truck would certainly leave a trail of dust behind it several miles long. An open two-seater at the best of times was something like a vacuum cleaner on dirt roads. Such sporting vehicles look handsome in motor-car showrooms but they can prove sheer purgatory in dust or rain. George thanked the two men.

" I swore you were chasing me," he remarked in parting. " Perhaps I'm too suspicious. I was all ready to push a shot-gun into somebody's eye."

They simpered. He drove on, still very suspicious. With two of them to share driving he would have difficulty in leaving the truck behind him. And with only the one road to Kilwa there was no prospect of losing them. He decided, however, to at least test their endurance. He simply gritted his teeth, tossed Kiyanda an extra blanket for his bed on top of the camp kit, and drove clean through the night without turning a head to worry how closely he was being followed.

At dawn George stopped for a meal and immediately discovered that Kiyanda was missing. The man must have been bumped out while he slept. There had been so many rough passages on the road it was impossible to know where he had made his exit. It might have been three hundred miles back. Kiyanda could certainly number his car journeys with George as notable experiences.

The only thing to do was drive on. Kilwa was little more than a few miles away by then. As soon as the cave was safely pegged, George could return and search for the missing passenger. He had pretty explicit directions about locating the cave. Actually, it was very simple to find the place. The local inhabitants knew about it, but they had never considered the cave to contain anything of value. A Swahili coconut farmer actually guided him to the place and watched with some amusement as he tried to enter it. The cave simply erupted bats. They tore out from every angle, showering him with liquid until he retreated for shelter. He had to spend a few minutes throwing stones into the cave in order to eject a proportion of its regular inhabitants. Some very odd little creatures emerged into daylight. When the rush was over he managed an entrance.

The torchlight revealed a substantial area of cave well-covered with guano. George eagerly examined the deposit. There was certainly enough of it. The trouble was that the cave was excessively damp. Much of the guano seemed soggy and mixed with sand. The stench was overpowering. He took samples as quickly as he could and then backed out of the place. Bob Sargeant was the expert on guano. From the samples he would have to determine whether it was worth exploiting the deposit. Meanwhile, all George could do was peg the claim and properly register it.

When he drove into the little port and administrative centre of Kilwa, the first vehicle he saw was the Ford truck of his fellow travellers. Kiyanda was riding in the back. The man gave him a broad grin and transferred to his original seat with the sheepish explanation that he had woken up to find himself lying on the road. His rescuers had driven up and discovered him desperately searching for something in the bush. His explanation that he had lost a photograph of what was at Kilwa prompted the two men to spend over an hour helping him in the search. Eventually they had found the photograph, a portrait of a rather plumpish-looking girl, and been so annoyed that they had wanted to leave Kiyanda to the lions.

Further argument about this proposal only brought fresh delay. George had been well ahead by the time they started. They did not seem particularly gratified when they were thanked for rescuing Kiyanda. George also rather exaggerated his description of the richness of the discovery, particularly as Sargeant later found the guano to be too soggy to be profitably worked. George, in fact, drove back to Mbeya in a mood of triumph only partly spoilt by the fact that in the evening, as they were nearing the end of the journey, Kiyanda was once again shaken out. This time George did discover his absence fairly soon after the event. Actually, he had just turned back on his tracks to find the man when he saw Kiyanda running along the road still clutching an unlighted storm lamp which he was holding in his hand when he fell. Incredibly enough, the glass was not even cracked, and on what particular part of his own anatomy Kiyanda always landed remained a mystery for he showed no ill effects from his two experiences.

Sargeant's opinion on the guano samples, when it came, was certainly a blow, but by that time George had experienced so many set-backs that he was almost immune to them. There comes a stage in a man's life, in fact, when he grows to anticipate disappointments. The one advantage of such a philosophy is that things can never be any worse than expected, while there is always the chance of a pleasant surprise.

This particular disappointment did undermine one castle in the air about a successful career in guano recovery. The economic set-back also induced George to accept another commission to act as a white hunter. A well-to-do fruit farmer, Harry Blackburn, from Elgin in the Cape, was interested in the services of a hunter for the months of September and October. Molteno had put him into correspondence with George, with strong personal recommendations for both of them. Blackburn, by all accounts, was an experienced hunter. Molteno considered him to be something well above the cut of the average pot-shotter who provided business for white hunters. He was keen on trophies and prepared to accept advice and discriminate in what he shot. The sad-looking heads which such individuals used to embellish the walls of their homes generally gave George the shivers, but, for what worth clients found in them, the search for suitable trophies at least provided some purpose to a safari. George was accordingly less reluctant to accept money for the conduct of one of the things than he normally was when only economic exigency forced him to take on such work.

He met Blackburn in Mbeya when the client drove up from the south in a brand-new Chevrolet truck specially bought for the occasion. It was at least a pleasure to start the safari in a vehicle not threatening to fall to pieces the moment it left the shelter of a garage. Notwithstanding a driver, a Rhodesian African named John, who had a totally blind eye for pot-holes, the whole trip went off with no more untoward an event than broken springs and one narrow escape for the client. He tried to photograph a cow elephant, tripped over a root when he was charged, and only survived to hunt again when George turned the animal with a high shot which furrowed the top of her head. For the rest, Blackburn proved better-mannered company than white hunters normally expect from their clients. In his turn, Blackburn secured a satisfactory bag and went off home without openly reckoning that he had been done down by his hunter. The outing was accordingly considered by both as an agreeable success.

George went back to the farm in a cheerful mood, all ready to assure an anxious wife of his survival from numerous dangers. As soon as she ran out to meet him, however, he could see that he would be the one to listen to a tale of hardship. Her first words, in fact, were to tell him that next time there was a client she would take the man out while George could stay at home. She was certain that she would be much safer with elephants in the bush than with the odd creatures who visited her on the farm.

CHAPTER TWENTY-TWO

LEOPARD IN THE NIGHT

" THE trouble," Eleanor said, as soon as she had given George a hug, " is that these beastly leopards know when you go. It's uncanny. It's almost as though they come down to take revenge on me because you're away killing other animals. Laza told me that and I'm beginning to believe him."

Old Laza, the tribal hunter, was standing on the veranda behind her as she spoke, making some attempt to shoulder arms with his muzzle loader. George was tempted to say:

" If leopards can sense when I go, it's nothing so wonderful as Laza anticipating my return, with a personal split-second appearance on his part to collect his tip. Well, go on, what happened?"

Over the meal, Eleanor treated him to quite a story.

" The first night you were away it was so hot that I slept with the bedroom door open on to the veranda. I had the watchman with his club sleeping in the kitchen. I kept your loaded revolver on the bedside table. Fanny was sleeping on the mat by my bed. Barney slept by the bedroom door and I kept a storm lamp burning on the floor. So I was well protected."

Fanny was their bull-terrier, while Barney was a rough-and-tumble airedale left for safe-keeping with them by the Costers. George visualised the scene in the house with some amusement. He would never have left Eleanor alone if he had not been completely confident of her safety. While he was home they all lived a free-and-easy life. The moment he left the house was turned into a fortress.

" Of course, you don't think it's necessary," continued Eleanor, noticing his look. "But this will show you that it is. At 2 a.m. I was awakened by the sound of a scuffle on the veranda. Then I heard a scream of pain from Barney. I jumped out of bed, grabbed the lamp with my left hand and the revolver in my right, and ran outside. I was just in time to see two animal figures roll over the edge of the veranda into the garden. I could hardly see in the light, but I could hear something being dragged through the flowers. I guessed that a leopard had caught Barney. They were having a terrific tug-of-war.

" I fired two shots from the revolver. What is it anyway, a cannon? The animals immediately tumbled over the edge of the terrace. I fired two more shots. I must say that they had some effect. The leopard released Barney and hurtled off with a great crash through the dry leaves under the wild fig tree. A few seconds later Barney scrambled back on to the terrace wall. I called him, but he simply stood there hanging his head. I ran to him. He was bleeding all over. I carried him into the house. The watchman came out and helped me. He fetched a bowl of water and we washed the wounds with permanganate of potash.

" Barney was gashed and torn all over his body, with a gaping wound in his throat. When we examined the garden in the morning we found a shallow furrow on the terrace, where Barney and the leopard must have dragged each other to and fro. And there were claw marks up the trunk of the fig tree where the leopard must have hidden after I fired the shots.

" The next night I went to bed early, hoping that the leopard had been scared off for good. Instead of that it came back with a half-grown cub to lend support. They kept up that ghastly noise of theirs all night, grunting around the house like donkeys starting to bray, with Fanny barking at them from inside, and the more she barked the more the leopards grunted and the hungrier they sounded. When we examined their tracks the next morning it was obvious that they had simply patrolled around the house all night, hoping the dogs would come out and provide them with a dinner.

" The third night was exactly the same. The watchman had a friend sleeping with him by then. They all said that they had never before heard leopards as noisy and as fearless as these. The female leopard had a particularly evil cry. I don't blame the Africans for thinking she was a witch. If I fired the revolver out of the window she simply paid not the slightest attention to the sound. If anything, her growling became more threatening, with the cub trying to imitate her like a demoniac echo.

" I couldn't stand much more of this. So I sent a message in to Mbeya asking the district commissioner to help me. But he was away on safari and his assistant was also on the verge of departure to a golf tournament at Tukuyu when my message arrived. So I had to send for Laza. He arrived with his muzzle loader and made his quarters for the night on the living-room floor. The watchman slept next to him with a club, while the third man was armed with a spear and a panga. They also had a petromax lamp kept alight but concealed under a packing case so that they could use it at a moment's notice.

" Laza had worked out a definite campaign. Just at midnight the leopard started to grunt outside the kitchen. I was in bed. There was a tremendous pandemonium on the back veranda. I heard the roar of Laza's muzzle loader followed by a vigorous tattoo beaten on an empty paraffin tin. I rushed out just in time to hear the leopard give a derisive grunt. But at least the creature was chased away and we slept until morning.

" When day came, Laza said he thought it was useless to try again. The leopard was a devil and his gun was impotent against black magic. I should rather see a witch doctor. As for Laza, he had business in town. He would see me another night.

" That afternoon Stewart and Griffiths very decently drove over from their farm and set up a trap gun in the garden. But that just made matters worse. The leopard sniffed about the thing and I spent the whole night lying awake tensely waiting for the gun to go off. Of course, it never did. I just lay there expecting the bang, and thinking how soundly you were probably sleeping in the bush.

" The next two nights were the same. Then Dr Jackson of the tsetse department passed this way. I told him about the leopard. He loaned me his shot-gun and some S.S.G cartridges. He advised that I should wait until the leopard was pretty close and then blow its bloody head off."

"And did you?"

She looked at George coldly for a moment and then went on.

" Well, I called on Laza to spend another night in the house and we planned a final show-down. The four of us, myself and the three Africans, sat up in the living-room waiting for the leopard. We kept the light on but draped blankets over the windows to make the house look dark. As soon as we heard the leopard near the kitchen we all rushed out the back door, first the man with the panga and the lamp, next Laza with his muzzle loader, then me with the shot-gun, and last the watchman with his spear and your revolver. What a farce! The lamp simply blinded us. The leopard just grunted and vanished. We all had to troop back inside and try to sleep. Next morning I sent a runner to Mbeya, ordered a taxi and abandoned the farm. I spent the last month with Lillian Eustace at Tukuyu. The only thing that brought me back was your letter saying that you would be returning today. And now you are here I jolly well hope that the leopard does come. Then you'll know all about it."

George tried to point out to her that even if the leopard did come there was no livestock on the farm which it could damage. The creature didn't drink coffee, so why not let it be? A more philosophic outlook towards the thing could even convert the disturbing qualities in its growl to something soporific. There were admittedly such things as man-eating leopards but there was certainly no record of one ever having entered a house by force.

Eleanor was not easy to convince. Her tension over the leopard, in fact, made him curious to encounter so redoubtable an animal. He sat up that night and waited for the creature to announce itself. A warm welcome would be provided when the animal did come. Shortly after midnight, when George was already half asleep, there was a grunting in the direction of the nearby gully. George slipped outside quietly. Eleanor followed with a revolver and a torch. She promptly kicked the dog's enamelled food bowl down the steps with a clatter. George sent her back inside and went after the leopard on his own. It was pitch dark, drizzling, and the rain on the long grass soon soaked his legs. The only sign of the leopard was one more subdued grunt in the distance. George assumed that the animal must have been alarmed by the noise of the food bowl, but Eleanor, when he returned to the house, was certain that it had smelt George.

"You'll see," she said darkly, " now that it knows you are here it just won't come again."

George scoffed, but the next night, when he heard a scratching on the roof while he was undressing and ran outside in his shirt, it was only the house cat, Winnie, although how she had made such a noise it was impossible to say. The leopard was heard no more, until, in fact, George had occasion to go back to the Lupa for a few days to clear up some business. Then Eleanor once again heard it in the night, but only far away. The watchman grinned at her understandingly.

"It's asking if the master is here," he said and, indeed, the grunt did seem to have more enquiry than venom in its sound. Eleanor simply gave it up. She shrugged. The matter was just beyond her comprehension. She went to bed while the watchman walked back to his post, nodding his head sagely and muttering:

"Well, what about the baboons? The madame knows they never come when the master is here, but the day he goes, they come. The madame knows. . . ."

On the Lupa, George had to attend to only minor affairs. He had no intention of going back to the goldfields to prospect. His financial position was such that some variety of regular income would be essential by the beginning of the new year. He just had no more cash reserves to finance any speculation on the Lupa. He had written once again to Philip Teare, the game warden, explaining the urgency of the position, and it was while he was awaiting a reply that he made his visit to the goldfields.

He found the Lupa in something of a ferment, with such bad feeling between the diggers and the government that there was even talk of a revolution. Molteno, at the head of a deputation from the Lupa Gold Diggers' Association, had flown down to Dar es Salaam to thrash the matter out with the governor. The trouble lay in a relaxation of the method of granting mining licences. Licences had always been granted fairly easily. A digger simply had to have his claim fee, be able to read the mining regulations, and be competent to properly mark off a claim with the simplest of implements. Now the authorities had relaxed their requirements so that anybody could register a claim simply by payment of a small fee. The result was a chaotic increase in gold theft, as even the completely illiterate labourers could peg some quite useless claim and by right of its ownership be legally entitled to sell to the gold buyers anything they had found or stolen, with no questions asked.

The threat to their livelihood completely upset the diggers. There were stormy meetings, threats to burn down the Government offices, and a great deal of hard-luck talk about men who had made something of a strike and then found that some member of their own labouring force had slipped through the bush ahead of them and registered the claim.

Prospecting in such conditions would be hazardous enough even if a man had adequate finances. Then, on top of these difficulties there was a general feeling that, at least as far as alluvial was concerned, the Lupa had been pretty thoroughly prospected. Reef discoveries like Lock's Luck might still be made, but they were hardly numerous. There was already a tendency for men to start drifting away from the Lupa. Others were abandoning claim working and taking employment on the bigger reef mines, like the Saza Mine and the Ntumbi Reef Mine, but there was little profit for the individual in such activity. George Nutting, an Australian, had found the Saza reef and made something worthwhile out of selling it to a company, but James Fraser Brown, the manager of this concern, eventually died leaving behind him a comfortable fortune for his old school in Britain, but for the country in which he had made it, only the reputation of having been one of the meanest men ever to live in Tanganyika. The Ntumbi Reef Mine was also run by a very tough individual indeed, McHugh, said to be the only man on the Lupa who, when drunk enough, could carry around in his teeth any one of the dining-room tables in the Goldfields Hotel. Like James Brown, he was not exactly of a philanthropic disposition to his employees and the only regret most of them ever had at leaving the service of such masters was that they had not left much earlier.

George simply completed his business on the goldfields and went back home. On the way he passed through Mbeya and found a message waiting for him in the bar of the Sluice Box. It was from Findlay Ross, the local forestry officer, and asked George to be sure and see him before going to the farm. George walked up to the forestry office. The news he received relieved him so sharply of the economic worries which had been oppressing him for years that it felt as though a physical weight had been lifted from his mind. There was a job going in the forestry department for a temporary field officer at Mbulu. It was a poorly paid post, only £350 a year, but there were pretty certain prospects of either joining the permanent staff or transferring later to the game department. There was also the privilege of regular paid overseas leave every thirty months.

The forestry department offered the position to George on the recommendation of David Pollock, the district commissioner of Mbeya, and in recognition of the work he had done in introducing trout to Tanganyika. It was the best news George thought that he had ever received. Eleanor was as delighted as he was when he returned to the farm and informed her of his acceptance of the appointment. She made the most of the opportunity to give him some news herself. She was going to have another baby. Some security in life was therefore particularly welcome.

Both of them realised that the change to their lives would be tremendous. The farm for one thing would have to be finally abandoned. There was no prospect of selling the place. They would just have to relinquish their grasp on it and allow the cultivation to revert to the wilderness from which they had taken it. Shedding tears over all their lost hopes was useless. The prospect of taking orders from somebody, after his lifetime of independence, might provide George with a few last-minute qualms, but the only thing to do was to face up to the realities of their situation. And there was always the consolation that he would be a long jump nearer his ambition of joining the game department.

They left the farm at the beginning of March 1938. They packed all their greatest household treasures, as well as Kiyanda and another African, the two dogs and a few other oddments, into the red Ford. The little vehicle seemed to contain everything, although its springs did take on a rather concave appearance. George drove it gingerly as far as the forest officer's house in Mbeya and then re-examined matters. Findlay Ross was frankly astounded that the vehicle had travelled as far as it had. To expect the springs to last for six hundred miles of pot-holes would be more than optimistic. They would either have to jettison part of the load or change to a heavier vehicle.

Here they had a piece of luck. One of the local garages had a Ford V8 box-body for sale. It was slightly more than second hand but could still go without much pushing. For a cash consideration together with the little Ford, the garage would part with this treasure. The transaction actually relieved George's banking account of its last few pounds, but at least he was now on the government payroll. Providing the box-body carried him to Mbulu without a major mishap he would be able to draw a small advance and keep the family in food.

The journey actually passed very well. The Great North Road as far as Dodoma had been much improved since the time seven years before when George had first brought Eleanor to the farm. The old rattle-trap pole bridges had been replaced by steel affairs which at least looked secure and many of the worst mud-holes had been filled. The weather was also pleasant, which was important, for they had no money for hotels and simply camped at any suitable spot when they stopped at night.

Eleanor had never been north of Dodoma, so she found the second half of the journey particularly interesting. Even the arid thorn-bowl country beyond the railway line had its fascination, with the wierdly shaped baobabs and the primitive Gogo tribespeople wandering through the wilderness with their herds of scraggy-looking cattle exactly as she remembered them from her first arrival.

North of Babati, Eleanor also saw her first really big herds of plains game. Even George found the excitement of his family to be infectious. Little Kate was bouncing up and down in her seat every time she sighted a herd of wildebeeste or zebra, while the ostriches and the almost tame giraffes who hardly deigned to clear the road for traffic made her chortle with delight.

For the first time Eleanor also saw the Masai on their home ground, with their strange, primitive hovels called *manyattas,* the thorn-walled cattle bomas and the tall, gaunt-faced young warriors tramping the roads as though they were on an African knights-errant.

George's immediate destination was Arusha. Their approach to that pleasant little town was on a beautiful clear day, with the family thrilled at the towering mass of Mount Meru and George rather heartsore at the sight of the coffee plantations. They were all obviously flourishing, with the ideal soil and climatic conditions of the area producing a far higher yield per acre than anything possible around Mbeya, and a convenient railway to take the crop cheaply to the coast. Eleanor's father had certainly been right in his original doubts. The only consolation for George was that he was not the only amateur farmer to rush into the wastelands and lose all his savings, where wiser men would have done little other than admire the view.

In Arusha, the family booked into an hotel so that they could all enjoy hot baths and a general sprucing up. Then George reported to Tom Lewis, the forestry officer, and made a start at learning his duties. It was certainly most pleasant work. His very junior position at Mbulu would call for more protective activity than anything else. He would have three magnificent indigenous forests under his care and his responsibility was to conserve them with the creation of firebreaks, the fighting of fires, and the proper control of any wood-cutting.

Tom Lewis took him out camping in one of the forest reserves on Mount Meru and gave him a short, intensive course on the practical side of a forester's life. It was all very fascinating and the pleasure very real of working in such cool and tranquil surroundings. By all accounts, Mbulu lay in equally high and almost as beautiful surroundings, and Lillian, Tom Lewis' wife, soon had Eleanor all agog with excitement at the prospect of occupying what was reputedly a very cosy little forestry house.

Eleanor actually was taking to the civil service life with very evident pleasure. She and Lillian Lewis stayed in the forest camp with their children while George was receiving his instructions, and the continuous chit-chat about service life and personalities, leaves and promotions, which George had formerly considered so vapid, certainly took on dimensions less trivial now that his own future was involved with their consequences.

By the time they returned to Arusha they were quite a family of junior civil servants, with Eleanor already marking off a little diary of the months until their first leave, when she would be able to see her children again and re-unite the family in a permanent home.

The night before they left Arusha it poured with rain. The prospects of an easy journey to Mbulu were not good. Most of the road lay over soil of the " black cotton " type, which stirred up to something like chocolate blanc-mange with the first addition of water. The Ford had no chains in its accessory box and there were none available in Arusha. George expected the worst, and in this he was certainly not disappointed. The major part of the journey, in fact, was only made possible by the presence of Kiyanda and his companion. They pushed, shoved, and poked grass and branches beneath spinning wheels, covering themselves with some pretty sleazy-looking mud in the process, but at least keeping the vehicle moving.

Quite early in the day George abandoned all hope of reaching Mbulu that evening. The first seventy miles were not so bad, as they had to retrace their route back down the Great North Road and then turn off on the track leading towards the Ngorongoro Crater. The trouble started from that point on and particularly when the road set out to climb the wall of the Great Rift Valley. Any consolation of magnificent views down upon Lake Manyara with its brilliant white soda beach was quite unappreciated.

There was a rest house at a half-way place called Karatu but the chances dwindled of even travelling as far as that when, in the late afternoon, the Ford bogged down in a mess of mud at the bottom of a steep hill. The most frantic efforts failed to budge it. George, who was pushing at the back with the two Africans while Eleanor drove, was about to give up and prepare for a cramped night in the car. But when he wiped the mud from his eyes he found five Masai warriors standing on the roadside watching him with a glint of amusement in their eyes. Eleanor was quite shaken at their sudden appearance. Nobody had seen the approach of the men. They simply seemed to have materialised, standing there with their long spears and shields, looking rather aloof and supercilious, their skins well rubbed with red ochre and for dress only a blanket casually knotted over one shoulder.

George greeted them in Swahili. He knew no Masai, but they seemed to understand him well enough.

" Help to push, I will reward you."

They recoiled with just sufficient reaction to register disgust at the mere idea of manual labour. The movement was a subtle expression of the fact that they were warriors and Masai warriors do not soil their hands. This was Africa. It was a place where women worked.

George wasn't amused. He did something which startled Eleanor as much as the Masai. He plucked their spears from their hands, one by one, and tossed the weapons into the back of the box-body.

" Now push," he said, " and when we are safely out of the mud you shall have your spears back."

The Masai burst out laughing. They pushed with a will. Soon the box-body was roaring up the slope.

" Don't try and stop," George shouted to Eleanor. " You'll stick fast again."

The car bounced and bumped up towards the summit with the men racing along behind it, the athletic Masai actually passing the box-body before it reached the top, and then standing cheering until the vehicle reached the safety of level ground. The episode put everybody into excellent humour, notwithstanding the mud and threatening clouds. George handed out gifts all round. Then he took the wheel and they had no further trouble along the road as far as the rest hut at Karatu.

There they spent a rather chilly night in the shelter of what was only a three-walled shack, very creaky and inevitably built with its open end facing the prevailing wind. Still, it at least provided a roof during an evening shower. In the early hours of the morning the weather cleared, leaving the stars to shine down as brightly as drops of sunlit dew glittering on a bed of velvet. The dawn would come sharp and clear. The mud of Africa soon settles and they would certainly reach Mbulu without further trouble.

Eleanor could obviously hardly contain herself to reach her new home. She talked herself to sleep about such momentous things as the size of the windows of the forest cottage and whether she had brought enough curtaining. The two Africans were full of curiosity to see the girls of the local tribe, who had some reputation as beauties. Only George admitted to a few lingering regrets. In some ways this was his last night of freedom. From the next day he would be the holder of an official position. He would be keeping the regular hours and following the routines of a conventional life which he had always considered intolerable. There would be reports to make and accounts to keep, wages to pay and respects to be made to men of whom he knew nothing, but who, by the very establishment of the civil service, even if they were still in their teens and fresh from Britain, would consider themselves to be very much the superior of a temporary forest officer. Even if the men were easy going, their wives, in so tiny a community, would soon put Eleanor in her place in the scale of precedence. Squabbles over such trivialities had made a misery of life in more than one outpost. The thought gave him some wry humour.

CHAPTER TWENTY-THREE

MBULU

MBULU lies in what is a quite striking portion of Tanganyika. The land-scape is a ruggedly fertile grassland lifted high between the Rift Valley in the east and the Lake Eyasi depression in the west. Between these two sink-holes of heat, fever and sleeping sickness, the Iraki tribe have found a healthy refuge for themselves where they lead a very isolated life preoccupied with the drudgery of the primitive peasant.

The Iraki are an amiable and good-looking people. Their women, parti-cularly, have delicately made features, walk well, and have an air about them of some superiority over their neighbours. In actual fact, the origin of these people is slightly mysterious. In the ceaseless storm of African tribal history they were somehow or other thrown up like exotic driftwood upon a strange shore. Speaking a guttural language quite foreign to anything else in Tan-ganyika, they were promptly nicknamed the *waMbulu* by their neighbours. The name means, literally, The People who Talk Foolishly. Understandably, they do not like this name, but it has clung to them through the years, attaching itself also to their district and to the diminutive " capital " where George and Eleanor made their new home.

Eleanor's notion of a romantic retreat in the forestry cottage came to grief as soon as they arrived in Mbulu. The road led through the usual non-descript collection of Indian-run *duka* shops and then curved with something of a flourish to rest in the shade of a stand of trees growing before a handsome example of one of the *Beau Geste*-looking types of fort which the Germans built during their years of rule over Tanganyika.

George went in to report to the district commissioner and found him to be a rather unusual-looking man with one blue eye and the other light brown. His name was Duncan. He promptly informed George that the forestry cottage was already occupied. As George had half-expected, temporary forestry employees were not much thought of locally and the cottage had been put to better use as a home for the assistant district officer. George and Eleanor could occupy quarters within the fort. Eleanor was not initially distressed at this news. The fort certainly had a romantic appearance. At first glance it might even be fun staying in the place.

The district commissioner showed them around. The fort was a whitewashed pile of masonry, single storied, but tall in the German manner. It was built around a centre square. Two sides of the fort were used as offices, storerooms and a courtroom. The third side consisted of a thick wall with battlements, loopholes, and a huge iron-shod double door of impressive weight. This was always barred at sunset when the flag was hauled down.

The fourth side of the fort contained the private quarters allocated to George and Eleanor. They were tolerably commodious but hardly cosy, and fitted with heavy Victorian furniture. There was a vast, bleak bedroom, a dining-room, and an enormous gloomy-looking kitchen in which meals for the original German garrison had once been cooked. In one corner of the fort there was also a tower which supported a Union Jack and contained a room which was included in the quarters as a sitting-room. Its windows provided a pleasant view of a rolling countryside, but this was certainly the only desirable feature to the entire place. For the rest, there was no vestige of privacy in living in a fort. The bare courtyard was filled all day with tribespeople squatting around waiting to be admitted to the courtroom as witnesses or spectators to trials. To relieve the boredom of the wait they ate, spat, picked their noses, and chattered in stentorian voices which seemed to reverberate from one side of the fort to the other.

In the evening when the humans went home, their place was taken by numerous wild creatures. The kitchen was the hunting ground for rats of the variety *Ratis giganticus* with a bulk rivalling that of young sausage dogs. In the attics there were screech owls with a habit of returning to and leaving their quarters with a horrible scrambling of their claws on the roof. Bees swarmed in the ceilings; the two askaris who guarded the fort at night had smokers' coughs, while the howling of prisoners receiving lashes could be heard at odd intervals from the adjoining gaol.

To complicate matters further, Eleanor soon discovered that the fort was reputed to be haunted. She came back from her first afternoon's walk with the information that she had noticed three distinct bullet holes in the door, while just beyond the walls there was a diminutive cemetery containing the graves of some fifteen South African soldiers killed in the neighbourhood by the Germans during the course of the First World War. There was a story that a German named Siedtendorf had crept up to the fort one night and called to the sentry that he wanted to talk to the officer in command. A lieutenant opened the peep-hole in the door and the German then very decently proceeded to shoot him in the face. Hence the bullet holes in the door and the stories of a ghost haunting the scene of so unpleasant an event.

The variety of occupants of the fort, both animal and spectral, were more distracting to Eleanor than to George. He engrossed himself in his new life and found the activities of a forester to be both strenuous and interesting. He was out all day and many a night planting wattles and gums or trying to persuade the tribespeople to conserve natural forests and plant trees themselves in order to provide firewood.

Occasionally, when he was busy supervising firebreaks in one of the indigenous forests, he would take Eleanor and Kate with him. They would enjoy a spell of camp life, living for several days on end in some roughly made but comfortable little grass shack erected in a clearing among the trees. George would be out from dawn to dusk attending to his duties while Eleanor would spend a lazy day relaxing in the shade or taking Kate on a stroll into the sorghum fields where the child could be entertained by watching the never-ending struggle waged against Nature by man in an effort to reap crops. As the sorghum ripened, prodigious swarms of grain-eating birds arrived on the scene. In an effort to defeat these plunderers, the peasants erected observation platforms in the centre of each field. Young boys and the women took it in turns to occupy the platforms. Each watcher had a sling. Balls of mud were placed as ammunition in the centre of the sling. The weapon would be whirled around at arm's length, one end of the sling suddenly released with a loud whip-like crack, and the ball would hurtle off to shatter with a crash against the sorghum stalks, sending startled birds swarming off in all directions. It was very easy for any spectator to develop a sneaking regard for the cheeky little birds but in such a false sentiment the peasants could have no share. To them the battle with the plunderers was a genuine matter of life and death with no quarter granted from either side.

In the evenings, when George was back from his labours, which certainly kept him fit, if tired, they often received visits from some of the local residents. Europeans, of course, were very scarce. Apart from the handful of Government officials at Mbulu, there were few settlers in the area; only a sprinkling of British, not doing particularly well in the heat near Lake Manyara, a group of Germans at Oldeani and a small Afrikaans community at Karatu.

The local African tribes, however, quite made up in variety for any scarcity of Europeans. They were, in fact, an odd lot. George only received his first inkling of their more interesting characteristics when an elderly Indian trader visited his camp one evening and entertained him with some gossip. George was camped at the time near the village of Babati, on the Great North Road, just below the forest-covered slopes of the extinct volcano known as Ufiyome. He was burning firebreaks at the time and the information given to him by the Indian trader provided material for considerable thought next morning as he climbed towards the lake which filled the original crater.

The trader had really wanted advice. He was a man who kept chickens and a few nights previously he had been aroused by a disturbance in his yard. He went out with a torch and a gun. In the torch light he found that a hyena had managed to force its way through the fence of the courtyard and was enjoying a chicken dinner. The trader put two bullets into the creature and then went back to bed. The real trouble started the next morning.

" I woke up," said the trader, " to the sound of lamentation in my yard. I went out. I found an old woman, a famous witch, crying over the body of the hyena. She was pouring dust over her head and wailing most piteously. When she saw me she went half-mad with rage. She turned the hyena over and pointed to a mark on its shoulder.

" ' This is my hyena,' she shouted furiously.

" She stormed up to me. She demanded to know what damage her hyena had done to cause me to shoot it. I told her that it was eating my chickens. She said this was nothing. She would have paid me ten times over. She threatened to kill me by witchcraft. She was so frenzied that I laughed at her. She ran back to the hyena. She took it into her arms and then went sobbing down the street. The people tell me that she is still half-dead with sorrow and frustration. They say that when I laughed she knew that her witchcraft was powerless against my own charms."

The man shrugged.

" I have no charms. Only disbelief in her magic. But the people believe in such things."

He eyed George half apologetically.

" They say that these witches have hyenas for their lovers. They say that all hyenas in this country of the Mbugwe people are owned by witches and all are marked with signs of ownership. They say that once a witch has a hyena for a sweetheart then all men are as innocents to them. It is of such things that I wish to ask you, for I am ignorant in these matters."

George had to admit to sharing in this ignorance. The Mbugwe people who lived in the alkaline flats below Ufiyome mountain were considered primitive even by their tribal neighbours. In bygone days they had found their way into a land so inhospitable that it would have been far better to have left it uninhabited. In the rainy season it was a swamp; in the dry season it turned into a desert. It was a place productive of little other than dust devils, tsetse fly, and the largest and noisiest mosquitoes in all Africa.

The drinking water was brackish and agricultural possibilities negligible. In an environment as miserable as this, the Mbugwe led lives of such hopelessness as to make them the despair of the administration and the butt of their neighbours. By that strange quirk of human emotion which often showers what is a stupidly exaggerated affection upon some totally worthless ground simply because it was the place of their birth, the Mbugwe resolutely resisted all efforts to persuade them that they would really be much happier elsewhere.

George had a few Mbugwe men on his staff. The very hardship of their home life made them excellent porters, and they traditionally found employment in this field. After hearing the Indian trader's story, George made a pastime of learning something more of the habits of the tribe. The porters were quite agreeable to discussing the private lives of their people. Around the camp fires at night they regaled him with a number of interesting details of the mysteries of their tribe.

They were certainly well riddled with superstition. Witches, were-hyenas and quite a few other gewgaws from the box of tricks of black magic haunted not only their nights but also their days. To them there was nothing particularly amusing or odd about the idea of the night being haunted by magicians riding full tilt on the backs of hyenas and carrying flaming torches made of the fat of the animals which bore them.

Hyenas played a major part in all Mbugwe witchcraft. They were the night cattle of wizards. The Mbugwe admitted to no wild hyenas. Every animal was owned by some magician, most of whom were female. Hyena pups were raised and trained for magic, while man-killing hyenas could be hired from their owners and employed to settle accounts with enemies. It appeared that, not satisfied with the natural hardships of their daily way of life, the Mbugwe had devised a very special hell for themselves at night.

Although game control was out of his province, and witchcraft a matter for the anthropologists, George had his curiosity sufficiently aroused to shoot a few hyenas in the area. Some of them certainly appeared to carry signs of human interference. Two of them had beads knotted into their fur, but whether by accident or design it was difficult to tell. Others had cuts in portions of their anatomy which looked too symmetrical to be accidental. The porters had no doubt at all about the nature and origin of these signs. They expected disastrous consequences to George for his slaughter of such special creatures. Nothing, however, happened. Only on one night, a black rhinoceros charged full tilt through his camp, scattered fire, tents and men in all directions, and then simply stormed on into the forest as though nothing had happened. According to the porters this was George's " warning off " notice.

The southern neighbours of the Mbugwe, the Irangi tribe, were said to be on even more intimate terms, if this was possible, with hyenas. The adjoining Tatog tribe, who lived around the slopes of the handsome extinct volcano named Hanang, had also developed an interesting pastime for themselves.

Their young women required all suitors, in exchange for their favours, to present them with convincing evidence of having barbarously murdered as many travellers and isolated persons as could be found exposing themselves unwisely to the hospitality of the country.

Against a background of such a variety of tribes, the small European communities in the district led lives of an almost unreal detachment. The three European women at Mbulu did not get on particularly well with one another. The men—the district commissioner, his assistant, Gordon Russell, a veterinary officer named Jock Gowan, a district foreman named Bobby Malan, and three civilians living in the village, a German with an American wife and an odd Irishman named Dudley O'Byrne with a pet pig called Denis—all just about tolerated one another, if only because they could find common ground by confining their conversation to professional matters.

The gulf between this European community and the surrounding tribespeople was so large through differences of language and culture that they could really be creatures who had originated on different planets. The tribespeople accepted the Europeans as judges, tax collectors and technical advisers. In exchange for this docility the tribespeople certainly received honest and well-meant administration of an almost fatherly, caretaker kind, and such benefits of medicine and education as the limited economic resources of the country could afford. The almost unreal mutual tolerance in the situation was emphasised each Friday when there was a regular ceremony in the late afternoon. A procession of African schoolboys, headed by a drum and penny-whistle band playing something which sounded like " Two Lovely Black Eyes," marched to the fort. With Eleanor and Kate peeping at them through the window, they formed up below the tower and saluted the lowering of the flag with a cheerful performance of " God Save the King." None of them could really be expected to know what the ceremony meant but at least the gesture was made.

The largest European community in the district was that of the Germans, most of whom were engaged on coffee-farming in the Oldeani area. Oldeani village was the centre for this community and it was far and away the most substantial settlement in the area, with a few European traders, a German boarding school and a very neat little hospital. It was there that Eleanor decided to have her baby. George secured the use of the Government rest house which was only periodically used by visiting officers, and Eleanor moved there in July as her time of waiting drew to an end. George went with her, arranging his work programme so that he could use Oldeani as a base for several weeks.

The change of community was interesting. Most of the Germans were rather on the grim side, and well saturated with the current Nazi vogue, complete with raised hand salutes, heel clickings, and carefully cultivated Hitler toothbrush moustaches. One or two of them, however, could relax slightly. There was a rather jolly butcher who wandered around shaded by a green Tyrolean hat and feather, and with his beefy thighs bulging out from the usual greasy-looking *lederhosen* supported by embroidered braces. He at least looked as though he would like to break into a yodel occasionally, while a trader named Schnabbe and his wife were also inclined to be human providing they were out of the company of the amateur politicians.

Everybody was very polite and kind. The local nurse, Sister Marianne, knew very little English, but by the aid of a pocket dictionary, assured Eleanor that there was no reason for any alarm at the absence of a doctor. She was an experienced midwife and if there were difficulties they could always rely on the aid of a retired veterinary surgeon who lived in the vicinity. Neither was there any need for George to loiter around, Eleanor was assured. The baby looked as though it would be late, and for a man to waste good working time simply waiting for a delivery was contrary to the nurse's ideas of efficiency.

As it happened, the baby was late; so late that Eleanor had to vacate the guest house in order to make way for a governor's visit, and remove to the school before there were any signs of the imminent advent of another young Rushby. The boarding school provided the only other possible accommodation and she had simply to brace herself against the giggles of what were normally a very prim and spruce set of children, and constant repetitions of the teachers' joke that she was getting young Rushby off to an early start in his lessons. Photographs of Hitler hanging on the walls above every bed also took some getting used to. Some of the spinster teachers attended to these portraits almost as though they were shrines, with bracket-vases of flowers kept freshly filled by the side of each photograph.

George took himself off to the Karatu area during Eleanor's days at the school. Working in this area gave him the opportunity of meeting the Afrikaans farming community. He found them to be a kindly if rather stoical and taciturn bunch. Their patriarch, and the head of an enormous family of sons, was a spare-figured, bearded man named Van Rooyen, a real Boer of the Smuts type who had fought the British for his independence during the South African War, then removed as a settler to Tanganyika and done his duty for the Germans in the World War at some cost and annoyance to his old enemies. He was now reasonably settled, just about tolerated the administration, liked the country, and with his sons, adored hunting with an almost fanatical fervour. In this connection, meeting a man like George was almost like a visit of the Pope to an isolated religious community. Strong men journeyed to his camp from miles around to discuss the finer points of marksmanship and tracking. The professional, whether hunter or photographer, is often baffled by the insistence of the amateur on the irrelevant trifles of their hobby. George was also not especially fond of the plain process of killing, but the Karatu enthusiasts were at least a rugged crowd. The older men, in particular, were such great individualists that he would not have been human if he had failed to be both gratified and flattered by their hospitality and esteem.

The German community also regarded George as being something different from their ideas of a conventional Englishman. Eleanor was aware of this from a companion she employed to look after Kate during the confinement. The companion was the well-bred and rather handsome young niece of a local baron who was keen on the girl having the opportunity of practising her English in a British home even though the wages were low.

Ingeborg, for that was her name, was also known as *Mouche* to her friends. She was partial to Hitler Youth songs and played martial music incessantly on her gramophone. She was a tall, boyish type with slicked-back hair, a liking for tweeds and an abhorrence of make-up. Such tastes might have given food for thought to casual acquaintances, but a gentleman friend lurking around the premises indicated that Mouche was healthily feminine beneath her exterior. She ate fantastic amounts of meat, particularly sausages, and it was a fortunate fact that the Tyrolean butcher was one of her admirers. She told Eleanor that the purpose of studying English was because her father wanted her to marry an Englishman. To her, personally, this idea was abhorrent. She regarded the English as being whisky swillers and physical runts. When Eleanor took umbrage at this and reminded her that George was English and hardly degenerate, she airily evaded the issue by saying that he wasn't really an Englishman, he was a hunter, a very much superior thing.

The baby eventually arrived two minutes before midnight on the 5th of September. George was away on safari at the time and the nurse and the veterinary surgeon did the job by the light of a pressure lamp. To make things difficult for them, it was a breech birth and quite a performance before Master John Rushby was hauled out by his feet and treated the world to a lusty howl after a particularly smart smack.

It was a relief to have it all over. George returned to find Eleanor smouldering under the enforced anticlimax of convalescence. Sister Marianne was inclined to be bossy at this time. She had a book written by a spinster specialist in Germany and giving frankly dogmatic instructions about the care of infants and the post-natal exercising of mothers. Eleanor found herself being exercised to the point of haemorrhage while the infant received similar Spartan treatment, with soft woollies " not allowed " (according to the book) and everything kept so sterile that Eleanor momentarily expected to be boiled herself.

There were dozens of visitors. The German community seemed keen to see the first British baby born in their hospital. They brought flowers and congratulatory cards festooned with fat little cherubs. They were all very much concerned at the time about the dangers of war over the current Czechoslovakian crisis. Sister Marianne's room, adjoining Eleanor's, acted as a variety of local short-wave listening post. The night Neville Chamberlain sold out the Czechs to Hitler produced quite a celebration. What seemed to be the entire local community poured into Eleanor's room, pumping her by the hand as though she had been personally responsible for the betrayal, and quite overlooking George's very evident disgusted opinion that he didn't know what the British were coming to.

Eleanor was ready to go home by then. No matter how comfortable the hospital or kindly its staff, the place is pleasanter to look back upon as you drive home at the end of the whole involved process of having a baby. George had also promised her a surprise, and when she had cleared the dust from her eyes as they drove in to Mbulu she was delighted to find that he had built for her a brand-new home.

The lack of privacy in the fort had proved too irksome to tolerate. So while Eleanor was in hospital, George built a rather picturesque-looking two-roomed shack of poles and rushes. There were no doors or windows. Rush blinds which rolled up in daytime provided light and ventilation, while the grass-thatched roof, if it was no guarantee against the rain, at least provided for nothing a full protein diet from the insects which tumbled from it into the coffee or soup.

From a security point of view, a back scratch from an elephant, or a good roar from a lion, could have pushed the place down. Perhaps it was just as well that the open plains around Mbulu sheltered very few animals save an occasional hyena. The only real danger to the place came from the weather. The very open-ness of the Mbulu plains allowed the winds to sweep around at will. With the grass hopelessly overgrazed in normal African fashion, dust devils had a real hunting ground in the place. They twisted erratically over the plain while Eleanor watched them apprehensively from her door. When any of them did pay her a visit, they simply wandered straight through the shack with the reed wall providing no apparent resistance at all.

The start of the wet season also emphasised the weakness of the shack. George was away planting when the first real storm came. With the shack built on a slight slope, the storm water simply poured through the walls. The roof sprang so many leaks it resembled a fire sprinkler, while the bowls and plates arranged to catch any water were soon floating about in pools of their own.

George, on his return, draped a tarpaulin over the roof and dug ditches to deviate water from the walls. The little shack with this protection looked as though it was outfitted with a mackintosh and galoshes. The tailoring stopped most of the leaks but the place was still damp and draughty. They were actually debating a rather ignominious return to the fort when the mail came one morning. And there for George was a notification from Philip Teare that at long last there was a vacancy in the game department. From the end of October 1938, George was offered the permanent post of a ranger, largely to be employed on elephant control in the Eastern Province where his skills and experience could be used to the advantage and welfare of Tanganyika.

He read the letter to Eleanor. She was as delighted as he was. On a pad of damp paper in the shack at Mbulu, George wrote out his acceptance of the offer. It was what he had been dreaming about since the failure of the farm. He was thirty-eight. For the last eight years, since he had first met Eleanor, he had tried to change his way of life to fit a mould which to him was really uncomfortably foreign. Now he could go back to the life he loved, to the long grass, the game and the elephants, and what was more, he could do it in a way which was tolerable to a wife and family. He had often wondered what his old companions of the ivory-hunting days would have said at his attempted transition to the conventional life of a farmer and civil servant. Jim Sutherland would certainly have bristled at the very thought. A hard-case prospector like Bill Cumming would have done an avoiding detour of a thousand miles around anybody even thinking of offering him a job. To really stubborn bush wanderers like these, slow starvation would be preferable to submitting to civilisation's stranglehold implicit in the wearing of a tie. On the other hand, neither of them was ever married; neither of them lived a life which allowed them to leave anything at all behind when they died save a memory.

The death of Sutherland had been miserable. As for Bill Cumming, before he had left the Lupa, George had tried to see the man in order to say goodbye. But the old prospector was so morose and withdrawn as to be quite unreachable in some private sanctuary in the bush. Actually, the prospector was suffering from diabetes. It was only long afterwards, in 1940, that George heard the news of the manner of Cumming's death. His diabetic condition eventually forced him into the Chunya hospital. Dr Latham tried to help him, but he was an unhappy patient.

Lambert Lock went to see him and tried to persuade him to stay in hospital.

" Doc reckons that he can patch you up," he said.

Cumming shrugged. He shook his head.

" I dunno," he said. " I feel that I'm going to die, and if I do I'd rather die in the bush. That's where I belong."

Lock argued with him. After a while the old prospector agreed to stay. But an hour after Lock left, Cumming changed his mind. He slipped away. Sandy Kerr took him back to his old camp on the Kasanga. There he died the next day. He was buried in the little cemetery at Chunya. The diggers passed a hat around to collect for a tombstone, but the money disappeared somewhere down the line. His grave was left unmarked, perhaps as he would have preferred it; just a pile of stones to keep the hyenas off and no more desirable a paradise for his restless spirit than the wild bush around him.

CHAPTER TWENTY-FOUR

NZASA

IT WAS, of course, pouring with rain when they left Mbulu. Having made them as uncomfortable as possible during the last few weeks, the gods of the weather seemed determined to inflict one last glorious drenching on their persons and impedimenta as they travelled. The only alleviating factor was that they had become so used to damp and cold in the leaky little shack that, by comparison, the cab of the box-body Ford was snug and the mud of the road at least not carried over the floor of their home by the floods.

The two servants were both certain that the downpour had been provoked by George's last act in the district. As a forester he had done something which was really not his concern. Two days before he left Mbulu he went to the Marang forest and shot a young bull elephant which had killed two of the local tribespeople. The animal had been wounded in his behind by peasants throwing spears in order to drive him off their land. In consequence he had become slightly irate against human beings. He was too inexperienced an elephant, however, to give George any trouble in the hunt. But Kiyanda and the other servant both had some notion that the creature had the power to impose supernatural retribution for his demise and the rainstorm was the consequence. If this was indeed the case then the elephant had managed to make no small stir over his death.

It took three days of travelling to cover the 120 miles to Arusha. As usual they started to move with the car hopelessly overloaded. The two servants made themselves comfortable with the bedding, the chattels and the two dogs in the rear. George drove, with Eleanor holding Johnny Jo on her knee and little Kate wedged between them on the front seat. Unfortunately Eleanor had been forced to put the baby on a bottle two days before they started and none of the stores in Mbulu had stocked either primus stove or thermos. The result was that every time the infant demanded food, George had to pull up to the side, hold a raincoat in one arm, and beneath its shelter

248

struggle to boil water over a few sticks soaked in paraffin. The fact that there was never any necessity to look for water was little consolation.

They covered forty-seven miles in the first day and then spent a miserably cramped night trying to sleep in the car while outside it poured with rain from sunset to dawn. By morning at least that part of Tanganyika appeared to have been reduced to a swamp. A boat might almost have made better going of it. The Ford swerved and skidded and occasionally managed a real acrobatic by sliding around in a complete semicircle. Eventually one of the wheel chains broke and had to be repaired with rope, which periodically needed replacing.

If anything, the Great North Road, when they reached it, was in worse state than the branch track to Mbulu. Just beyond the junction they found Jock Gowan, the stock inspector of the district, with his car bogged down to its axles in a mud-bath of black cotton soil. Saying goodbye to him in such circumstances was not particularly cheerful. He had already sent for help so there was nothing they could do save wish him farewell and be thankful that while he was stuck they were still under way.

George had something of a technique in driving through mud. Either that, or one of the Ford's ancestors had been indiscreet with a tank. Whatever the secret, the vehicle kept going. There was even some humour to be found in the sight of the heavy transport vehicles, which were largely responsible for churning the road up in the first place, now stuck fast in their own muck, while the Ford somehow or other managed to slither past. Towards evening they also found a smart car packed with young German men from the Oldeani settlement, all elegantly dressed in lounge suits and originally destined for some wedding. The wedding was long past, assuming that the bridal couple had reached the church, and this particular car-load of guests had composed themselves for a damp night. The wedding photographer was one of their party. He was making up for what business opportunities he had missed by taking photographs of all and sundry as souvenirs of the day they were stuck in the mud.

George parked the Ford for the night close to the Germans. At least the rain had dwindled to a drizzle. The night seemed slightly more cheerful. At dawn it was even possible for George to help the others to extricate themselves. The rest of the journey to Arusha passed off relatively easily. At the worst mud-holes, Eleanor walked, carrying the children in her arms, while George practically thrashed the Ford across. They reached Arusha just before dark and made their way self-consciously through the hall of the hotel. They had as much mud as clothing on their persons, but a bath, a dinner and a comfortable bed put them all back into good humour.

The next morning George went to report to the warden at the game department. He felt curiously ill at ease reporting to a new boss. He could still not quite accustom himself to the idea of working for anybody. The smartly uniformed African game guards, the clerical workers who eyed him curiously as he entered the general office, all made him feel as though he had simply once again returned from the bush to renew a hunting licence or answer some complaint about poaching. To his disappointment he found that Philip Teare was away on leave. The deputy warden, Major Jock Minnery, however, called him into his office as soon as the clerk at the enquiry counter carried in news of George's arrival. He shook hands affably and kicked out a chair.

" It's great to have you with us after all these years," he said. " Philip always wanted you on our side of the fence—George Rushby, ivory hunter, poacher, prospector, farmer, forestry officer and now game ranger. You've certainly crowded enough into your life up to the present. How old are you?"

" Thirty-eight."

" Well, we haven't caught you too late. You're at the peak of things now. You've got all the knowledge and experience that the bush can give. We could never teach you all that. In fact," he grinned, " you could teach us a lot."

" Like how to be a successful poacher?"

" Not only that, but how to shoot straight, and how to understand elephants."

" You're not a bad shot yourself."

Minnery shrugged. He toyed with a small brass badge lying on his desk. George glanced at it. It was the badge of the Tanganyika game department, the head of a buffalo. Minnery noticed his glance.

" Philip and myself were never elephant men," he said. " Philip has always gone for buffaloes. That's why he chose them for our badge. Did he ever tell you how we got these?"

" No."

" We'd always wanted a badge for the department but the Government would never give us the money. Somebody higher up reckoned a badge was an extravagance. Then we had a millionaire Yank out here on a hunting safari a few years back. For a change he was also inclined to do something useful. He considered that we had done him some favours, so when he finished his safari he said that he would like to do something for us. Philip had already told him about our disappointment over the badge. We'd gone so far as to have a Birmingham firm quote on the job and they had sent us a sample. So when he offered to pay the bill, naturally we didn't refuse. It was rather decent of the Yank, I thought. We'd never expected him to do anything like that."

He pushed the badge across the desk.

" You can have this one if you like. You don't have to wear it, of course. The African staff, the game scouts, wear it on the front of their pillbox caps. They're very proud of it. But the European staff have never had a uniform. It would be a bit foolish to attach the thing to a bowler hat. Just keep the badge as a souvenir of the day you became a game ranger on the generous salary of £360 a year. You also enjoy the usual privileges, of course; pension, medical aid, and long leave every thirty months so that you can clear out to a civilised climate and try and purge your system of fever, bilharzia, a touch of sleeping sickness, and any damage to your hide done in the course of your duties by the wild life of the territory."

George grinned. The overseas leave was one of the attractions of the job to Eleanor. They would be able to travel to Cape Town, see her parents and perhaps reclaim the two eldest children. Since they had been left in the Cape for the sake of their health at the beginning of the previous year, Ann and little George had been taken over to England by George's mother.

" What about my duties?" he asked.

Minnery nodded. For the next hour he explained the routine of a ranger's life. George was destined to be posted to the range of the Eastern Province. The previous ranger, a man named J. F. Gabbutt, had been sent back to England after a losing bout with fever. He had died in April 1938, during his sick leave. The range had been vacant ever since his departure.

" You'll really have to start from scratch," Minnery said apologetically. " You'll even find that most of the former game scouts are in jail for poaching. It's been the usual case of mice playing while the cat's been away. You'll just have to recruit and train a fresh staff. If any of the original scouts are worth keeping, you can retain them, but we'll give you a free hand about that. There's nothing we can do to help you from this end. We'll give you one orderly before you leave here, but whether you'll find him any use is another matter. Most of your fellow rangers seem to dislike men trained at headquarters on principle."

" When do I start?"

" We'd like you to get to the range immediately but there's a snag. I'm afraid you'll have to go to Iringa first. There's a bit of a panic on at the moment about rinderpest. It's nothing that really worries us. As you know, things like that are really veterinary matters. Rinderpest is a cattle disease, even the name means that, and not a game problem at all. But the South Africans and Rhodesians are alarmed that the present outbreak might be carried south by infected game and spread to their domestic herds. We want you to go to Iringa, recruit a temporary staff and organise patrols in the bush. Have a good look at the game. Destroy anything that looks sick and send us reports. The proper ranger of the Southern Province, Dusty Arundell, is away on leave. In any case, this type of work is not really a ranger's affair. A ranger is fully employed on his normal duties. Arundell also has some special problems on his hands in the Njombe district. The lions there seem to have a tendency to eat people.

"As soon as possible, however, we'll get you off to your proper range. Meanwhile we'll have to place you on this special duty. Let's hope things don't get worse. Whenever they do there's always some fool in the administration who starts blaming everything on the wild life. You know yourself that if you want to rally idiots to your banner in Africa, you simply raise a cry demanding instant destruction of every wild animal or bird. You'll find that the game department is always the whipping boy for quite a few troubles."

There were several minor matters for George's attention, and the family had one more day's rest in the hotel. By the time they set out for Iringa the weather had cleared. With a dry road the journey to the south was a pleasure. The only lugubrious member of the party was the new orderly, Juma. He obviously preferred the routine life at headquarters. Also, he claimed to have been to Nzasa, the game ranger's base for the Eastern Province and, having been there once, was quite frank about the fact that he had no desire to ever go back. The others, however, were in too cheerful a mood to pay much attention to his depression.

Actually, it was not until the beginning of February 1939, three months after he had started with the game department, that George eventually reached his proper range. The intervening time he spent on rinderpest patrol. It was dull work, although shooting sick animals could at least be marked down as an act of mercy. With Eleanor reasonably comfortable in quarters in the old German fort in Iringa, at least somewhat modernised and far more private than their haunted home in Mbulu, he spent weeks patrolling into the bush country on either side of the Southern Highlands.

Rinderpest is a disease endemic amongst domestic cattle in the Horn of Africa. It would appear to be nature's way of controlling the number of scrub cattle kept by the more primitive tribes. These cattle, economically quite useless, with little milk and worse meat, are more nuisance than asset to mankind. With their pastoral owners they roam through the bush country creating havoc with erosion and reducing arid plains to deserts. In exchange for this destruction the cattle supply little other than blood to the Masai, and dismally small quantities of milk. To their bemused owners the scraggy creatures nevertheless have some charm as capital possessions, cherished and seldom to be slaughtered for food. To nature, however, they are an abhorrence. Periodically, when their numbers become unwieldy, rinderpest or a drought sweeps off the surplus and the countryside becomes the better as result of at least a temporary relief.

European administration in these areas attempts to fight nature by simply combating the inevitable with specifics and not offering any solution to the basic problem of overstocking. The result is naturally a series of contradictions. The long, cattle-carrying ridge which runs like a backbone down the centre of Africa periodically becomes overstocked. Everybody knows it is overstocked but nothing is done. Nature then obliges with rinderpest. The disease is carried from one infected animal to the other from the Horn of Africa to the south. Southern Africa blocks the advance with a veterinary buffer on its borders. Moist-nosed game, principally wild pig, buffalo and kudu, living in the bush-covered lowlands verging on the ridge also become infected from the cattle and their mortality is high. Dry-nosed game is less susceptible. Zebra, elephant, rhino, hippo and monkeys are immune. The further away into the bush from the central cattle ridge, the less virulent the disease, as the tsetse fly performs its age-old task of protecting the game by destroying the cattle.

The duty of searching for diseased animals involved George in endless walking. It was hopeless trying to use a motor vehicle. Sick animals invariably retreat to the most impenetrable thickets where only a man's feet could carry him. It was easy to diagnose the trouble of any animal found in such retreats. Rinderpest is a wasting disease. The animal also betrays its presence and ailment by incessant attacks of diarrhoea. Liquid discharges from eyes and nose are also so acid as to carry away fur from the animal's face. Buffaloes, which are particularly susceptible to rinderpest, become very aggressive, attacking on sight, and the human intruder to their sanctuaries does so at grave peril. The practice they gave George in speedy avoidance and rapid shooting soon polished off any rust his trigger finger and hunter's wits had acquired after the recent years of comparatively easy living.

The whole of the three months was not spent at Iringa. Shortly before Christmas, George was instructed to move south to the Rhodesian border and he suggested to Eleanor that she might like to travel back to their old farm near Mbeya. The little house would still be habitable, they had always maintained an African caretaker over the property, and such news as they had received of the place had indicated that everything was at least still standing.

Eleanor was enthusiastic at the prospect of seeing their first Tanganyikan home once again. All she remembered of the place was its pleasantness. No sooner had she arrived, however, than Thomas, the caretaker, reminded her of the former nights of terror. He informed her that there were now two leopards at large on the property, both busy at night taking dogs, livestock and poultry. Thomas was certain that the original leopard was one of the pair. No other leopard to his knowledge had ever operated in so brazen a manner or advertised its presence so impudently.

Eleanor's enthusiasm at being home again promptly vanished. George, as usual, tried to laugh her fears away, and while he stayed on the place over Christmas everything of course was completely quiet. It was just rather melancholy reminding themselves of the shattering of their original hopes. The coffee plantation looked hopelessly neglected, while the farm paths were completely overgrown. Both of them were sorry they had returned. Re-opening half-healed wounds is never profitable.

After the Christmas break, George commenced his patrols in search of rinderpest in the game along the Rhodesian border. This activity perforce left Eleanor alone and the leopard immediately returned. The wretched creature was almost like an ex-lover trying to stage a come-back as soon as the husband was away. When George returned he had a full account to listen to of sleepless nights, of blood-curdling grunts and snarls, with the dogs barking and the children crying and a whole armament of weapons and African bodyguards enrolled into the defence of house and home. Without the supporting evidence of these people he would simply never have quite believed Eleanor. Every night he was back was completely peaceful.

They eventually left for Nzasa at the end of January. For totally different reasons they both thoroughly enjoyed the journey. To George, every mile they travelled took him nearer to his new post. To Eleanor, every mile they travelled took her further from the pestilential leopard. She at least fervently hoped that some miracle might produce a buyer for the farm before circumstance ever made George take her back there.

Apart from such feelings the journey would still have been pleasant. They had no trouble on the well-remembered road to Dodoma, and the train down to Dar es Salaam made a comfortable change. It was also nice to be on the coast again, to see the sea instead of the bush, even if Dar es Salaam was hot and listlessly sticky with its seasonal humidity and breathless nights.

They stayed at the Splendid Hotel for two days. George had official visits to make while Eleanor shopped for her new home and took the children to the beach where they could play in the lukewarm water, watch the dhows putting to sea with their billowing sails, and the always lovely spectacle of ocean liners sailing in to a tranquil tropical port.

Nzasa was inland, about sixteen miles from Dar es Salaam. So far as George could discover the place had experienced a somewhat melancholy history. The single house had originally been built as a residence for district officers. Two of these individuals in succession had died there of blackwater fever. The place had then been hastily handed over to the game department as quarters for a ranger. Gabbutt, a bachelor, had been the first to be stationed there. He had soon come to grief, and when George and his family drove up to occupy the house it had been standing vacant for nearly a year.

From their car the Rushby family viewed their new home with interest. A neglected but fortunately short road through thick coastal bush had led them as far as a clearing. The house stood waiting for them in this island in the enveloping bush. It did not exactly have an atmosphere of being glad to receive them, but Eleanor was delighted with the place. It was far and away the best home she had so far had since her coming to Tanganyika. There were three airy rooms with their doors opening on to wide front and back verandas. Mosquito gauze reinforced by heavy trellis-work of expanded metal protected the whole place from insects. The necessity for this defence was emphasised as soon as night fell. When Eleanor ventured outside to see if she could still smell the sea, her first deep breath practically choked her with mosquitoes. She retired coughing and ventured out no more at night, which was wise, for she found later that the metal trellis-work was a very essential addition to the house in order to keep out lions.

The place was even hotter than Dar es Salaam. It had much the same climate, but the bush shut it off from any sea breeze. There was also no refrigerator and by morning all things such as butter and cheese had dissolved to oil, the meat had turned bad, and the children were irritable. Kate had woken up screaming during the night. She had some tale that she could see a figure glaring through the mosquito net at her from the end of the bed. She was in such an hysterical state that Eleanor was obliged to crawl into her little bed with her and remain for the rest of the night, despite the heat and discomfort.

Next night Eleanor left a night lamp burning, but even so she had to sit by the bed until Kate dropped off to sleep. Eleanor had hardly returned to her own room before she was recalled by an ear-splitting scream. This time Kate was not only awake, but so frightened that she was standing rigid in her bed. Eleanor lifted her out and carried her to a chair, meaning to comfort her, but she screamed louder than ever, saying " Look, mummy, it's under the bed. It's looking at us."

Neither Eleanor nor George could see anything. They searched for any possible rat or bat but there was nothing. The house conveyed no sinister feeling to them. Kate, however, refused to ever sleep in that particular room again.

The only human occupants of the establishment at the time of George's arrival were two Africans, a clerk named Daniel, and Asmani, an elderly game scout who acted as caretaker. Juma, the orderly from Arusha, of course accompanied his chief to Nzasa, but the two domestic servants remained in their proper homes at Mbeya. Juma's description of Nzasa had been sufficient for them. Eleanor had been forced to find substitutes in the persons of a rather dignified and scrupulously clean Mohammedan cook named Hamisi who hailed from Dar es Salaam, and a rather timid houseboy with an excessively plain wife who accepted the post as *ayah* (nursemaid).

The morning after Kate's nightmare, the houseboy remarked that he had heard the child screaming. He asked what had happened. When Eleanor told him he carried the news to the caretaker. Asmani waylaid Eleanor that afternoon and gravely informed her that the room used by Kate was haunted by a *shaitani* (devil) who hated children. While he was alone in the house he had slept in the same room with his wife and small daughter. The child had gone through the same experience as Kate although Asmani had never seen anything himself. Eleanor could only shrug and George laugh it off with the remark that it must be pretty dull being a ghost wasting eternity in the useless occupation of trying to scare people. They had, however, to humour Kate. George moved into her room while she joined Eleanor and the baby. George could sleep through a stampede of elephants. Even a really grisly ghost firing its own head off through a cannon would have had a thin time trying to arouse him.

While Eleanor settled down in the house, George examined his new post and responsibilities. Connected to the house by a short track was a group of disused huts intended for the accommodation of game scouts. Near to them there was an office and a storeroom. With the house, these buildings were all contained in about one acre of sandy clearance in the bush, where nothing had been allowed to grow save a few acacia trees, a small patch of sour-looking citrus, and a rather revolting milky desert bush called *manyara*. The clearing was contained all around by a dense wall of thorn bush. When George made a casual effort to penetrate this wall he was forced to return hastily to the house to collect his rifle. " It's lousy with buffaloes," he said shortly to Eleanor. He strode off. With a sigh she watched him go and realised that her daily walk with the children would always be the same, down the track to the office and then smartly back again.

During the months before George's posting to Nzasa the range of the Eastern Province had been loosely administered from the adjoining Southern Province, whose ranger, an Englishman of Greek descent, Constantine Ionides, paid as much attention to the place as his numerous preoccupations allowed. George had been told about Ionides. In East Africa it was almost customary for people to talk of others as being at least " queer," if not well off their heads. Ionides, or Iodine as he was more generally known, was a snake lover, a herpetologist, which alone would have been enough to brand him to his fellow men as crazy. On top of this he was inclined to reclusion, but by some quirk contrived always to appear a really top-drawer gentleman, even though he affected the most extraordinary clothing.

A few days after George's arrival, Iodine came to hand over the range. He was a likeable little man, very knowledgeable about most things, but somewhat reluctant to accept their hospitality even for the night. He had come prepared to spend the night in the cramped quarters of his tent. When George pressed him to stay in the house away from the mosquitoes he replied with the flat statement that he preferred the insects. This was no reflection on the Rushbys. He just disliked Nzasa, particularly the house. In past visits he had always slept in the office. Beyond this information he would offer no explanation for his mood.

He and George spent the evening poring over maps, browsing over the files in the little office, and discussing the state of the range. Iodine did not have much personal knowledge of the Eastern District. He had his hands full enough in his own range and had been able to do little else save keep an occasional eye on the house at Nzasa. For the rest, the Eastern District was

41,600 square miles in extent, completely wild and with communications even worse than normal in Tanganyika. After the months of neglect, George would certainly find the place somewhat chaotic and, so far as Iodine was concerned, he could have it.

The heart of the range was the largest portion of the 10,000 square miles of the Selous Game Reserve. This reserve was a pure animal paradise, especially for elephant, buffalo and hippopotamus. It was almost completely untouched by man. No tourists or amateur game conservationists ever visited the place. There were only about 150 Africans living in it. There were no roads and very few paths other than the erratic trails of the game. One main path wandered through it from Kisaki to the Rufiji River. On its way this path passed Behobeho, where the namesake of the reserve, the renowned hunter and pioneer of Rhodesia, Frederick Selous, had been buried beneath a nondescript concrete slab after losing his life there during the war with the Germans.

There was very little for any ranger to do within the Selous Game Reserve. The animals could be left quite happily to their own devices. It was around the verges of the reserve that any ranger of the Eastern District would find the bulk of his work. To the south of the reserve, in the valley of the Rufiji River, there was a dense human population engaged on the growing of rice and cotton. In the north-west there was another agricultural settlement in the foothills of the Uluguru mountains, where maize was the crop. With some 30,000 elephants in the Selous Game Reserve and a countless number of hippos living in what is pre-eminently Tanganyika's district of rivers, there was inevitably a clash between man and animal over the question of who had the right to reap crops.

Raiding elephants and hippos could produce acute local famines unless crops were protected and the animals carefully controlled. The ranger of the area was essentially the disciplinarian over a most unruly company. His only future could be one of hard walking, judicious killing, and all the frustrations of training African assistants to the dangerous job of elephant control. A strong physique, tireless legs, a hide impervious to mosquitoes, a cool head, clear eye and a steady trigger finger were the most desirable qualities of any ranger of the Eastern District. The ideal qualities required from his wife would have made an equally interesting list.

CHAPTER TWENTY-FIVE

THE RANGER'S LIFE

THE first task George set himself was to become familiar as quickly as possible with his range. What Iodine could tell him, and the files in the little office at Nzasa, provided some background to the area, but a personal inspection was essential. He also wanted to meet such of the African game scouts as remained on the staff, decide which of them were worth retaining, and begin the process of recruitment in order to restore their numbers to the allotted fifty.

Even a cursory inspection of the files showed that, apart from the results of a breakdown of discipline, the normal wastage of game scouts was considerable. It was, after all, a risky business. The 1936 annual report of the game department, for instance, was quite instructive in its list of casualties in this portion of the country.

" Game Scout Mohamedi bin Abdullah was killed by a hippo in the Selous reserve, Mahenge district. Scout Mohamedi together with Scout Sulemani bin Likumba were on patrol in the Selous reserve and wished to cross the Ruaha River. A local Native agreed to take them in a small canoe. Soon after the party had left the river bank a hippopotamus charged the canoe and upset it. The scout could not swim and sank at once. His son who was with him tried to save him but was unsuccessful. The hippopotamus again appeared and it is thought that the beast took Mohamedi in its jaws. The rest of the party were saved.

" On the 13th November, game scout Asmani bin Sulemani was killed by a cow elephant near Kisaki in the Morogoro district. It appears that he followed a small herd of four cows and calves and came up to them in open country, approaching downwind. They, of course, winded him and turned. Asmani fired and wounded one, which killed him before he could reload.

" Game scout Ali bin Salim was killed by an elephant in the Liwale district on the 13th December. He was following up a wounded elephant in dense bush. He had fired four shots and was killed whilst firing the fifth shot. The elephant was found dead nearby."

There was no year in all the reports that was without casualties. For men receiving 30s. a month, the going was apparently heavy. Gabbutt had been kept on the move whenever his health allowed him to leave his bed. The Rufiji River valley had obviously been the man's principal headache. In 1933 an intensive campaign had been commenced there against hippos. By the end of 1934 some 2,600 of the animals had been shot, with Gabbutt putting in such heavy single days as the shooting and recovery of carcasses of sixty-seven hippos in a river stretch of not more than a quarter of a mile. From the more recent reports it appeared that the slaughter had not much affected the hippos. Their normal rate of increase was considerably above that number.

In 1936 and 1937 Gabbutt had also carried out a large elephant-driving scheme. This was calculated to push the entire elephant population out of the Rufiji valley and away from areas of human cultivation. A very great number of elephants had been shot. The drive was still under way when Gabbutt had gone down with his last illness. George's instructions were to continue with the scheme as soon as he could muster the men necessary to aid him in the task. The prospect of such wholsesale slaughter was not particularly pleasant, especially as Iodine had assured him that there were now more elephants in the area than before the shooting had started.

It was very necessary that George visit the Rufiji area as soon as possible. He could reach the river by car with reasonable ease, going down first to Dar es Salaam and then taking the coast road to the administrative post of Utete on the south bank of the river. As soon as he could leave Nzasa, therefore, he packed his camp kit into the box-body and, with the reluctant Juma as company, set out early one morning on the first of his safaris to the outlying areas of the range. The last he saw of his family for three weeks was Eleanor and Kate waving goodbye from the door of the house. They both looked slightly odd. As his parting act, Eleanor had induced him to cut her hair very short. Kate's shoulder-length curls had also been consigned to the garbage pail. It was just too hot for such luxuries. Even without hair, with the baby only in napkins and the two females in the bare minimum of cotton sun-suits, they looked shiny with perspiration.

George gave them a parting wave as he drove off. He wondered what account of night visitations he would receive on his return, assuming, of course, that the resident ghost didn't take over entirely. It suddenly occurred to him that he had a very long-suffering wife. He would obviously be spending far more of his time away from Nzasa than there. He could shrug the place off. Sweating it out on her own in so miserable a hole, however, would certainly provide Eleanor with an experience somewhat different from anything she had ever had while teaching in Rustenburg Girls' High. George tried to give her another wave, but she had already gone into the house. With Juma looking at him in mild surprise, he simply had to turn back to driving and steer the Ford past the pot-holes down the track to Dar es Salaam.

His first duty was to visit the district commissioner of the Dar es Salaam rural area. Visits to district commissioners by game rangers always followed a pattern. There would be a stream of official complaints about the misdeeds of wild animals, and a demand that everything indigenous on four legs be shot on sight. There was really not much of a density of game in the vicinity of Dar es Salaam, but an occasional hippo did drift down a river and present itself in the harbour amongst the shipping. An elephant would also appear periodically in somebody's garden, while now and then a pride of lions would wander through the northern suburbs. There were actually a fair number of lions in the vicinity, mainly doing good work by eating the wild pigs. Occasionally, however, they could go slightly off convention and start eating people. Gabbutt's records at Nzasa listed a fairly steady number of animals with appetites for humans. In 1936, for instance, there were nine known man-eaters operating in the range. Six were accounted for by spearing or shooting and a seventh was despatched by a trap gun. Man-eating, however, was always a recurring problem for any game ranger. Like measles in children it just had to be expected, at least in moderate amounts, so long as there were lions and, to a lesser extent leopards, living in close proximity to man.

With nothing currently so serious in the Dar es Salaam area that it could not be left for a while, George went on to the south. On the way down he encountered the district commissioner of Utete holding a baraza at a wayside village. They camped together for a night and had a general discussion. The district commissioner was a rugged individual named Dallas with one of his legs left behind on some battlefield of the First World War. He provided George with an up-to-date account of the Rufiji valley and its affairs. The tribe resident there was the waRufiji, a miserably backward crowd, riddled with witchcraft, full of silly feuds, and what was known on the coast as *fitina,* or spite against their neighbours.

There were very few Europeans in the area. George was surprised to learn that one of these was the same individual with the long name, R. de la Bere Barker, whom he had last seen half-dead with blackwater fever at Kilosa sixteen years previously. Barker, after some rather extraordinary adventures of his own, was now living a hermit-like life in the humidity of the mangrove swamps of the Rufiji delta. He had pushed some of the mosquitoes aside on an island there in 1930, settled down, and found a useful occupation for himself even in this outlandish place by writing articles and shooting hippos. Hippos, classed as vermin by the game department, provided a marginal profit to any hunter as they yielded small tusks, the leather from their backs, and a type of fat known as *Karafat,* much used by the Arabs for smearing, as a protection from barnacles and toredo worms, on to the bottom of their dhows.

Apart from Barker there were half a dozen other odd characters of various European nationalities who ostensibly claimed hippo shooting as the reason for their presence on the Rufiji. There was also an uncommonly large number of Arab and Indian traders managing stores up the length of the river. The district commissioner was non-committal about these individuals. It was difficult to see how they could all make a living honestly. Perhaps they did; if they didn't, the only possible racket in which they could be involved was poaching. That was a matter for the attention of George. When the district commissioner asked him innocently whether he had any knowledge of poaching techniques he had to burst out laughing. It was really rather funny sitting there beneath a coconut palm, in the presence of the personification of local law and order, and realise that he was now himself on the side of the administration.

He explained something of his past to the interested district commissioner and that individual frankly conceded that the local poaching community might be in for some unfortunate surprises. So far as the superfluity of traders was concerned, George was glad they were there. Like blow-flies attracted by a corpse, the more useless type of Arab and Indian trader was always to be found gathered at the scene of corruption. Their mere presence served as a useful betrayal of social rot. Their own lack of personal spine prevented them from ever participating in the racket in anything other than the character of receivers of stolen property or financiers of criminals. If his coming action against poachers was really successful, however, the traders would simply wither away. By the implication of their silent departure they would serve at least one useful purpose in their lives in keeping him advised of the effectiveness of his own measures. In this opinion the district commissioner concurred.

The next day George drove on to Utete. It consisted of a cluster of stores and huts built around the usual German fort standing above the flood level on the only high ground available for many miles along the banks of the Rufiji. The fort was an impressive double-storied example of its kind,

with a substantial courtyard built around a central water well. The upstairs
portion was used for the accommodation of the various civil servants and
their families stationed at Utete. Remembering the atmosphere at Mbulu,
George liked to imagine how happy they all were living in so gregarious a
state.

The first thing he did on arrival was to summon for inspection the remaining game scouts who had been based on Utete. There were only three
left, but at least one of these, Mohamedi by name, was a real stalwart. He
and his two companions would certainly be the nucleus for a revival of
game department operations along the Rufiji and this was at least something
of a relief. Mohamedi also had a lively knowledge of affairs along the river.
He knew the background of the early attempts at elephant and hippo control
and also had few illusions about poachers. According to him practically
everybody along the Rufiji, including one group of four European pseudo
hippo-hunters, were making what they could out of elephant tusks and
rhino horn. With all due allowance for the pleasant local habit of slandering
one's neighbours, it still appeared to George that there was a fair amount of
disciplinary work to be done amongst the human as well as the animal
population of his range.

Taking Mohamedi with him as a guide he drove up the track which
follows the south bank of the Rufiji. On the way he introduced himself to
the various chiefs, headmen and traders who lived on the banks of the river.
They were all polite to the point of obsequiousness. Virtue oozed out of
nearly every word they said. He answered their common complaints of
raiding animals by assuring them that his policy would be to shoot out of hand
animals raiding settled areas, as well as humans raiding animal areas.
This information did not seem to leave many of them quite as happy as
law-abiding persons should be. At least, however, they understood what he
meant. It would certainly be necessary for him to prove his intentions
with deeds, but this he fully intended to do at the first opportunity.

Leaving Mohamedi to act as a recruiter for game scouts, George then
returned to Nzasa. The safari had occupied three weeks and his programme
was if possible to spend the last week of each month at Nzasa where he could
attend to documentation, pay the staff and enjoy some family life. Arriving
home in fact, became one of his few pleasures. Even late at night the watch-
dogs, Fanny and her son Paddy, would hear his approach long before any
human ears. They would stir and whimper. Next in the chain of reactions
would be a cough from old Amisi who slept on the back veranda. He would
turn up his lamp and then hurry out to rouse the house servant. While he poked
the fire, Eleanor would be up, combing her hair and powdering her nose. The
rest of the staff would also arrive out of the shadows. By the time the car
bumped into the clearing there would be quite a reception committee, with
much shouting of the time-honoured East African greetings, " *Jambo,*" and

"*Habari ya safari*," while the dogs, beside themselves with excitement, rushed around like lunatics.

The generous nature of the welcome was not entirely altruistic on the part of all concerned. George could always be relied upon to bring the post, bundles of newspapers and magazines, fresh meat and other supplies. Then, after a day clearing up official work he would load practically the entire population of Nzasa into the back of the box-body Ford and take them off on a spree to Dar es Salaam where they could shop, and Kate and Johnny Jo could have a spell on the beach. In the cool of the evening they would all come back again, the Rushbys and the Africans equally relieved of a good part of their wages, but all happy after a day of relaxation.

For his second safari in the range, George went to the area of the Uluguru mountains. This settled area lay on the north-west corner of the Selous Game Reserve and, like the Rufiji valley, it was a place of conflict between man and wild animal. As with the Rufiji people, the tribe of the Uluguru were agriculturists who planted crops, maize, rice and cotton, in the foothills of the 8,000-foot range of mountains which provided so handsome a change from an otherwise swampy, flat, bush- and mateti grass-covered landscape.

To reach the area George went by car along the Central Road from Dar es Salaam to Morogoro town and then down a track along the eastern side of the mountains to still another of the original German forts. This was a small specimen of its kind built at Kisaki. The place had been long abandoned as an administrative post. The game department used it as a headquarters for that part of the Eastern District, and as at Utete, George found one of the old guard, Head Scout Sayidi by name, still faithful to his colours and waiting patiently for some superior to give him instructions. The rest of his fellows, apart from one other relic of the former staff, had dwindled away. Sayidi was living with his family in a shack erected outside the walls of the fort. He declined to go inside. The place apparently had even more than the usual share of demons and other gaseous vertebrates among its inhabitants. These phantoms had long since ejected all rightful human occupants from the fort. According to Sayidi, the sound of carousel could frequently be heard from the deserted interior. There were also tales of old executions and floggings which had given the fort a reputation for evil.

It was not really profitable trying to laugh these stories off with the Africans. Actually, a ghost was a remarkably good caretaker to any abandoned building. The Nzasa phantom, as Eleanor had had nothing further to say of it, was obviously tolerant of anybody not sharing its room. Its reputed presence might provide Eleanor with some added protection from human interlopers in her solitude. As it was, she had quite happily informed George that the only disturbance came from lions. They snuffed and grunted around the house nearly every night but she had little fear of them. They

weren't sneaky creatures like leopards, and the sound of old Asmani reassuringly coughing and clicking the bolt of his rifle on the back veranda
always put her back to sleep even in the midst of a full demonstration of
roaring.

At Kisaki, George completed his inspection, began a recruiting campaign
for staff, and then returned home leaving Sayidi to prepare for the first foot
safari which he planned to make into the Selous Game Reserve. In the
meanwhile George spent a few days at Nzasa, and then paid a short visit to
the third and least troublesome out-station of his range, the old Arab slave
port of Bagamoyo. There, again, the original head scout, Kaloko, was the
only man surviving of the former game department staff. With only a few
elephants and hippos in the district, however, Bagamoyo was quiet. It was
mainly notable for the convenient use illicit ivory traders made in smuggling
their wares in dhows sailing out of the numerous creeks and bays scattered
among the coconuts along the coast.

The foot safari into the Selous reserve promised to be interesting. To do
it, George went by train to Morogoro, then hired a truck to take him and
his camp kit down to Kisaki, where Sayidi had organised porters for the
coming journey. George planned, actually, on a relatively short walk of little
more than one hundred miles, ending on the Rufiji River, from where he
would canoe down to Utete.

The purpose of the safari was to provide him with some idea of the
topography of the Selous reserve, the density of its animal population and
the character of its few human residents. The place proved to be a huge
wasteland of swampy scrub bush and tall-grass country, which, apart from
a few nondescript hillocks, had only gentle undulations. The rivers of the
reserve were its handsomest asset, with fine shade trees along their banks
and countless pools for a hippo population probably more numerous than
in any other part of Africa. To animal tastes, in fact, this wasteland had
charms of grazing and water which obviously made it their special paradise.
It was literally teeming with game—elephants, buffalo and hippo were the
leading inhabitants in point of numbers. But close to them were impala,
wildebeeste, waterbuck and zebra, with a few rhinos, some greater kudu,
and large quantities of warthog. The elephants were notably short tusked,
the result of years of slaughter by ivory hunters from the nearby coast,
while the numerous lion population was made up of curiously poorly maned
animals.

The human residents of the place were a thoroughly miserable crowd.
In an area of mosquitoes and swamps, a healthy life was impossible. Agriculture was out of the question and George simply listed the 150 people
as a parcel of poachers and their families. The best thing to do would be
to clear them all out to a healthy area. A game reserve was an impossibility
so long as it had this type of humanity among its residents. They would

really be far happier making a living from agriculture or honest work instead of being dependent on the hazards of poaching and the largesse of the crowd of crooked traders on the Rufiji. Before he ended his walk, George informed such of the residents of the reserve as he met that he would be moving them out within the next three months. He could rely on the news spreading very quickly. In fact, traders were already discussing the matter on the Rufiji when he reached Mpanga at the end of the foot safari.

At Mpanga, George hired canoes to take Juma and himself down the river. It was an interesting hundred-mile journey, with the Rufiji a very handsome stream and, like all African rivers, full of interest and life. The journey was also extremely unfortunate for certain poachers. Stopping at a village for supplies, George was informed that there was a camp of four Europeans a few miles down river. They were all poachers. Two of them had left for parts unknown a few days previously taking with them quite a stock of ivory. One of them had just arrived. The fourth was an old hand at his trade and apparently none too popular with the local tribespeople, hence the information.

George had heard of this party while he was in Utete. Both the district commissioner and old Mohamedi had been suspicious of them without any definite information. He went on immediately so that there would be no chance of the poachers receiving a warning of his presence. It was hardly a pleasant surprise for them when the canoes swept around a bend with the current and made a landing opposite the tents. George stepped ashore and introduced himself. The one man was a German named Dillner, the other was an individual of less clear-cut nationality. Apart from some argument that they were honest hippo hunters, they had no satisfactory explanation for the presence in their camp of six rather poor tusks and two rhino horns. Without further ado George confiscated their armament, a fine single-shot ·500 Webley and a 9·3 Mauser. He also arrested the German and gave him half an hour to prepare for the river journey to Utete. The second man was obviously an amateur at the game. He was left to pack up the camp and make his way down river as best he could.

For the rest of the river journey George had somewhat sour company from the German. The glumness of the man was only really comprehensible when George led him into the office of the one-legged district commissioner at Utete. The district commissioner, it appeared, was well known as having a personal score to settle against Germans. By the time he and George had finished grilling the poacher they had a complete signed statement from him of quite a few interesting activities. On its information the two missing partners were arrested in Dar es Salaam as soon as they made their way home with innocent faces after hearing of the break-up of their camp on the river. The enterprise of the quartet ended in substantial fines.

Apart from one German doctor George arrested a short while later on the lower Rufiji, he had no further serious trouble from European poachers in the range. A European trying to operate illegally and systematically in such an isolated area would be as conspicuous as an elephant on roller skates. Fortunately they had enough sense to realise this and accordingly took their activities elsewhere.

For the next few months George was preoccupied in training his new staff, in shifting the residents out of the Selous Game Reserve, and recommencing the work of elephant and hippo control. The training process had to be done most carefully. In recruiting new scouts, George gave preference to men who had been born in elephant country and preferably had used a muzzle loader against those animals. Anybody attempting to kill elephants with a muzzle loader had to have something to his backbone better than jelly, and this was the type of man George wanted.

The recruits were concentrated at Nzasa where George gave them a basic training in the game laws and the use of a modern rifle. For practice there was a rough rifle range at Nzasa but the best training was to take the recruits out on an actual elephant hunt. If they survived a couple of these outings with some credit to themselves, when shooting had to be done under pressure from a highly dangerous target, then the recruit was accepted as a game scout and issued with a paybook entitling him to 30s. a month. They also received their uniform of khaki drill shorts and bush shirts, pillbox cap and badge, a heavy leather belt with ammunition pouch, a haversack, groundsheet and blanket. At first they were left bare-footed, but later on when the game department had more money to spend, sandals and puttees were issued to them.

For armament, the scouts received a Vickers ·404 magazine rifle, if they were on elephant control, or a ·303 Lee Enfield for lighter work. Ammunition books were also issued entitling them to draw on stocks kept in the various outlying administrative posts. Each month the scouts were required to make a return of animals killed and ammunition used, while ivory had to be handed in to the administrative posts. From the returns, George could check the performance of each man. A scout averaging more than four rounds of ammunition for each elephant killed was not considered any good.

The scouts were posted out to such areas as were menaced by crop raiders or were strategically situated on pathways used by counter-raiding human poachers into the Selous Game Reserve. The actual border of the reserve in no part followed any natural line. There was not even a fence to separate it from the surrounding country. The original surveyors had simply blazed a boundary line through the bush and the game department had nailed to the trees at regular intervals a number of enamelled signs bearing the name " Selous Game Reserve." Neither animals nor man were inclined to pay much attention to so arbitrary a division. None of them could read, and the process of teaching them to remain in their respective territories could only be lengthy and bitter.

Just how bitter this struggle could be George learned in June when he was returning from an elephant control safari in the Bagamoyo district. He had been in the bush for the usual three weeks. On the way home he stopped at Dar es Salaam to collect the post and was immediately informed by the district commissioner that one of the game scouts in the Maneromango area had been murdered by poachers. A party of police had already been sent out to search for the murderers but they had returned after a fruitless investigation.

George had expected to have to be tough with poachers before the community really accepted the idea that their pursuits were unprofitable. To have the poachers take the initiative in so belligerent a way was a real declaration of war. In a state of some rage he set off for Nzasa immediately, collected some of his best men, and without losing more than an hour at home drove on to the site of the murder.

He found the local tribespeople all agog over the affair. There was no difficulty in finding out what had happened. Game scouts were each entitled to one young porter who not only carried their belongings on safari but also acted as a variety of apprentice to the trade. According to the murdered man's porter, they had come across a band of poachers in the bush. The poachers were carrying a load of meat, mainly from a giraffe which they had just killed. The scout attempted to take their names. There had been a squabble, and the poachers had stabbed the scout to death. The porter had escaped by running away. Neither he nor the local people admitted to the slightest knowledge of the identity of the culprits.

The police party had visited the site of the crime, recovered the corpse, asked a few questions, and then gone home, considering that the poachers must have been strangers to the area. The crime would remain open until suitable information was received in the usual way from paid informers or disgruntled women.

To George, however, the delay of waiting for information was intolerable. He was pretty certain that the poachers were local men. They were not likely to be carrying meat for too great a distance. The local people also seemed to be slightly too virtuous in their innocence. The logical thing was a private interview with the local headman. A hippopotamus hide sjambok to his backside soon produced the necessary information. The poachers subsequently received seven years for manslaughter after trial in the Dar es Salaam circuit court.

It was certainly not a pleasant affair but it at least had one satisfactory consequence. It was notable very shortly after the trial that the superfluity of traders along the Rufiji went into evident decline. One after the other they closed their shutters, packed up their stock and left. With no tangible reason for such a pronounced depression in their business, none of them would volunteer an intelligent explanation. When George encountered any of them on the road in the process of moving, they declined anything more than an evasive answer when he asked why they were going. Only their women looked sulkily at him with an expression which suggested quite simply and to his satisfaction that he was to blame.

CHAPTER TWENTY-SIX

WILD ANIMALS AND MEN

GEORGE was on safari in the Rufiji area when a messenger reached him with news of the outbreak of the Second World War. Most people had been more or less expecting it. There were already routine preparations and secret orders against so calamitous an event. Nevertheless, it was a shock to put such plans into action. All over the territory, people who had once been at least acquaintances, if not friends, had to be interned overnight as enemies. In an entire country of 362,688 square miles, four times the area of the United Kingdom, there were at that time less than 10,000 Europeans. The great bulk of these people were civil servants and their families who constituted the skeleton caretaker administration running the country under the British mandate from the League of Nations. Even at the best of times there were barely sufficient men for the tasks of basic government. To have half of them summarily called up for army service could do more harm to Tanganyika than their combined efforts were likely to do against the enemy.

George was only in the army for six weeks before the inevitable, nicely worded letter reached him from the government chief secretary requesting his immediate return to his former duties. Under war conditions the question of food crops was too vital a matter for them to be left to the appetites of hippos and elephants. The government, on the contrary, would be forced to launch a large-scale emergency rice-growing scheme in the Rufiji area and the long-standing quarrel with the animals over the question of harvesting would be likely to develop into quite a war on its own.

Eleanor, at least, had something to be grateful about to the war, for it contrived her removal from Nzasa. The first she heard of hostilities was a note sent to her through the bush by George. It simply informed her of the war, that he was automatically drafted into the King's African Rifles as a lieutenant, that all the scouts had also been mobilised and would be reporting at Nzasa for their military service, and Eleanor must pack as quickly as possible. The wives of civil servants drafted into the army could obviously not to be left in isolated stations. They would be housed elsewhere in one of the towns. By the time George arrived the next morning, Eleanor was all packed up to go and more or less waiting on the veranda with the children. The game scouts were also gathered at Nzasa, all looking very spruce, well washed, ironed, polished, prim and slightly bemused. They obviously didn't know what it was all about, but whether to war or to a church parade, they were prepared with equal stoicism to follow George.

Eleanor left Nzasa without a backward glance. Even George admitted that he was not sorry to see the last of the place. By the time the army had regurgitated him from the splendour of a rather ill-fitting uniform and the two pips of a lieutenant's rank, the family had already been installed in a house one hundred miles inland from Dar es Salaam at a little town named Morogoro. As the town was included in George's range, and should have been the logical place in which to station a ranger in the first place, he had no great difficulty in inducing the game department to allow him to remain. The stupid base at Nzasa, far from the post office, telephone or any convenience in transport or communications, was quite abandoned, the house dismantled, and whatever it was that provided the place with so unpleasant a reputation scattered to the winds.

Morogoro was a complete change. It was a sprawling little township lying next to the Central Railway line and dominated by the heights of the Uluguru mountains. The place had been founded in German days as a centre of some importance. It was blazing hot, but at least without the coast's humidity. For coolness the Germans had planted the streets with flamboyant acacias and magnificent shady mango trees. With their colonial style of architecture very evident in public buildings and the residential houses built on the slopes of the mountains, Morogoro had managed to retain something of the atmosphere of the lost days of German East Africa.

Eleanor revelled in the little town. She had a small but snug house standing on the outer perimeter of the residential area. In Morogoro, houses were allocated to civil servants on a strict seniority basis. With the Rushbys only credited with twelve months of service, they could not expect to be anywhere nearer the centre of town than the next best thing to a safari journey away. But at least there were comforts, companions for the children and for Eleanor, and the knowledge for George that no matter how often or far he was away from home, the family had the security of being within reach of friends.

George was actually away from home even more than when he had been stationed at Nzasa. To allow for wartime depletions in staff, the size of many of the ranges in Tanganyika was increased. The Eastern Province received the additions of the Mahenge and Kilosa districts and this gave George charge over a total area about three-quarters the size of England, inhabited by a very varied company indeed of animals and men.

The Mahenge district was a particular responsibility. With Liwale, where Iodine was stationed in the Southern Province, Mahenge sheltered the greatest density of elephants in Tanganyika and, for that matter, probably in all Africa. Back in 1923 George had hunted in parts of this area. It was there that the Mbunga tribe had accepted him into their brotherhood of hunters. Returning to the area after the lapse of so many years, he found with pleasure that he was still well remembered by the tribe. He had also by no means forgotten the skill and courage of the primitive hunters, and henceforth most of the men he recruited as game scouts were drawn from the Mbunga people. Their experience was invaluable to him in effecting control over such a rugged area of wilderness, but he was still kept constantly on the move himself with endless problems to solve.

One nuisance which the war actually stimulated was the activity of illicit ivory buyers, mostly Arabs based on Zanzibar. These gentlemen had always regarded Tanganyika as being something of their private looting-ground and the slightest relaxation of Government control was always immediately exploited by a resumption of the ancient trade in ivory, if not in slaves. The war years certainly provided such an opportunity. The only coast guard left on duty between Dar es Salaam and the Kenya border was one African on a bicycle, and his efforts were obviously somewhat limited.

The Arabs smuggled a great variety of trade goods into the country. As a game ranger, however, George was only interested in what they smuggled out, mainly ivory obtained by illicit buyers all over Tanganyika. In the bush these tusks were cut up with fine-tooth wood saws into the three commercial sections which could easily be concealed and transported to the smugglers' landing beaches, from where it was carried in dhows over to the open market on Zanzibar island.

The trade was a curse, for demand always stimulates supply. The poachers themselves normally had a fairly short life, either the elephants or George liquidated them, but the Arab buyers in the bush would immediately beguile somebody else into entering the business, and with no fixed trading stations to give the game away, as they did on the Rufiji, it was a traffic almost impossible to suppress without adequate staff.

George went down to the coast as often as the all-important elephant-control operations would allow him, but it was invariably a frustrating experience. Just how frustrating was perfectly demonstrated to him once at Kunduchi Creek, about ten miles north of Dar es Salaam.

On this occasion George received positive information that a shipment of ivory was to be taken off one night by a dhow. With his informer as guide he drove up to within a few miles of the place, and then walked through the evening shadows to reach the actual creek. Sure enough there was a big dhow lying at anchor just off-shore but there was no sign of life on the beach.

George and the informer hid and waited. It started to rain with the warm drizzle of a tropical shower, while occasional lightning gave the scene an additional touch of dramatics. At 3 a.m. a truck arrived and signalled to the dhow by flipping its headlights. George had his rifle with him and he planned to provide an unexpected climax to the scene. On this heroic intention, however, he very soon had second thoughts.

A motor-boat came off from the dhow. When it approached the shore from the darkness George saw that it was filled with half a dozen resolute-looking Arabs, all armed to the teeth with daggers, swords and modern rifles. Discretion indicated some prudence in George's plans for a climax. He had the mortification of keeping his peace while he watched the smugglers exchange goods for four boatloads of handsome-looking ivory. In that lovely little creek the spectacle was like watching an adventure of the days of the pirates. The only consolation George had for his inactivity was that he could identify most of the shore-based smugglers. He would certainly go out of his way to make things unpleasant for them whenever opportunity occurred in the future.

Unpleasant things actually did happen quite often to the poacher-smuggling community. Once George went with Theodore Pike, the district commissioner of Bagamoyo, on a raid on the dhow port of Sadani. This was a real resort of all manner of sly gentlemen whose low salaams and innocent smiles were exasperating evidence on this occasion that they had been forewarned of the raid. Nothing, of course, was found in any of the stores. Only some time afterwards, George heard news of a very satisfactory consequence of the raid. A large shipment of ivory had been made during the previous night and two big truckloads of sugar and scarce trade goods received in exchange. The smugglers were actually in the process of transporting their cargo to Dar es Salaam when news of the coming raid reached them. It was an awkward moment. They were forced to stop at a poverty-stricken roadside village and hastily negotiate in cash with the headman for the hirement of a few huts. Into these huts they packed their goods and then drove on to Dar es Salaam with empty trucks. After the raid they returned to collect their goods. They found the huts just as innocently empty as their trucks had been. Nobody in the village admitted to having ever heard of such things. The headman simply asked, " What goods?" There was nothing anybody could do about it. George liked to imagine that the headman had heard something of his own technique with poachers. A good hiding administered in the bush could never produce any complaints to the police from such compromised gentlemen.

The great bulk of George's time was of course occupied in elephant and hippo control. The responsibility of shooting at least 500 hippos and 1,000 elephants each year provided him and his scouts with a life of the most strenuous activity. An extract from his diary for June 1942 provides an example of a typical month in his life at this time.

3. W.   Left Morogoro in Bandali's lorry. Reached Melela's village. Lorry stuck and could not get further. Camped.

4. Th.   Safaried to Msongosi with porters and camped.

5. F.   No news of raiding elephant here. Safaried to Mahalaha. Killed six elephants *en route* near to Mahalaha. Five rounds of ·577 and four rounds of ·375. Two male and four female (two of them no-tuskers).

6. Sat.   In camp. Runner left for Morogoro.

7. S.   Safaried to Mibamba.

8. M.   Hunted out to the south, country very hilly. Elephant appear to have cleared the area. Signs of one herd travelling south, possibly part of herd I shot on Friday near Chiganga. They had passed yesterday. A hard day.

9. T.   At Mibamba, letters and papers arrived from Morogoro. News came in of elephants raiding at Figugu. Arranged to go there tomorrow.

10. W.   Safaried to Figugu, climbing a very steep and high hill with a fine view of Mgeta valley from top. Elephants appear to have moved on.

11. Th.   Hunted to the west, killed nine elephants, three of them no-tuskers.

12. F.   Returned to Mibamba; sent eighteen tusks and letter to D.C. Morogoro.

13. Sat.   Left for Nyamgwa; arrived noon. Five hours. Extremely hilly. No elephant here.

14. S.   Safaried to Lugengi; country very hilly and hard going. Six hours. Crossed Mgeta River five times; thigh deep, thirty yards wide. Most of people have left here because of elephants and moved to Kisaki and Mahalaha.

15. M.   Went out westward, followed spoor of three young bulls. Shot two with one shot each. Never saw the third bull. Lions very near to tent during night.

16. T.   In camp.

17. W.   Safaried to Lufutu.

18. Th.   Went out westward, saw no fresh spoor. On way back to camp saw yesterday's spoor of large herd which had gone east.

19. F.   Went out northward. Got a single bull which charged.

20. Sat.   Left with fresh porters and arrived Mbakana noon. Five hours' very hard going. Mbakana name of village and stream which joins the Mgeta River here, Mbakana being the larger stream of the two.

21. S.   Safaried to Kisaki; arrived 11 a.m. Saw Game Scout Martin here on leave from Utete. Had lost his hat and badge whilst being chased by a rhino in game reserve on way here.

22. M. Safaried to Dutumi six hours, good going but hot. Mkamba and twenty-four of his men had settled near Kikosa. The remainder not yet moved.

23. T. At Dutumi.

24. W. Left in T.C.C. lorry; arrived Morogoro early afternoon. Shot a few baboon *en route*.

The years of living and working in close proximity to elephants yielded George a wealth of experiences which were sometimes as curious as they were dangerous. One of these experiences came to him on an afternoon in the Ulanga valley, the principal elephant stronghold of the Mahenge district.

George was watching a herd of elephants moving slowly across the wind in his direction. There is always entertainment and instruction to be found in watching elephants, for those great animal individualists can reward an observer with some really surprising sights.

On this occasion, George was squatting on a low mound, concealed behind a small bush. He had calculated that when the herd actually passed him he would be reasonably out of their way. In actual fact, however, they were uncomfortably close as they ambled past his hide. The nearest of the herd was a cow and her very young calf whose course took them within ten feet of George's bush. The cow was ahead of her calf and she paused just beyond the bush in order to allow her offspring to catch up.

To George's astonishment, the calf walked straight up the mound to the bush, pushed its small trunk through the leaves and for a full minute proceeded to smell and feel over his chest and face. It then turned and ran off to its mother. It lifted up its trunk and blew into its mother's mouth as if trying to convey to her for identification the scent of the strange object squatting in the bush. The cow did not seem particularly interested. She gave her calf a light box on the ear with her trunk and started to move on. The calf promptly squealed a protest, twined its trunk round one of its mother's front legs and tried to halt her. The cow turned round, treated the calf to another cuff, allowed it a quick snack from the local milk supply, and then wandered on to join the herd.

Experiences like this tended to make George philosophise about elephants. Notwithstanding the fact that he certainly killed more of the creatures than any other known human being, he liked them with something of the regard which a rancher has for the pedigree stock in whose breeding he takes such pride even though the animals are destined for the sudden end of slaughter.

It was this basic liking which made him search for a solution to the problem of game control far beyond the traditional idea of massive destruction and the confinement of a few survivors to reserves or national parks where their sole value would be that of display. What he looked for, in fact, was a new conception of game control, a way of life in Africa in which there would be room for wild animals as well as man, and the true value of game properly appreciated and exploited. In such appreciation and even in controlled exploitation, he considered that the wild animals had their greatest chance of continued existence alongside of expanding human settlements.

The prodigious waste of crude elephant control appalled him. From the records he could compute that since this means of crop protection was first started in Tanganyika in the early 1920s, the game department had killed close on 80,000 elephants whose carcasses would have yielded some 300,000 tons of meat. The history of this wanton effort at elephant control revealed its own stupidity.

Back in 1923, when he had first hunted in Tanganyika, George had participated in the initial effort at elephant control made by the British Government. He remembered very well the original " Governor's Licences." As a means of elephant control they had proved a fiasco. The men who had secured these licences had all been professional ivory hunters like himself. None of them had hunted for any altruistic motives. They had wanted ivory. Shooting crop raiders was, to them, a waste of time. The big bulls who carry worthwhile ivory are seldom crop raiders. They are conservative characters by nature and in diet. They know what they want to eat and where to find it. The wilderness has always been their proper feeding ground and home.

After the " Governor's Licence " scheme had been dropped, the game department appointed a ranger named C. Goss, aided by a team of scouts, to the task of ruthlessly clearing elephants from parts of the Mahenge district. Some 150 elephants were shot in quite adventitious fashion before the scheme was abandoned. C. F. Swynnerton, the then game warden, had admitted to George that the whole effort had been a complete failure, a waste of good elephants and something he would not try again.

Within a year, however, pressure from the administration over crop raiders forced a large-scale action by the game department. A number of Europeans were engaged in 1926 as elephant-control officers. They were stationed in areas of Tanganyika where elephants were doing heavy crop damage. Assisted by scouts they commenced a systematic slaughter which again was completely unselective in all but a desire to make the effort pay for itself as much as possible by yielding tusks. Once again this meant the slaughter of the best herd bulls, this time on a considerable scale. The effect of this type of shooting, as George had observed so often in his own ivory-hunting days, was to produce, as the runts took over the breeding tasks, a notable deterioration in the quality of elephants and especially in the size of their tusks.

As for the density of the elephant population, this massive shooting must obviously have had some effect. George estimated, however, that some 80,000 elephants, at least as many as had ever been shot, were currently living in Tanganyika. Of these, about 30,000 were breeding cows who reproduced every four years. This gave a gross increase to the elephant population of 7,500 a year. The game department was shooting about 2,000 a year under elephant control. Another 1,000 a year were being privately shot by licensed hunters and poachers. Natural causes accounted for probably another 1,000 each year. This left a net increase of 3,500 a year to the total population, so notwithstanding everything done against them, the elephants were definitely on the increase.

George's instructions from the game department were simply to destroy indiscriminately all crop raiders or attempt to drive them deep into the Selous Game Reserve. His own instructions to his game scouts were never to shoot any big bull unless in self-defence. Cows and no-tuskers were to die, but only, of course, if they were actually doing crop damage. No animal was to be shot outside of a five-mile radius of a village. With these instructions he hoped to prevent a further deterioration in the quality of the elephants and, by the only possible argument of bitter experience, teach them that they were safe if they stayed well clear of man, and particularly his crops.

This type of control was, however, a superficial answer to the problem. It ignored the fact that over the greater part of tsetse-infested Tanganyika, and in many other parts of Africa where the keeping of cattle was impossible, the only source of protein for the human population was game or fish. No game department, not only in Tanganyika but anywhere in Africa, had ever really faced up to this. They all had the basic game-preservation-at-all-cost attitude, the legacy of the European gamekeeper. Crop protection was an unfortunate necessity required of them by the administration. Ideally, the really enthusiastic conservationist would like the whole country to be uninhabited by man, one huge wilderness where animals could be observed providing they were not disturbed, and shooting very much of an expensive privilege for licence holders only.

The entirely revolutionary idea of game management and systematic cropping had always fascinated George from the early days when he had started providing meat for the workers on the Beira-Nyasaland railway. In a country like Tanganyika, whose principal wealth lay in its enormous wild animal population, such a plan would be the only one of perpetual benefit for all the inhabitants, both human and animal. Without it, man was simply at indiscriminate war against the riches of his own environment. He wilfully destroyed that which could serve him more profitably and better than all the exotic crops and livestock which European government often dreamed of introducing to Africa if the expenditure of countless moneys could only clear the land of all its indigenous wild life.

The problem was to persuade man to this logical approach. The African had never on his own attempted to domesticate a single indigenous creature although his continent had the world's richest variety of wild life. The European settler throughout Africa had come to the continent with a veritable lust for blood. The early history of South Africa, of Rhodesia and other parts, is a discreditable record of the most ruthless and idiotic slaughter with no single creature spared, and only the presence of tsetse fly saving the game in certain areas by literally driving man out.

The system of elephant control currently practised involved the shooting of large numbers of animals over a short period of time, mainly during the season of harvest. During this period there was a glut of elephant meat available only in the areas where shooting was taking place. Much of it was wasted, whilst the rest was simply gorged by the local tribespeople. In the long non-shooting periods in between crops, the elephants were tolerated by the Africans, for they were doing no damage even if they were in close proximity. They became bold through their own immunity, forgot any lessons they had been taught during the previous harvest, and prepared themselves for the next seasonal raids. With the killing of elephants too hazardous a matter to tempt primitive hunters simply for the purposes of meat, the tribespeople turned on the soft-skinned game as their source of protein. Trying to stop them from such hunting on grounds of poaching was an interminably frustrating activity which quite drained the energies of any game department.

The only sensible course, once one accepted the fact that the elephant population was far from being in any danger of natural decline, was to visualise a systematic year-round cropping of their surplus numbers. The slaughter would have to be properly planned, the meat dried or smoked on the spot and efficiently distributed. The same process could be applied to any other game like the hippos and buffaloes whose numbers were in no danger of any decrease through natural causes.

The prodigious antelope population, especially in areas like the Serengeti Plains, where half a million Thomson's gazelles, some 240,000 wildebeeste and over 170,000 zebra wander around in company with many other varieties of game, deserved to be preserved untouched as one of the great natural wonders of the world, but if necessary, even these animals would be susceptible to some form of cropping rather than extermination to make room for farmers. Domestication and selective breeding of animals like the magnificent eland would provide nature's true answer to the tsetse. With them, man could produce meat and milk in quantities even in the most heavily infested fly country. Simply put, it was ludicrous that in a continent like Africa, with all its wealth of naturally healthy and finely flavoured animals, there should ever be a protein shortage, or man obsessed with the introduction of exotic livestock against the grain of local parasites, diseases and unsuitability of climate.

In one report after the other George detailed his views on the whole conception of game cropping and domestication. He invariably ended his reports by requesting the views of the department, but no views were ever received in reply. A game warden, in fact, holding his job against pension in the conservative caretaker government of a mandated territory, would probably have risked some suspicion of insanity if he had recommended prizes on agricultural shows for fat eland rather than for Jersey cows; or more money for a buffalo stud farm than for a research programme on the problems of acclimatising Scottish Highland cattle to the tropical areas of Africa.

CHAPTER TWENTY-SEVEN

LYAMUNGA

THE four years they spent at Morogoro were very happy ones for both Eleanor and George. The restless, arduous type of life was of the kind to which he had become accustomed before his marriage and reverting to it was very much to his liking. He felt fit, he was free of any financial cares for the first time in years, and the company of elephants still suited his temperament just as much as it had done in the old days of ivory hunting and adventuring.

Eleanor was equally content. Life in Morogoro was, to her, very much like living in any small town in South Africa. There were several other women there from the same part of the continent. They found agreeable company with one another, interminably knitting for the war effort, gossiping, and generally being completely suburban even though the heat did its best to keep them aware that they were really in the heart of tropical Africa.

There was one spell of leave, and this was really George's final confirmation into the civil servant's way of life. The whole process of preparation, packing, departure and safe return was something of a ritual. The technique of farming-out pets and pot plants to the care of friends, without losing friends, was always considered in East Africa as revealing the real class of any civil servant. With game rangers this process generally demanded a special aptitude. Their livestock was often rather varied. At the time of his leave, March 1941, George had accumulated among his dependants a rather impudent pet guinea fowl named Susan, two ducks named Molly and Polly, and a waist-high baby elephant named Winston who had been rescued from a rather unfortunate predicament when his mother had abandoned him in a mud-hole. Finding homes where the birds would be cared for rather than eaten, and the elephant allowed the three table meals a day and sundowner to which it had become addicted, involved a careful assessment of the tolerance of quite a few acquaintances.

It had been eleven years since George had enjoyed a holiday. He would inevitably spend most of the time wondering what was happening in his range, for there was no replacement; but even he had to allow that the leave was necessary. Kate, for one thing, was due to start her schooling and Eleanor was expecting another baby. As the war precluded any chance of going to Britain to see the two absent children, the idea was to sail down to Cape Town. Kate could be left there with her grandparents. Eleanor, if there was any danger of a repetition of the last performance at Oldeani, could also remain and have her confinement in a modern hospital.

Everything, however, proved this time to be the right way up. After a stealthy voyage down the coast in a blacked-out ship, they enjoyed a relaxing two months in the cool shadow of Table Mountain. Then they returned, minus a rather wistfully brave little Kate, and with no greater alarm about the coming baby than a last-minute doubt as to whether the captain of the ship would be prepared to accept Eleanor as a passenger in her interesting condition. The baby, a vigorous 9 lb. 10 oz. boy named James Caleb, was actually born in Morogoro without a hitch on the 25th August 1941, just a month after their return from the holiday. With a big, domed and completely bald head, the newcomer to the Rushby family was known in Morogoro as Mussolini.

George resumed his duties with enthusiasm as soon as he returned. He managed to be home for the birth of the baby but Eleanor saw precious little of him after that. If it wasn't a serious raid by the elephants against the crops on the Rufiji, it was some impudent piece of poaching or the trampling to death of a game scout at Mahenge which kept him permanently outdoors and on the move. And then, in the second half of 1942, he received one particularly interesting special assignment which took him away on quite a safari.

For some time the game department had heard rumours of a remnant of a race of chimpanzees inhabiting the remote mountain country overlooking Lake Tanganyika, just north of the port of Kigoma. As the rumours also indicated that the chimpanzees were rapidly dying off, the department decided on investigating the matter and George was selected for the task. It turned into a very pleasant outing.

He found the chimpanzees quite easily. Their last stronghold in Tanganyika was in the mountains overlooking the lake shore north of Kigoma, near a small village named Mitumba. The village was inhabited by men earning their living largely by cutting down the remnants of evergreen forest in order to provide the faggots used by fishermen on the lake. The fishermen, who netted the tasty little sardine-like *dhaga*, worked at night with a fire burning on the prows of their canoes. The light attracted the fish. With several thousand fishermen out nearly every night, the demand for good, brightly burning wood had caused no insignificant destruction of natural forests around the shores of Lake Tanganyika. It was this destruction which was actually the principal threat to the chimpanzees, for their forest consisted largely of a reddish timber which burned particularly brilliantly and longlastingly.

The forests inhabited by the chimpanzees occupied less than four hundred acres. They were narrow strips of forest remnants running alongside the streams which coursed from the mountain ranges through gorges to the shore of the lake. It was a very wild and beautiful part of the country, with the high peaks of Malenga and Kangalunga looking steadfastly out over the deep waters of the lake. In this retreat some 150 chimpanzees had found a happy home for themselves until the woodcutters had started their work of destruction, with no effort being made at all at replanting the trees they destroyed.

There was no direct animosity between the woodcutters and the chimpanzees. On the contrary, the apes appeared to enjoy something of the same veneration given to them in the Moyen Congo. As a result they were not particularly wild. They liked man to keep a reasonable distance, but beyond this they had no resentment at being observed. George spent some absorbingly interesting days watching them. They wandered around in families and small clans with a friendly cheerfulness to their way of life, an intelligence and discipline of behaviour which was salutory to any watching human. Like gorillas, each member of a chimpanzee family made a separate bed for himself, usually in a common tree, and it was possible to accurately count their numbers all the way down from the large beds of the parents to the diminutive couches of the infants.

They appeared to be a bigger and heavier breed, and certainly darker in colour, than the chimpanzees George had seen in West Africa. The woodcutters had numerous accounts of the animals visiting their huts in search of such delicacies as salt. George was also shown one small boy with a badly scarred nose. As a baby he had been snatched up by a visiting chimpanzee. When his mother had rushed screaming to his rescue, the chimpanzee had bitten him on the nose, placed him reasonably gently on the ground and then jumped for the trees.

Protecting the chimpanzees was rather a matter of protecting their forest home than of themselves, for they had no enemies save perhaps an occasional visiting leopard. Without the forest, however, they would die. In the wet season they did wander out, but in the dry months towards the end of the year the dwindling forest home was their only possible retreat. There they found shade and water and the fruit of the wild oil palms which was their principal food. Trying to protect them without protecting the forest would be like protecting a fish and then draining its lake.

At the current rate of cutting, George estimated a life to the forest of

not more than five years. At best, therefore, the woodcutters had a limited
future. Their trade was also facing ruin from the normal march of progress.
As fast as war-time conditions allowed, the revolution of the paraffin pressure lamp was coming to the fishermen. The flickering glow of the fires
was yielding to the steady brilliance of the lamps. Not only were the lamps
more compact, with no demands for tinder space in cramped canoes, but
their light was a far more irresistible lure for the teeming little fish. The
almost magical spectacle one sees at night on Lake Tanganyika, when glittering towns of light seem to materialise on its dark waters wherever the
fishermen collect, is also, in its way, the real saviour of the isolated little
colony of chimpanzees. George's report on them did result early in 1943, in
the establishment of a chimpanzee sanctuary known as the Gombe Stream
Reserve. It was, however, the decline in the demand for their product which
made it easy to persuade the woodcutters to remove their activity to some
other field and really left the chimpanzees in a lasting peace.

For the rest of 1943, George worked almost ceaselessly on the task of
elephant control. One of the few proofs that he had been at home for any
time at all during this period was that Eleanor, at the exact moment that
the sound of hooters and firecrackers exploding in Morogoro marked the
beginning of the Moslem celebrations at the end of Ramadan, produced
another little hunter. This was a 10 lb. 3½ oz. effort named Henry William
who, oddly enough, was born with a faint birthmark in the shape of a
crescent moon above his left eyebrow. His advent, like the new moon to
the Moslems, was indeed very welcome but, with a family of eight now
scattered between Morogoro, Cape Town and Jacksdale in England, both
Eleanor and George were determined that this newest addition would
also be the last. Three little boys, a baby elephant, Susan the guinea fowl,
and the inevitable hutch of guinea pigs, were handful enough to Eleanor. On
top of it all, George was transferred.

The transfer came in March 1944. Philip Teare had retired and inevitably
there was a change around in the game department. The new warden was
Captain Monty Moore, V.C., who had originally come to Africa as an
officer in the King's African Rifles, liked the place so much that he left the
army, joined the game department, and attained some renown at his post
at Banagi in the Serengeti Game Reserve where he contrived to half-tame the
local lions by regular free meals of antelope meat. George's transfer was to
the post of ranger attached to game department headquarters, and he did
not at first take too kindly to the change. It seemed to threaten more desk
work and less action. The prospect was not exciting, although experience
proved the change to have quite a few consolations.

Apart from the process of late-night farewell parties, leaving good friends
and moving the household, Eleanor welcomed the change for the same reason
that George was suspicious of it. Her friends had all made some habit of

warning her that her husband's activities with elephants would inevitably one
day be the end of him. The delusionary idea that George would be sitting
at a desk in headquarters rather appealed to her. She had also heard that
the game department headquarters, then at Lyamunga, was most pleasantly
situated, high up and cool, near the little town of Moshi and quite dominated
by no less a scenic marvel than the snows of Kilimanjaro.

To Eleanor, accordingly, the physical move to Lyamunga was the only
real disadvantage to the change. In the event it certainly was not too pleasant a journey. They always seemed to have a habit of making such moves
during the wet season. The two trucks which conveyed them the 160 miles
to the railway station of Korogwe on the Tanga-Moshi railway line, took a
full day of slithering in mud to do the journey and then, when they reached
the station, part of the line had been washed away and the train was twelve
hours late. Eleanor promptly went down with fever, James ran into a low
wall and blackened both his eyes, and by the time they did eventually
arrive at the Lion Cub Hotel in Moshi, George was more than ever sorry
that he had left his elephants. Even Kilimanjaro was brooding behind an
impenetrable screen of clouds and the only relieving factor was that he found
an old acquaintance named Eccles, whose wife, Mollie, obligingly came to
the Rushbys' rescue, washed and fed the infant and organised Eleanor comfortably in bed.

The next day things started to improve. George drove out the sixteen
miles to Lyamunga and found the place, to the eye at least, not so bad.
Properly speaking Lyamunga was a government coffee research station. It
lay in the foothills of Kilimanjaro surrounded by a very lush expanse of
countryside indeed, with the rich green of coffee plants and the lighter
shade of the banana groves completely blanketing a sleepy jumble of hills.
During the war, the normal agricultural staff had been drastically reduced.
To the annoyance of the proper head of the place, the vacant houses and
part of the office buildings had been taken over temporarily by the game and
the labour departments. There was some social ill-feeling of the more
absurd kind. The agriculturists obviously considered everybody else to be interlopers and they were inclined to be very distant over the matter.

As usual, however, such bickerings affected the women more than the
men. So far as George was concerned, he received a most cordial welcome
from Monty Moore and the agreeable news that far from being confined to
an office, his new range would include what were considered to be all the
real show places of Tanganyika from a wild animal point of view, not only
the Tanga and northern provinces with the Masai steppe, but also the Ngorongoro Crater and the Eastern Serengeti. Safari would be very much the order
of the day. A particular reason for George's transfer was also to inaugurate
a control scheme in the coastal area near Tanga where elephants were
challenging sisal farmers the right of cultivating their ancient feeding grounds.

George broke the news to Eleanor with as little evidence of cheerfulness as he could manage. At least she had the consolation of a really modern and roomy house with a fine garden, an equitable climate, and certainly a view whose overwhelming quality she only really appreciated on the second day after moving from the hotel. Late in the afternoon of that day, when the children were playing on the lawn outside and she was hanging curtains, she heard John suddenly exclaim, " Oh, Mummy, isn't it beautiful! " She ran outside and there before her, emerging from a veil of cloud, she saw for the first time the mighty dome of Kilimanjaro with the setting sun tinging its snows an exquisite shade of pink. In all Africa there is no more stunning scenic spectacle than this. It is a spectacle which has the alchemy of such infinite change that each time the slumbering volcano reveals itself through its covering of clouds it shows some subtle difference of colour or mood. In the long weeks while George was away on his duties, the mountain was a never-ending wonder to Eleanor and the children, adding, by its changing moods, something different to every passing day.

George's first preoccupation in his new range was with the elephants near Tanga. Quite a poignant little crisis had developed in that part of the country and a solution was urgent. The area inland from the port of Tanga had always been a favourite area for elephants. Unfortunately for them, it was also a good area for what was the principal cash crop of Tanganyika—sisal. The great estates, first established in German days, had steadily eaten into the elephants' area, cutting down the bush and converging from all sides in a most unfortunate manner on one remaining central island-thicket about forty miles from Tanga where the remnants of the elephants had been compressed into a last refuge.

To this elephant stronghold the planters had been serving notice for years. The animals had been harried and hunted, wounded by the injudicious efforts of sporting amateurs with light rifles, and sprinkled with missiles of varying size and shape propelled from the muzzle-loader guns of plantation guards.

The embattled elephants had simply despaired in their crumbling stronghold. They had no means of knowing that beyond the encroaching plantations there was still a prodigious expanse of their beloved wilderness. To them, they must have seemed to be the last of their kind and, if they were to die, they were creatures of too much courage not to give some account of themselves against man for the honour of their most ancient line.

George felt genuine sorrow for them when he first examined their retreat. The whole problem could have been solved so easily if only there was some means of communication between man and elephant. They were such sagacious creatures that a whisper of warning, some sensible advice about a place of safety, would certainly have been heeded. He estimated that there were only 150 of the animals left. They would just have to go. He looked involuntarily at his rifle. It was a double-barrelled ·577 Stensby, a pretty murderous example of the gunsmith's art. It had cost him over £200 to buy. The loving care and perfection which had very evidently gone into its manufacture made it an almost incongruously superbly-finished instrument of death. He remembered with regret Colonel Sherwood-Kelly's remark back in Mbeya in 1930, when they had returned from a duty rather similar to this one. " It is perhaps a rather unfortunate fact that the basic tool of the game ranger's trade is his rifle, and one of the best skills he can have is the ability to use it with maximum efficiency when the judicious occasion demands." Poor Sherwood-Kelly; retrenched by the game department during the depression, he had been found alone and unconscious in a London park. In hospital he died of cerebral malaria, and only then did anybody discover who he was and remember his record of service and adventure.

George shrugged. Feeling emotional about sudden death at this stage in the game was not profitable. With a twist of humour he remembered how well primed his head had been with juvenile rubbish when he had first come to Africa. How he had devoured all the stupid, trashy books of gentlemen whose only claim to fame came from their wanton destruction for sport of the most beautiful animals of Africa.

He dismissed the memories from his mind. Death was now a duty, even if he was reluctant. The only hope was that if he so terrified the elephants in one violent attack, their sanctuary would become so much of a nightmare that the survivors might flee the place in horror, stampede across the sisal fields and then find that they could lose themselves in perfect safety once again in the primeval bush.

George stood up. The breeze was blowing steadily into his face. The early afternoon light was dazzling bright for the weak eyes of elephants. There was little chance of the animals detecting the approach of a hunter. He turned to see whether the game scouts were ready. They were all picked men. Selecting and training them had been responsible for his few grey hairs. Each scout had survived the final test of standing next to him in the face of an elephant charge. Those recruits who had run had been allowed to continue their journey all the way back to their homes. Doubtless they were sitting there in the sun now, consoling themselves with the thought that fear had at least taught them to be wiser men than hunters on elephant control.

The bush was of the dense, coastal thicket type: shrub with an occasional big tree. Firing range would be very short, not more than fifteen yards, and then only if the hunters were lucky. George checked his cartridges and moved forward. The elephants were feeding, finicky as they usually are, plucking tender young shoots from the tops of thorn trees. George selected two cows feeding from the same tree. By their position he calculated on hitting them both in the brain with the two shots of his double-barrelled rifle. If anything would make the herd stampede it would be so devastating an initial calamity.

He watched the cows closely, waiting for them to move into correct position. Fate could have saved at least one of them by leading her away. Instead, the two elephants turned into ideal profile. The whim behind that move was the last either of them ever had. Pandemonium broke loose as their two bodies crashed to the ground. Elephants have an astonishing variety of sounds produced from their trunks. The shrill, amplified cornet blast followed by staccato screams of rage, when heard at close range in the bush, is one of the most terrifying sounds on earth, especially if it is followed by a crashing charge, with a living battering ram pushing over everything in its way straight at the hunter.

George cursed. The whole herd seemed to be converging on him in a storm of fury. Even if his rifle had still been loaded, it would have been a slender straw in such a hurricane. He raced straight for the bodies of the two cows. The move confused the herd. They lost sight of their enemy. George saw them sniffing over the ground and in the air with their trunks, like a pack of bloodhounds trying to find a trail, or a blind man groping for something lost. It was an alarming spectacle. Once, in the Eastern Province, he had found it difficult to believe the story told to him by a young district officer, of how he had attempted to shoot an elephant and then, pursued by the whole herd, been forced to ignominious flight, thanking his stars for a notable prowess at athletics. A few days later, when he re-examined the site of his mishap, he found tracks on the ground to prove that the elephants had followed his trail for over two miles. Although he was out of sight, they had scented him right back to the road where he had reached his car. There the animals had obviously milled around in frustration at the point where he had tumbled into the vehicle and disappeared at speed.

Such vindictiveness was formidable in animals of the strength of elephants. George reloaded as fast as he could. Before the herd had discovered his hiding place he opened fire from the cover of one of the dead elephants. It was quite a war while it lasted. By the time the dust had settled there were nine dead elephants on the ground. The survivors had turned and fled deeper into the bush. It was obviously going to take no little effort to even teach them never to charge back on a shot, let alone flush them out of the thicket.

The process actually took two months and the killing of fifty elephants before the remainder lost their nerve. For the first time they turned their backs on a hunter. This was the initial crack in their courage. Ten more of the herd had to die. Then the survivors really panicked. One night they fled. No man heard them go, but when dawn came the thicket was deserted. Rather than continue with the terror, they had ventured themselves into the unknown. It was pleasant to imagine their relief when they discovered that the rest of the world was not all covered with sisal.

In the records of the game department this exercise in elephant control could be written down as a complete, if melancholy, success. No elephants ever returned to the ill-omened thicket island. The sisal estates in future could be very simply protected by a few game scouts patrolling their outer perimeters. Those elephants who were tempted to raid the young sisal in order to chew the juicy base of the leaves were regularly taught the error of their ways and crop damage was reduced to a minimum.

There was, fortunately, no need for measures as drastic as this in any other portion of George's new range. Most of the area was an arid plain which had for its human occupants the members of the Masai tribe. Their pastoral inclinations, lack of interest in agriculture and dislike of venison as a dish, allowed them almost complete tolerance of game, except for any onslaughts made on their cattle by lions, and they were perfectly capable of handling such occasional problems for themselves. Patrolling their areas was a pleasant relaxation compared to participation in the running warfare taking place between man and mammal in the agricultural areas. All, in fact, that he had to watch for there were poaching forays made mainly by Greek farmers of the type known to the Africans as second-class Europeans. These individuals considered that the cheapest way to feed their labour was by massive shooting of antelope.

Even Eleanor and the three little boys could accompany George on such patrols. He would pack the whole family, with Mabemba, his new orderly, and a pair of game scouts, into a three-ton truck and lumber off in the vehicle, almost as though it were a motor-boat chugging its way across a bumpy but otherwise almost completely flat sea. Roads were non-existent, the few tracks were little more than unmade navigation routes linking the principal centres, and with the seemingly boundless horizon, the dark blue dome of heaven as a roof above, the total absence of fences, the almost non-existence of landmarks, all contributed to a unique experience of travel.

They would jolt along across the plain, the radiator pushing aside the long grass, and George finding a way expertly between the scattered thorn trees. Antelope grazed all around, fat zebras, the cavorting wildebeeste, the long-necked gerenuk, the dainty little dikdik. Ostriches raced the truck needlessly, while tall giraffes watched their passage with a curious air of disdain and casual immobility.

Occasionally they would hear the tuneful jangle of cattle bells and come upon the humped-back Masai herds grazing in the bush. Even less frequently they would see the primitive villages of mound-like mud huts surrounded by an outer boma or enclosure of thorn bushes as a defence against lions and hyenas.

The people were as wild as their land. The herdsmen, more than half-naked but completely unselfconscious, invariably regarded the novelty of a truck with an air of almost petrified astonishment. The young warriors, like knights of old, wandering the land in search of adventure and romance, were more cheerful and sophisticated dandies, with their bodies beautifully oiled and ochred and their long hair most elegantly arranged. The women were even more colourful. With none of the agricultural chores common to the rest of their sex in Africa, they could occupy most of their time in titivation of their persons. This, unfortunately, included the rubbing into their skins of a mixture of rancid fat, cattle dung, and something which had the scent of cat's urine. Added to their normal body odour, this perfume had a formidable potency, but at least they were attractive to look at.

They wore skirts of dressed goat-skin, knee length in front but ankle length behind. Their arms from elbow to wrist, and their legs from knee to ankle, were encased in tight coils of copper and galvanised wire. All of them had their heads shaved and in some cases bound by a leather band embroidered in red, white and blue beads. Circular earrings hung from slit earholes, while their handsome throats were encircled by stiff wire necklaces strung with brightly coloured beads and so graded in size that they formed deep collars almost, but not quite, covering their breasts.

Flies, smells, clouds of stifling volcanic dust from the hoofs of cattle, and an indescribably miserable supply of drinking water—liquid filth simply screaming of amoebic dysentery—seemed to be the principal characteristics of the land of the Masai. The visitor was inclined to simply write it off as one of those areas on earth where man would be much better off if he simply moved away, and yet the very savagery of the place had some charm. There was a brooding solitude to the nights, a mystery about the people and their way of life, a curious quality to the legends their elders told when George had them gathered for some *baraza,* a wondrous magic to the enormous herds of game and a complete detachment from all the concerns of the outside world, which always, when the safari was over and George asked the family—" Well, was it worth it?" would make the little boys chorus. " Lovely, let's go again soon," and Eleanor simply say with a sigh, " If only Ann, George and Kate could have gone with us too."

CHAPTER TWENTY-EIGHT

MEN AND LIONS

THE Second World War ended, so far as Tanganyika was concerned, in victory parades by the King's African Rifles, in entertainments by the inevitable Italian prisoners of war, and such a prolonged succession of parties in a multitude of isolated stations that even Captain Monty Moore, V.C., who had no mean capacity to enjoy such things, found the going a trifle heavy. His first safari after the war was down to Dusty Arundell's range of the Southern Highlands Province and he returned to the game department headquarters at Lyamunga looking slightly the worse for wear.

George, of course, had acted as warden during his absence. That was one of the duties implicit in being the ranger attached to headquarters and it was one of the duties which he least liked. Confining himself to paper work for weeks on end and doing the polite to visiting personages of importance always bored him. It was one of the aspects of life at headquarters which had made him reluctant to accept transfer there in the first place and always left him with a lurking desire to be sent somewhere else.

He went into the office shortly after Monty's return and found the warden propped up in his chair with his feet on the desk. He was a heavy man with reddish jowls and he mopped a rather cold-looking perspiration from his face as, with a weak grin, he rewarded George's greeting.

"That was quite a safari," he said. "I think perhaps it is time that this late war was considered as having been properly buried under empty bottles." He paused a moment and looked at George reflectively. Then he added, "We have a slight problem on our hands as a result of it."

George looked at him questioningly.

"Dusty Arundell," explained Monty, "couldn't quite take this last round of festivities. In fact, I have a medical report to the effect that if he isn't sent back very smartly to some place like England he's going to die. Apparently he's been in bed with a haemorrhage ever since we ended the safari."

"So?"

"I'll have to send him off. The trouble is, we have no relief for him. You know how bad the staff position is. The Southern Highlands is too important a range to leave for any indefinite period without a senior man in charge. There's a big staff of game scouts there, a few European game observers to control, and the task of maintaining the game-free area along the Rhodesian border. If we let rinderpest slip through we'll never hear the end of it from the people in the south."

He thought a while in silence.

"I was thinking of sending Swynnerton down there. His Lake Province is pretty quiet. Perhaps we could leave it without a ranger for a while?"

"This range is also pretty quiet," George said meaningly.

Monty looked at him.

"Do you mean that you'd like to go? You don't have to, you know. That wasn't exactly my idea in raising the matter. I just wanted advice." He paused, and then added, "On the other hand, you might be the best man for that area. You always were pretty good with a rifle. There's a matter down there that needs very definite cleaning up. Those Njombe lions are something more than a joke. There are quite a few complaints. I think it's time that we had an end to them."

This was an opinion which George heartily shared.

"I've heard of them," he said dryly. "They seem to have eaten a good few people. Why hasn't Dusty liquidated them? They've been operating for some time."

Monty stirred rather uneasily. Dusty was a particular friend of his.

"He's had a few personal problems down there. That's one reason I think it's wise to get him right out of the range. If he recovers, I'll send him somewhere else. Perhaps I should have done that before. It might have saved some botheration and grief." He coughed and mopped at his brow with an oversize handkerchief. "There's also something else to the business. It's not just a matter of lions eating people. That's clear-cut. These Njombe man-eaters seem to be mixed up with some jiggery-pokery—witchcraft and all that sort of thing. I don't know much about it. But you had better investigate their background. It may at least be partly a police matter." He paused again. " It might even pay you to visit Singida on your way down and learn from the experience the people there have had with the lion-men."

George was slightly startled. He had not heard before of any supernatural complications to the appetite of the Njombe lions.

" Do you know anything about the lion-men?" Monty asked.

George shook his head.

" Only what I've heard."

He told Monty about his period as a forestry officer at Mbulu, the accounts he had heard about the hyena cult of the Mbugwe people, and his shooting of a few of those animals which seemed to carry some signs of human interference or ornamentation. There had also been a recent report of the ranger in the area having shot a hyena which was found to be wearing a pair of men's khaki shorts. The creature's human, or sub-human, sweetheart had been making some stir about demanding compensation from the government for the loss of her lover.

The Singida district, south of Mbulu, had always been a centre for what was known to the tribesmen as *mbojo,* or lycanthropy, the black magic of man changing into animal. The Turu tribe who lived in the Singida district were a primitive, apathetic, superstitious people. The wilderness of thorn trees in which they lived had always been a great place for lions. Further back than local traditional history could remember, a horrible perversion of animalism had also appeared in the way of life of the tribe. Almost inextricably confused with the normal killings of lions, there began a long series of barbarous murders committed by creatures known individually as *MtuSimba* or collectively as *WatuSimba* (Lion-men). These killings were accepted by the tribespeople as matters of witchcraft. They were resigned to the position and had no remedies to suggest to any would-be helpers. They considered that the were-lions had been created originally by those in authority as a means of liquidating politically odious individuals. Then the convenience of the idea had penetrated to the general public. In later times it was possible for anybody to hire such a killer from its controller and use the creature to settle a grudge or dispose of unwanted acquaintances.

So much was fairly general knowledge. There appeared to be always some activity among the lion-men in the Singida district, but occasionally there was a real spate of murders. One of these peak periods had been in 1920 and this had first attracted the attention of the outside world to the extraordinary nature of the business. The political officer of the area at that time had apparently experienced something of a lively tour of duty. In that one year he had been called upon to investigate some two hundred killings, largely in the Usure area adjacent to Singida. All of these killings had been accepted by the people as the work of lion-men.

Some years after this the political officer concerned, writing under the name of Captain W. Hichens, had contributed to the famous old feature "The Queer Side of Things" in the *Wide World* magazine, three very fascinating articles on his experiences. These articles had given the lion-men an international renown.

According to the author, after disposing of eight genuine man-eating lions he discovered for certain that there were witchdoctors who not only practised extortion by threatening people with death by real lions which they claimed to control or to be able to change into, but also perpetrated murder through the medium of assassins. Hichens mentioned one lion which was hunted down after attacking a party. It proved to be a sturdy youth dressed in a lion skin, with its clawed paws worn like gloves over his hands and feet. He was hired out by a witch to her clients for five shillings a time. His technique was to spring on his victims from behind, drive a knife through the heart and then claw the body to resemble the mauling of a man-eater. The youth seemed to be well drugged with what was apparently hashish (dagga).

The party he had attacked remained convinced that a proper lion had been the culprit. One of the curious points emerging from all investigations, in fact, was that survivors of attack were always certain that the creature responsible appeared in the guise of a proper lion. There were innumerable accounts of attempts made to track such lions, and the pursuit abandoned in terror when the pug-marks inexplicably changed into the footprints of a human being. It was easy to find people who positively claimed to have personal experience of such lycanthropy. For the official record there were such things as statements made separately by persons giving identical and detailed accounts of how they had witnessed not only human beings but also dogs being changed into lions. There were numerous rumours, as well, of men living with lions, hunting with them, and threatening to direct the animals on to human victims unless payment was made. Similar payments were demanded from clients for the services of these lions in ruining any personal enemy by destroying his cattle. It was exceedingly difficult to discover just how much substance there was to these various claims and stories; whether, in fact, some of them were true, or whether others were simply made by opportunists seeking personal prestige from their supposed ability to motivate lions in personal vendettas.

In the atmosphere of a land infested by lions and aggravated by an occasional tendency towards genuine man-eating, the Turu people were firmly convinced that the animals never attacked human beings unless directed by some malign influence. When such attacks did take place, the victims' relatives, if they wanted vengeance or reparation, did not consult a hunter. They went straight to a witchdoctor who was employed to divine the reason for the grudge and the name of the person who was responsible for employing the assassin. The same assassin, either a lion, a lion-man, or some other animal reputedly changed into a lion by a magician, might even be quite happily engaged to settle accounts in reverse with the original employer. Life was really not highly valued in such dismal areas of thorn bush, heat and aridity.

The information that the Njombe man-eaters might also be involved in witchcraft intrigued George. He had no doubt that the best medicine for the business would turn out to be a few well-directed bullets. But if there were any witchdoctors mixed up in proceedings, he would take them in his stride. He had heard of many odd things in Africa, but never of any efficacious magical antidote to either an accurate marksman or a hangman's rope. He made a mental resolve to test the real mettle of the Njombe lions at the earliest possible moment.

As soon as he finished with Monty he went home to inform the family of the coming change. He had thought that Eleanor would be irritated at still another move, especially when they had so pleasant a home and she would have to lose her beloved view of Kilimanjaro. She received the news, however, with something more than equanimity. Apart from the curse of the leopards at their old farm, she had pleasant memories of the area which had been her first home in Tanganyika. The game ranger of the Southern Highlands was always stationed in Mbeya. The house there was said to be reasonably pleasant, the climate tolerable and, above all, the Government had taken over the old German school at the outbreak of war and it had been developed into a substantial establishment. As things were, Eleanor was struggling to break John into education on a correspondence course sent from Dar es Salaam, and it was heavy going expecting a small boy living in the shadow of Kilimanjaro to welcome instruction in the usual mealy-mouthed drivel of the "Run Rover run" or "Mother plays with baby" variety. He was putting up a strong resistance to the stuff. In a school he might be more receptive when he saw that other children were also obliged to digest such reading matter even in a continent as exciting as Africa.

They left for Mbeya in the last week of October 1945. George had thought of travelling by way of Singida in order to learn what he could of the lion-men, but several factors dissuaded him from following this route. For one thing, the truck supplied by the game department for transport had such threadbare war-time tyres that he was certain it would be lucky to complete the journey even on the relatively well-kept and frequented Great North Road. The side road through Singida was not only bad but also very deserted in the event of a breakdown. There was also the consideration that things were apparently reasonably quiet in lion-man circles at the moment. There was not likely to be any official still stationed in the place who would have had any personal experience of the last big outbreak of murders. It would be better for George to take his family direct to Mbeya, see them settled and then, if the Njombe trouble did have any roots in sorcery, he could always go up to Singida for any purposes of comparative study.

As it happened, the truck failed to even travel down the Great North Road any further than Babati before its tyres started to go. After a miserable night in a tumbledown hut, George arranged for a lift on a truck owned by one of the local traders, Sher Mohammed. This contraption, when it arrived, looked in far worse state that the game department vehicle. Doors and canopy had long since been shaken off but at least it managed to rattle its way through to Dodoma where they had a night in the hotel and the next morning continued the journey by the scheduled railway bus service. It was a relief to reach Mbeya three days later with no worse a family casualty than one travel-sick dog and possibly the foundations for any future attack of lung trouble from the amount of dust breathed in on the road.

After the lush green vegetation of the slopes of Kilimanjaro, the Mbeya country looked brown and dry. The game ranger's house was also something of a blow. It was a diminutive affair built of sun-dried bricks by some original German owner who had lost it to the Custodian of Enemy Property at the outbreak of the war. At least, however, the house was overlooked by the heights of Lolesa Mountain and it boasted a pleasant garden more than half-buried in carnations planted there by Dusty Arundell's wife.

Dusty had already left for Britain when George arrived in Mbeya. The only way to learn anything of the running of the range was by enquiry from the African game scouts and reading through the files in the poky little office. The latter pastime was not particularly profitable. Dusty's ideas of keeping a file appeared to be to stuff all paperwork into one folder. When this was too full he simply extracted material from the bottom and threw it away. There were only minor references to the Njombe lions in any documents which had survived this process of unnatural wastage.

The game scouts were not much more helpful. If they really knew anything about the man-eaters they were certainly not inclined to talk. If it wasn't for his prompting, they gave the impression that they would never even have mentioned the lions. Even then, what they had to say was valueless. No lions had been shot in the area. The scouts were all employed on normal duties of patrol, crop protection, and work on the high bush pole fence erected along the Rhodesian border to prevent the spread of rinderpest. They seemed more virtuously concerned with the onslaughts of white ants and bush fires on this pole fence than on anything else.

If it hadn't been for the fact that the scouts always pointedly evaded mentioning the lions as anything other than *dudu ya porini,* or insects of the bush, George might have been inclined to dismiss them as being of slighter consequence than he had first imagined. But when armed game scouts were so frightened of lions as to avoid mentioning them by name, it was suggestive of serious trouble. Throughout Africa there has always been a belief that to mention a man-eater by name is courting disaster. It is thought that by some secret means the man-eater will know that his name has been used and the speaker will be marked as a future victim.

The matter of the lions of the Njombe district would obviously require some personal study before George would really know much about them. Meanwhile, there was certainly enough to do in the range. Apart from the question of the man-eaters, the Southern Highlands occupied 45,000 square miles of territory. There was a fair amount of crop-protection work, with about 250 elephants to be shot each year, and there was the real government top priority job of the game-free area along the border fence. This was a headache for any ranger in the area. If the endemic rinderpest of the north managed to penetrate this contrived barrier and caused in Southern Africa even a shadow of the chaos and ruination of the famous 1896 outbreak, the international repercussions would, in the very least, cause the head of one local game ranger to fall.

Dusty Arundell had obviously been preoccupied with this duty. Apart from African game scouts patrolling the fence there were four Europeans employed on shooting at sight all animals, wild or domesticated, found within five miles of either side of the fence. Whilst they did the actual dirty work, the ranger of the area had the task of supervision and all the chores of administration—pay, stores, ammunition, transport, co-ordination of returns and detailed reports. On the face of it, at least, the Southern Highlands range looked as though it demanded even more desk work than the post at headquarters. The prospect made George groan.

He was still busy three days later trying to organise something of an office routine when he received a telegram. It was addressed to him from W. Wenban-Smith, the district commissioner of the Njombe district. The wording was simple and to the point.

" I beg you to apply earliest attention to man-eaters stop Conditions in this district pathetic."

George remembered Wenban-Smith. He had been assistant district commissioner at the Dar es Salaam rural office when George had taken over the range of the Eastern Province at the end of 1938. He was a level-headed and conscientious type of political officer, not a man likely to exaggerate anything simply for effect. George was still considering the contradiction between the urgency of the telegram and the lack of information about the man-eaters in his own game department office when he had a visitor, a wiry, dusty-looking man, who practically shouldered his way into the office and, in rather an abusive tone of voice, said—

" Hey, man, what the hell are you going to do about these lions? I've worked like the devil to make this Great North Road, and now half of my gang have been eaten, and the rest won't work there any more. All you fellows in the game department ever seem to do is draw your pay. The rest of us have to work, and that's hard enough without being eaten by lions."

George was about to take effective practical offence at the man's attitude when he realised that the intruder was obviously an individual with something on his mind.

"Who the heck are you?"

The man looked at him sharply and his attitude seemed to change.

"Oh, hell!" he exclaimed. "I thought you were that chap Arundell. I only met him once. I see you are somebody else. I'm sorry, man, but I've got these damned lions under my skin. It seems to me that the Government must be leaving the things alive just to keep the population down. Where do I find the ranger?"

George introduced himself and explained that Arundell had left. The visitor relaxed. His name was Watermeyer. He was a road foreman engaged on maintenance of the Great North Road and he certainly seemed to have just cause for complaint. The section of the road from Mbeya to Iringa carried heavy transport traffic and its gravel surface deteriorated rapidly unless under constant care. Maintenance in Tanganyika at the best of times consisted of little more than a few Africans stationed at fixed camps along the wayside and employed in dragging branches of trees along the road in order to sweep loose top-surface into the hollows of corrugations. Most travellers regarded with some disdain the efforts of these road sweepers, but as Meneer Watermeyer tersely put it,

"Now that they've all been bloody well eaten, people are starting to miss them."

According to his reckoning, the roads department had lost seventeen of its maintenance staff from the section of the Great North Road running through the Njombe district. There was no prospect of securing any replacements.

George placated the road foreman and saw him off with assurances that the lions would receive immediate attention. He would have to make one hurried inspection of the game-free area, but immediately this was concluded he planned on a thorough investigation into the whole matter of these lions. It was obvious that only personal knowledge would prove whether Watermeyer was exaggerating and Wenban-Smith in an unjustified panic. The local authorities in Mbeya were too typical of their kind. They were so absorbed in the affairs of their own district that, apart from admitting to having heard about such things as man-eating lions, they were hardly concerned with any unfortunate events in Njombe. Only the veterinary officer, Mike Molloy, whose range was partly the same as George's, expressed some concern at attacks on cattle. That the herdsmen had been eaten as well was another matter. He had heard something about this, but men simply were not the responsibility of his department.

The contradictions and elusiveness of information about the man-eaters was provoking to George. He completed his inspection of the anti-rinderpest organisation as rapidly as he could. Fortunately it seemed to be functioning reasonably well. The European men on the patrol were a rugged crowd, with few complaints and quite able to look after themselves. With relief, he left them to their duty of slaughter and finally turned his full attention to the lions. The actual shooting of the creatures he expected to be routine. Shooting lions was always dull stuff to any professional elephant hunter. It was the background of witchcraft which gave the Njombe lions their added interest, together with the thought of bringing retribution for the odious horror of man-eating.

According to his reports, the territory of the man-eaters lay on either side of the Great North Road where it traversed the southern edge of the Buhoro Flats. He knew the area well. The prodigious view from the point where the road twisted down to the flats from the heights of Mbeya brought memories crowding back to him when he drove along it. From the heights, the wasteland of the flats had almost the appearance of some enchanted sea. The dense covering of trees and shrubs and long grass shimmered in the heat haze with the same restless movement as the surface of water. The smoke of a distant fire—most inseparable of companions to the African bush—seemed to be creating a thunder-cloud canopy on the northern horizon. The whole landscape seemed almost as unreal as a dream, a harsh wilderness of thorn bush contained in the north, south and west by sinister-looking mountain ranges and, in this prison, tortured on a rack of heat.

He had hunted in the area when he had first come to Tanganyika. The site of Vivian Lumb's ruined store at Ruiwa was close to the route of the road as it twisted down the escarpment. It seemed incredible that twenty-three years had passed since the odd partnership between himself, the irrepressible old trader and the taciturn Bill Cumming. He remembered how they had wandered alone and at will, like many other European adventurers and explorers, penetrating the most desolate reaches not only of these flats, but of the entire continent, and all with an impunity only really threatened by mosquitoes. He had certainly experienced some wild nights and days since he had first seen the Buhoro Flats. Perhaps he owed Africa something as fair exchange for all its indulgence. If ridding its people of the nightmare of man-eaters and lion-men was any return service, then the task would be a pleasure.

CHAPTER TWENTY-NINE

THE MAN-EATERS OF THE NJOMBE DISTRICT

AT THE bottom of the descent to the Buhoro Flats, George picked up two elderly African hitch-hikers. African foot-travellers are invariably loquacious. They move at such a leisurely rate that they collect all the gossip of the road. It is often possible to hear very illuminating fragments of information, particularly if the travellers are elderly and knowledgeable in local affairs.

George took one of the men into the driving cab, while his orderly, Mabemba, moved to the back of the truck with the second hitch-hiker. Mabemba knew very well what to do. He and George had resorted to such a means of securing news during many a search for poachers in the Eastern Province. If the man in the front cab was shy of Europeans, then the second passenger in the back of the truck might be inclined to talk.

They drove on. After a spell of exchanging the usual inconsequences, George said to the man:

" Is there no danger in walking here? I am told that there are creatures in this bush."

It was always curious, as well as irksome, to see how an African could close up his mind to an outsider with almost the physical action of somebody lowering and bolting steel shutters. There was the merest glint of fear, then the man's face went blank. It was easy to guess his thoughts. If the man-eaters were indeed were-lions, there was no means of knowing who they were in human form. Such a degraded animalism could reputedly involve a man's friends and neighbours or even his own family. A horrible doubt over the matter assailed the reason of even the most intelligent of primitive Africans. They became terrified to discuss such a matter even with their own wives for fear that one of them was a were-lion who would resent such mention of her deeds and, in retribution, kill the speaker.

All the man would say was—

" Such things are further on, beyond the Ruvaha River. We do not walk there."

He seemed to shiver. George did not press the matter. Mabemba at the back was equally frustrated. Nothing would have been gained by any obvious attempt at cross-examination. The rest of the journey was completed in silence. The men were travelling some forty miles up the road to a place where there was a trading station and hotel on the banks of a stream known as the Kimala. George stopped to let them off and then turned into the hotel grounds.

On their way to Mbeya the bus had left George and his family in this same hotel for a night. It was a comparatively newly developed amenity in this part of the world, a picturesque grouping of bungalows, bougainvillaea, and petrol pumps all making the most of some tall shade trees growing on the side of the Great North Road. The owner, James Cormack, was one of those surprising characters who turn up in the oddest places of Africa. He was an athlete of some renown, a former champion half-miler of Scotland and, in 1906, the first British-born man to accomplish the distance in the marathon race at the Olympic Games. After emigrating to a job in the South African public works department, he had been sent up by his superiors on a temporary task of attending to war graves in Tanganyika. In his travels he had passed the site of his future hotel, liked the situation, and bought what were originally a couple of old German farms. When he retired in 1933 he moved to the place, built a few bungalows, and there George, at the time of the bus journey, had first seen him with his head so far jammed into a radio loudspeaker that he was beyond the reach of terrestrial conversation.

On the second visit Cormack was more approachable. He joined George in a drink in his little bar and explained away his distraction on the previous occasion. He had been trying to disentangle British election and political matters from the atmospherics of Tanganyika. With the handicap of a run-down battery and some rather explosive opinions of his own on the matter, this had not been easy. George eased him down from high politics to realities on the Buhoro Flats. Worrying about whether the United Nations would switch the mandate over Tanganyika from Britain to Soviet Russia or give the place its independence were problems which George had not so far considered. Cormack grumbled that he should remember that politicians were far more dangerous to Africa than any man-eaters, but he did, however, admit to having heard of the lions. Fortunately his hotel lay a few miles west of the Ruvaha. He confirmed that the creatures had not so far ventured on his side of the river. All he knew of them, therefore, was by repute.

"They possibly know that we have enough troubles here as it is," he said, "from the leopards."

He pointed through the window at the gaunt cliff faces of the overlooking Poroto mountains. There was always a fairly dense population of leopards along this escarpment and on the high Uwanji Plateau which acted as the roof of the range. The leopards enjoyed an adequate supply of natural food in the form of baboons, monkeys and small game, but sporadically they turned on human beings. Leopards, however, are seldom consistent man-eaters. They simply seem to like an occasional change of diet.

There was a legend on the Uwanji Plateau that many years ago an African man came from a distant country and settled near the village of Matamba. This stranger farmed well but, unfortunately for him, not at all wisely. In any primitive community it never pays to do better than one's fellows. The price of success can only be increased demands for tribute from the chief, and the dangerous envy of neighbours. The primitive Kinga tribespeople of the plateau watched the progress of the newcomer. Inevitably they concluded that his success came only from some magic charm in his possession. They therefore decided to kill the man and use parts of his body in fertility rites for their own soil. Since that day, ritual killings have been common on the plateau with a regular cult known as *Buda* whose technique is to cut away the portions of the victim required for their rites. Then they throw the mutilated corpse down the cliff faces and palm the tragedy off upon the leopards.

"We have this trouble around here in spasms," Cormack said. "It's impossible to disentangle fact from fiction and find out where animal killings leave off and murder takes over. Everybody is too frightened to talk. Even the name of this place is said to be properly *Kimaleke,* meaning to wipe out. It refers to some such visitation of death in the past. From the same reasons of terror, I haven't heard much about these lions across the river. Even a man who lost his child to a man-eater the previous night would be loath to discuss the matter in the morning, and certainly not prepared to even mention it to any stranger. I suspect that you are going to have quite a task ahead of you to clear up things in the Njombe district. Perhaps you should rather invite the politicians there. Those lions might at least do one really worthwhile thing by eating them."

George left him to his radio and drove on across the river into the territory of the man-eaters. He could understand the Great Ruvaha acting as a barrier to the lions. The road hugged the foot of the Poroto mountains on the extreme southern verge of the Buhoro Flats. It bridged the river just where the Great Ruvaha came rushing out of the wild valley in which it found its source. Immediately beyond the bridge the river flattened out on the plain into a series of impassable swamps. He had hunted for ivory there once, as far down as where the Madawi tributary fed the Ruvaha. It was definitely no place for lions. Only elephant and crocodiles could live permanently in such shallow morasses of mud and water. The elephants spent their lives as prisoners of their own environment. From years of wading through the swamps feeding on the giant star grass, their feet were so pudgy and tender on account of saturation of water that they became increasingly reluctant to ever again walk on hard ground.

George had heard no murmur of any trouble with man-eaters from the tribespeople resident in the area at the time of his first hunt. He remembered the people well. Just across the river the inhabitants were an overlap of the Sangu tribe living under a sub-chief stationed at the village of Rujewa. Beyond them the Great North Road went on westward into the lands of the Bena people, the principal tribe of the Njombe district. The whole area, although so densely bushed, had never been a great place for game. The tribespeople were cattle keepers and peaceful men with little stomach for adventures. What precisely had brought their present trouble upon them was something of a problem. Before the appetite of the lions could be finally satisfied with a generous ration of bullets, the whole affair certainly promised to make a rather interesting study.

The Njombe administrative station was the first place in the district to which George directed himself in search of information. The government centre lay fifty miles down a branch track leading off the Great North Road. It was not only somewhat south of the actual area of the lions, but also high above it. The original founder of the station, *Jumbe* Northcote, had made an admirable choice for the place. It was situated over 6,000 feet up in a world of its own of green grass and misty hills. A waterfall tumbled down through the centre of the little settlement and the whole place could rather have been a hamlet in Europe than an outpost in Africa plagued with the grisly horror of man-eating lions.

The relief with which the district commissioner of the station, W. Wenban-Smith, received George in his office soon shattered any delusionary notions of the tranquillity of the area.

" Thank the Lord somebody has come from the game department," he said, " and brought, I trust, an armament of rifles. This district of mine has become so demoralised it is literally falling apart into a rabble of terrified people."

He unrolled a map of the Njombe district on his desk and proceeded to give George his first authentic details of the man-eating. It was a dismal story.

As far as Wenban-Smith knew, the killings had started about 1932. He had no idea how they had started. It was assumed that the business had more or less followed the usual history of man-eating. Some lioness had possibly become incapacitated and turned to eating men as the easiest way of securing food. She had passed the taste on to her successive batches of cubs. There were certain stories current about black magic, but the police had never found the slightest indication that the killings were the work of anything other than lions. All the signs seemed to reveal the technique of the stereo-typed lion attack, with the tracks of the animal leading up to the final spring, with the victim dragged off in the lion's mouth for several hundred yards into the bush, and a broken neck as the characteristic form of death. The remains also indicated normal consumption by a lion, the skin torn off and the meat literally licked away by the file-like tongue.

Since the beginning of the killings, successive district commissioners had done what they could to end the matter. Various parties of African police constables had been sent to patrol the area. Four African game scouts were also permanently stationed in the Njombe district. These men were well armed for their normal duty of crop protection. They had been regularly instructed to hunt the lions, but the sick dread which the tribespeople had for the man-eaters appeared to be contagious. No lions had ever been shot in the district in all the time of the killings. The game scouts had some story that when they followed the tracks of the lions, the tracks invariably turned into those of a human being. This was their excuse for never proceeding with any hunt. The policemen were equally superstitious. Their investigations were completely negative.

George was increasingly puzzled.

" What about Dusty Arundell ?"

Wenban-Smith shrugged.

" He came here quite often. But it was incredible how the chap was always called away on some other priority duty or obligation or personal problem at home just as he was on the verge of starting something. It was as though fate had contrived a deliberate sequence of events carefully calculated to provide immunity to these cursed lions."

It sounded like quite a situation to George. The type of situation, in fact, which any witchdoctor worth his salt could exploit with considerable profit. What an enhancement to the prestige of any magician if he could claim re-sponsibility for the immunity of the lions!

" How many people do you think have been killed?"

The district commissioner pointed to the map. He confirmed that the lions seemed to confine most of their activities to three sub-chiefdoms, those of Bernardi at Mtwango, of Majengwa at Rujewa, and of Jifiki at Wangin-gombe. Each area had been equally troubled over the same length of time. The total area hunted by the lions covered some 1,500 square miles. When the trouble began, the tribespeople were living widely scattered in their cus-tomary small family units. There was no means of the administration having any check on their casaulties. After the trouble started, the people gradually concentrated for their own protection into villages for at least a negative form of defence.

Even then it was difficult to know exactly what was happening. The reluctance of the people to talk defeated any detailed investigation. Only the sub-chief Jifiki attempted to keep any record. He was a man of intelligence and integrity. He was frightened of the lions but not too superstitiously overawed by them. The lions had hunted in his area from 1932 to 1940, but he had kept no record of their killings during that period. During 1940, for some inexplicable reason, the lions abandoned his area. Jifiki was reluctant to discuss this period, The lions had returned during the following year. It was from this time that Jifiki had kept a list of the names of his own followers killed in the local area of Wangingombe. The list did not include casual visitors or travellers walking through the area. The district commissioner handed the list to George. He looked at it with some shock.

In the four years since 1941 the names of 230 people were listed as having been killed at Wangingombe. The implications of the list were staggering. The eight years previous to the keeping of the list were considered by Jifiki to have been equally bad. The killings in the two neighbouring sub-chiefdoms were said to have been at least equal at Mtwango and certainly worse at Rujewa. George worked things out on a piece of paper. At a rough guess it looked as though the total figure must have reached the 1,500 mark quite some time ago. The district commissioner watched the expression on his face and grinned rather wryly.

" That's why I sent you the message as soon as I heard that you had arrived in Mbeya. I suppose you thought that I was an alarmist. But I think you'll agree that something pretty drastic should have been done about these creatures quite a few years ago. So what are you going to do now—tell me that you have something more important to do?"

George looked at him.

" No," he said, " there is nothing I could have to do more important than liquidating this business. All the time I possibly can I'll spend here until the lions are finished, that I promise you."

The next morning he set out on a thorough tour of the affected area. Before he could plan any systematic action it was essential that he know the whole district, meet the sub-chiefs concerned with the area, hear their version of events, secure news about the present whereabouts of the lions and, if possible, devise some form of reliable information about their movements and doings in the future.

For two weeks George travelled through the district, doing most of his driving at night in the hope of having the fortune to pick up one of the lions in the headlights of his truck. It would have been marvellous luck to have started the hunt with such an easy success, but he never even observed the tracks of any lions on the dusty surface of the road, let alone saw the slightest glimpse of the creatures.

Stories about the lions were more easy to come by than information about their current whereabouts. There were two mission stations in the area, and, if the fear of the tribespeople inclined them to the prudence of silence, then at least the missionaries were loquacious. Both missions had experienced a grim time from the lions. Both considered themselves to be in almost a state of siege, with children never allowed to play beyond the safety of their own homes.

At the Swedish Lutheran station of Ilembula, the missionary in charge, the Reverend Martin Nordfeldt, had also kept some record of the losses suffered by his community. His list only covered the previous two years but it included over two hundred names. He was quite frank about the matter to George. If the Africans considered the activities of the lions to be the result of black magic, he was certain that the whole affair was a visitation of the devil. The glint of amusement in George's eyes failed to even irritate him.

" I think, Mr Rushby," he said, " that by the time you really get to know these monsters for yourself you will agree with me. They may look like lions; I suppose that they are lions; but they do not behave like them and I will be interested to hear your opinion after you complete your study."

The atmosphere at his own mission was tense. A few evenings before George's arrival the kitchen servant had knocked off late, just after sunset, and set out for home with a hurricane lamp to light his way. Just as he disappeared through the jacaranda trees growing around the side of the handsome mission church there was a sudden bellow of sheer animal terror. Nordfeldt and his assistants ran out with torches and rifles. They found the hurricane lamp lying on the ground. A blood trail led them to the disembowelled body of their servant, abandoned in a maize field.

A month before this event another member of the mission had been carried off in broad daylight. The lion had dragged him into a thorn thicket. On the way one of the thorns had fortunately penetrated the animal's face. With a howl of pain the lion dropped the man and tried to paw the thorn from its face. The victim, up till then, had been petrified with terror. As the lion dropped him he recovered sufficiently to commence such a stentorian bawling for help that the man-eater took fright and bolted. It was not often that any victim had so fortunate an escape when he had actually been in the jaws of death.

The Kidugala mission also had a record of frightening events. During the war the place had been converted into a Polish refugee camp, mainly for women and children, with a few Italian men who did the maintenance work. When he discovered that the lions were killing off the tribespeople around the mission the Commandant of the camp, a Mr Wagner, erected machans in a few trees down a valley through which the man-eaters seemed to have the habit of travelling.

Over a considerable time, Wagner spent at least two nights of each week in these machans hoping for a chance of a shot at the lions. He never had a sight of them. Two of the Italian prisoners of war were also interested in trying their aim against the man-eaters. They usually sat up with Wagner. Oddly enough the only time the lions actually came close enough to the machans to allow the chance of a shot was on a night when Wagner was called away. The two Italians were left on guard with rifles, blankets, torches and thermos flasks.

At 1 a.m. the lions came. They reached the bottom of the tree and started grunting, while one tried to claw its way up to the machan. This was too much for the Italians. In a wild scramble higher up the tree they dropped their rifles and torches on to the heads of the surprised lions. Until dawn the Italians clung to the topmost branches of the tree, half-frozen and more than half-frightened to death. They were still there when Wagner came in the morning to find out what had happened to them.

At least the Italians had made an attempt to hunt the lions. The African population, although the men were nearly all armed, had done precisely nothing. Talking to them about the matter was so frustrating that George was half-inclined to line the whole population up and spend some time in planting a kick squarely into each man's backside in the hope that it might at least shame him to some form of activity in his own defence. Travelling through the tribal lands was simply depressing. On every side could be seen deserted and ruined huts and hamlets. Entire settlements had packed up their belongings and fled as though from a visitation of the plague.

The atmosphere was, admittedly, oppressive. Even without the ingredient of black magic, these lions appeared to be diabolical enough and with more than their share of the cunning possessed by most man-eaters. They had developed some very awkward habits. They were partial to attacking villages in the night, jumping on to the roofs of huts, scratching their way down through the thatch until they could fall inside and then playing havoc with the occupants. The lions had obviously become arrogant through their own immunity. Only very occasionally did George meet anyone who had attempted to resist them. One man living near Rujewa told George that he had lost his beloved wife early one evening when a lion simply stormed straight into a village street, bowled over several people and seized the woman in its jaws. There were other lions waiting outside the village. Together they dragged the corpse off and started to feed on it in a thicket.

The husband, in a frenzy of grief and rage, immediately ran to his hut and found his muzzle-loading Tower musket. He called to his neighbours to help him but none of them would move. On his own he advanced towards the thicket where he could hear the animals snarling over the choicest pieces of the feast. Suddenly a lioness broke cover and advanced towards the man. Her face and chest were stained with the woman's blood. In her mouth the lioness carried one of the woman's legs. She stared at the man with that cold and baleful glare which only the larger cats can give. This so unnerved the man that he became rooted to the ground, trembling so much that he shook the percussion cap right off the breech nipple of his gun, making it unusable. Then the lioness contemptuously turned her back on him and slowly walked away.

Panic is like an infectious disease and the people of the Njombe district were obviously dying of it. There was a prevailing horror of ghosts in the night, of shadows which moved, of darkness with eyes, of the flaming fury and ruthless savagery of these monstrous creatures. Hunting them was obviously going to be a complex and tedious affair. Those of the headmen who were even prepared to discuss the lions were emphatic, not only in their opinion that hunting them would be a waste of time, but that no African in his right senses would make a move to help. They at least would have sufficient brains to know that such a display of hostility towards the man-eaters could only result in the most violent retribution.

Jifiki was the only responsible African in the district who seemed to have kept his head. His oddly named little capital of *Wangingombe* (The Place of the Stolen Cows) stood by the side of the Great North Road in a pleasant grove of jacaranda trees. He was a youngish man and Wenban-Smith's opinion of him proved perfectly correct as an individual too intelligent to be quite overawed by black magic, even if he believed in it. Sitting at night in the room he used for his court, Jifiki told George the background to the man-eating.

As Wenban-Smith had said, the trouble had started in 1932. In that year Matamula Mangera, headman of Iyayi village on the Great North Road and a renowned witchdoctor in his own right, was deposed from his post by his tribal chief on accusation of corruption. Whether the lions killed people in the Njombe district in any significant numbers before that event was unknown. But it was after the deposition of Matamula that complaints started to be heard of the activity of man-eaters. A story became known to the people of the Buhoro Flats that the lions belonged to Matamula. It was said that he had an assistant named Mkakiwa who lived with and herded the lions in a secret area between the villages of Igawa and Rujewa. A second assistant, Hamisi Sayidi, was said to have the task, on receiving instructions from his master, of taking over selected lions from the herdsman and conducting them to appointed places where they would kill any person on order.

So much was said by others, as well as the rumour that the terror would continue until Matamula was once more chief. These things were not publicly claimed by Matamula. Whence came the story in the first place nobody knew. But it was implicitly believed by every tribesman. They were convinced of the power of the witchdoctor. They offered him gifts of propitiation and begged him to accept substantial payment to protect themselves or to

direct his lions to the persons of enemies or unwanted relatives and neighbours. It was said that Matamula had become enriched from all the payments
made to him. It was said that it was useless to oppose the lions. Not only
were their acts directed by a human brain but they were themselves not
simple lions, but *simba ya mtu,* were-lions, some changed from living human
beings, others the revived corpses of the dead.

As for Jifiki, he would say no more. When George asked him whether
he believed such things he simply shrugged. When George discussed the number of killings with him and reached the point where the lions had left his
district in uneasy peace in 1940, Jifiki became extremely diffident. He side-
stepped the question. When pressed for a positive answer he ended the
discussion with some indication of fear, and left the meeting room in order
to go to bed.

The whole safari had certainly provided George with enough food for
thought. He returned to Mbeya the next morning still mentally ruminating
on all he had been told and the set of human characters he had met living
on the scene of this most curious tragedy. Matamulu was the one key figure
he had still to meet. He had resisted calling at the man's residence. In the
conventions of Africa, this might indicate to the tribesmen that he had heard,
and believed, the tales of the witchdoctor's control of the lions. The meeting
with Matamula would come later. For the present, George's head was full
of schemes of action against the lions.

As soon as he returned to his office he would send off wires calling in as
many game scouts as could be spared from outlying posts. He would also
wire Monty Moore, at the game department headquarters, telling him of the
true extent of the terror, requesting as many trap guns as could be spared,
and informing the warden that he would be on the trail of the man-eaters
full-time until their complete elimination.

All these telegrams were, in fact, sent off. Unfortunately, one other had
also to go. This one was to Wenban-Smith informing him with deepest
regret that, in the midst of preparing in Mbeya for the campaign against the
lions, George received an order from the government. The order was to
drop everything he was doing and give urgent priority to the operations currently being taken by the International Red Locust Organisation against an
outbreak of locusts in the Rukwa valley. The order was categorical and had
to be obeyed.

CHAPTER THIRTY

THE TRAIL OF BLOOD

IT WAS not until the middle of January 1946 that George found it possible to
return to the Njombe district. For two months he had been completely involved in the campaign being waged against locusts in the Rukwa valley. The
humid wilderness of high grass around Lake Rukwa was one of the principal
breeding grounds in Africa for the plague of the red locust. For years the
number of these insects would remain static in the valley. Then for some
reason, possibly part of a cycle or as a result of some delicate balance between climate and their own parasites, they would suddenly breed in enormous numbers. Prodigious swarms of them would set off on proper invasions
of the surrounding territories, doing such damage to crops and vegetation
as made the red locust share with the mosquito the reputation of being the
principal curse of Africa.

To control this pest the International Red Locust Organisation had been formed, with a staff of scientists in command of a field task force made up of a pretty rough-and-ready set of international recruits. This crowd poured down into the wonderful game country of the Rukwa valley as though their interest was to wage war on the animals rather than the insects. Fortunately their scientific command, Dr Bredo, a Belgian, and a British biologist, Vesey-Fitzgerald, soon realised that the game were responsible for keeping the high grass under some control in the valley. The locusts, in their primitive form, lived in this grass. The grass-eating game, therefore, were the true allies of anyone attempting to combat locusts. The policy of the locust control organisation promptly became definitely conservationist, and George was able to return to his preparations against the lions with at least the satisfaction of knowing that the trigger-happy set in Africa had once again been frustrated in their ambition to use any excuse as a reason for wholesale shooting of wild life.

For his campaign against the man-eaters George selected six of his best African game scouts. These men he stationed permanently in the disturbed area; two of them at Wangingombe, two at a small hamlet near Jumbe Musa's, while the other two were instructed to be continuously mobile, following up the slightest rumour as to the whereabouts of the lions. Twenty trap guns were also erected in different parts of the district. The guns were carefully placed over the narrow entrances of small circular bush pole enclosures. Any animal attempting to enter an enclosure would be forced to push against a cord running vertically to the gun trigger from a point in the ground in the centre of the entrance, and would immediately be blown to its glory by a bullet straight through the top of its head. The bait for the traps was temptingly varied through a whole menu of bleating goats, yelping dogs, human remains recovered from killings, live game scouts and, on numerous occasions, George himself. During the long and involved hunt for the man-eaters, no lion ever ventured near the traps.

From the beginning of the hunt, George speculated about the number of creatures, whether lion or lion-man, involved in the killings. There was no immediate answer to this problem. Normally, lions do their hunting and travelling at night and spend the daylight hours relaxed in some nearby hide, where it is comparatively easy to find and see them. The Njombe man-eaters certainly did most of their killing in the early evening, but when exactly they relaxed was another matter. They appeared to spend most of the night feasting and sporting with their kill, like cats with some unfortunate mouse. With the dawn they abandoned what was left of the victim and moved away, travelling so hard all day that by the time news of the kill reached a hunter and he arrived at the spot, the trail of blood was already cold. It was as though the creatures had a guilt complex and deliberately tried to get as far away from the scene of their crimes as possible.

Even with a good start, it was difficult to follow their trail. The ground in the country of the man-eaters was hard, dry and stony. The man-eaters had also developed a really awkward habit of rapid dispersal of their numbers. An entire pride of the creatures was capable of attacking a single village. But in the daylight, during their flight from the scene, they tended to scatter into small groups, pairs, or even single animals who would hunt alone in a seemingly quite haphazard manner for many nights on end. Then groups of them would band together again for another combined attack. They never duplicated an attack two nights running on the same place and had never been known to remain in any single area for successive days.

So far as George was concerned, the first three-week hunt after the man-eaters had to be debited to experience. He simply had to abandon any delusions that conventional hunting methods would soon liquidate the lions. It was obviously going to be a painstaking business unless some phenomenal stroke of luck occurred and he was actually in one of the villages when it was attacked. There would certainly be some fun if that event took place, but arranging it would not be easy.

What he decided to do was to improve his channels of information as much as he could. The one possible weakness to the man-eaters' hunting ground so far as the killers were concerned was that it was cut not only by the Great North Road, but also by two branch roads to Njombe. These roads were under scheduled traffic by government transport trucks and buses. The drivers could all be enrolled as news-gatherers. They could be relied upon to pick up information about overnight killings.

The plan George formed for his second hunt was to establish his base camp on the side of one of the roads. As soon as he received information of a recent killing he could drive to the place concerned, follow the tracks until their direction seemed to be at all purposeful and then try to guess to which area the lions were heading. If this area was isolated, he would just have to leave it to its fate. If, however, it was reachable by road, he could drive there as fast as possible, spend the afternoon hunting back in the direction from which the lions would be coming and then, if there was no sign of them, spend the night waiting in a tree or a hide.

Before he could launch this new plan of campaign, George had to return to Mbeya for a week and attend to his normal administrative duties. He also had the pleasure of seeing Kate again. Now that they were settled in a reasonably healthy little township like Mbeya, with a good school available locally, there was no sense in leaving the children so widely scattered. Kate had experienced a very happy five-year stay with her grandparents in Cape Town. Seeing her arrive at Mbeya airport, a bright, pretty and modern little girl, and listening to her chatter of school events and holiday activities which the speed of an aircraft had allowed her to leave only the day before, emphasised the whole remarkable contrast of the African continent. That the same Great North Road could have its start in a pleasant twentieth-century city like Cape Town and then, some 2,500 miles away, traverse the setting of the nightmare events in the Njombe district was almost too incongruous to believe.

George returned to the hunt at the end of the week. The total failure of his first pursuit of the man-eaters had irritated him to a considerable extent. Inevitably the tribespeople regarded any such failure as proof of their own opinion that it was useless to even attempt to hunt the lions. Unless he had a rapid success the game scouts were also likely to become infected with local superstitions, and with such notions in their heads they would become as spineless as the tribespeople. A couple of them already seemed slightly uneasy about their work. He would certainly have to replace them.

One hopeful sign on his return was that the information service seemed to be working well. Each day the transport drivers brought news of killings to his roadside camp. Nearly every night he sat up until dawn in a hide at some village, hoping that the man-eaters would attack. He began to hate the creatures, not only with disgust at their killings, but with a personal feeling of frustrated annoyance at his own lack of success. Practically every day he had to examine the debris left behind from a previous night's feast. The creatures certainly made it hearty in their eating habits. If the Singida lion-men always made a token meal of selected parts of their victims then the Njombe killers if nothing else, certainly had substantial appetites. The scraps which they left behind were often hardly worth placing as bait in one of the traps. The killers seemed to be particularly fond of human brains. They always carefully cracked open their victims' skulls. One of the few fragments of their meal was invariably a cleanly licked-out brain pan.

The man-eaters were obviously thoroughly confirmed in their choice of human food. There were considerable numbers of domestic livestock all around them, with the cattle sheltered at night in such fragile enclosures that even a calf, let alone a resolute lion, could push its way through the waist-high walls of brushwood. The disinterest of the man-eaters in beef was perfectly proved by the fact that the cattle showed very little fear of them. They even failed to stampede when the man-eaters on several occasions charged into the very midst of a herd, snatched the herdboys who habitually rode on the backs of the bulls, and then made off without so much as a scratch to the flank of a calf. The man-eaters, on the other hand, did seem to have some feeling about pigs. Very often, in the course of his tracking, George found the carcasses of wild pigs. They had been killed as though for sport and left with their stomachs ripped open. Their squeals had no doubt provided some amusement to the man-eaters and this was the probable reason for the killings.

Sitting up all night certainly provided George with ample opportunity to think of the man-eaters. There are few things more miserably uncomfortable than a tree-top machan in an area habitually swept by cold night winds.

He very soon switched this part of his campaign to sitting in the shelter of a pit. A pit had the disadvantage of a restricted view but at least such devices were snug. They were dug about three feet deep by three feet wide and four feet long. A piece of tarpaulin was placed over the pit and pegged down on three sides. The fourth side, facing away from the prevailing wind, was raised so as to provide an opening four feet long and one and a half feet high.

In such a pit George would spend the nights sitting on a box with his rifle beside him and no other company save his thoughts and the dismal remnants of some human being deliberately scattered in front of the hide as a bait. After three weeks all he could show for his patience was one wild pig, two hyenas, one leopard, one jackal and one stray goat. These innocents simply paid the price of approaching the hide. Although, looking out from the dark pit, the starlit night was comparatively bright, it was still difficult to identify any movement in the surrounding bush. In any case, George's experience of this type of tense and rather nerve-racking hunting over a bait induced him to shoot first and attend to such matters as identification afterwards. He had a torch strapped to his head, with the switch next to the trigger on his rifle, but it was still best to shoot at the first sign of movement and then switch the light on later.

The failure of the plan to anticipate the movements of the man-eaters was unfortunate. The creatures obviously habitually changed their direction even when they were at the very outskirts of a village. At the end of three disappointing weeks, when George returned to Mbeya, he had to take two of the game scouts with him. Their nerve had completely failed. The remaining four were also not particularly happy about their work. Unless something happened in the third hunt they would have to be replaced, and there were limits to the number of new men he could introduce to the task. The two scouts returned to their normal duties had both seriously suggested that the best way to deal with the man-eaters was to negotiate with Matamula. They had obviously been listening to too many tales.

For his third hunt after the killers George brought with him two of the most level-headed of all his African staff, game scouts Alfani and Fungamali. Alfani was the same individual who had once been George's cook on the coffee farm near Mbeya. Distant Somali ancestors had bequeathed him a hooked nose and a countenance so fierce that he had even been able to eject George's mother from the kitchen on one memorable occasion, simply by rolling his eyes and flapping his large brass ear-rings. He was not a man likely to be much over-awed by lions, magic or otherwise. George stationed the two men at Jumbe Musa's, at that time one of the most badly troubled areas. To familiarise them with the work of patrol he hunted with them for three days. There was no sign of any man-eater.

On the fourth day the transport drivers brought news of a bad night at the village of Mambego, some fifty miles away. George moved there immediately. The village was in a state of disintegration. Most of the inhabitants had fled the place. When he walked to the huts he found the relics of two human beings scattered over the floor of a goat corral. The man-eaters had not even bothered to drag their victims to the bush. A few goats were still standing about staring wonderingly at the remains.

George walked into the village calling out the traditional " *Hodi?*" (" May I come in?") The only sensible person apparently left in the place was one little girl about eight years old. She maintained the honour of her village by gravely replying with " *Karibu* " (" Come near "), and emerging from a hut to receive the visitor. She had been overlooked there when the villagers had fled. The only other inhabitants were a few old people abandoned to their fate and too bemused to provide any coherent account of events. The little girl simply told him that on the previous night the insects of the bush had forced their way into two of the huts. She had been asleep under a blanket. In the uproar some skins hanging from the roof had fallen on top of her. Petrified with terror at the screaming going on around her, she had actually lain silently under this covering until dawn. Then she had emerged and found her family gone. She was not sure whether they had been eaten or had simply run away.

It was approaching night and too late to make any effort to track the man-eaters. George scouted through the bush surrounding the village but there was no sign of any lions other than numerous pug marks. By the tracks, the animals had literally surrounded the village, regarding the place from various vantage points until they judged the time suitable for their attack.

From the negative experiences in the past there was little prospect of the killers returning for a second raid on the village. It was dull going sitting in a pit all night when you knew that the chances of a shot were negligible, but on the slender offchance George instructed the two scouts with him to prepare a suitable hide. He also ordered the remaining inhabitants of the village to gather for the night in one of the huts where the game scouts could guard them. The atmosphere of the half-deserted village was wretched but at least there was plenty of food and drink. Just before sunset the little girl came and invited him into the hut. The child had boiled some eggs for him and secured a bottle of fresh milk to complete his supper. The game scouts and the old people were even inclined to be slightly merry on some pots of beer which had been in store at the time of the attack.

George left them all packed into the one hut and retired to his pit. It was a long night, with not even the whimper of a hyena to break the monotony. All George could do when the dawn came was curse himself for being so stupid as to wear himself out in such a useless vigil. He scrambled out of the pit and went to the hut where the little girl again provided him with food. He was still eating when several former inhabitants of the village came back.

One of them was the little girl's father. Her mother had been eaten during the night in the village to which they had gone in hope of safety.

George gulped his food. Then with one of the scouts, the girl's father and two other tribesmen he set out to try to intercept the man-eaters by guessing at the route they would take away from the scene of the last attack. The three tribesmen did not exactly volunteer their services, but George needed guides too badly to listen to excuses.

Three hours after leaving the village they cut fresh lion tracks. The tracks were of four lions. They were following a small upper tributary of the Mbarali River, heading in the direction of the Kidugala Mission. They were the freshest tracks George had so far found. He looked exultantly at his companions and was surprised to see how miserable they all seemed to be. Even the game scout was frightened.

They set off on the trail. The going was not easy. The thorn bush was thick and the weather scorching. George thanked his stars that he at least had the ideal rifle for the task, a double-barrelled ejector 9·3 mm. German Magnum, deadly accurate in both barrels, hard hitting, well balanced, fast to use and light enough to be carried all day. On such a fresh trail he would be prepared to follow to the bitter end even if it meant sleeping in the bush. A heavy rifle would have been wearisome.

They tramped along, keeping as silent as possible. The thorn bush crowded them so closely that they had very little vision in any direction and there seemed hardly any air to breathe. The four Africans were glistening with something more than the perspiration of heat. They were watching the trail so fixedly that George could guess the fearful nature of their thoughts. Whatever they found at the end of the trail would certainly provide them with quite a climax.

Just before noon they pushed through a wall of thorn shrub and suddenly saw the lions. The four animals were standing close together in the shade of a tree. They had probably been resting and had been startled at the hunters' approach. If the thorn thicket had obscured the view of the hunters, it had also done the same for the lions, and the stillness of the air had killed any chance of scent. George heard the Africans' gasp behind him. He dropped to his knee. The nearest lion was a young female. Before she had recovered from her surprise he took careful aim and fired. The explosion was startling in the taut silence of the bush. The bullet splintered the right front upper leg of the lioness. Pandemonium broke loose as she tried to claw and bite her own wound.

The other lions started to move off. George was inclined to put his second bullet into one of them but it was too important that he at least have an absolutely definite kill. He let them go and aimed again at the lioness. She was growling and rampaging around in small circles. The second shot went straight through her head. George reloaded and gave her two more very deliberate bullets. It was only after he had fired that he realised that he had never before wanted to be so certain that an animal was dead before he went near it. He glanced at the four Africans. The expression on their faces was an almost indescribable mixture of fear and incredibility. Their eyes were fixed on the lioness with a horrible expectancy. They obviously expected the animal to be transformed before them into some dread demon. George realised that deep down it was through a precisely similar feeling that he had wanted the lioness to be so very dead.

He almost laughed at himself and walked up to the carcass. It was a young, sleek and obviously very well-fed animal. He called the Africans over and examined the carcass in front of them. There were no signs of any human interference with the animal. Her coat was glossy, her teeth superb and her body in excellent condition. The Africans sat down on their haunches and stared at her. After a few minutes one of the tribesmen said:

" She may not have been one of the insects of the bush."

George shrugged. He was pretty certain about it himself, but there could be no absolute guarantee that she was a man-eater. In any case, it was not particularly important. The important thing was that in killing the lioness he had broken the ice. Every tribesman in the district would soon know that there were real lions roaming around in the bush; that they could be killed with impunity and at least some resistance to being eaten was perfectly feasible.

Maximum publicity for the killing was essential. There was a small village about one mile away. George sent off two of the men to summon the inhabitants. Within half an hour every man, woman and child arrived on the scene. They stood around the lioness, all strangely quiet. After a while George asked the men to skin the animal. No one would touch it. He had to do the job himself while they continued to watch in silence. Once the skin was off they seemed relieved. After he had cut the skull off they were prepared to touch the creature. A few of them even volunteered to help carry the trophies back to Mambego. It was quite a triumphant return. The little girl even managed to find a full dozen eggs and present them to what was now definitely her hero. Somebody had obviously told her that Europeans lived on eggs and George couldn't find the heart to explain to her that the things gave him heartburn.

The next day he took the skin and skull to Wangingombe. Jifiki was overjoyed at news of the kill. He promptly displayed the trophies in his court room and George was assured that the news of the success would be spread by every means. The local excitement was very considerable, with people streaming in to stare at the trophies and gingerly touch the teeth, as though wondering what it must really have been like to have been held in such a fearsome jaw.

George left them to their glee. At Mambego he had found a message waiting for him from his two scouts at Jumbe Musa's. They reported a continuing series of killings in their area. They had not been able to track any of the man-eaters but the creatures were obviously lurking there in strength. They particularly asked George to return to them immediately.

George camped with them that evening. He had been rather afraid that the urgency of their message indicated that his two new scouts had already lost their nerve. He found them, however, to be in excellent fettle. They were just highly irritated that the local tribesmen not only refused to give them the slightest aid, but actually seemed antagonistic at the mere idea of anybody provoking the man-eaters by hunting them. The news of George's first kill was very heartening to the two scouts. They realised as well as he did just how profoundly such a success could affect the tribespeople. If only they could have a similar success in their own area it would make all the difference between a hostile and a friendly atmosphere for the scouts.

Even without this consideration, George had resolved to hunt in Jumbe Musa's area himself. From all reports the man-eaters were finding the local people so much to their liking that they were becoming regular if unwanted guests in the district, and man-eaters with regular habits were exactly what George wanted.

He set out at dawn the next morning. Ignoring the local tribespeople entirely, he and the two scouts hunted hard for three full days. In an area where people were being killed nearly every night it was both infuriating and baffling to explain how the man-eaters could avoid so persistent a trio of hunters. At least, if the creatures had made an effort to attack them it would have brought a greater atmosphere of reality to the scene. As it was, the dark nights, completely still, other than for the sound of the insects and the rustlings of a cold wind, were the ideal medium for the spread of the infection of terror.

What the scouts were thinking about it all, George could easily guess. He had never felt particularly happy himself in the territory of the man-eaters, and expecting others to be jolly at their work would have been rather too much. As it was, the three of them would simply sit and brood around their fire, the Africans occasionally making an attempt at minor conversation and George, for some reason, often thinking of Cormack in his hotel listening to his radio and wondering whether the United Nations were going to take the country over or give the place its independence. Politics had never really interested George. So far as he was concerned, a handful of British officials, with the co-operation of a friendly population, had for nearly thirty years run the place with a remarkable absence of trouble but at little profit and no small cost to themselves in time, patience and health. If somebody else wanted to take over the task of dealing with such things as the man-eaters of the Njombe district he would be inclined to present his rifle to them with the kindest regards.

It was a wonderful relief from all the tension when, on the fourth morning, they cut a beautifully fresh trail of what seemed to be quite a substantial pride of lions. They were still trying to determine the number of animals in the pride when they caught up with what was apparently the rearguard. It was a strapping-looking young male who turned and snarled warningly at them while the rest of his pride disappeared into the bush. The three men all fired within a split second of each other. Which of the shots actually killed the lion was of purely academic interest. George was happy that there would be some confusion about the matter. It would be far more impressive to the tribespeople if the game scouts could boast of a kill. Whatever a white man did would always be regarded as something slightly outside the local curriculum.

The game scouts were quite overjoyed. They skinned the lion with such glee that they could obviously hardly wait to show the proof of the killing to the tribespeople. There was going to be a really glorious amount of boasting about the result of this hunt and George was delighted. He egged the scouts on by doubting that his own bullet had inflicted the fatal wound and jibing at the cowardice of the tribesmen. By that evening in fact, the change in atmosphere at Jumbe Musa's was remarkable. The people were so jubilant that they were running about carelessly even after dusk, and this was dangerous. George had to point out to their headman that the killing of this one lion in his area hardly meant the end of the terror. It was certainly a fine beginning, but there were likely to be quite a few more deaths among the people before the man-eaters were all liquidated. Meanwhile they must remain as cautious as ever, only heartened by the sure knowledge that the killers were just as vulnerable as any normal lions.

The next day George had to leave the area. The scouts would continue the hunt on their own until he could attend to the usual accumulation of administrative matters at Mbeya. He had every intention of returning within a few days. One of the pleasures which he had promised himself, now that the first two lions had been shot, was to satisfy his own curiosity by arranging a meeting with the famous Matamula. It would be something in the line of a rather interesting social occasion.

CHAPTER THIRTY-ONE

MATAMULA

NEARLY one and a half months had to elapse before George could return to the area of the man-eaters. This was a serious and most disappointing delay which quite neutralised most of the earlier good results of the hunt. It was caused by the fact that when George made a hurried inspection of the game-free area on the Rhodesian border he found one of the European supervisors, a man named Charles Chitty who was in charge of the western section of the fence, to be very seriously ill. He had to be taken in to Mbeya for the trouble to be diagnosed and then flown down to Dar es Salaam where he died miserably of cancer of the bladder. Winding up the dead man's affairs and finding and training a successor took time. The rest of the range, including the locust area around Lake Rukwa, was also clamouring for some attention. It was only at the end of March 1946 that George found himself once more at Jumbe Musa's.

He arrived expecting the worst, but was at least gratified to learn that game scout Alfani had followed the tracks of a pride of lions in the direction of Kidugala, and had shot and killed the rearguard. This was encouraging, although the remaining five scouts could report nothing other than a continuing terror of killings by the man-eaters.

George postponed any immediate intention of visiting Matamula. Although three lions had been liquidated in the district since the start of the hunt, the atmosphere was still so miserable that some large-scale success was imperative. The fact that a game scout on his own had killed a lion without himself suffering the least ill-effect had certainly been noted by the tribespeople, but their general despondency was alarming. A deputation had recently been sent to the paramount chief begging him to reappoint Matamula to his original post. There was some talk that the man had promised to call off his lions providing he was restored to his petty-chieftainship. George's return to the hunt was greeted by the tribesmen with a subdued hostility. They just did not want anybody to disturb the delicate supernatural nature of the business with such a crude antidote as shooting.

For three days George hunted around Jumbe Musa's with the two scouts. Then he moved to Wangingombe, hunting there for two days, also without any luck, but at least making the most of the opportunity to discuss things with Jifiki. The chief seemed even more perplexed about the business than when George had first met him. He was very much a man struggling to free himself from the dark superstitions of his ancestors but finding it increasingly difficult to resist the pressure of his people to simply recognise the power of Matamula by reappointing him. George did his best to rally the man, and then decided to move on to the Njombe administrative post. It was time that he saw the district commissioner again and thrashed out some solution to this continuing question of witchcraft.

George took the southern turn-off road to Njombe, stopping at every hut and hamlet along the way to ask for news of killings. Near to Ihanyawa, just before 8 a.m., he noticed a small hamlet of half a dozen huts situated some five hundred yards from the road. He parked his truck on the roadside and, carrying his rifle under his arm, walked over to the huts.

As soon as he approached the hamlet he realised that there was something wrong. The women were standing close to the doors of their huts with the children all inside. Three men, two armed with muzzle-loading guns and the other with spears, were watching a small shallow cultivated depression. George asked what was wrong. One of the men said that about half an hour earlier he had started off to work in the cultivated area. He had seen a lion on the other side of the depression, some 150 yards away. He had run back to give the alarm. As he ran he had lost sight of the lion. He did not know whether it had moved off or was lying hidden beyond the depression.

George moved forward. The man with the spears reluctantly agreed to accompany him. The other two said they would stay and guard the huts in case George missed the lion. Just beyond the depression, George picked up the fresh tracks of a single lion. He followed steadily, with the spearman seeming to gain more confidence as they travelled.

Two hours passed. Then they saw the lion. It was a young male animal with a half-grown, reddish-coloured mane. He was about fifty yards ahead, crossing a flat, shallow little dried-out marsh. He was within range but moving steadily ahead and offering only a stern shot. George followed silently, hoping for a better target. Five minutes passed. Then the hunters came to a bank of loose gravel with an exposed sheer side about four feet high. George jumped down it silently but the spearman, following about three yards behind him, slipped in a shower of rubble.

The lion immediately turned his head at the sound. He saw his pursuers and swung round at tremendous speed. George raised his rifle and fired. As he did so the lion started a full-blooded charge. The bullet simply kicked up a puff of dust behind the animal. The lion seemed to be coming like a thunderbolt. To the hunters, he looked all mane, teeth and claws. His tail was cocked up stiffly and whirling about at a forty-five degree angle. The mane hairs stood out on end as if electrified.

The recoil from the Magnum was slight, but by the time George had brought the second barrel back into line and could press the trigger, the lion was only ten yards away. He was really travelling. Fortunately the second bullet smacked straight into his brain. He somersaulted over the grass with a thud and crumpled up. George reloaded and put a second shot into the animal's head. Then he walked up and examined the creature. Like all the others, he was a youngish animal in excellent condition and with no pecularity other than what did appear to be a characteristic of these Njombe lions, a slight tendency towards smallness in size, with hair, on the other hand, inclined to be luxuriant, glossy and long.

The spearman had bolted. George did not blame him. After a deal of calling and hollering, the man returned. George sent him back to the hamlet for aid. By the time he returned with a few men George had skinned the lion and cut off the head. The men carried the trophies back to the huts. They seemed as serious about the matter as if they were carrying home the body of a chief. At the hamlet the people simply gathered around and stared at the skin in a listless manner.

George felt slightly disgusted at them. There was certainly not much pleasure in hunting the man-eaters if their victims preferred to be eaten. He indulged in some straight talking to them about the whole idiotic idea of black magic. They agreed with everything he said in the same lack-lustre tone which indicated that they were not even properly absorbing his arguments.

For the next three days George hunted in the area of the hamlet, sleeping in his truck at night. He found no other fresh traces of lions and the nights were completely peaceful. On the fourth day he decided that it was useless remaining in the area. He gave the tribespeople one final talk and then drove on to Njombe. Discussing the matter with the district commissioner might at least maintain his own sense of balance. It was too easy to start picking up fancies when you were isolated with the superstitious Africans.

The problem of the total number of man-eaters in the district still puzzled George. After his first investigation he had been inclined to think that there was something like under ten of the creatures. If this was true, then the shooting of four of them should start having a significant effect on the total number of human casualties in the district. In his central position of district commissoner, Wenban-Smith had a better chance of keeping check on the casualty figures. He did consider that there seemed to be some sign of a decrease in killings, but there was certainly no considerable relief in the district as yet. Either not all the lions shot had been man-eaters, or else there were considerably more than George's original estimate.

So far as the witchcraft side of the business was concerned, government policy was to completely ignore such notions. Wenban-Smith had heard of Matamula and knew the details of the man's original deposition. The present headman of the Iyayi area, one named Ulaya, was satisfactory in every respect. He was carrying out his duties in an exemplary manner, especially in view of the fact that he was only too well aware of the agitation for his replacement by so doughty a figure as Matamula. It was unthinkable that the administration would not give him complete support. Restoring Matamula would simply be official acknowledgment of the whole rigmarole of black magic. The final liquidation of all the man-eaters remained the best answer to all the stories of were-lions.

George continued his tour of the district. None of the game scouts could report the least success. Jumbe Musa's area still seemed to be the most consistently troubled. Mambego, on the other hand, was having a quiet spell with most of the inhabitants of the place back in their homes and the two game scouts stationed there having a rather easy time. They were staying with the husband of the woman killed in the last attack and the little girl, as friendly as ever, gave George the inevitable welcome of a few fresh eggs and a pleasant smile.

There was also a letter waiting from Eleanor. George's return to Mbeya was essential. The game department had sent a message that he was to be ready for an important communication. He cursed. The incessant string of distractions was a nuisance. All he could do was warn the scouts to persist with their patrols. He would return within a few days. Then he set off down the Great North Road back to Mbeya.

There was one thing, however, which he was determined to do before he left the district and that was to at last make the acquaintance of Matamula. The Great North Road actually ran through the village of Iyayi. It was easy to stop there, call in to present his greetings to Ulaya and reassure him of government support. The headman was a likeable and serious character who seemed mightily relieved at knowing that he had official friends. His village had experienced its full share of the terror but he was as reluctant as any of the other tribespeople to discuss the matter of the man-eaters. He would much rather have pretended that nothing was happening, and a diplomat could have learned a lesson from him in guarded language when it came to mentioning Matamula.

George wandered through the village, ostensibly talking to the people and enquiring about their losses. They seemed to regard him with indifference. Matamula's hut was on the west side of the road. The game scouts had often pointed it out when they had driven past the village. Just before he completed his visit, George walked across to the place and called out, " *Hodi?*"

Matamula came out to meet him with the usual " *Karibu.*" George introduced himself with the customary title for a game ranger, *bwana nyama,* and the two men looked at each other appraisingly. What Matamula thought of his visitor it was impossible to say. He was a medium-sized, well-built, clean-shaven man of about forty years of age. He was dressed in the usual white gown known as a *kanzu* and seemed affable enough. George chatted about a few trivialities. Trying to assess a man's character from his answers to such questions as " How are the crops?" is not particularly rewarding. Matamula appeared to have a ready wit, an easy ability to evade any issue which he disliked, and a depth to his nature which would resist something more than a mere superficial probing.

Only at the end of the visit did George mention the matter most on his mind. As he left, he said quite casually:

" The insects of the bush are not having a very good time. Four of them are dead."

Matamula looked at him with an odd little smile. He shrugged almost imperceptibly and said:

" *Labda* " (" Perhaps ").

They parted on this word. George drove on to Mbeya. The news he received on his arrival was that, in the post-war shortage of shipping, an unexpected opportunity had occurred for Tanganyika civil servants who, like him, had been unable to enjoy overseas leave since the beginning of the war, to sail immediately to Britain, on the old British India liner *Mantola.* Six months' leave was accordingly granted to him. He was instructed to pack, hand over the range to the senior European employed on duties in the game-free border fence area and present himself and family at Dar es Salaam docks as quickly as possible. Eleanor was already half-packed and almost as excited as the younger members of the family. For eight long years she had not seen her two eldest children at school in Britain and she was full of speculation as to what they would look like, and foreboding that they would not even recognise their parents. To even suggest to her that leave should be declined while George completed operations against the lions would certainly have provoked the first major disturbance of their married life.

George retired to his office to think things out. The succession of delays and postponements had certainly undermined a great part of his campaign against the man-eaters. When he had started off in the range he had been tempted to blame Dusty Arundell for not having ended the terror years ago. Now he could understand that if the man had experienced a similar series of official distractions on top of any personal problems then the immunity of the lions was becoming understandable.

To the good, at least four of the creatures had been shot. The game scouts would also continue their activity in the area, although this could be expected to have a diminishing effectiveness the longer he was away. The relieving man, *Twiga* Rogers, was reliable and conscientious. He might manage to do something although he was no experienced lion hunter. George had discussed the matter with him before and he had been somewhat opinionated about using large numbers of armed tribesmen in organised drives. Assuming that the tribesmen could be induced to turn out for such an effort, a few lions located as a target, and the drive so disciplined as not to degenerate, as they usually do, into a disorderly rabble of panicky men shooting one another on sight, then there might be some results, although George had his doubts.

Anyway, he supposed that he had best take the leave. He would have to write to Wenban-Smith and explain the new set-back, but the district commissioner would certainly understand. Leave was too much of a sacred cow to civil servants for any man to ever be expected to decline it, especially after so long a wait and in such circumstances of family separation.

George remembered how often he had been infuriated in the past by the civil servants he had badly wanted to see nearly always being either absent on leave or hopelessly preoccupied with the process of going or returning. He had fumed then about the delays and discontinuity of administration inevitable in the process of long leave. He had thought then that if a country could not support a permanently domiciled administration, it was hardly worth running. Now he knew that the prospect of leave was one of the few consolations many a man had for spending the best years of his life in some lonely and dreary post, conscientiously struggling to do a job which very few people would ever appreciate.

With a sigh he filled in the leave papers, wrote to Wenban-Smith and, within a few days, was on the way to the coast. From the bus as he passed Iyayi he pointed out to Eleanor, Matamula's home. There was no sign of the owner and they soon left the place behind them in the dust.

The leave, of course, seemed to pass very quickly. There was the grand re-union, with the two children waiting for them at the bus terminus at Jacksdale and, to Eleanor's relief, demurely submitting to their mother's kiss as though they had only parted eight days rather than eight years ago. There were the charabanc trips for the family around the English countryside, the sight-seeing in London, the egg-powder breakfasts, with food still on ration, the inevitable rather stupid musical show, and the chance meetings in crowded streets with old Tanganyika acquaintances. Then it was all over and an overcrowded *Winchester Castle,* still in its wartime troopship austerity dress, deposited the re-united family safely back on the shores of East Africa at the port of Mombasa. From there an even more overcrowded little tub, the *Al Said,* owned by the Sultan of Zanzibar, transhipped them, along with its usual cargo of cockroaches and stinks, to the palm-fringed harbour of Dar es Salaam.

It was the end of October 1946. It was good to be back again in some familiar place even though the old port was broiling hot, and for one night, until they could catch the train to the interior, they had to practically burst the seams of hospitality at the New Africa Hotel by sleeping on makeshift beds in a screened corner of the lounge. The place was packed with civil servants waiting their turn to board some ship for overseas leave, and George looked for someone among them who might provide him with news of events in his range.

Unfortunately there was nobody from the Southern Highlands in the hotel. Most of the crowd seemed to have come from the Lake and the Central provinces. From them, apart from a great deal of chatter about some new idea of a ground-nut scheme to revolutionise the moribund economy of Tanganyika, he did hear one item of particular interest. There had been a definite revival of activity by the lion-men in the Singida district. It was still all very confidential and under careful investigation. It was at least no secret, however, that upwards of thirty killings had taken place in the area since the beginning of the outbreak in May of that year. Rumour tended to implicate witchdoctors and lion-men. Nothing definite was known about the matter as yet. It was complicated, according to the informants, by some unrest in the district over the suspension from duty for various misdemeanours of a chief named Matwi. The suspension had also taken place in the month of May. The information provided George with material for thought all the way back to Mbeya. Whatever else he did during his coming tour of duty, he would certainly do his utmost to finally settle the Njombe trouble. Parallel events in the Singida district, which was well out of his range, would be watched with interest.

Twiga Rogers was waiting for him at Mbeya. His report was illuminating. The killings in the Njombe district were continuing at precisely the same level as when George had left. One more lion had been eliminated. Near Mdandu, the seat of the Paramount Chief of the Bena tribe, a single lion had been seen skulking around a small hamlet. Three tribesmen armed with muzzle loaders had stalked the animal. The three men had fired simultaneously and killed it. News of this event was very pleasing to George. It not only meant that five lions had now been eliminated, but that at least some of the tribesmen had found enough spirit to oppose the man-eaters.

So far as his bold idea of a mass drive was concerned, *Twiga* Rogers was rather crestfallen. By dint of an impressive persuasion he had, in fact, organised such a drive. On his second visit to the area he had also managed to locate three lions which, like the one killed by the tribesmen, were seen near Mdandu. The paramount chief had exerted pressure on his followers to join in the drive and by the use of motor transport a considerable number of men were rushed to the area. All the men were armed, either with muzzle loaders or shot guns. *Twiga* Rogers, fortunately, had occupied a strategic position behind a low bank when the hiding place of the lions had been surrounded. There had been quite a battle royal. When the dust had settled, the score was two Africans shot dead and several wounded, one of them dying later in hospital. The lions got clear away and, by pure luck, so did *Twiga* Rogers.

George took over the range as rapidly as possible. He had to check stores, rifles, ammunition, and restore office routine. A quick inspection of the range was also essential. Inevitably he struck one unexpected problem which still further delayed his return to the Njombe district. The northern section of Lake Rukwa had dried up after a number of poor seasons. At the climax it left its substantial population of hippos to a miserable death in a few extremely saline mud-holes. The plight of the animals was hopeless. The spectacle of the normally easy-going hippos packed like sardines, the dying on top of the dead in the stinking graveyard of the few mud-holes, was pathetic. To add to the agony of the animals, the hot sun on their backs had split their skin open and the salt had produced ghastly sores. The only thing which could be done was to put as many of them out of their misery as possible.

It was over two weeks before George finally reached the Njombe district and made a circuit of the various game scouts and chiefs. Their reports all indicated a slight decrease in the number of killings. Only nineteen people had been eaten in Jifiki's area since George's departure, but the chief mentioned, very uneasily, a continuing pressure for the restoration of Matamula. A month earlier a considerable deputation had actually gone over his head to see the Paramount Chief. The members of the deputation had been extremely annoyed when, on Government instructions, they had been declined a hearing. There was likely to be much more agitation over this matter unless something was done about the lions, and that very quickly.

George had already warned Eleanor that he was likely to be away in the Njombe district almost permanently until he had finalised the matter. It was fortunate that he could leave her in Mbeya in some comfort, settled in a larger house, with her children safely in school around her, an amiable social life of friends, and the diversion of a pleasant little club. If she had been living among the lions with the children, staying, perhaps, in a ghastly hole like their first station at Nzasa, then the whole business would have been a personal nightmare. As it was, he could understand the horror of the tribespeople when they saw their own families killed in front of them. What was unforgivable was that it was largely through their own supine acquiescence that the matter had ever been allowed to develop to this stage at all. Jifiki could only shrug when George mentioned the matter.

Accompanied by Game Scout Alfani, George went on to Mambego. He planned to camp there. It was as good a base as any for the hunt and he happened to like the people of the village. He had his pocket full of sweets for the pleasant little girl, but the first thing he heard on his arrival was that she had been eaten four days ago. The village was practically in ruins. The few people still living there were almost numb with their own apathy.

The next morning George started the hunt. Before he had gone on leave he had been forced to sell his double-barrelled Magnum in order to settle his store bills and have some pocket money in England. On his return he had tried to buy the weapon back but its new owner declined to part. For the second leg of the hunt, therefore, George was using a Westley Richards ·404 magazine with a Mauser action. It was good enough for the job, although his heart ached for the Magnum.

With Alfani, he hunted out southwards towards the Mbarali River and its upper tributaries. He was determined to get rapid vengeance for the death of the little girl. On the third day out the two hunters cut the fresh trail of a pride of lions moving north-westwards in the direction of Igawa. They followed quickly. Just before noon they caught up with the pride. The hunters worked to a carefully prearranged plan. The scout took one lion while George concentrated on another. It was the usual difficult thorn country for a stalk, but one advantage from the lion's long immunity was that they hardly expected man to hunt them and they were inclined to be incautious.

George and Alfani fired simultaneously. The scout hit with his first shot but his second bullet whined harmlessly away. George dropped his lion but by the time he could reload the animal had clambered to its feet. It tried to make off rather unsteadily but the second shot brought it to the ground stone dead.

The scout's target had been a lioness. She was making some commotion, growling, clawing and biting at the base of a nearby sapling, thinking that it had been responsible for her pain. George gave her two more fast shots and killed her. While he was reloading, Alfani saw a glimpse of a third lion as it was moving off through the secondary growth. He took a snap shot at the animal and certainly hit it, but not seriously. They followed a diminishing blood trail until late that afternoon before losing the tracks entirely. There were two other lions keeping company with the wounded animal and the speed at which they were moving proved that there was nothing much wrong with the invalid.

At least, however, two more of the Njombe lions had died, and with luck these were members of the pride which had last attacked Mambego village. They were certainly man-eaters, with the same glossy coats and opulent look which was common to their kind. Skinning the creatures gave George and Alfani a good opportunity for careful examination of what certainly did appear to be remarkably well-kept hides for creatures living in the thorn bush. George remembered the story that the lions were supposed to have a human herdman. It was a story too ridiculous to consider. He mentioned it to Alfani as they sat on their haunches, each man skinning his lion. The scout had heard the tale. He did not appear as amused about it as he should have been. George reminded him that black magic certainly hadn't turned their bullets. In the final analysis it would be the bullets which would count, not any supernatural herdman. Alfani shrugged. He supposed so.

They returned to Mambego, looking forward to telling the villagers of the success. The first person who came forward to meet them, however, was an African police constable from Iringa. He had an urgent message for George. The township foreman of Iringa, Bill Marshall, had been trampled to death by an elephant. There was an angle to the killing which required some investigation and the immediate presence of a game ranger was imperative. George groaned. With the end of the year approaching he would be snowed under quite enough with annual reports and recurrent administrative duties. Now he would have to lose still more time away from the lions. It was infuriating. All he could do was instruct Alfani to remain at Mambego and patrol the area. Then he drove off with the constable to Iringa.

On the journey he was slightly cheered by one piece of good news. At the Malangali turn-off he learned that two days before, a young Hehe herdman had, single-handed, speared and killed a lion. The lion had rushed a herd of cattle. The youth had run in from the side and thrown a spear which had the good fortune to penetrate the animal's heart. Whether the animal was one of the man-eaters was rather doubtful. Unless the creatures were suddenly starting to turn honest, it was more likely that the lone lion belonged to a more normal breed of beef eaters. He had been killed on the outer perimeter of the normal hunting ground of the man-eaters. Whatever the animal, however, the killing was a very stout effort on the part of the young herdman, and certainly one more lion less.

The news at Iringa was less pleasant. Marshall and a local cattle trader named Cathles had gone out hunting. Twenty miles north west of Iringa they had found a herd of elephants. They had fired at the biggest animal, missed, and the entire herd had charged. Cathles had jumped to his left and fallen backwards over a bush. Marshall had run to the right. One of the elephants had caught him, knelt on him, tusked him and then stormed on into the bush. An African game scout in the area claimed to have heard the first shots, gone to investigate, found Cathles with Marshall's body, tracked the elephant responsible and killed it. Marshall's body had then been carried to the Dodoma road and conveyed back to Iringa. Cathles had submitted a claim of eight shillings to the estate for the cleaning from his clothes of bloodstains left when he carried Marshall's body to the road.

There were other peculiar features to the affair. To prepare for the inquest George went with the game scout and a policeman to the scene of the mishap. The tracks in the earth told rather a curious story. After a certain amount of pressure the game scout told an even odder story. He had been with the two hunters all the time. The purpose of the hunt was to find any elephant, kill it, and then ring the changes between its tusks and a truly magnificent pair which the scout had obtained in the course of his duties. The three men would split the profits of the scheme between them.

Such was the new story of the scout. There were certain other oddities in the tracks but they were difficult to interpret. At any rate, George dismissed the scout, confiscated the ivory, cancelled Cathles' hunting licence and placed him on the black list. The man was a peculiar character in many respects and incredibly mean. One of his false economies was never to completely fill up the petrol tank of his car. He had some idea that evaporation accounted for a large proportion of fuel in a tank. Shortly after the inquest on Marshall, he was driving up the steep gradient of the Great North Road, where it enters Iringa from the valley of the Little Ruvaha River. His car ran out of fuel. He replenished from supplies carried in sealed cans. Then he tried to start, but the battery was flat because he never topped up the acid. He ran the car backwards to start the engine. The engine started but the brakes failed because he never replenished the hydraulic fluid. He went in reverse over the side of the road, down the escarpment and killed himself. By the time of that sad event George was already back in Mbeya and too busy to mourn.

CHAPTER THIRTY-TWO

THE LION-MEN OF THE SINGIDA DISTRICT

THE end of the year was always a hectic time for any ranger. It was nearly Christmas before George was freed from the Marshall enquiry and it was not simply the family obligations of the holiday season which forced him to return to Mbeya. There was paper work by the boxful clamouring for attention, with little red stickers reading "Urgent," and all the preparations to be made for the coming harvest season when crop protection from raiding elephants was imperative unless dire risk would be taken of local famine.

Throughout January 1947, George was busy on the range and attending to the needs of the game-free area. It was only in the beginning of February that he was free for another round with the man-eaters. He drove back to the Njombe district and immediately received two satisfactory reports from the game scouts. Jumapili had killed a definite man-eater at Mterengani. Two other lions had been shot towards Mawindi, just outside the recognised area of the man-eaters. Although these two animals had been mere cattle raiders, it was still better to be rid of them in case they moved into the territory of the man-eaters and learned a few bad habits.

The score was now eight man-eaters eliminated and there had been a definite effect on the rate of killings in the district. Jifiki, in fact, estimated that the weekly average of persons reported eaten in his district had dropped by half. This was very interesting news, and for the first time George began to feel that the reign of the man-eaters was drawing to a close.

The most recent killings had been of three people in the Ilembula-Malimzenga area. George looked at his map. If the lions were following their usual strategy they would already have left this area and be travelling on an irregular course, each leg being true and at a sharp angle to the previous one. When one of the legs over-ran a human settlement, the lions would feed, and then move off on the first stage of another involved course of confusion. Just how the lions had devised this complex scheme of travelling was a problem, and trying to guess their present whereabouts, a game with intriguing possibilities. George decided on a shot in the dark. He made his camp at the small village of Halali, some ten miles west of the scene of the recent killings. With any luck, the man-eaters would over-run this place in their present travels.

Before dawn the next morning George set out to hunt in an easterly direction, hoping to encounter the lions. There was no sign of them, however, and after six hours of hard searching he returned to the village for food. To his fury he immediately learned that an hour after he had left his camp a pride of lions had impudently walked into the village, killed a man and, in full view of the rest of the people, taken it in turn to carry the corpse off some little distance, where they proceeded to make a leisurely meal. They had obviously been rather hungry. Normally, if their victim was young, they consumed the whole body, including bones. With older victims they were inclined to be fastidious, but although their latest victim was on the elderly side all they had left was the saucer-like top of the skull. In other killings George had investigated, the man-eaters had left so many identical fragments, all licked scrupulously clean, that it was almost like finding their visiting card.

George swallowed a hurried pot of tea. Two of the villagers, a man and a sixteen-year-old youth, volunteered to accompany him in a search for the lions. It was a pleasant surprise to have such co-operation from any of the tribespeople. With the two men he set off after the lions. The youth was a magnificent tracker. George had never before had the pleasure of so keen and fearless an assistant to a hunt. They made excellent going.

About 4 p.m. they reached a large area covered in brachystegia and combretum. It had once been a cultivated field, but abandoned several years ago when the lions had terrorised the peasants into flight. The secondary growth that had sprung up was dense and shoulder high. It was a nasty area in which to hunt.

The three men entered the bush, with the youth in front following the tracks, his spear at the ready. George was at his heels, rifle cocked and keeping a lookout ahead. The second tribesman was in the rear. They moved forward slowly and as silently as possible. After about fifty yards they heard a slight movement ahead. They stopped and listened. They heard the movement again. It was so slight it could have been a game animal or even a bird.

George waved the two Africans back. He moved in front. He went ahead slowly, crawling on his hands and knees. Visibility was slightly better at ground level. He crawled forward for about twenty yards. Then he saw a young lioness. She was lying on her stomach with her front legs stretched out before her and three-quarters facing George. She was about five yards away. She saw George at the same moment that he saw her. Whether it was because she had recently fed, or because of surprise, she made no move. George brought up his rifle and shot her straight through the brain.

He jumped up to reload. There was some scurrying in front. Then, about thirty yards to his right front, a big lioness took a long, high bound at right angles to him. She appeared to be in more open bush than that in which George stood. She took a second bound. George snapped a hurried shot at her, firing shot-gun fashion. He hit her hard but a trifle too far back to be fatal.

The lioness seemed to tuck herself up in mid-air as she received the bullet. She landed on the ground and all hell was let loose. She rampaged around tearing at the surrounding bush, grunting and growling. George re-filled the magazine, sat on the ground and waited. From the rustlings in the bush he guessed that there were at least two other lions nearby. He suddenly remembered his African companions. He looked around. To his astonishment the youth was still with him, close on his heels. The second tribesman had fled.

After about a quarter of an hour the noise subsided from the wounded lioness. For another ten minutes there was only an occasional grunt, then dead silence. George was slightly perplexed. He thought of going back to camp and returning the next day. Then he realised that he was afraid, and deliberately gave up the idea. To ease his tension he filled and lighted a pipe. He sat smoking, giving himself and the wounded animal a long chance to cool off.

When he had finished the pipe he whispered to the youth to stay where he was. Then, with the utmost care and caution, he went after the wounded man-eater. He moved very slowly towards the place where she had been making the commotion. About half-way there he heard a slight movement ahead. This made him even more tense. He concentrated straight ahead on the sound. He took three more steps forward.

There was a heart-chilling bellow of sound a few feet to his immediate rear-left. He whirled, with his rifle cocked and ready to fire from the hip. It is strange how fast one's thoughts can work in such a time of emergency. He thought. " Oh, God! It's too near, no matter how fast I shoot it'll get me."

He looked into the face of death itself. There was a big male lion with a thick brown mane behind a bush within five feet of him. They stared into each other's eyes for a split second. Then the lion turned and made off, hurtling through the thorn bush. George felt an almost physical pressure of cold fear on his heart. Then he thought—he had his chance and failed to take it. I'll have my chance with him one day. I'll take it.

He sat down, filled his pipe again and smoked it slowly. After a while he called for the youth. The young spearman came without hesitation. Together they moved on towards where the lioness had been, the youth at George's heels, with his spear at the ready. They reached the spot. Apart from the clawed-up earth there was a fairly heavy blood pool where the animal had been lying.

They continued slowly on her trail. About forty yards further on they found the lioness. She was facing them in a half-crouch. George didn't wait to discover whether she still had enough strength left in her for a charge. He put two rounds into her before she could move. She fell over on her side, kicking spasmodically. The youth touched George on his shoulder.

" Can I put my spear into her?" he asked.

George looked at him.

" Why?"

" My father was the man who was eaten at the village."

George understood.

" Stab her quickly," he said, " she is not yet dead."

The young spearman gave the lioness her *congé*. Then they walked back to the first dead lioness. The youth plunged his spear into her heart. George watched him with sympathy. They were both nearly exhausted from exertion, nervous tension and, on the part of the youth, with what George now knew was grief. It was also drawing towards evening. When the youth had finished his act of vengeance they set out for the village, retrieving, as they went, the second tribesman who had found a very sensible refuge in a tree.

For the rest of the month George hunted from the village, hoping for at least a chance at the two lions who had escaped. He would dearly love to have met again the big male lion who had given him such a fright. He was not normally a collector of hunting trophies. The dead man-eaters were always skinned simply to have proof to display to doubting tribespeople. But the head of that male lion was a prize George was determined sooner or later to obtain, even though for the present it was denied to him.

There was little prospect of him being able to continue the hunt into March. The crop season would be in full swing and it would demand his complete attention. All he could do, as February drew to a close, was to exhort the game scouts to maximum effort. Then he returned to Mbeya. On the way he passed through Iyayi. He imagined that news of the hunt had already reached the people of the village. As he drove past Matamula's hut, however, he noticed the man standing outside. George stopped, reversed, and beckoned the man over. It was the first they had seen of each other since George's return from leave.

" Two more insects of the bush have died," said George, " Ten of them are now finished."

It was impossible to interpret the man's reaction. On the surface, Matamula seemed very faintly amused. What was going on down in the depths was possibly another matter. There was again an almost imperceptible shrug.

" You have hunted very well," he said. " It will be interesting to see the end of this matter."

George nodded and drove on. The stories about Matamula were so absurd that he was annoyed with himself for allowing them to even linger in his mind. In hunting the lions he had certainly found nothing positive to indicate human interference with the animals. The stories about their tracks changing into human footprints had not been borne out in fact. The curiously well-groomed, glossy appearance of the lions, along with the slightly stunted size, was probably due to the special peculiarities of their diet. Just how they had learned some of their tricks of attack and avoidance, and why their behaviour was so different from that of normal lions, was something of a problem. But, again, this warping of their nature might be the consequence of the specialised requirements essential in hunting human beings. Thinking about these problems made him wonder what was happening in the Singida district. He had heard that affairs there had reached the stage of massive police investigation. He decided to pay a visit to Singida as soon as opportunity offered. A comparative study of events in the lion world there and in the Njombe district might clarify some of the peculiarities of the business.

The crop protection duties, actually, were prolonged until the end of April. For some reason the elephants were particularly troublesome that year. They not only raided the standing crops, doing more damage by trampling entire fields underfoot than by what they ate, but they also followed the crops once the harvest was in. In the nights, the more impudent animals started a regular campaign of raiding villages, breaking down the wattle and daub bins and looting them of their freshly reaped contents of maize. A full year's supply of food for an entire village could vanish overnight in this fashion. The only prevention was in ruthless counter-hunting, the destruction of the habitual raiders, and the driving of the rest back into their proper feeding grounds in the wilderness.

For two months George practically lived in a world of maize cobs, elephants and bullets. It was certainly quite a way of celebrating a harvest home. When it was over he returned to Mbeya and found urgent instructions waiting for him to finally close down the anti-rinderpest operations along the Rhodesian border. The danger of the disease spreading to the southern areas of Africa had receded. The staff employed on the game-free border area had to be discharged, their stores checked, camps broken up and everything conveyed back to Mbeya. Getting rid of the whole business was, actually, rather a relief. It was not simply a matter of one less responsibility. At best the anti-rinderpest operation had been a filthy process of butchering countless thousands of head of small game simply because they unwittingly wandered within five miles of the border. Only a moron could derive pleasure from such an occupation. It was for this reason that George was glad to see the last, not only of the whole idea, but also of one or two of the individuals employed on it.

He was still busy clearing up this work when the game department sprang on him one of its periodic visitations by a very important personage. He groaned when he saw the letters V.I.P. marked by Monty Moore at the head of the letter of introduction. With the blessings of the Colonial Office, the Empire Fauna Society had sent out a personage to conduct another one of the interminable series of surveys on the game position in the East African territories. Practically every year some well-meaning individual from Europe or America arrived on a similar mission. Some of them were sensible but most were hopelessly emotional and quite impractical in their whole approach to wild animals.

If possible, most rangers remembered dead grandmothers at times of such visits or took other avoiding action. Even if the visitors were amiable, they were still very demanding on the services of local staff. With very few of these overseas experts ever allowing themselves time for anything other than the most hasty of studies of their subject, the superficiality of their reports could be anticipated in advance, as well as the unlikelihood of them ever having any significant results. What Tanganyika really needed was the painstaking study of basic research which could only be given to it by some future indigenous institution like a university endowed, as it should be in so wonderful a country of wild life, with the richest chair of zoology in the world.

The current visitors were Captain Keith Caldwell and his wife. They were at least a pleasant and sensible couple. If George had not had the lions on his mind it would have been more of a pleasure taking them on a safari. As it was, he simply did what was expected of him, showed them the game country of the Rukwa valley, and then saw them off across the Rhodesian border on the continuation to the south of their tour of inspection.

It was already June and what George particularly wanted to do was to pay a short visit to Singida. He had heard that the high court session there during that month would see the trial of a substantial number of Africans implicated in lion-men killings. The information he could derive from a visit to the place might be very helpful.

Singida was a long day's drive north of Mbeya. It was the usual type of Tanganyikan small town, a handful of Indian shops standing at a respectful distance from the inevitable German-built fort. The town was situated in the midst of the real howling wilderness of thorn-bush-covered plain which makes up the heart of Tanganyika. It had, however, at least the local landscape features of some remarkable outcrops of granite and a couple of shallow saline lakelets, one of which had given the town its name.

George spent an interesting evening exchanging experiences with some of the officials stationed there. The two senior officers on the station, the district commissioner, A. R. Bate, and the police inspector, R. H. Stewart, had quite obviously had more than their fair share of troubles in the district. Both of them had been transferred to Singida in January of that year and found the Turu tribespeople to be in the grip of a most degrading terror.

As George had already heard, the current wave of killings had started in May 1946, and gained in momentum with not the slightest effort made by the tribespeople to oppose them. Bate, the new district commissioner, was, fortunately, a pretty resolute individual. He had taken over his duties on the 4th of January. As soon as he had learned about the dismal reputation of the Turu people for periodically indulging in what was something like their special tribal pastime of *mbojo* (lycanthropy), and had studied the recent reports of thirty killings concerning which rumour implicated lion-men rather than lions, he decided to summon all the headmen of the area to a discussion in his headquarters.

The meeting had been held five days later, on the 9th of January. It was a gathering of individuals who, like the people of the Njombe district, were only too obviously sick with a grisly fear. Nobody wanted to face the realities of the business. There was even an attempt to evade the whole issue by blaming it on the neighbouring Barabaig tribe who traditionally had the monstrous custom of indulging in killing as an essential part of courtship. Some apologists for the local crop of murders tried to shrug them off by suggesting that the Barabaig young men, searching for presents of noses, ears, or even of entire corpses for their sweethearts to mutilate, were raiding into Turu territory.

There was nothing to substantiate this suggestion of Barabaig raids. When the killings had first started in May the work had been at first simply blamed on lions. Game scouts had been sent to destroy the lions. They had reported that they could find no lions and that witchcraft was responsible. Early in December a police detective had then been sent to investigate. He had confirmed that the thirty killings were indeed murders. Securing evidence about them, however, was extremely difficult. One woman who had survived an attack, badly wounded, at first made a detailed statement describing her assailant as a man wearing the skin of a lion. As soon as she had recovered from her injuries, however, she retracted her statement before a magistrate and said that her attacker had been a proper lion.

The whole series of killings made an exceedingly complicated study. Basically there were numerous real lions in the district and a certain amount of recurrent man-eating by them was inevitable. Then there was an unfortunate weakness in the Unyanganyi chiefdom in which the killings had taken place. Throughout the world, when the hand of authority slackens, all manner of human perversions, follies and barbarisms seize the opportunity of emerging on the surface from the darkness of human nature. Africa is no exception to this rule, and with people living there in so primeval an environment it should not, perhaps, be too surprising that that which emerges from very shallow cover can be both vicious and brutish.

The chief of the area troubled with the killings had been deposed for being idle, weak, drunk, and whipping without authority. He had been re-placed by his brother, and then recently re-elevated when the brother had been found even less suitable to hold authority. The rivalry of the two men had released upon their people some very primitive passions. The game scouts in the area, infected with the same fears as the tribespeople, were firmly convinced that the killers were lion-men sent by a *mganga*, or witch-doctor, who was partisan in the quarrels of the chiefs. Trying to trap or hunt such creatures was useless. With a human intelligence they would obviously eschew such crudities as traps and the only way to subdue them would be to trace the witchdoctor and pay him to lift the spell.

This view of the matter was shared by the Chiefs and headmen. The only variation they could suggest to the district commissioner was that they thought that more than one witchdoctor was behind the killings. The lion-men were always directed to their kills by some human escort, and although every effort was made to mutilate the victims in a manner similar to the vicious clawings of a lion, the footprints of the human escort in proximity to the pug marks of the lion-man always betrayed the real nature of proceed-ings. Nobody, Chiefs or tribespeople, would be happy to divulge the identity of witchdoctors or lion-men for fear of direct reprisals.

From the Chiefs present at his meeting, Bate had selected three of the best of them, Pahi, Salim and Senge, whose homes were out of the centre of the area of disturbance. These men were instructed to proceed to the village of Mgori where most of the killings had taken place, and aid the police in their investigations. The result had been rapid and gratifying. On the 29th January 1947 the Chiefs and the detective in charge had returned to Singida with eight accused and forty-five other persons implicated in the killings. Remands had eventually been asked for against twenty-seven of these persons. Confessions implicated twelve of this number. No lion-men had been arrested but their names were known. They were said to be completely subordinate to the will of the witchdoctors and three of these practitioners were among the arrested persons.

This was a major police success but it had no appreciable effect on the killings. There had been ten more victims of the lion-men during January while the investigations were proceeding. Eight more people had been killed in February, even though Bate had gone to Mgori himself on the 6th of that month and held a large public *baraza*. He had pleaded with the people to work with the police and secure the apprehension of the actual lion-men. The shameful business had ruined the reputation of the entire district. It was up to them to at least help outsiders purge their country of the evil. By combining forces it would not be an impossible task. The four hundred tribespeople sitting around had simply stared at him in bewilderment. They seemed obsessed with the idea that there had always been such things amongst their people and always would be. Arresting witchdoctors and clients was one thing but a genuine lion-man could never be arrested no matter what reward was offered. Such creatures were invisible to the human eye and therefore immune. Bate could do nothing to enlighten the tribespeople. Their Chief, Matwi, failed to attend the *baraza*. There was even some air of general resentment about the arrests already made. Bate returned to Singida wondering, as George had done in the Njombe district, whether the people liked having lion-men murder them. There was certainly little other explanation for their completely negative attitude.

Investigations had continued in preparation for a high court trial. The police painstakingly worked through the human population while the game ranger of the province, B. "Walky-Talky" Cooper and a staff of game scouts, laboured hard in the area hunting real lions. Both police and game ranger had some successes in their particular spheres. From their combined efforts there emerged some very curious facts indeed.

From the lion point of view the game ranger included in his bag several rather odd animals. Among them was a lioness shot near Ikungi. Her teeth had been filed to points. The skull was sent for examination to Sir Frank Colyer, of the Royal College of Surgeons in London, but conclusions could only tend to confirm the common stories that lion cubs were brought up by various persons and used for a variety of purposes. There was certainly nothing illegal about taming lions, but the police could certainly be interested in some of the tricks being taught to them.

Police activity in the area had been steadily increased. Plain-clothes men mixed with the people while the uniformed staff patrolled throughout the area infected by this horrible animalism. What they hoped to catch was an actual lion-man to include among the principals in the coming high court trial. That the lion-men were very active was proved by the corpses they left. During March and April 1947, under the very eyes of the police patrols, twenty-four more people had been killed. No lion-man was seen or apprehended by the police, but information received about them not only established their personalities but revealed the infamous methods used by the witchdoctors in obtaining and training them for the purpose of murder.

One of the lion-men was said to be named Halota. The police reports on him were appalling. His wife, Geli, stated that he had vanished six to eight years ago when on a journey to Singida. He was said to have been held captive and trained as a lion-man by two witchdoctors. The police considered that it was probable that he had been turned insane by drugs and made homicidal by further drugs immediately prior to the commission of a murder.

" From statements recorded," went on the police report, " it would appear that the two witchdoctors hire Halota out for the sum of forty shillings to persons desirous of using his services and that the person having achieved his purpose rehires Halota to others for a lesser sum in order to reimburse himelf for the original sum expended. There is very little evidence against the two ' owners ' of Halota, who has not been arrested nor are his present whereabouts known. It may be possible that, due to vigorous police action in the area, he has been disposed of. He has been positively identified on the scene of one murder. Witnesses have described him as wearing a lion mane over the head and obscuring his face, with baboon skins covering the entire body.

" In his killings he used two knives of about eighteen inches in length. As he is under the influence of drugs at the time of the murders he must be directed to the desired victim. A horrible feature of at least one murder is that he cut off pieces of flesh from the victim and consumed them, presumably to make it appear that a real lion was responsible."

Another lion-man was Morhango, an imbecile also turned homicidal by drugs. He had never been known to speak even when addressed. It was said that his tongue had been torn out by his owner. He was dressed in similar fashion to Halota and hired out at the cut-rate price of fifteen shillings a time.

Women could also be lion-men. Siyanda was one such a female *mtu-simba,* dressed exactly like the men. Another lion-man was Sumbayi, of whom there was a very complete description given by two persons arrested as principals in a killing committed on the 16th April 1947. These two persons offered an explanation for the presence of lion-like pug marks at the scene of this and other killings. They said that the hands of the *mtu-simba* were covered with a form of gauntlet complete with lion pads and claws. The feet were placed in a special pair of sandals manufactured from old motor tyres and shaped into the form of a lion's pads. The impressions left by these sandals at the scene of the crime were identical with those of a real lion, but with certain differences.

Real lions were also so mixed up in the killings that it was quite impossible for any investigator to really distinguish between man and animal. Women desirous of learning witchcraft were always required to allow one of their own children to be devoured in front of them by a lion. Children were themselves in great demand among the witchdoctors for training as lion-men. It was reported to the police that these children, either kidnapped or given voluntarily to the witchdoctors, were kept hidden in dark food bins or other secret places with ceilings so low that they could never stand upright.

In such places the children were so terrorised that they eventually became mental cases. Their wrists were broken and tied back on the forearm until they simulated the pads of an animal. The tendons behind the knees were so treated at the same time that the legs could be straightened and the future lion-man enabled to walk as an animal, as several witnesses stated they did.

The process of training these future lion-men was detailed in a statement made to the police by a witchdoctor named Mondulu.

" We agreed to take Siyanda, the daughter of my relation, Kingi, then about eight years old, and turn her into a *mtu-simba*. Siyanda at that time was subject to epileptic fits. We abducted her from her guardian's house, one of her parents having gone to Arusha, the other having died. We took her to my house and there slaughtered a goat. Amongst the goat meat we mixed some drugs. The drugs were prepared by myself and Ninahi. The drugs were to change her into the form of a lion. After five days she commenced to change into the form of a lion. We covered her with a lion skin. Her habits changed into those of an animal.

"After seven years we started to hire the new *mtu-simba* out at the rate of thirty shillings a time. She was passed from person to person for thirty shillings. Like all lion-men she is invisible while indoors and can only be seen by a witchdoctor. Outdoors, a *mtu-simba* is visible to anybody.

" If it be desired to change a person into a *mtu-simba* one uses the following drugs: the pounded roots of the tree *msatu* and the roots of *mdubu* and *mkulukundu* (known preparations of the strychnos family). This drug makes a person strong and fat and makes the voice deep and husky. This drug we gave to Siyanda. The food given to a *mtu-simba* is honey, ugali and meat. Many years ago I was taught witchcraft by Ninahi, at that time a headman in the area. To prove the efficacy of my training I was instructed to kill my brother, Maguni. He was younger than me. Ninahi gave me a concoction of flour and pounded root. This I gave to my brother in beer. He died after an illness of about a month. I paid Ninahi two cows to be taught the art of witchcraft."

What exactly it was like to be turned into a lion-man was revealed to the Singida police during the month of May 1947, when they recorded the first detailed statement ever made by one of these creatures. It was a revelation of the lowest depths of animalism, ferocity and depravity to which a human being is capable of being degraded.

CHAPTER THIRTY-THREE

THE MASTER OF THE LIONS

THROUGHOUT the month of May 1947, lion-man killings continued in the area of the Unyanganyi chiefdom, with the village of Mgori as the epicentre of the trouble. The diligence of the police only had one significant result, but at least that was of major importance to a better understanding of the inner secrets of the lion-men. This result was the statement made on the 21st of May by Mande, the son of Mgu, who confessed to having been a lion-man.

"Many years ago," his statement read, "I was turned into a *mtu-simba* by Mama Kitoto. I was then a child of about twelve to fifteen years. One day I was in the bush guarding my father's cattle. I met a man named Mwiru, the son of Soghombo. The man told me to go home alone. I refused. Mwiru then persuaded me to go home alone. On the way I became lost and my senses left me and I was taken into the bush by an unknown person. When I recovered I found myself in Mama Kitoto's house. Nobody was there. In the evening many women came in and some men. Then a cow and a sheep were slaughtered and skinned. Then they cooked the flesh.

340

" Four women were there already turned into lions. They wore skins of dressed hide on their bodies and monkey-skin cowls. I saw a trench dug in the floor of the house. I was told to peep into the trench. I did so and as I bent over to look they threw a skin over me. It was a monkey skin and covered me from the neck to my waist. It was tight fitting. Then I was given a pair of shorts made of a stiff material, something like feathers—not feathers actually. It had red and white stripes on it.

" On my legs they put a kind of long stockings which reached to the thigh. On the feet of these stocking-like contraptions were the pads of a lion, complete with claws. Similar things were put on my arms and hands and my fists were clenched. At the end of these gauntlets were the paws of a lion complete with claws. There was no tail.

"After I was dressed I was led into the pit of the house and by an underground tunnel to some native-type houses where I was kept with four other lion-men, two male and two female. These houses were above ground and near some ant-hills. There I was kept for a long time. There was a person who cooked and fed us on meat and much beer. I was very fat and strong. The five of us had separate rooms in the house. I was alone most of the time and did nothing. I saw Mama Kitoto from time to time. She asked me about my food. She used to ask the other lion-men how many persons they had killed. When I was left alone I was covered with a large pot after having been covered with a medicine. The medicine made me incapable of thinking. I was also given a medicine to drink which made me dizzy.

" The other lion-men went out quite frequently to kill people. I saw them go out early in the morning. Before they went there was a rush of wind and then I saw them go out armed with knives and pangas. From time to time men and women were brought for the lion-men to copulate with. When this happened the lion-men performed in a manner similar to animals. I myself was too young to have anything to do with women. Each night I took off my skins and put them on in the morning.

"After I had been there a long time, Mama Kitoto said to me one day that I should try and kill someone and that if this was successful that I should kill my sister, Baha. I went out with the other four lion-men. There was the usual rush of wind and I found myself outside (*Police note.* This is probably a rush of fresh air into a dark atmosphere. It is probable that the house he speaks of was in ant-hills at the end of the tunnel). I was given two knives and a panga. I put them in sheaths on my thighs. I was taken to a place where some women and children were pounding grain. A man who accompanied us directed me to kill one of the children. I went towards the child but before I reached it one of the women struck me with a pestle on the back and I fell down. The man who was helping me rushed up and dragged me away by one leg, thereby damaging my left knee."

The damage to his knee actually saved Mande from further ill-use. He limped for the rest of his life and was considered to be a failure as a lion-man. He was moved to another area. The dosage of drugs ended and eventually he was allowed to return to his proper home. In interrogation he appeared to be quite sane, but of retarded mentality. Mama Kitoto died some time after this event. In her day she was one of the most notorious witches in the entire Singida district.

The problem of coping with such aberrations of human behaviour was not easy to solve for administrative and police officials more familiar with the routine law enforcement required by the cattle theft and assault cases which make up the normal crime list of an African tribe. Continuous police action would obviously produce arrests and eventual convictions, but whether such punitive action was the final answer to the business was doubtful. At best it would probably only suppress the lion-men, force them back into the dark where they would lurk until some other time was more opportune for their activity.

In an effort to find some long-term answer to the lion-men, the government sociologist, H. Cory, was called in at the end of May 1947. He was of opinion that the general breakdown of traditional methods of tribal government was responsible in a large measure for the impunity of the killers. If the tribespeople were incapable of spontaneous resistance to the process of being murdered, then something would have to be organised for them. More power would have to be given back to the clan elders and lists drawn up of important people who would aid the enforcement of law. Administration itself would always have to be strong and the police permanently vigilant in the area.

These measures did in fact appear to have some effect on the killings. At the time of George's visit to Singida there was a definite lull in proceedings with no murders reported between the 6th and the 20th of June. A total of 103 people had been killed since the outbreak of the trouble. With the high court sessions due to start on the 23rd of June it was rumoured that the lion-men had gone to cover. Too many eyes were watching for them at the time. They would resume their business later, which was exactly what they did. Although twenty-seven out of fifty-seven accused at the sessions were sentenced to death, with two others added to the capital list later at a trial at Dodoma, a new case of killing was reported on the 11th of July. For the rest of the year 1947 the terror was destined to continue with the Turu country, in November, being officially declared a disturbed area. The lion-men remained rampant and themselves largely immune from all police action until, for reasons which still remain conjectural, the terror subsided in 1948. It did not reappear to any large extent until ten years later, in 1958, when the whole business started all over again with twenty-two killings reported.

George had not waited for the high court sessions. His day in Singida had shown him the difference between the killings going on there and in the Njombe district. The two areas of killing seemed to have little that was in common other than the basic presence of real lions and the acquiescence of the tribespeople to the idea of supernatural influences. In both areas the killing off of real lions would certainly undermine some of the troubles. Until the supernatural aspects could be rooted out, however, either by ruthless punitive action or by the enlightenment of the tribespeople into disbelief and resistance to the whole idea of black magic, the terror would be likely to continue with the stories of lycanthropy simply transferred to any other predatory animal common to the area. On the Kinga plateau and the heights of the Poroto mountains overlooking Cormack's little hotel, the witchdoctors mixed their killings up with leopards, so lions were no essential part to black magic. Even the hyenas in the Mbugwe country had been used for murder, as George remembered from his camp there on Ufiyome Mountain.

Accepting the impossibility of a human being changing anything other than his mentality into the degenerate form of an animal, the Singida trouble seemed to stem from an elusive handful of homicidal lunatics directed and controlled by witchdoctors and at times inextricably mixed with lions, also tamed and trained for murder. Apart from the singular elusiveness of the actual lion-men, the whole disturbance could be explained as a rather fancy-dress version of the infamous profession of the hired assassin. The number of killings could be written down to a combination of the tempting cheapness of rates coupled to the inflammatory passions of primitive people.

The Njombe disturbance was another matter entirely. The curious behaviour of what were undoubtedly real lions remained the basic puzzle of the killings. If one accepted this as an aberration produced purely as a result of the specialised requirements of man-hunting then the killings were also understandable. The tales of Matamula controlling the lions could then be dismissed as either a stupid public fancy or an ingenious fraud. In both the Singida and the Njombe districts the wretched, all-pervading ignorance and superstitious fear of black magic paralysed the mental processes of the people and made them appear so spineless. With a basic belief among them that even the smallest misfortune was the consequence of magic, it would not take too self-assured a confidence trickster to successfully exploit so credulous a public. All such a person would need to really establish his reputation as the master of the lions was an initial piece of luck in predicting their killings. The general atmosphere of superstition and terror would do the rest.

The task now was to finally liquidate the lions. Then, as Matamula had already said, it would be interesting to see how it all ended. If no more was heard of black magic in the Njombe district then the hunt could be classed as a complete success.

George drove straight from Singida to the Great North Road and then down into the Njombe district. He arrived at Wangingombe the next after-

noon and made his camp close to the village. Jifiki came over to meet him
with great cordiality. The chief had the pleasant news that the doughty
Alfani had killed a definite man-eater ten days earlier. The rate of killings
had declined so much that there could not be more than two or three of the
man-eaters still active. Something also seemed to have happened to these
creatures. They were no longer hunting with their original habits. They appeared to have lost much of their sinister skill and unpredictability of
technique. They were now much more like normal lions.

The game scouts confirmed this interesting news when George toured the
area the next day. The only locality in the hunting ground of the man-eaters
where killings were still reported was within a fifteen-mile radius of Jumbe
Musa's village. That had always been the most troubled area. Now it seemed
to have become the last stronghold of the man-eaters. They were concentrat-
ing there, abandoning their former technique of rapid dispersal, and seemingly expending their last viciousness on one community of people.

Such sudden regularity of eating habits was curious, but it was certainly
exactly what any hunter required. George gathered all the game scouts and
immediately concentrated them in the last troubled area. He shifted his own
camp to the actual village, where the headman, Jumbe Musa, gave him a
rather uneasy welcome. His people had been plagued by man-eaters since
the very beginning of the trouble. They had never regarded hunters as being
anything other than a dangerous provocation to the killers. The sight of
such a gathering of game scouts together with George, instead of being a
reassurance, seemed to frighten them. During the evening George tried to explain to the headmen and elders that the concentration was only because
the last man-eaters were lurking in the vicinity. This information hardly
seemed to cheer them. When he set out the next morning on the start of the
hunt he noticed that they were gathering for a meeting. He hoped that the
previous evening's talk had at least stimulated them to some active concern
for their own defence.

For seven days George hunted through the bush with the scouts without
finding any sign of lions. On the eighth morning George dispersed his men
into pairs with instructions to work in various directions. Game Scout
Jumapili remained with him and it was early on the following morning that
they found the fresh trail of two lions. The tracks were very clear when they
first saw them. The lions had walked across the dew so they could not be
more than a couple of hours away. This was not the only excitement of the
find. The tracks looked as though they were those of a male and a female
and the pug marks of the lion were uncommonly similar to those left by the
big animal with whom George had experienced his brief encounter on the
previous hunt.

This was one lion which he badly wanted for himself. As they followed
the trail he told Jumapili about the narrow escape. The game scout could

fully appreciate his feelings about the matter. They agreed that if they found the lions, Jumapili would attend to the female. George would settle accounts with the male.

After three hours of tracking they overtook the lions. There was almost something of an anticlimax about the end of the hunt. There had always been an air of tension about the previous encounters with the man-eaters. The dread and superstitious expectancy of the tribesmen they had formerly used as trackers or escorts had probably been contagious. Perhaps because George and Jumapili were on their own and free of this influence, the hunt seemed to go with the calm customary to a thoroughly professional affair. Whatever it was or wherever it came from, the indefinable feeling of evil which had been so inseparable a companion to the man-eaters was distinctly absent.

They found the two animals resting in the shade of a thorn tree and being very affectionate with each other. As the hunters approached, the male heard them and ceased his attentions to the female, advancing slightly from the shade into the sunshine to see what was happening. George recognised him immediately. The features of the animal were engraven in his memory too clearly for him to be mistaken. It was the same strapping lion with the handsome brown mane which had stared him in the face for those heart-stopping few seconds. Only this time he seemed more of a normal lion and less of a demon out of hell. Perhaps it was his spell of romance which had mellowed him.

Whatever it was, George put a bullet straight through the animal's shoulders into his heart while Jumapili caught the female with a hard-hitting shot through her lungs. She collapsed choking on the ground and the scout finished her off as fast as he could reload. They walked up and examined the animals. There was no doubt about the identification. George looked into the dead lion's face and remembered the last occasion on which they had met. The difference in circumstance was remarkable. If it hadn't been for what he knew of the record of the lion, George would have been sorry for the animal. He looked completely innocent, lying there like an over-grown tom-cat killed in a road accident. What evil had motivated him in the past was certainly gone for ever.

George and Jumapili sat down, skinned the two carcasses and cleaned the skulls. They both felt that these were the last of the man-eaters. It would be a real pleasure to inform Wenban-Smith of the final ending of the terror. The district commissioner was being transferred at the end of that month to the secretariat in Dar es Salaam. He would certainly be gratified at being able to leave his successor a district completely purged of all its former trouble and horror.

George and Jumapili carried their trophies to the nearest village and secured porters to help them back to Jumbe Musa's. At the chief's place, the villagers received them with their usual rather irritating hostility. The rest of the game scouts were still out hunting. On the offchance that there might still be an odd lion roaming around it would be safer to leave them in the area for some time. George instructed Jumapili to keep them all vigilant. The scout needed no instruction to make him display the relics of the lioness to the villagers. George warned him not to taunt the tribespeople too much over their lack of resistance to the lions. Then he drove back to Mbeya and sent a telegram to Wenban-Smith informing him of the final liquidation of the man-eaters and wishing him well in his new post. The reply was quite heart-felt, simply the Arabic words for " Praise be to God!"

George reverted to his normal duties for the first time in one and a half years without a feeling of frustration that he was not away hunting lions. He was still engrossed on bringing his administrative chores up to date at the beginning of the new month when he received another telegram from Wenban-Smith. It was terse—" You're wrong George. Regret. Woman eaten yesterday at Matipu village."

George really cursed. The telegram must have been one of Wenban-Smith's last official duties at Njombe. Instead of being able to leave for his new post with the satisfaction of having heard the last of the man-eaters, he must have left on the same day he sent the telegram. His successor would not be taking over until later in the month so the whole wretched business would have to remain an open issue in his reports.

There were several things which George had started in the range which he could not simply drop. He dealt with them as quickly as possible, however, meanwhile sending a message to the game scouts instructing them to do their utmost to avenge the new killing. It was only on the 16th July 1947 that George managed to return to the Njombe district. He was determined to remain this time, even if it took months, until the animal responsible for the unexpected killing had been found.

Matipu village was in the area where the game scouts were concentrated. He drove straight to Jumbe Musa's. When he arrived he found the villagers an entirely changed people from the sulky crowd who had received him on previous visits. The women were busy making beer, livestock were being slaughtered, with all the indications set for a feast. Everybody was full of smiles and friendly greetings. The scouts were not there, but George found a message asking him to go on immediately to Sindagosi village, a few miles away. The scouts, hunting together, had tracked the animals, two lionesses, who had been responsible for the last killing and had shot them on the previous day midway between Matipu and Sindagosi. The scouts were positive that the man-eating was now completely over.

George was as delighted as the villagers of Jumbe Musa's. He drove over to see the game scouts and congratulate them. They spent an evening together reminiscing about the whole affair. The final score was fifteen definite man-eaters killed after all the long months of effort, frustration, delay and hazard. In the same period five other lions had been eliminated, although these were of doubtful man-eating habits. Two other lions had been seriously wounded in the various hunts. As nothing more had been seen of them it was pretty certain that they were dead. This made a maximum total of twenty-two lions which, along with any animals which may have died a natural death, could have been responsible for what was without doubt the greatest and most sustained record of man-eating ever known in Africa.

The next day George left the scouts to routine patrols. He drove off to Wangingombe to see Jifiki and give him the glad news. Curiously enough, the chief seemed less jubilant about the information than George had expected. He seemed to have something on his mind which he was reluctant to disclose. George allowed him to find his own time and they sat for a while beneath the jacaranda trees, enjoying a pull of beer and talking about past occasions and future hopes.

It was only as George stood up to go that Jifiki said, rather awkwardly:

" You've been a long time in Africa, Mr Rushby, you must know this place and its people very well."

George looked at him and wondered what was coming. The Chief walked with him towards his truck.

" I suppose that one day you will be the head of your department?" Jifiki asked.

George shrugged.

" Perhaps, but I rather think I started too late in government service for that kind of promotion. I'll reach pension age and be considered a dotard before that opportunity comes."

" Will you remain in Africa then?"

" Yes, of course; I love it. I could go nowhere else."

Jifiki touched him on the arm.

" Mr Rushby, don't think that we will ever forget what you have done for us about these lions."

He hesitated a moment as they reached the truck.

" But don't expect the people to ever believe that the ones you shot were the lions that were killing them."

George stared at him.

" Why not?"

Jifiki seemed embarrassed and slightly distressed. After a while, he said:

" The people of Iyayi and Jumbe Musa's heard that Mr Wenban-Smith was leaving. They formed a big deputation and sent it straight to the Paramount Chief at Mdandu. They begged once again that Matamula be replaced in his post. They pleaded that only this would end their trouble. They told the Paramount Chief that he could easily make the change before the new district commissioner arrived."

" So?"

" The Paramount Chief agreed. He deposed Ulaya at the end of last month and once again put Matamula in his place. The people are now very happy. They are holding beer drinks and dances. It is said that Matamula has called off his lions. It is said that no man will be killed from now on because Matamula has his rightful place."

George looked at him in silence for a while. Then he lit his pipe carefully and drove off along the Great North Road, back to Mbeya where Eleanor and the children were waiting. There were no more killings by lions in the Njombe district.

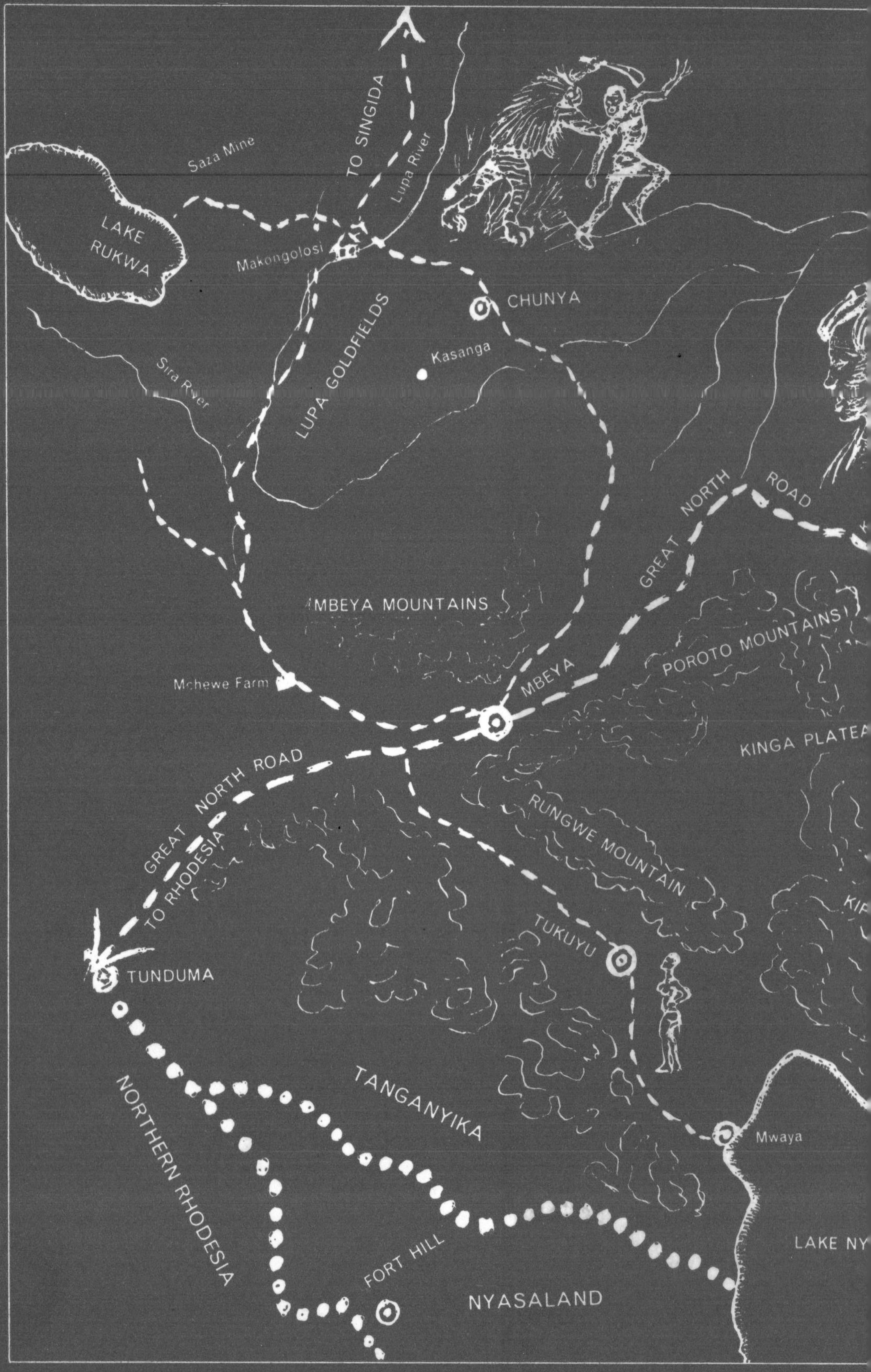
TO SINGIDA
Lupa River
Saza Mine
LAKE RUKWA
Makongolosi
CHUNYA
Kasanga
LUPA GOLDFIELDS
Sira River
GREAT NORTH ROAD
MBEYA MOUNTAINS
POROTO MOUNTAINS
Mchewe Farm
MBEYA
KINGA PLATEA
GREAT NORTH ROAD
TO RHODESIA
RUNGWE MOUNTAIN
TUKUYU
TUNDUMA
TANGANYIKA
Mwaya
NORTHERN RHODESIA
FORT HILL
NYASALAND
LAKE NY